Volume 3

By M. Alice LeGrow

HAMBURG // LONDON // LOS ANGELES // TOKYO

Bizenghast

Contents

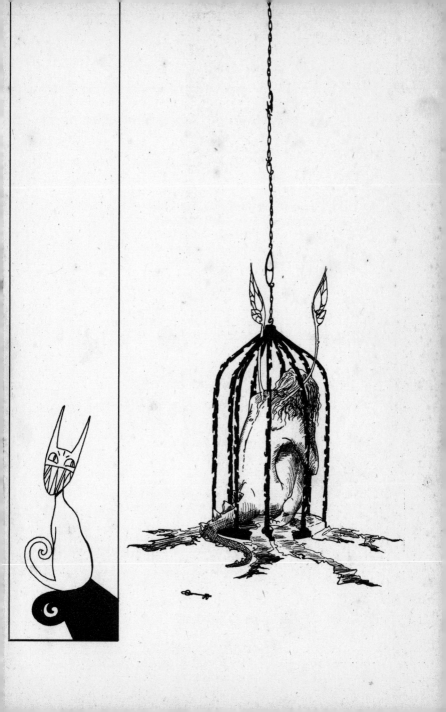

Bizenghast Vol. 3
Created by M. Alice LeGrow

Development Editors - Jodi Bryson & Aaron Suhr
Lettering - Lucas Rivera
Toning Assistant - Katherine Schilling
Cover Designer - Al-Insan Lashley

Editor - Lillian Diaz-Przybyl
Digital Imaging Manager - Chris Buford
Pre-Production Supervisor - Erika Terriquez
Art Director - Anne Marie Horne
Production Manager - Elisabeth Brizzi
Managing Editor - Vy Nguyen
VP of Production - Ron Klamert
Editor-in-Chief - Rob Tokar
Publisher - Mike Kiley
President and C.O.O. - John Parker
C.E.O. and Chief Creative Officer - Stuart Levy

A **TOKYOPOP** Manga

TOKYOPOP and ⊙ are trademarks or registered trademarks of TOKYOPOP Inc.

TOKYOPOP Inc.
5900 Wilshire Blvd. Suite 2000
Los Angeles, CA 90036

E-mail: info@TOKYOPOP.com
Come visit us online at www.TOKYOPOP.com

ISBN: 978-1-59532-745-1

First TOKYOPOP printing: August 2007
10 9 8 7 6 5 4 3
Printed in the USA

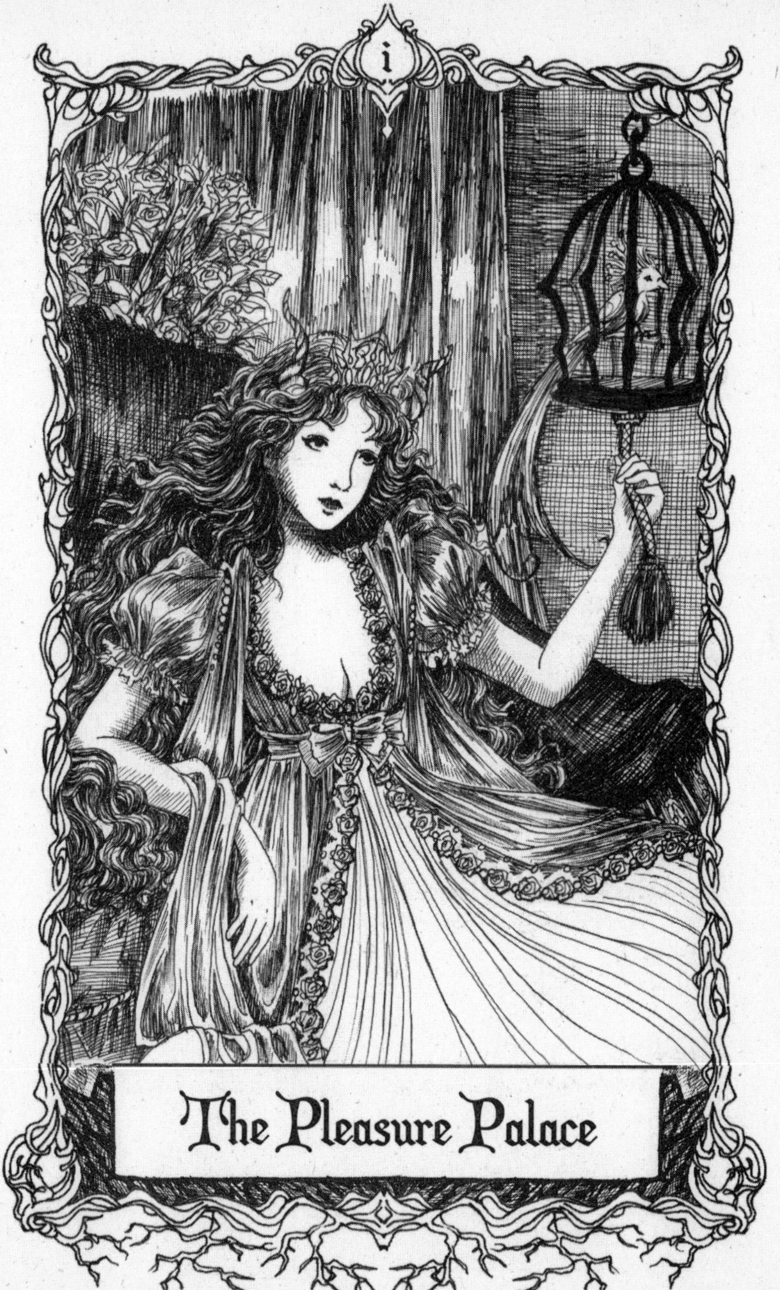
i
The Pleasure Palace

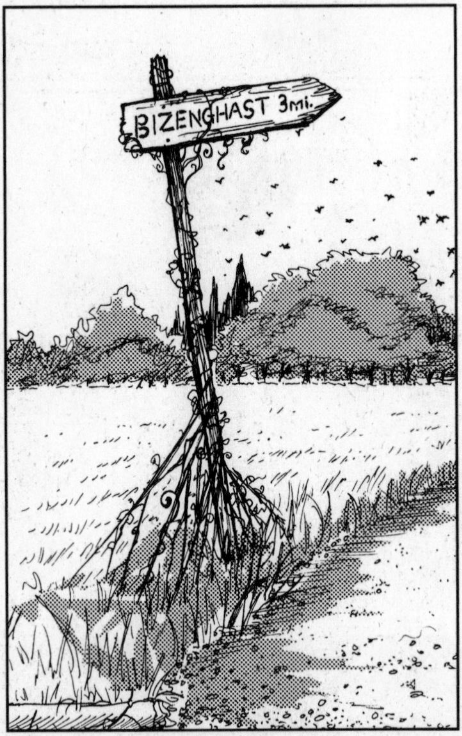
BIZENGHAST 3mi.

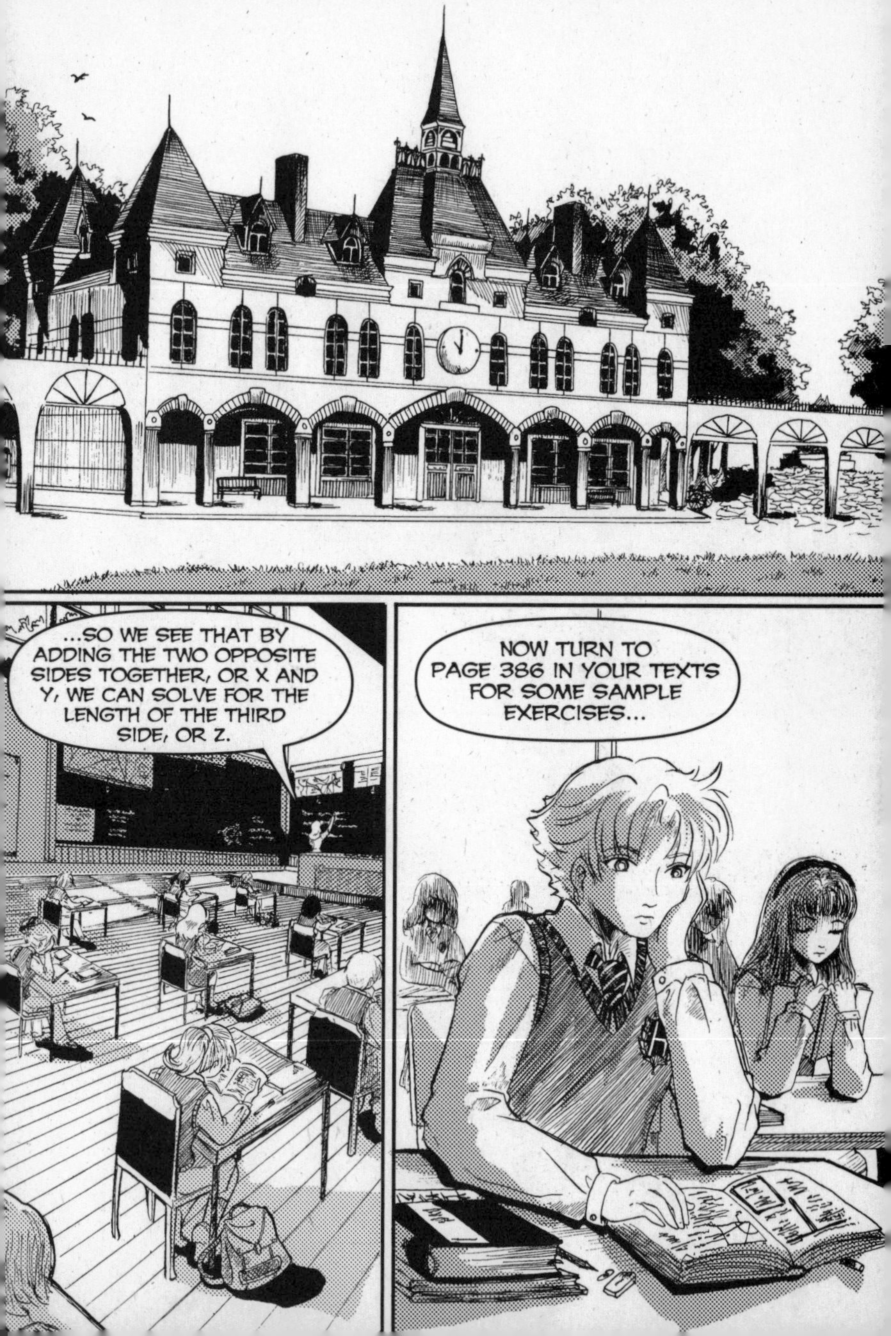
...SO WE SEE THAT BY ADDING THE TWO OPPOSITE SIDES TOGETHER, OR X AND Y, WE CAN SOLVE FOR THE LENGTH OF THE THIRD SIDE, OR Z.
NOW TURN TO PAGE 386 IN YOUR TEXTS FOR SOME SAMPLE EXERCISES...

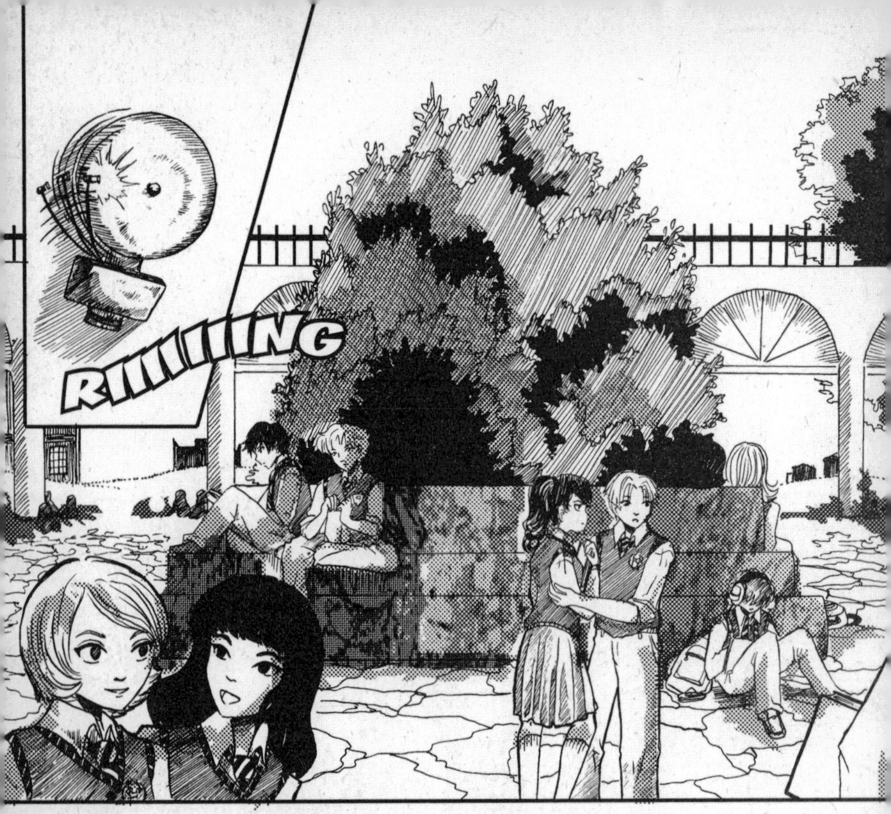
RIIIIIIING

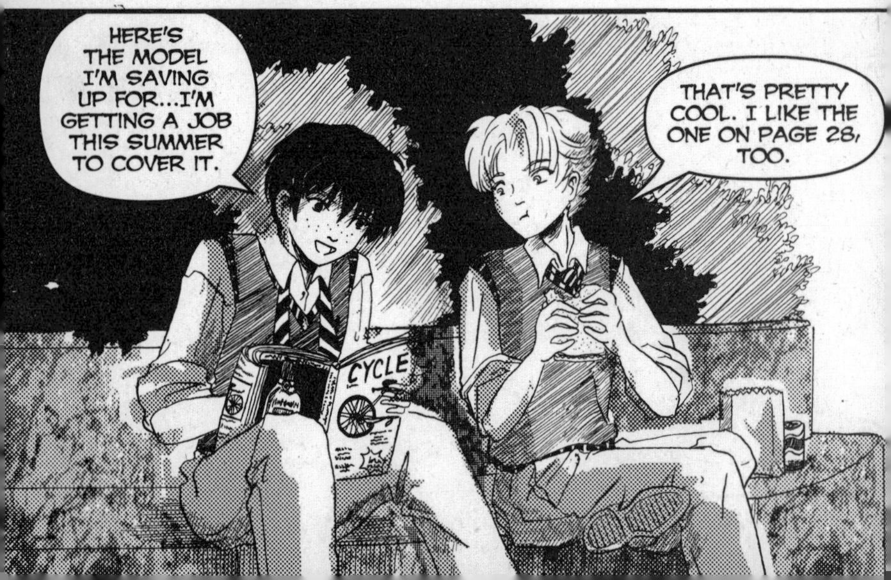
HERE'S THE MODEL I'M SAVING UP FOR...I'M GETTING A JOB THIS SUMMER TO COVER IT.
THAT'S PRETTY COOL. I LIKE THE ONE ON PAGE 28, TOO.
CYCLE

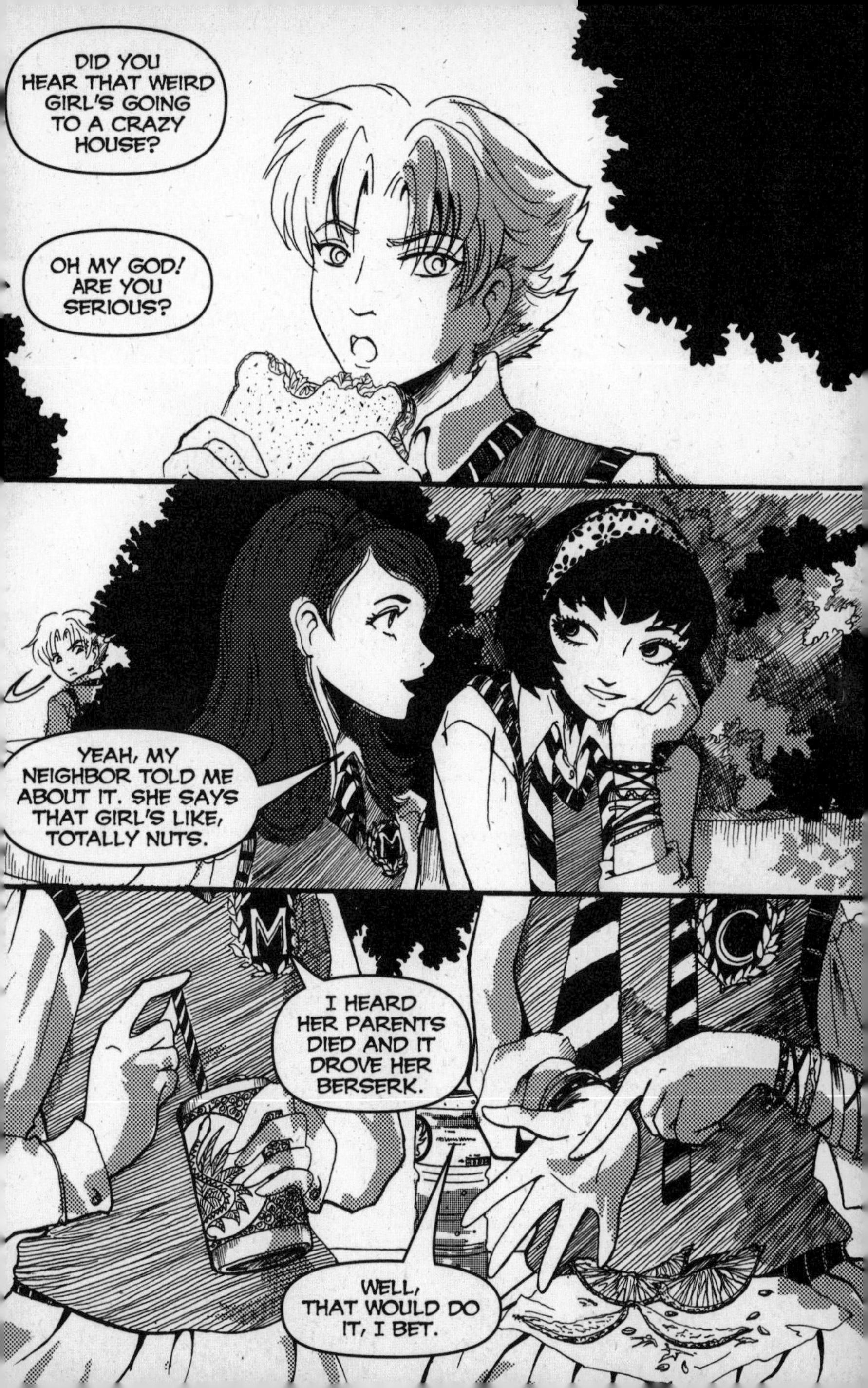
DID YOU HEAR THAT WEIRD GIRL'S GOING TO A CRAZY HOUSE?
OH MY GOD! ARE YOU SERIOUS?
YEAH, MY NEIGHBOR TOLD ME ABOUT IT. SHE SAYS THAT GIRL'S LIKE, TOTALLY NUTS.
I HEARD HER PARENTS DIED AND IT DROVE HER BERSERK.
WELL, THAT WOULD DO IT, I BET.

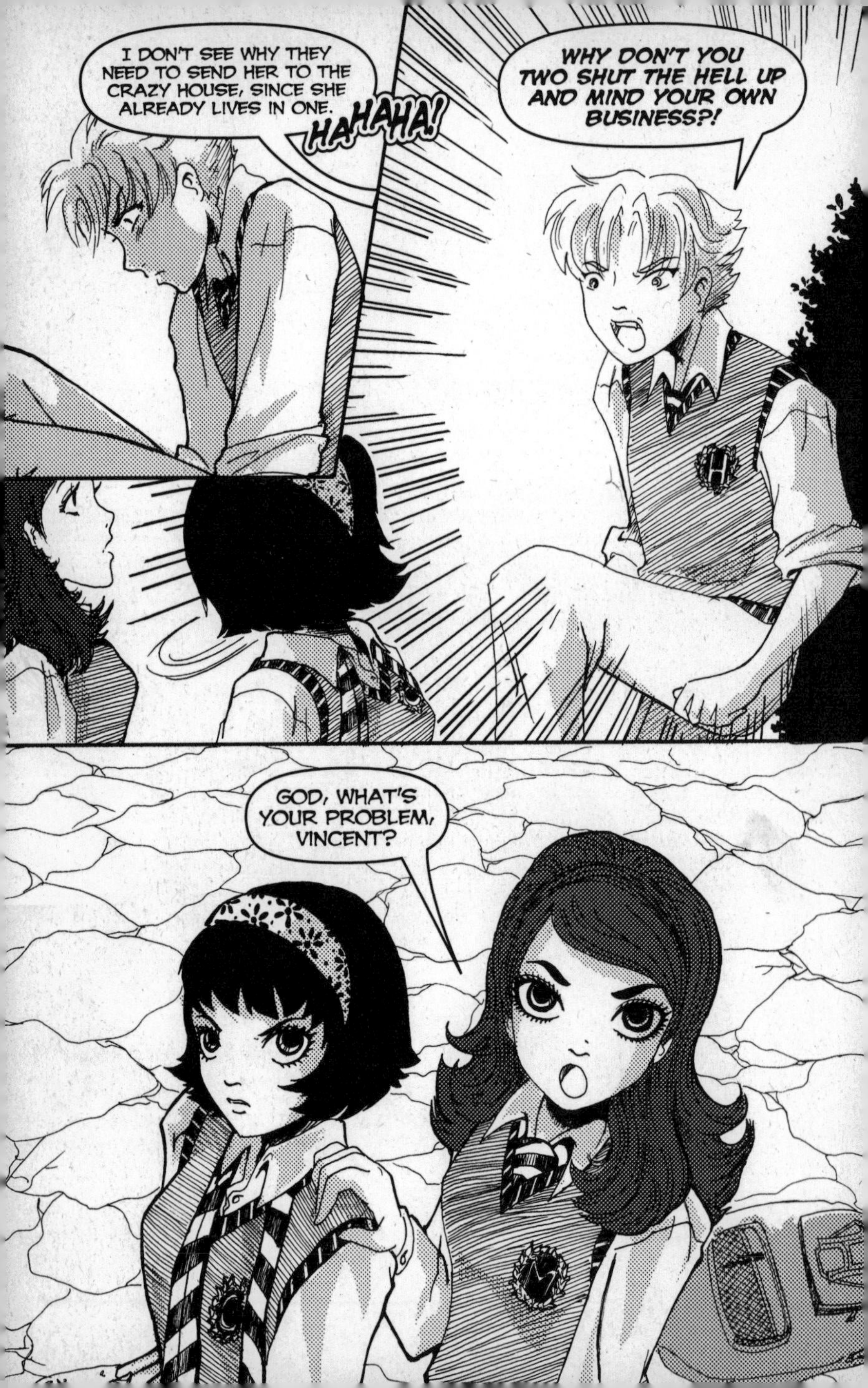
I DON'T SEE WHY THEY NEED TO SEND HER TO THE CRAZY HOUSE, SINCE SHE ALREADY LIVES IN ONE.
HAHAHA!
WHY DON'T YOU TWO SHUT THE HELL UP AND MIND YOUR OWN BUSINESS?!
GOD, WHAT'S YOUR PROBLEM, VINCENT?

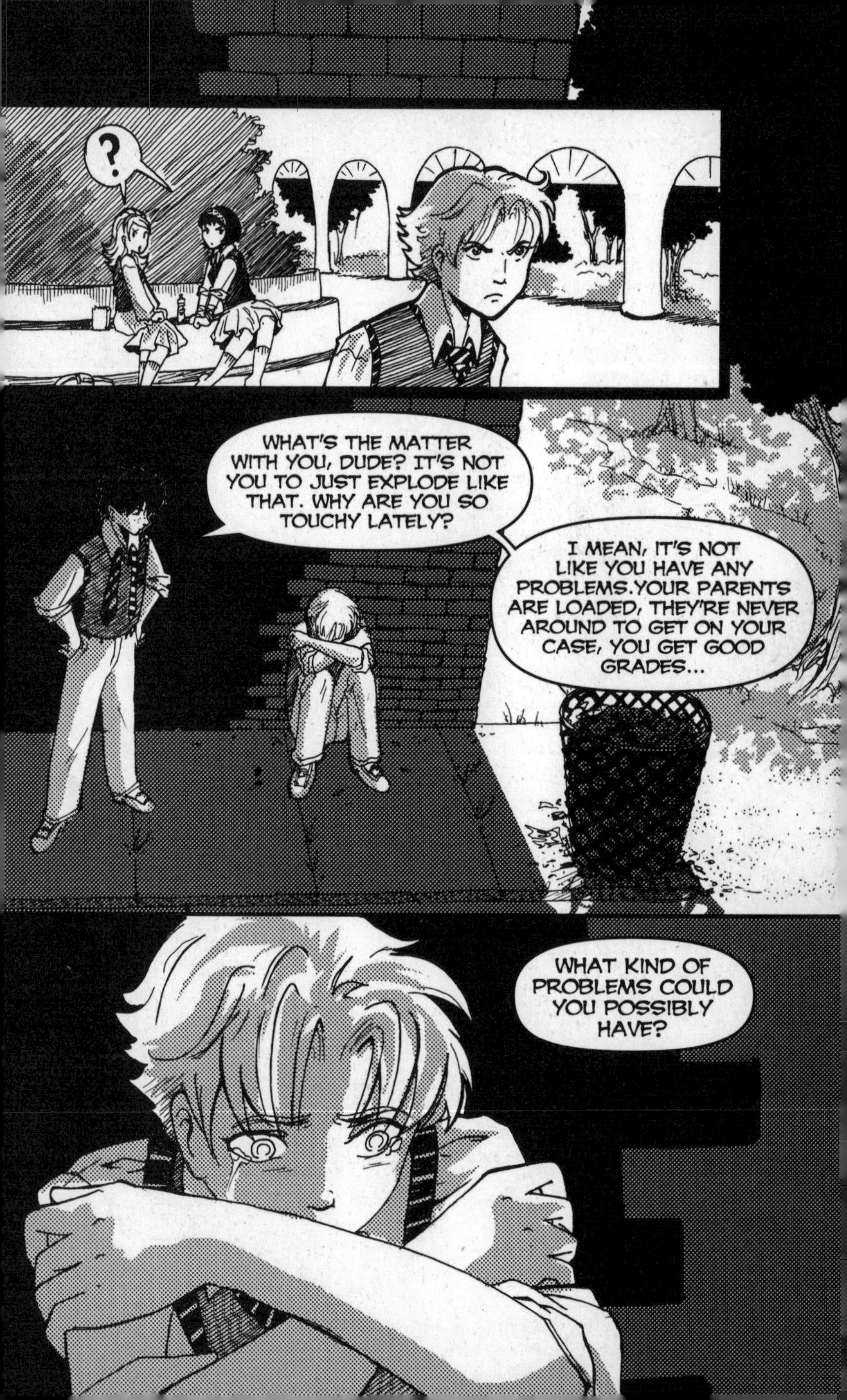
?
WHAT'S THE MATTER WITH YOU, DUDE? IT'S NOT YOU TO JUST EXPLODE LIKE THAT. WHY ARE YOU SO TOUCHY LATELY?
I MEAN, IT'S NOT LIKE YOU HAVE ANY PROBLEMS.YOUR PARENTS ARE LOADED, THEY'RE NEVER AROUND TO GET ON YOUR CASE, YOU GET GOOD GRADES...
WHAT KIND OF PROBLEMS COULD YOU POSSIBLY HAVE?

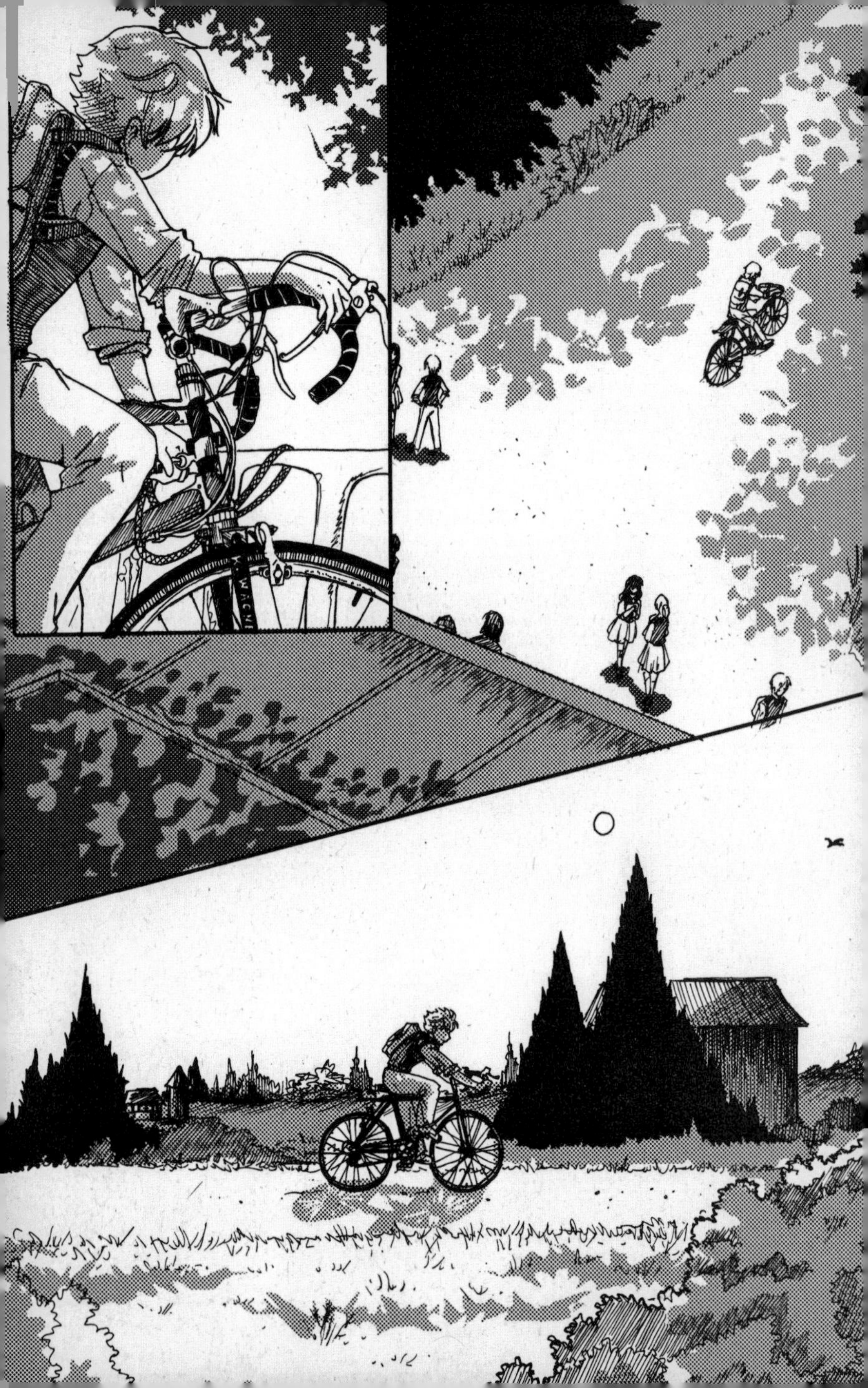

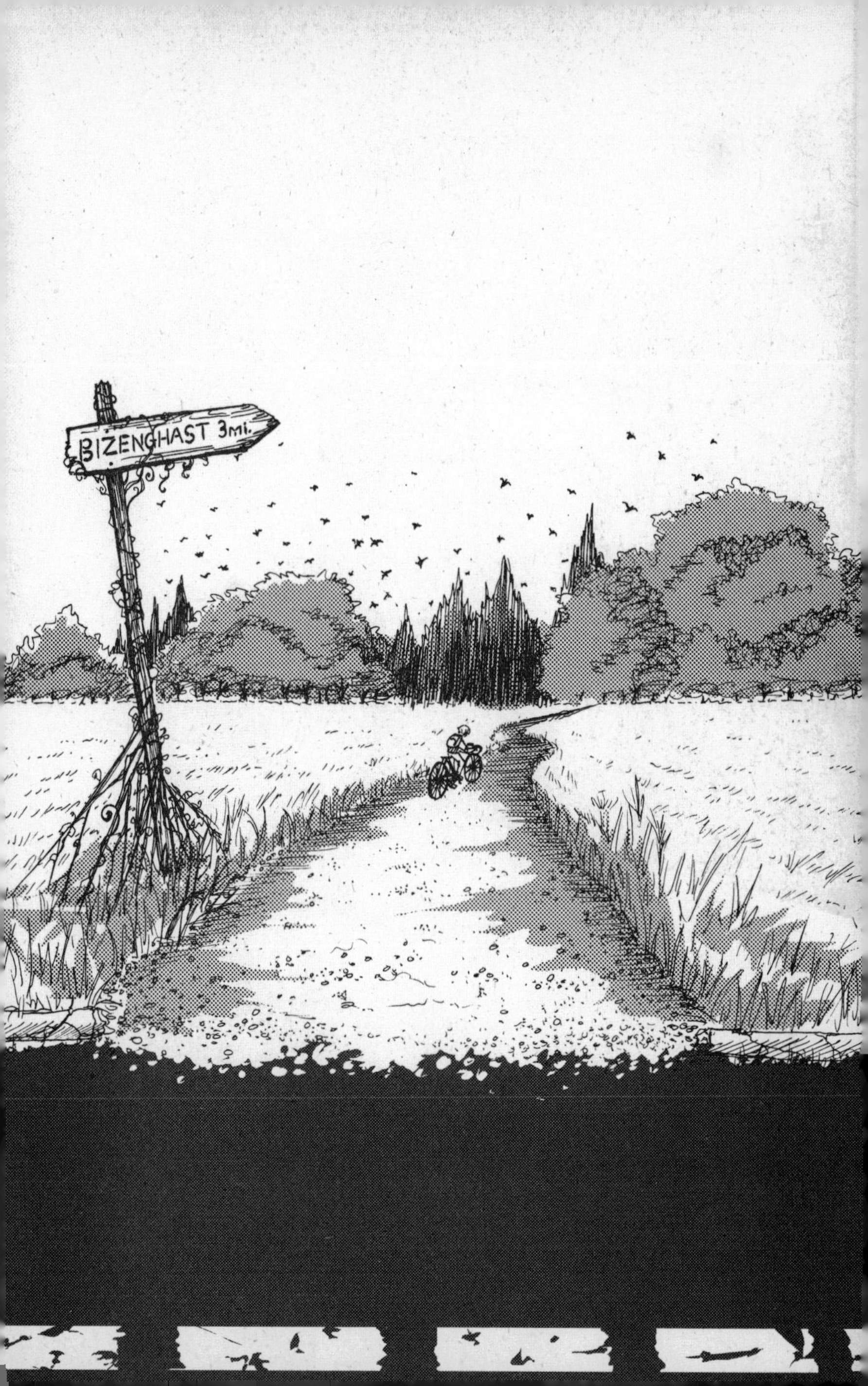
BIZENGHAST 3mi.

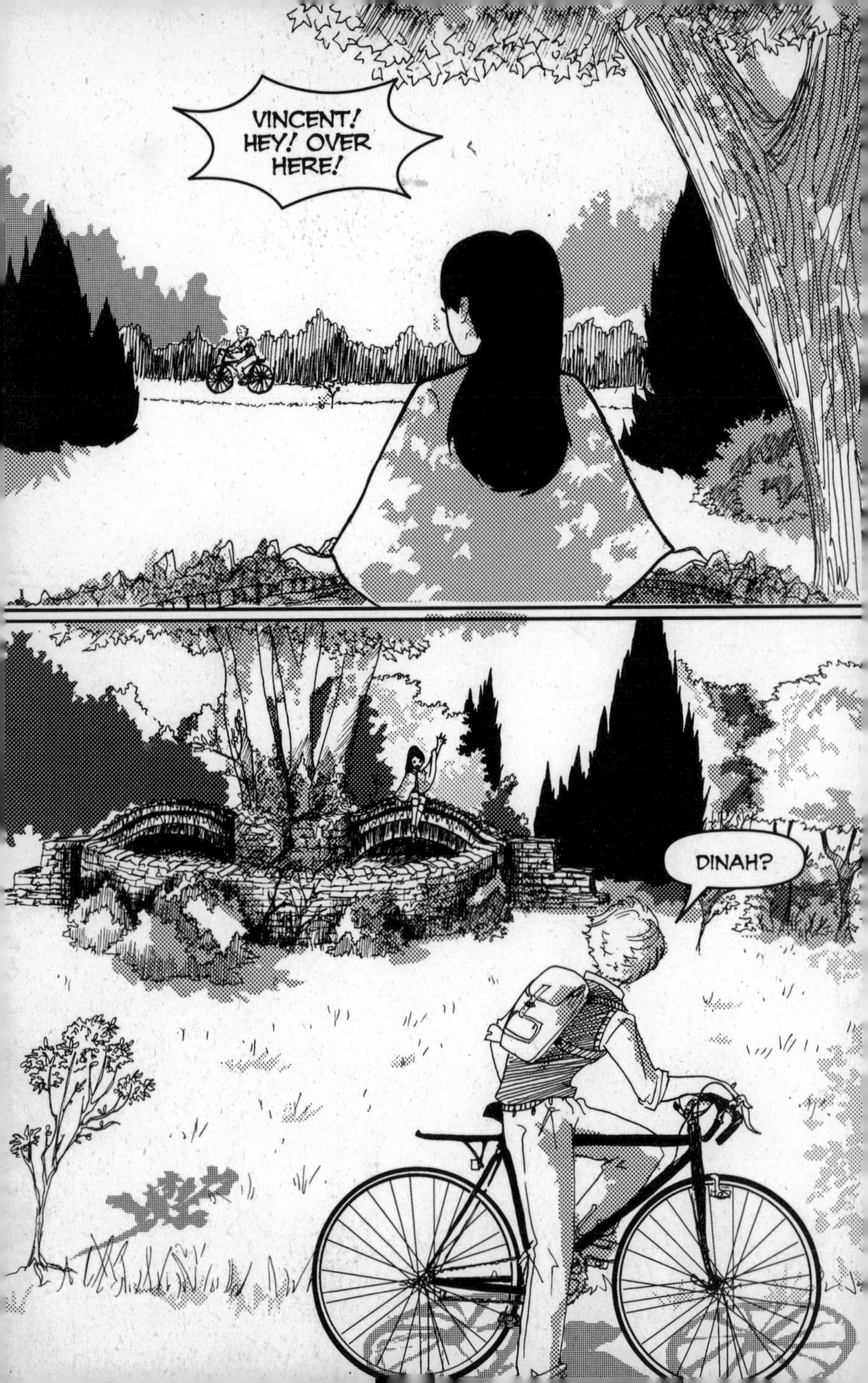
VINCENT! HEY! OVER HERE!
DINAH?

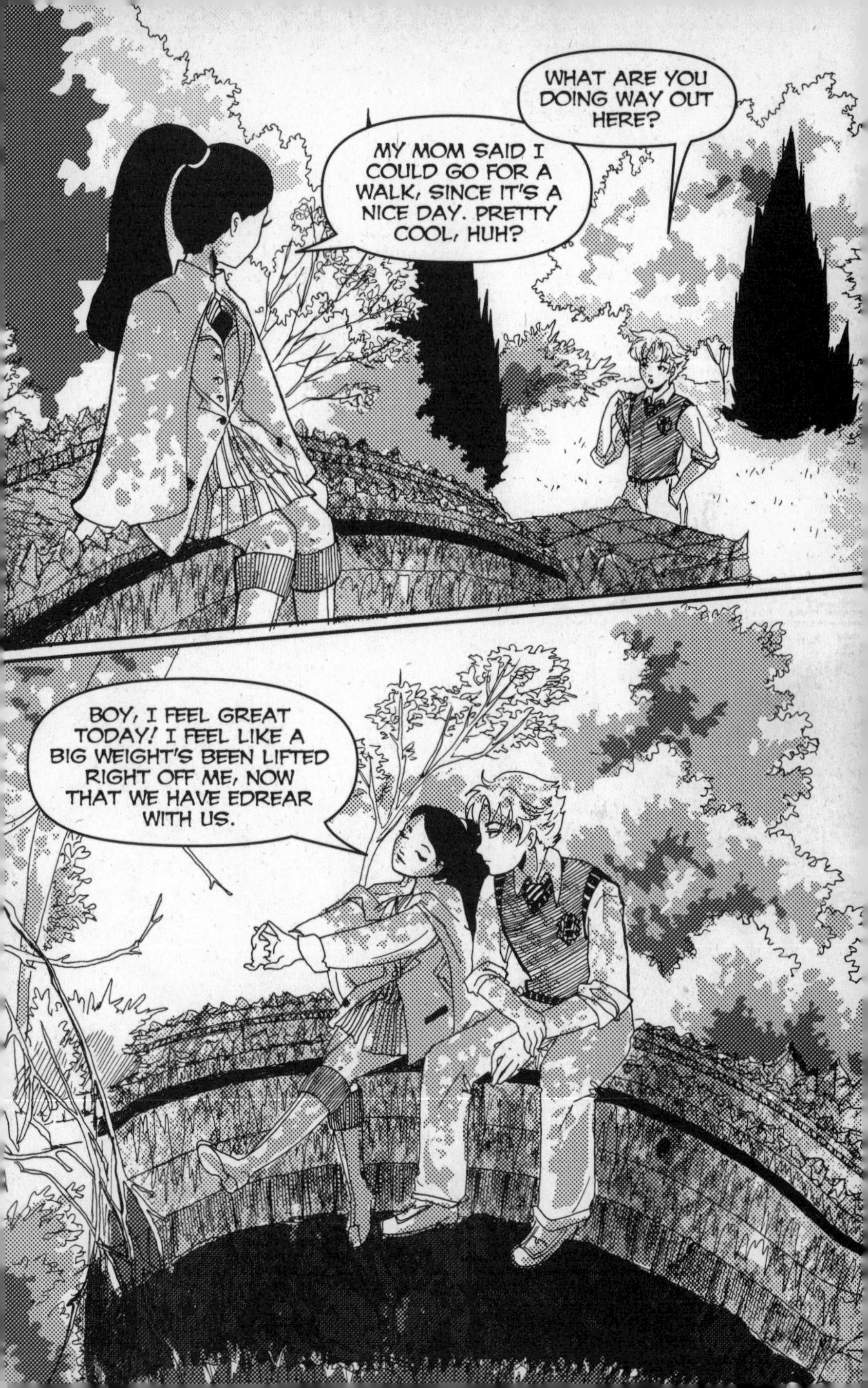
MY MOM SAID I COULD GO FOR A WALK, SINCE IT'S A NICE DAY. PRETTY COOL, HUH?
WHAT ARE YOU DOING WAY OUT HERE?
BOY, I FEEL GREAT TODAY! I FEEL LIKE A BIG WEIGHT'S BEEN LIFTED RIGHT OFF ME, NOW THAT WE HAVE EDREAR WITH US.

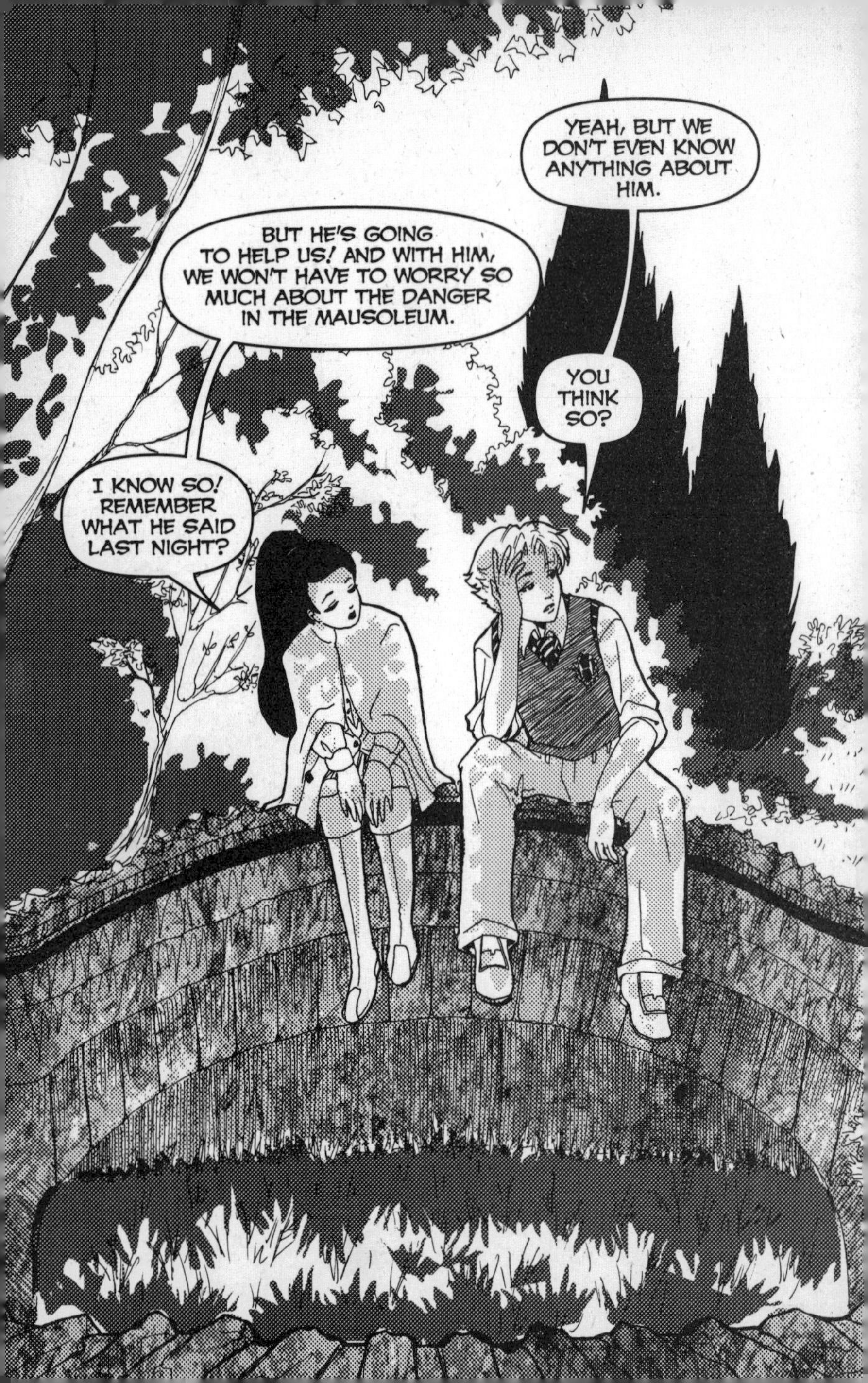
YEAH, BUT WE DON'T EVEN KNOW ANYTHING ABOUT HIM.
BUT HE'S GOING TO HELP US! AND WITH HIM, WE WON'T HAVE TO WORRY SO MUCH ABOUT THE DANGER IN THE MAUSOLEUM.
YOU THINK SO?
I KNOW SO! REMEMBER WHAT HE SAID LAST NIGHT?

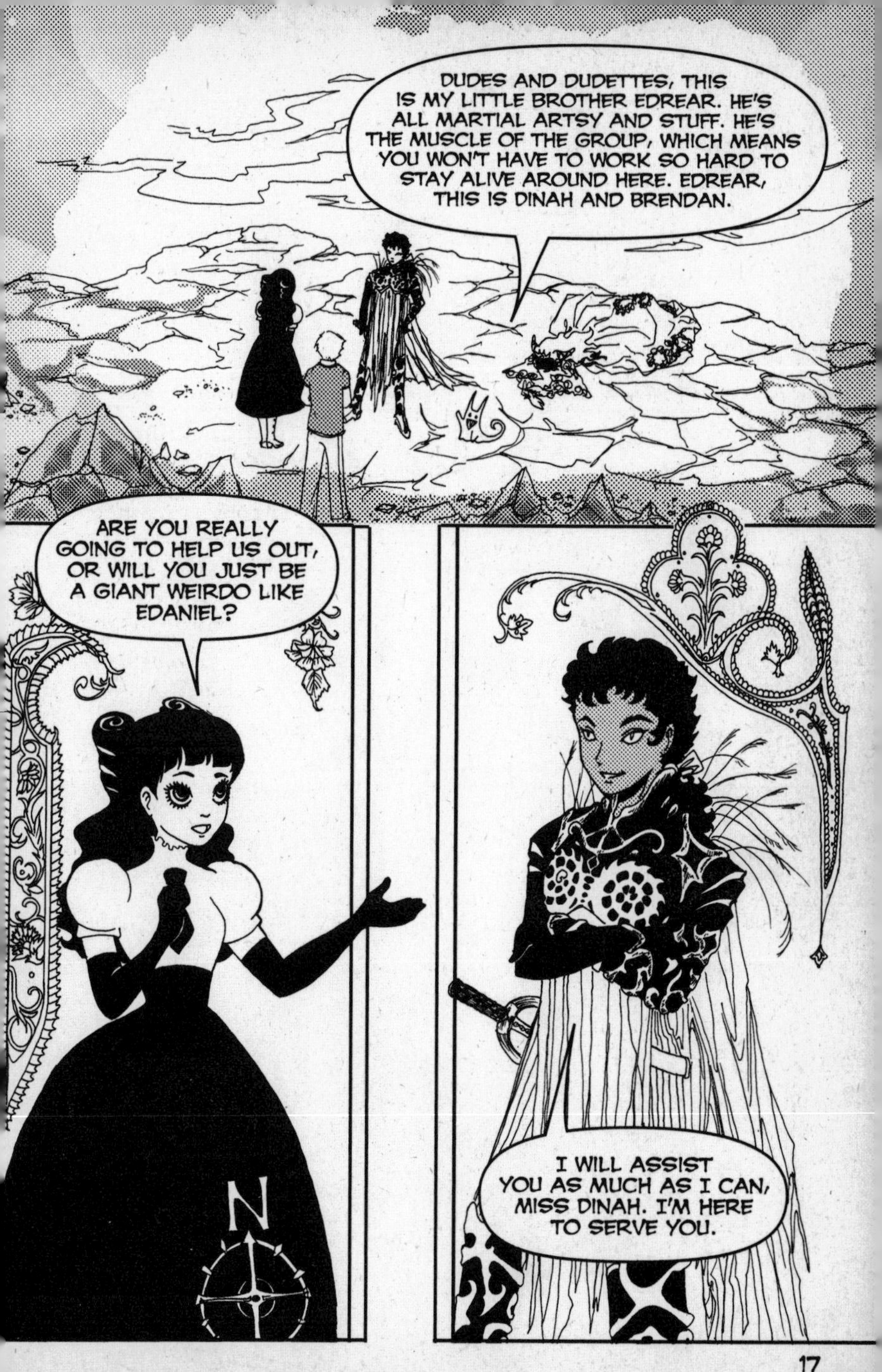
DUDES AND DUDETTES, THIS IS MY LITTLE BROTHER EDREAR. HE'S ALL MARTIAL ARTSY AND STUFF. HE'S THE MUSCLE OF THE GROUP, WHICH MEANS YOU WON'T HAVE TO WORK SO HARD TO STAY ALIVE AROUND HERE. EDREAR, THIS IS DINAH AND BRENDAN.
ARE YOU REALLY GOING TO HELP US OUT, OR WILL YOU JUST BE A GIANT WEIRDO LIKE EDANIEL?
I WILL ASSIST YOU AS MUCH AS I CAN, MISS DINAH. I'M HERE TO SERVE YOU.

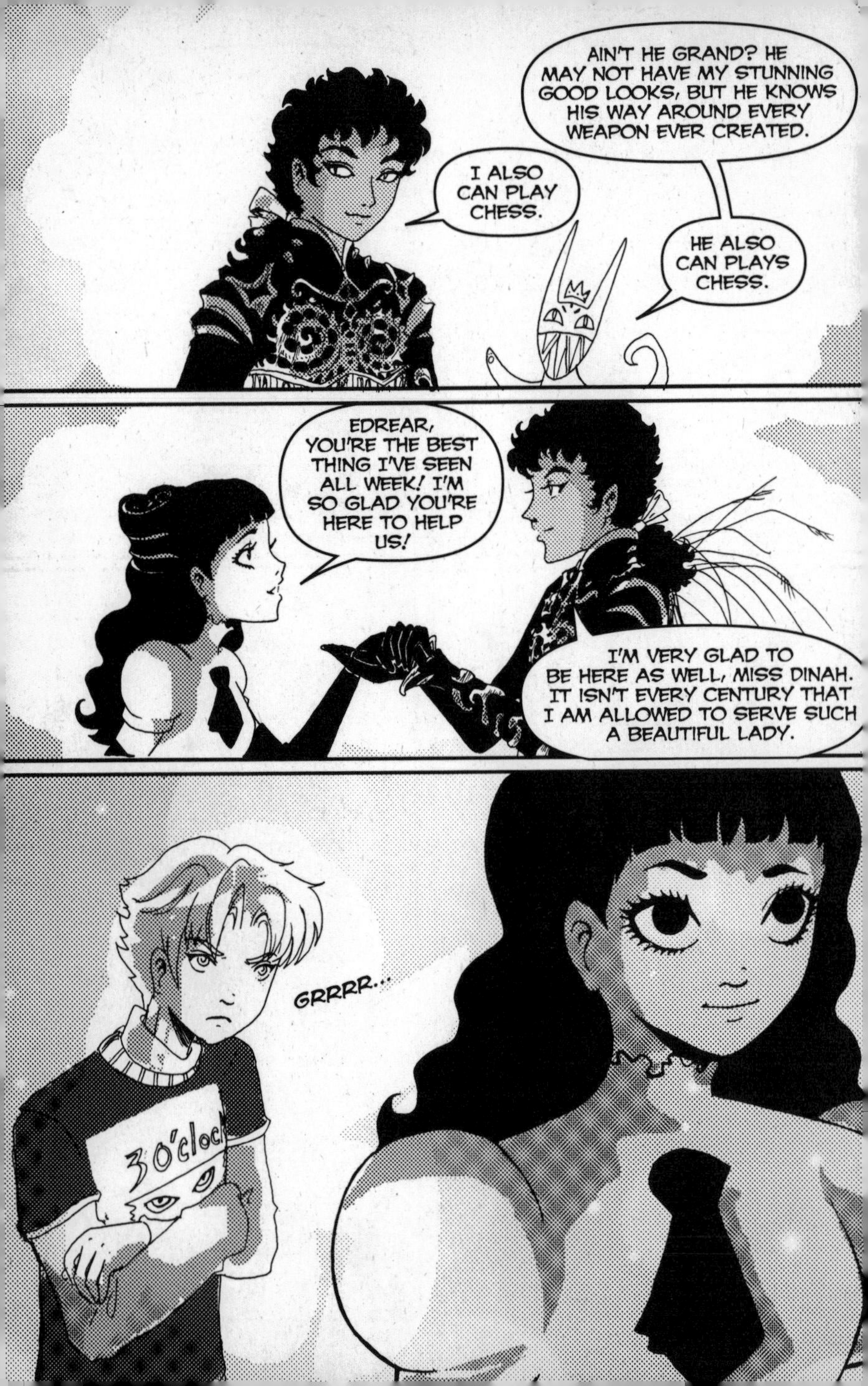
AIN'T HE GRAND? HE MAY NOT HAVE MY STUNNING GOOD LOOKS, BUT HE KNOWS HIS WAY AROUND EVERY WEAPON EVER CREATED.
I ALSO CAN PLAY CHESS.
HE ALSO CAN PLAYS CHESS.
EDREAR, YOU'RE THE BEST THING I'VE SEEN ALL WEEK! I'M SO GLAD YOU'RE HERE TO HELP US!
I'M VERY GLAD TO BE HERE AS WELL, MISS DINAH. IT ISN'T EVERY CENTURY THAT I AM ALLOWED TO SERVE SUCH A BEAUTIFUL LADY.
GRRRR...
3O'cloc

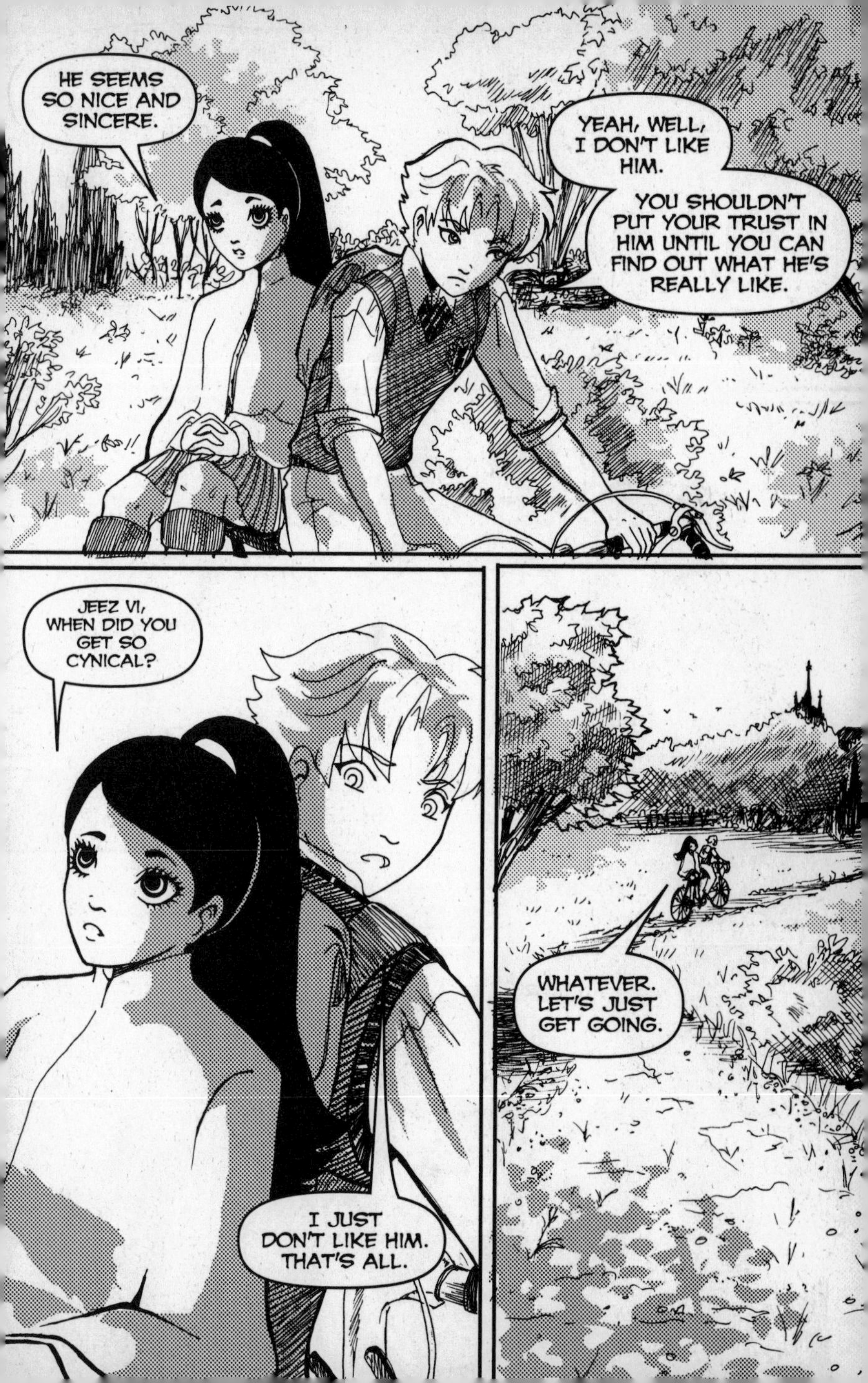
HE SEEMS SO NICE AND SINCERE.
YEAH, WELL, I DON'T LIKE HIM.
YOU SHOULDN'T PUT YOUR TRUST IN HIM UNTIL YOU CAN FIND OUT WHAT HE'S REALLY LIKE.
JEEZ VI, WHEN DID YOU GET SO CYNICAL?
I JUST DON'T LIKE HIM. THAT'S ALL.
WHATEVER. LET'S JUST GET GOING.

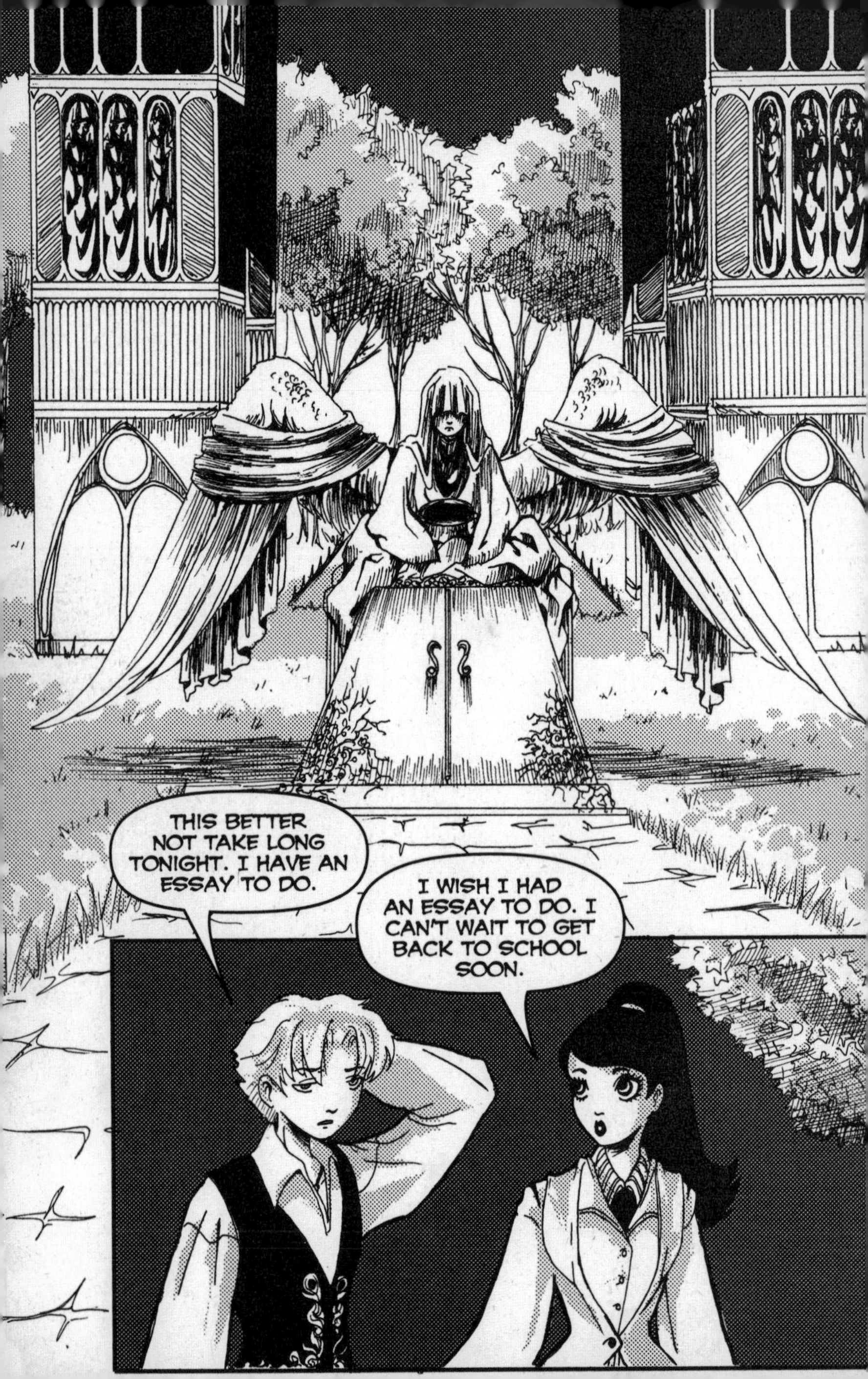
THIS BETTER NOT TAKE LONG TONIGHT. I HAVE AN ESSAY TO DO.
I WISH I HAD AN ESSAY TO DO. I CAN'T WAIT TO GET BACK TO SCHOOL SOON.

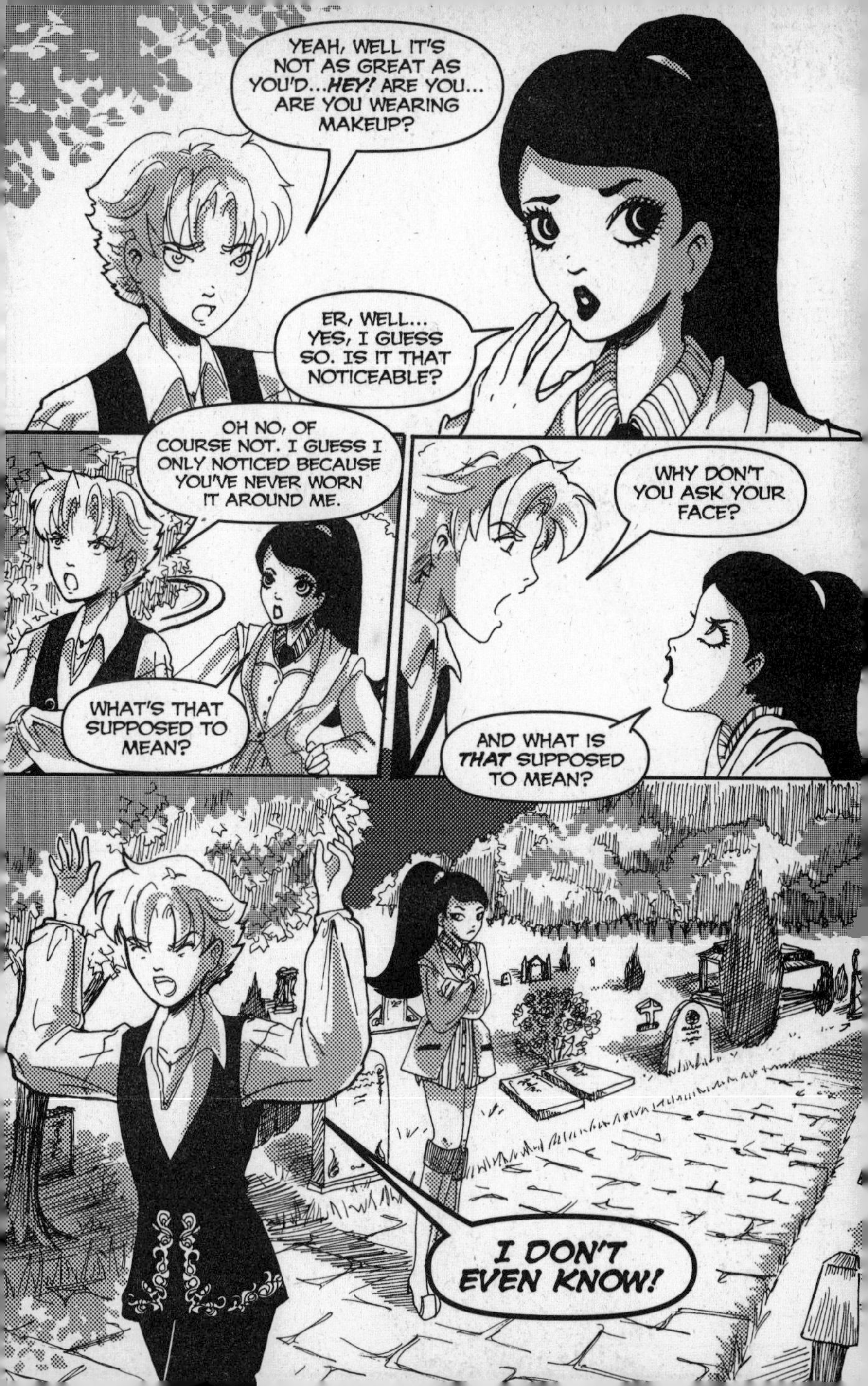
YEAH, WELL IT'S NOT AS GREAT AS YOU'D...*HEY!* ARE YOU... ARE YOU WEARING MAKEUP?
ER, WELL... YES, I GUESS SO. IS IT THAT NOTICEABLE?
OH NO, OF COURSE NOT. I GUESS I ONLY NOTICED BECAUSE YOU'VE NEVER WORN IT AROUND ME.
WHAT'S THAT SUPPOSED TO MEAN?
WHY DON'T YOU ASK YOUR FACE?
AND WHAT IS *THAT* SUPPOSED TO MEAN?
I DON'T EVEN KNOW!

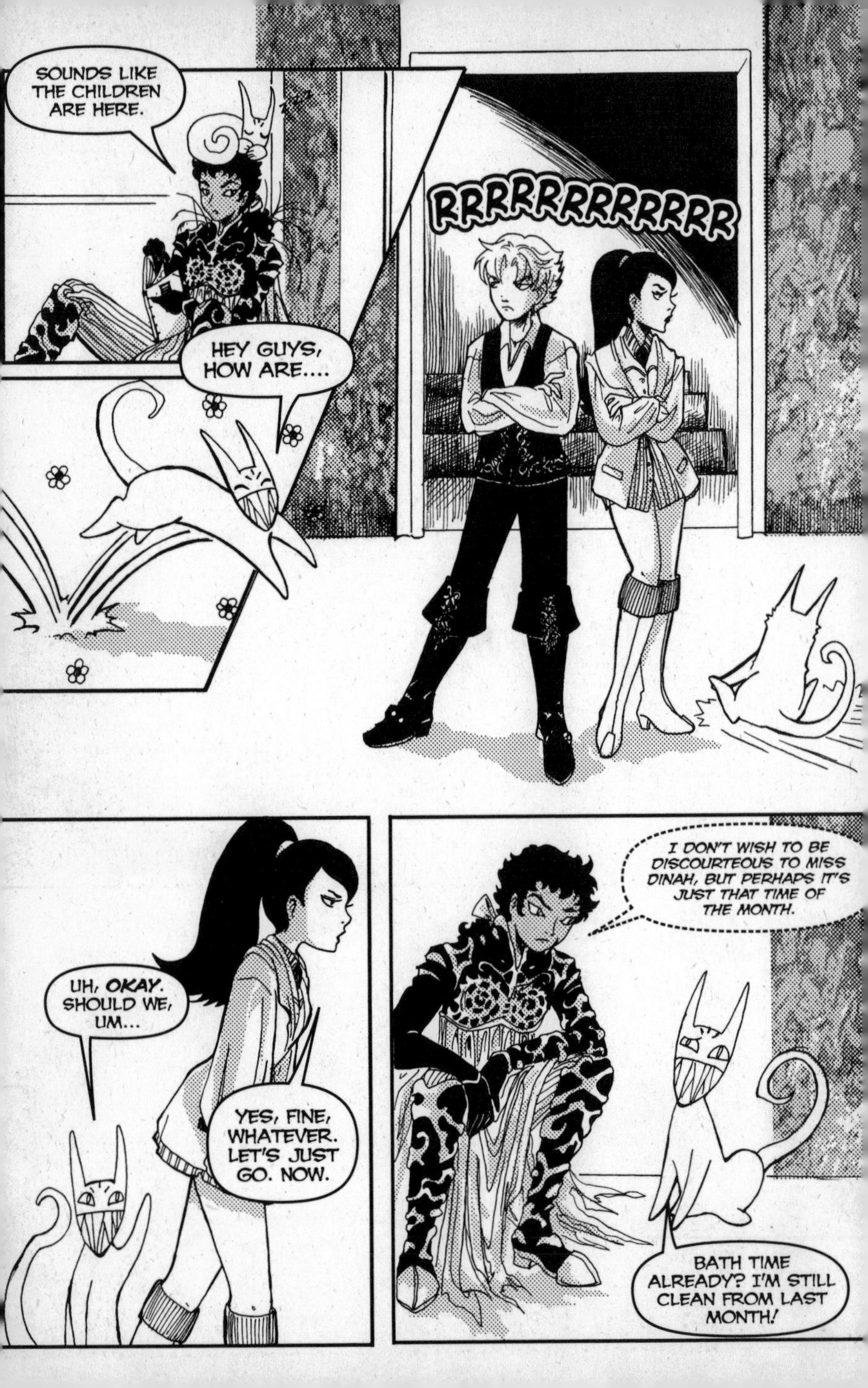
SOUNDS LIKE THE CHILDREN ARE HERE.
HEY GUYS, HOW ARE....
RRRRRRRRRRRRR
UH, *OKAY*. SHOULD WE, UM...
YES, FINE, WHATEVER. LET'S JUST GO. NOW.
I DON'T WISH TO BE DISCOURTEOUS TO MISS DINAH, BUT PERHAPS IT'S JUST THAT TIME OF THE MONTH.
BATH TIME ALREADY? I'M STILL CLEAN FROM LAST MONTH!

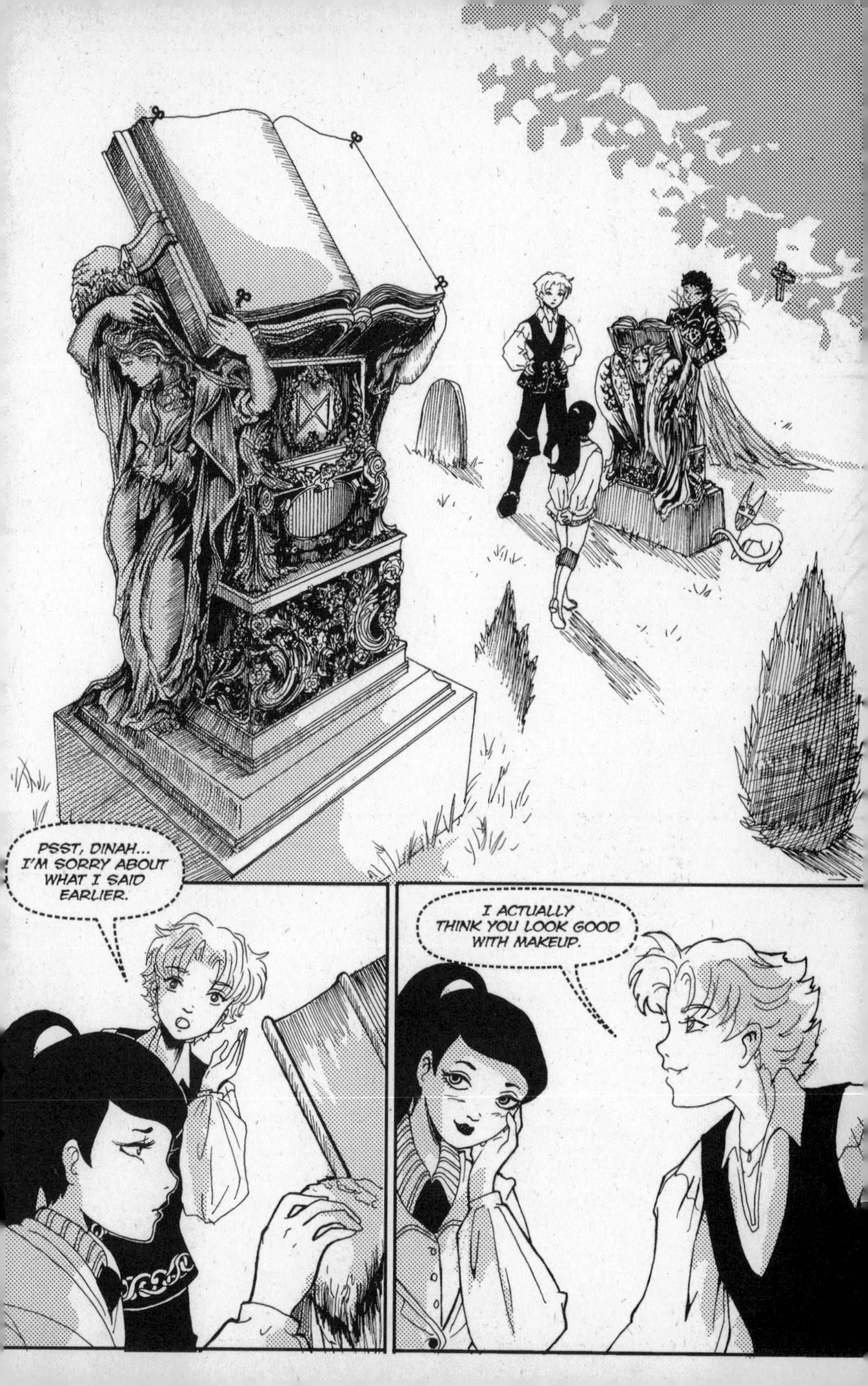
PSST, DINAH... I'M SORRY ABOUT WHAT I SAID EARLIER.
I ACTUALLY THINK YOU LOOK GOOD WITH MAKEUP.

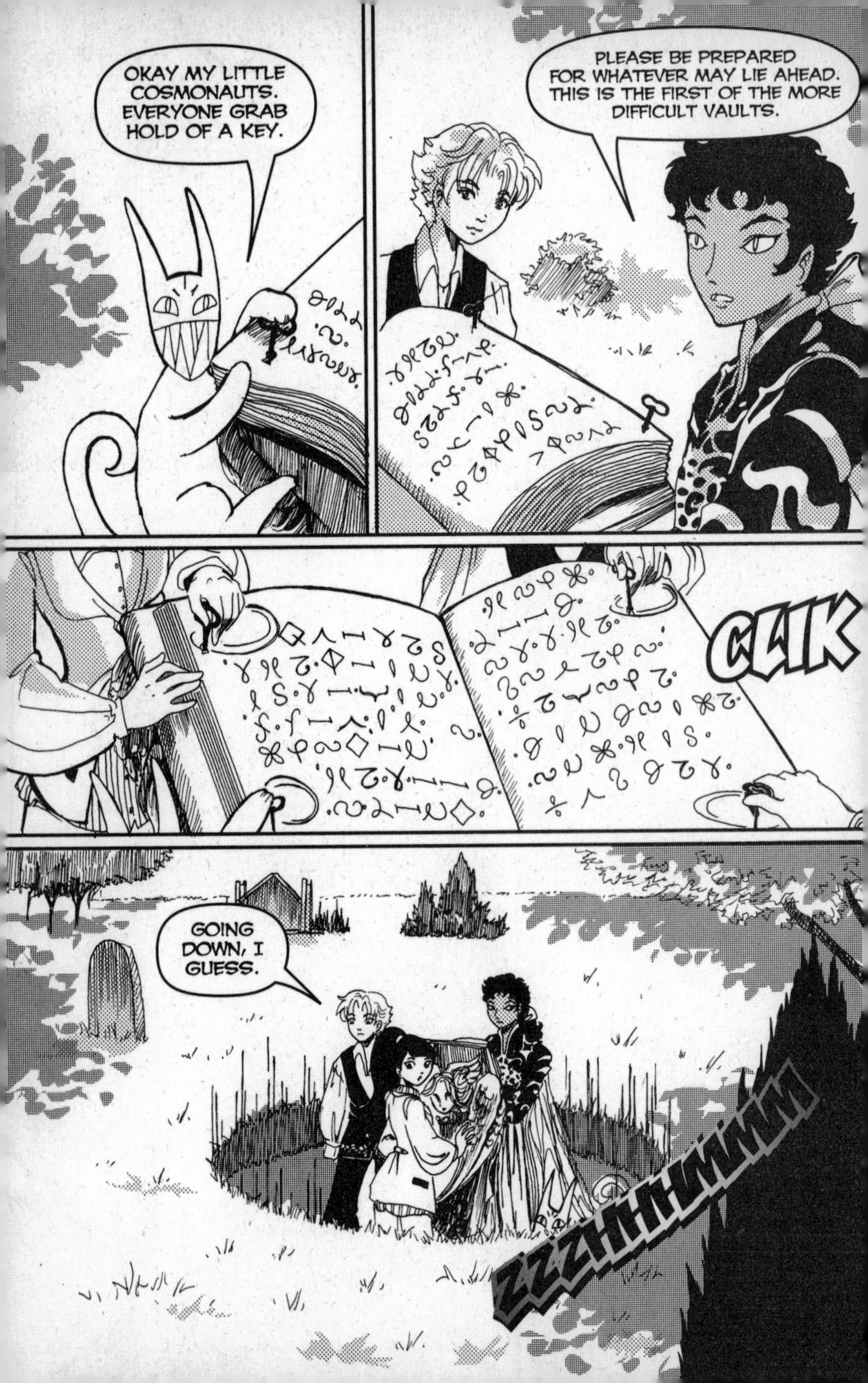
OKAY MY LITTLE COSMONAUTS. EVERYONE GRAB HOLD OF A KEY.
PLEASE BE PREPARED FOR WHATEVER MAY LIE AHEAD. THIS IS THE FIRST OF THE MORE DIFFICULT VAULTS.
CLIK
GOING DOWN, I GUESS.
ZZZHHHMMMM

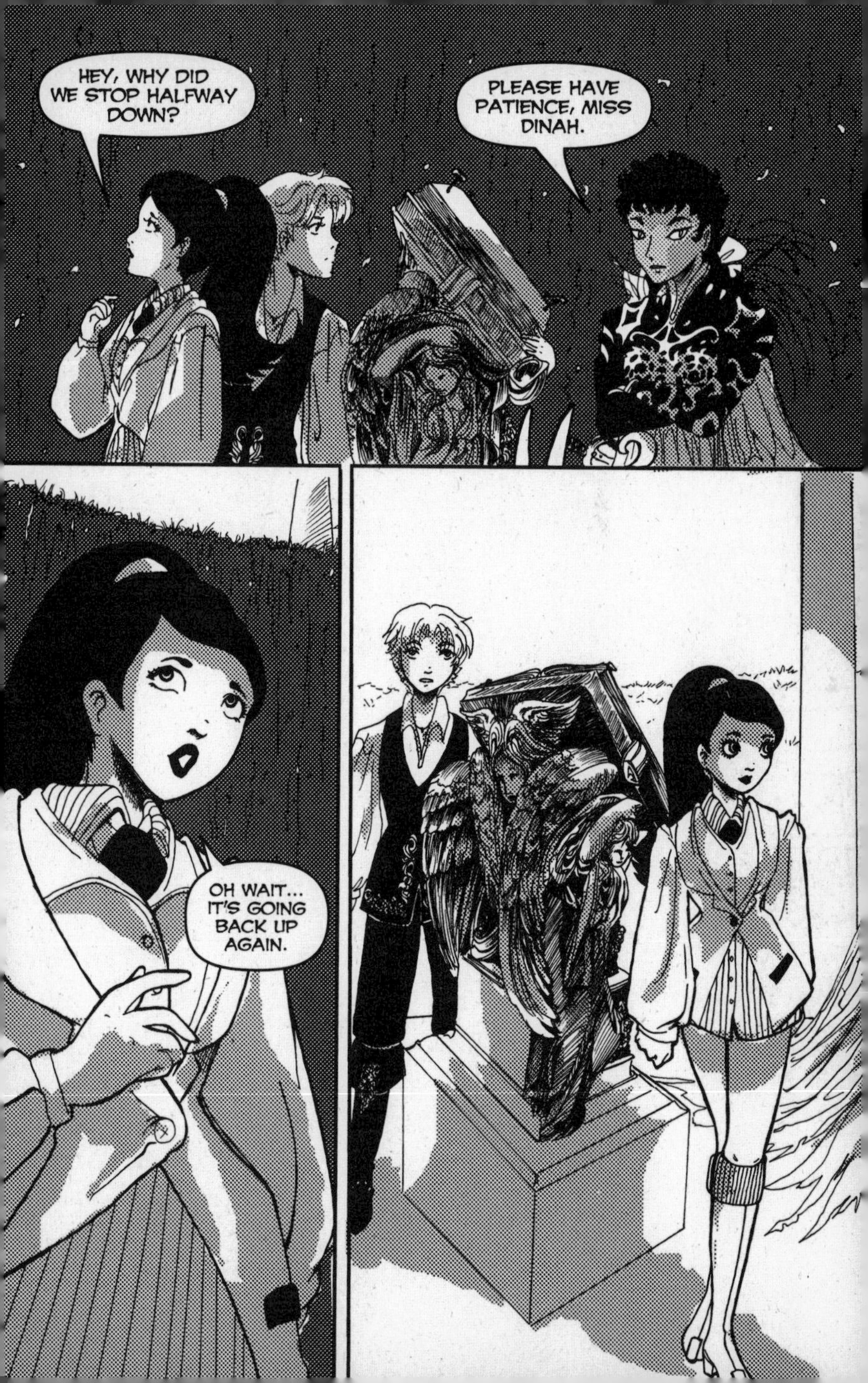
HEY, WHY DID WE STOP HALFWAY DOWN?
PLEASE HAVE PATIENCE, MISS DINAH.
OH WAIT... IT'S GOING BACK UP AGAIN.

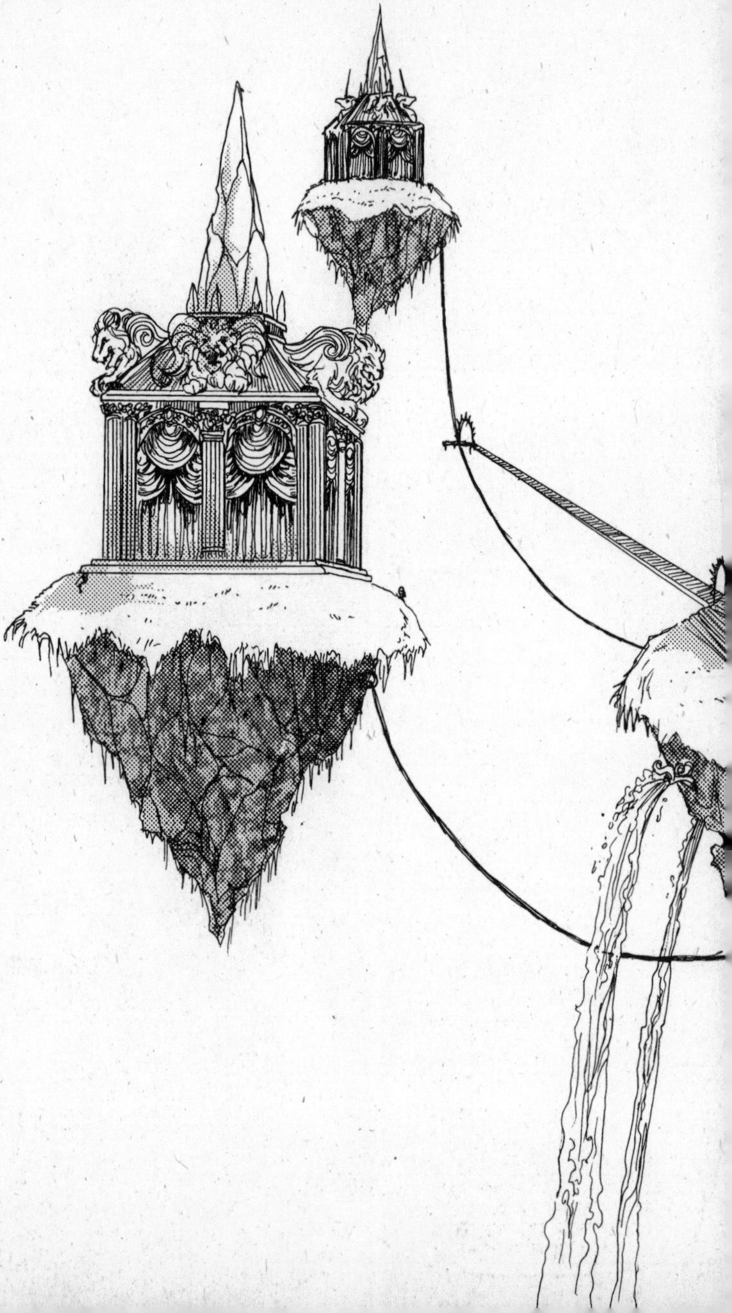

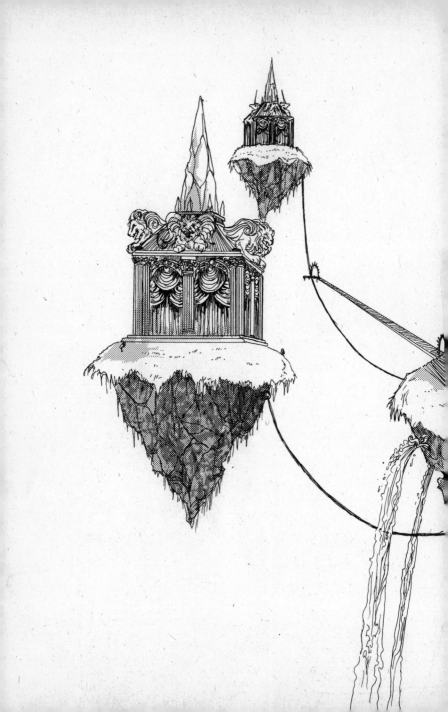

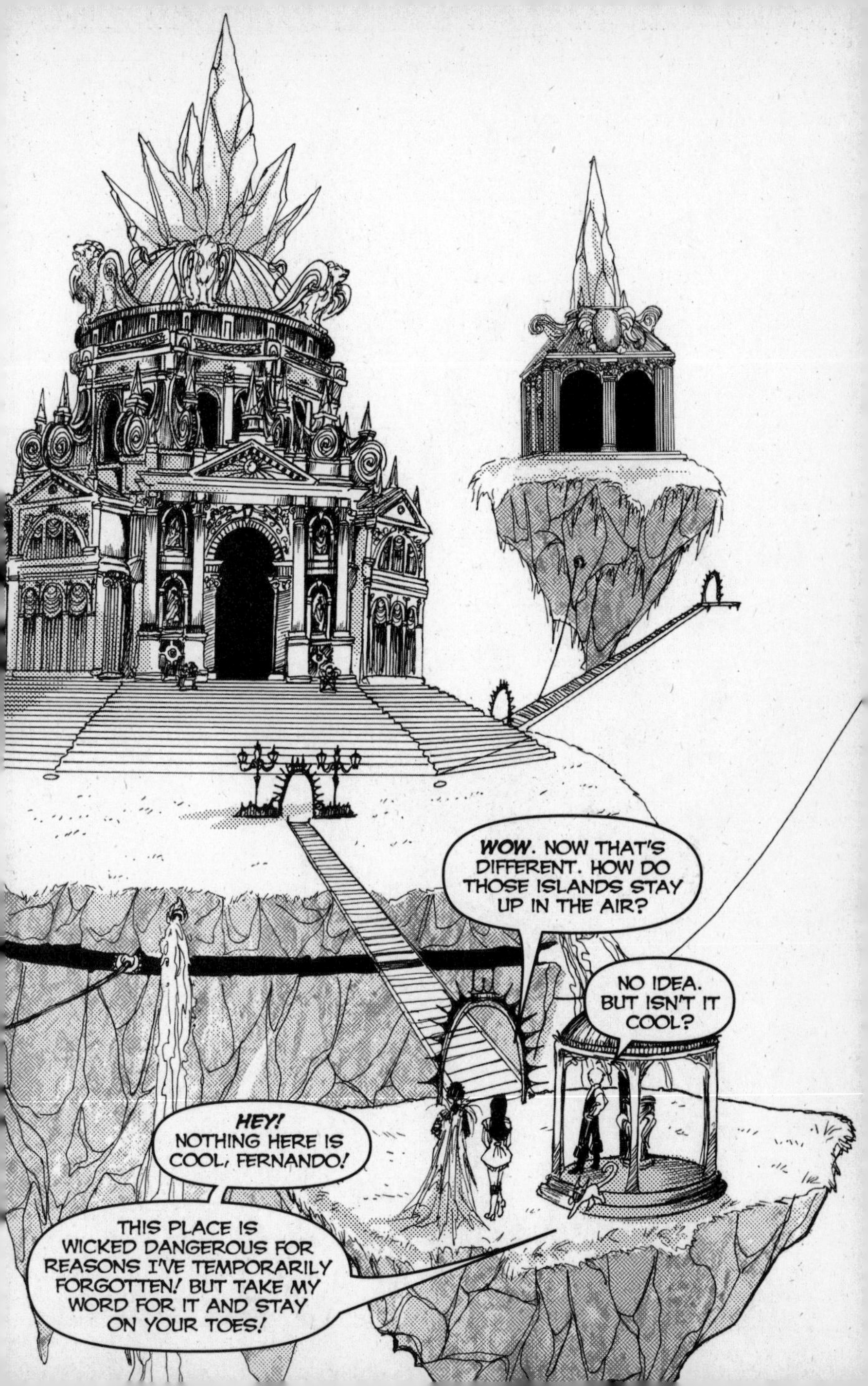
WOW. NOW THAT'S DIFFERENT. HOW DO THOSE ISLANDS STAY UP IN THE AIR?
NO IDEA. BUT ISN'T IT COOL?
HEY! NOTHING HERE IS COOL, FERNANDO!
THIS PLACE IS WICKED DANGEROUS FOR REASONS I'VE TEMPORARILY FORGOTTEN! BUT TAKE MY WORD FOR IT AND STAY ON YOUR TOES!

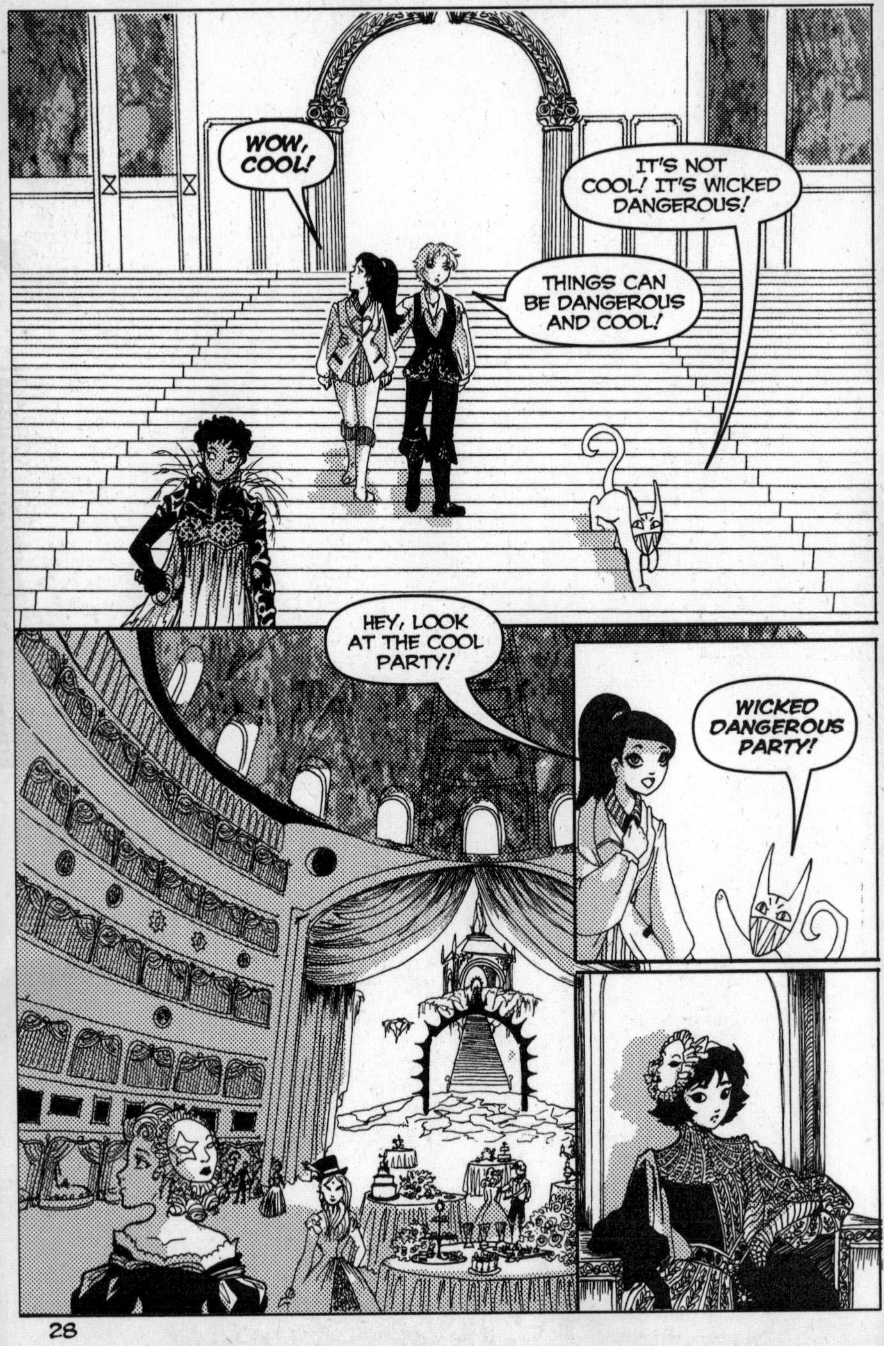
WOW, COOL!
IT'S NOT COOL! IT'S WICKED DANGEROUS!
THINGS CAN BE DANGEROUS AND COOL!
HEY, LOOK AT THE COOL PARTY!
WICKED DANGEROUS PARTY!

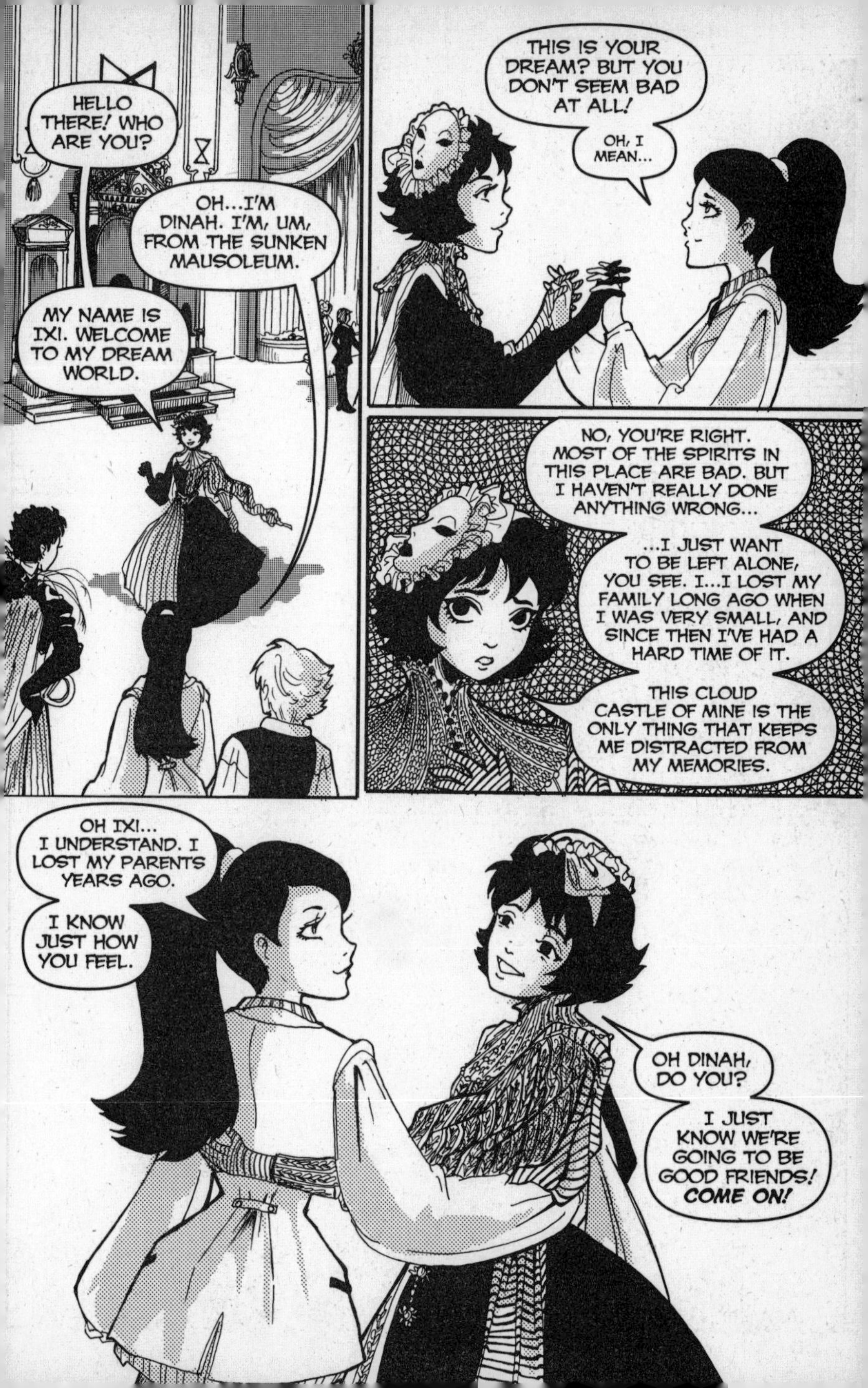
HELLO THERE! WHO ARE YOU?
OH...I'M DINAH. I'M, UM, FROM THE SUNKEN MAUSOLEUM.
MY NAME IS IXI. WELCOME TO MY DREAM WORLD.
THIS IS YOUR DREAM? BUT YOU DON'T SEEM BAD AT ALL!
OH, I MEAN...
NO, YOU'RE RIGHT. MOST OF THE SPIRITS IN THIS PLACE ARE BAD. BUT I HAVEN'T REALLY DONE ANYTHING WRONG...
...I JUST WANT TO BE LEFT ALONE, YOU SEE. I...I LOST MY FAMILY LONG AGO WHEN I WAS VERY SMALL, AND SINCE THEN I'VE HAD A HARD TIME OF IT.
THIS CLOUD CASTLE OF MINE IS THE ONLY THING THAT KEEPS ME DISTRACTED FROM MY MEMORIES.
OH IXI... I UNDERSTAND. I LOST MY PARENTS YEARS AGO.
I KNOW JUST HOW YOU FEEL.
OH DINAH, DO YOU?
I JUST KNOW WE'RE GOING TO BE GOOD FRIENDS! ***COME ON!***

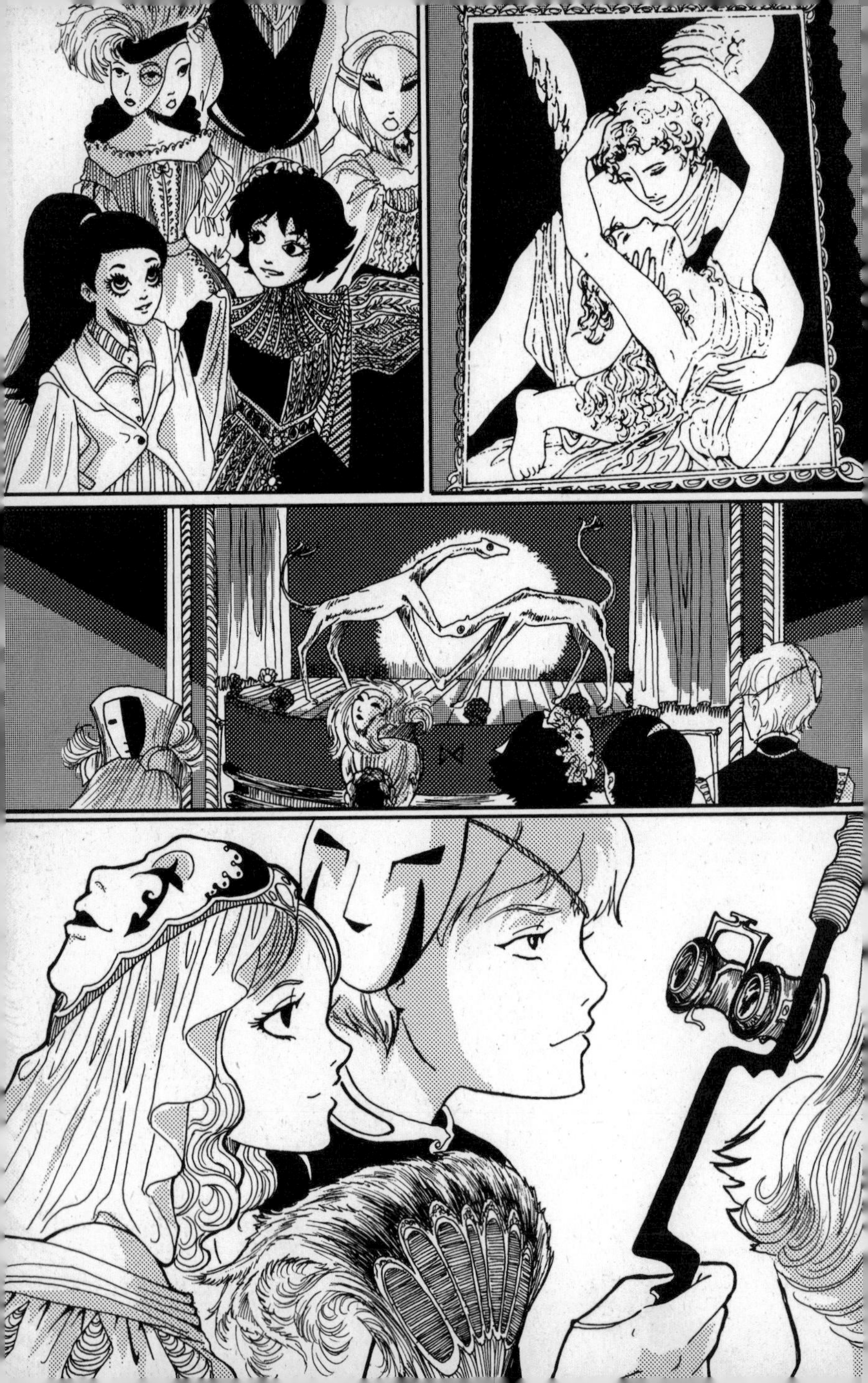

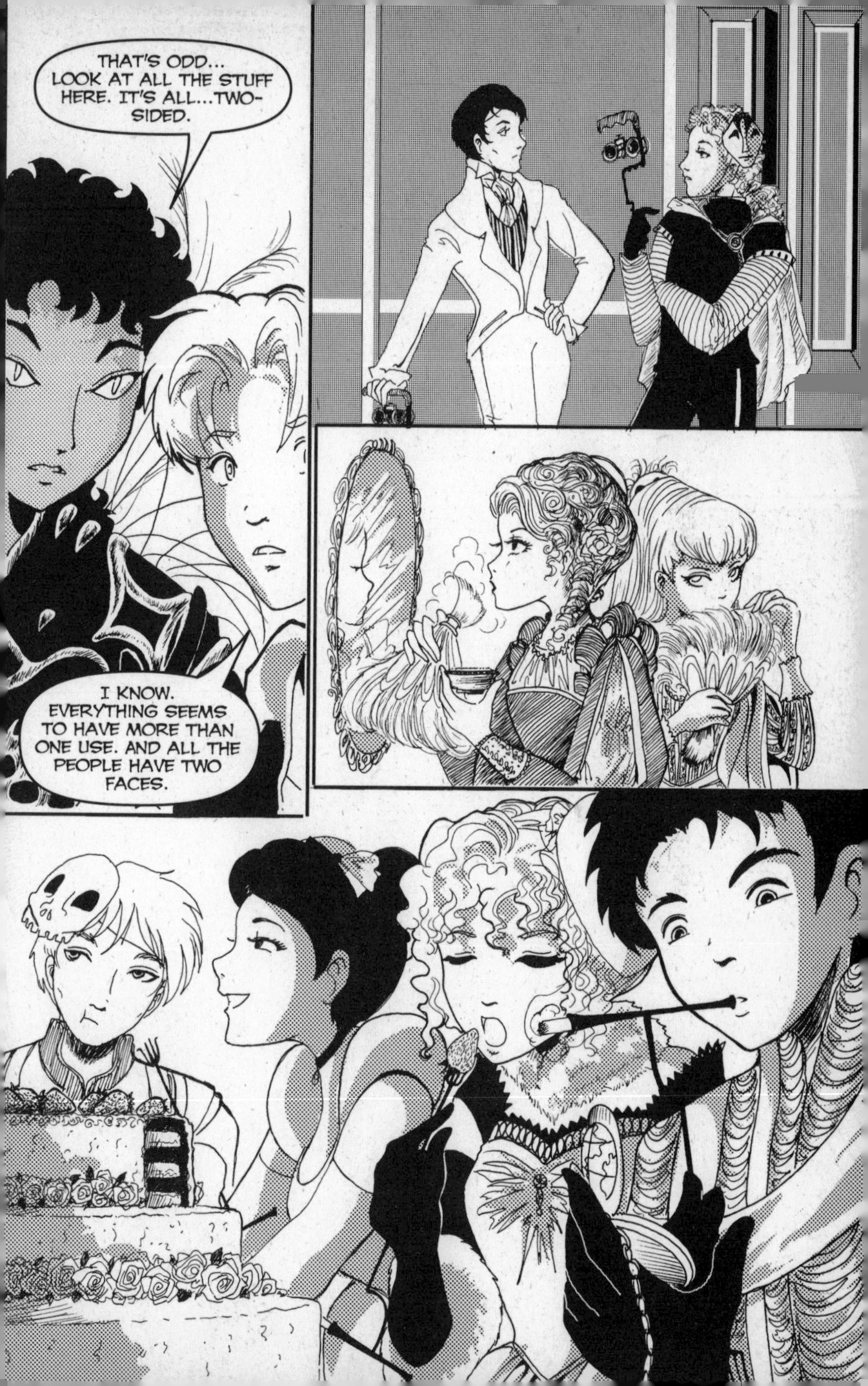
THAT'S ODD... LOOK AT ALL THE STUFF HERE. IT'S ALL...TWO-SIDED.
I KNOW. EVERYTHING SEEMS TO HAVE MORE THAN ONE USE. AND ALL THE PEOPLE HAVE TWO FACES.

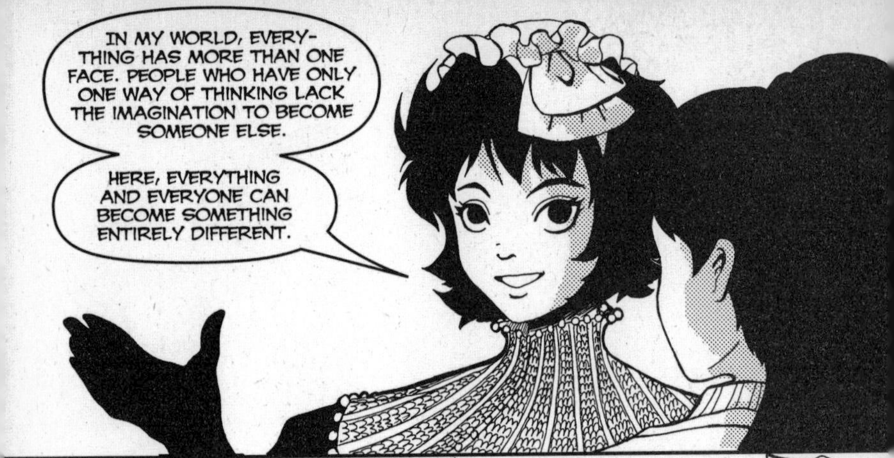
IN MY WORLD, EVERY-THING HAS MORE THAN ONE FACE. PEOPLE WHO HAVE ONLY ONE WAY OF THINKING LACK THE IMAGINATION TO BECOME SOMEONE ELSE.
HERE, EVERYTHING AND EVERYONE CAN BECOME SOMETHING ENTIRELY DIFFERENT.

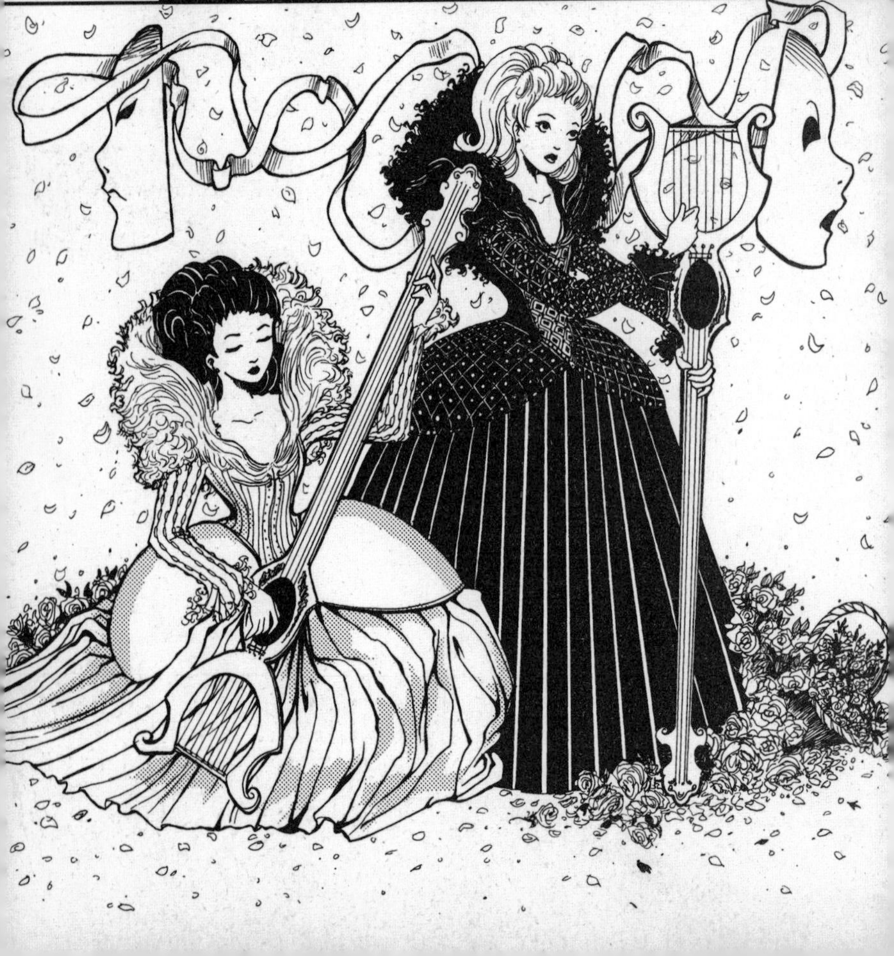

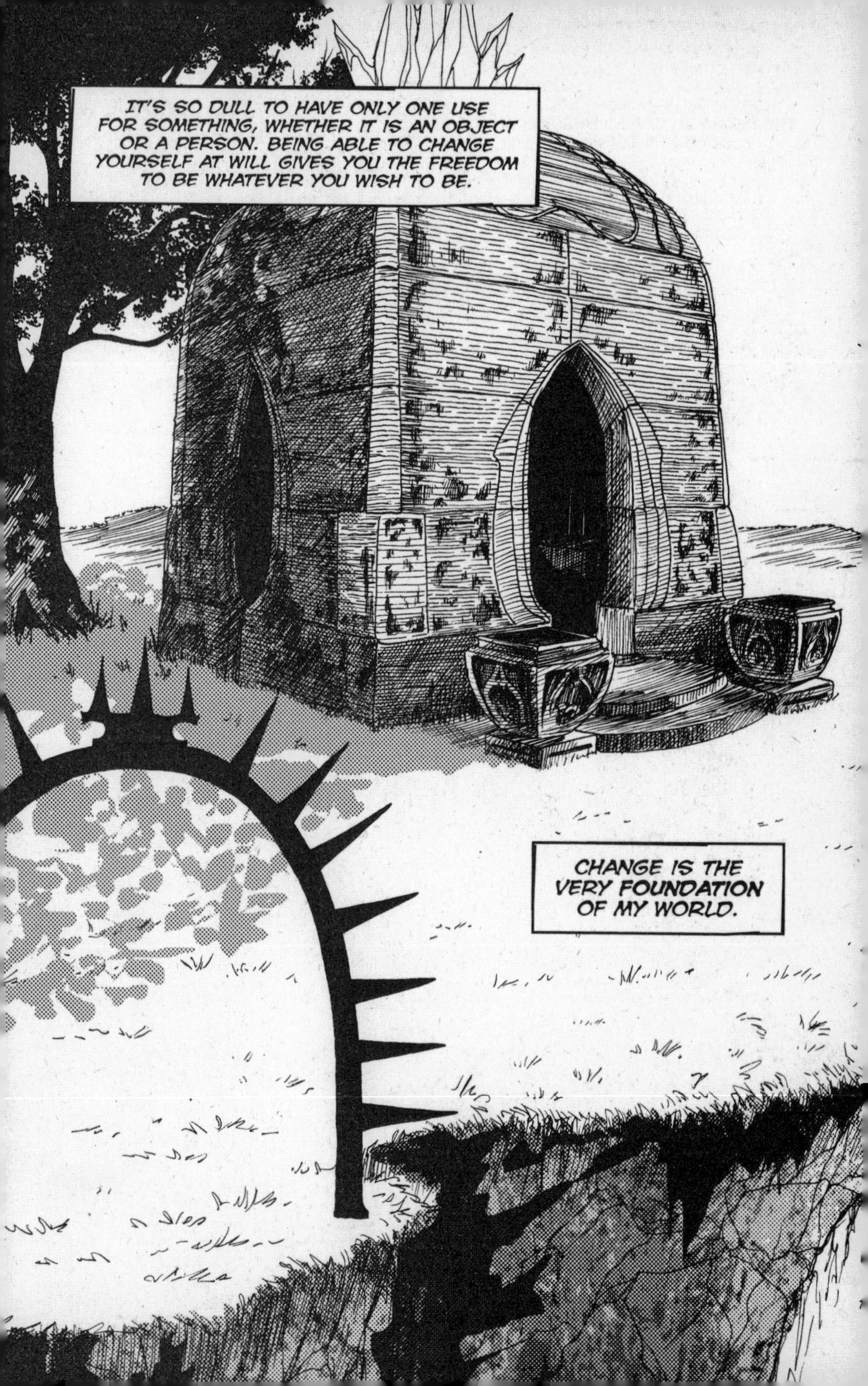
IT'S SO DULL TO HAVE ONLY ONE USE FOR SOMETHING, WHETHER IT IS AN OBJECT OR A PERSON. BEING ABLE TO CHANGE YOURSELF AT WILL GIVES YOU THE FREEDOM TO BE WHATEVER YOU WISH TO BE.
CHANGE IS THE VERY FOUNDATION OF MY WORLD.

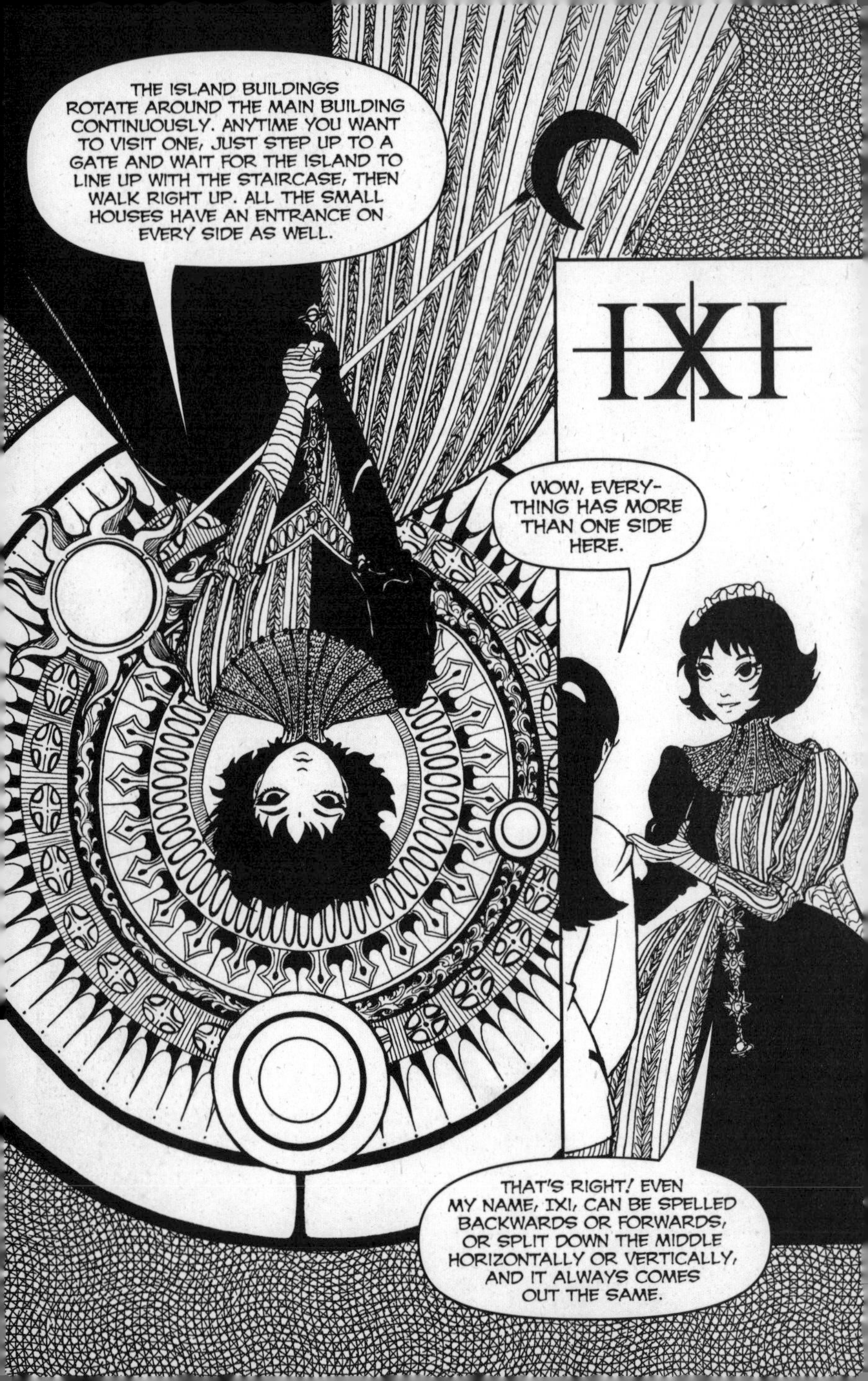
THE ISLAND BUILDINGS ROTATE AROUND THE MAIN BUILDING CONTINUOUSLY. ANYTIME YOU WANT TO VISIT ONE, JUST STEP UP TO A GATE AND WAIT FOR THE ISLAND TO LINE UP WITH THE STAIRCASE, THEN WALK RIGHT UP. ALL THE SMALL HOUSES HAVE AN ENTRANCE ON EVERY SIDE AS WELL.
IXI
WOW, EVERY-THING HAS MORE THAN ONE SIDE HERE.
THAT'S RIGHT! EVEN MY NAME, IXI, CAN BE SPELLED BACKWARDS OR FORWARDS, OR SPLIT DOWN THE MIDDLE HORIZONTALLY OR VERTICALLY, AND IT ALWAYS COMES OUT THE SAME.

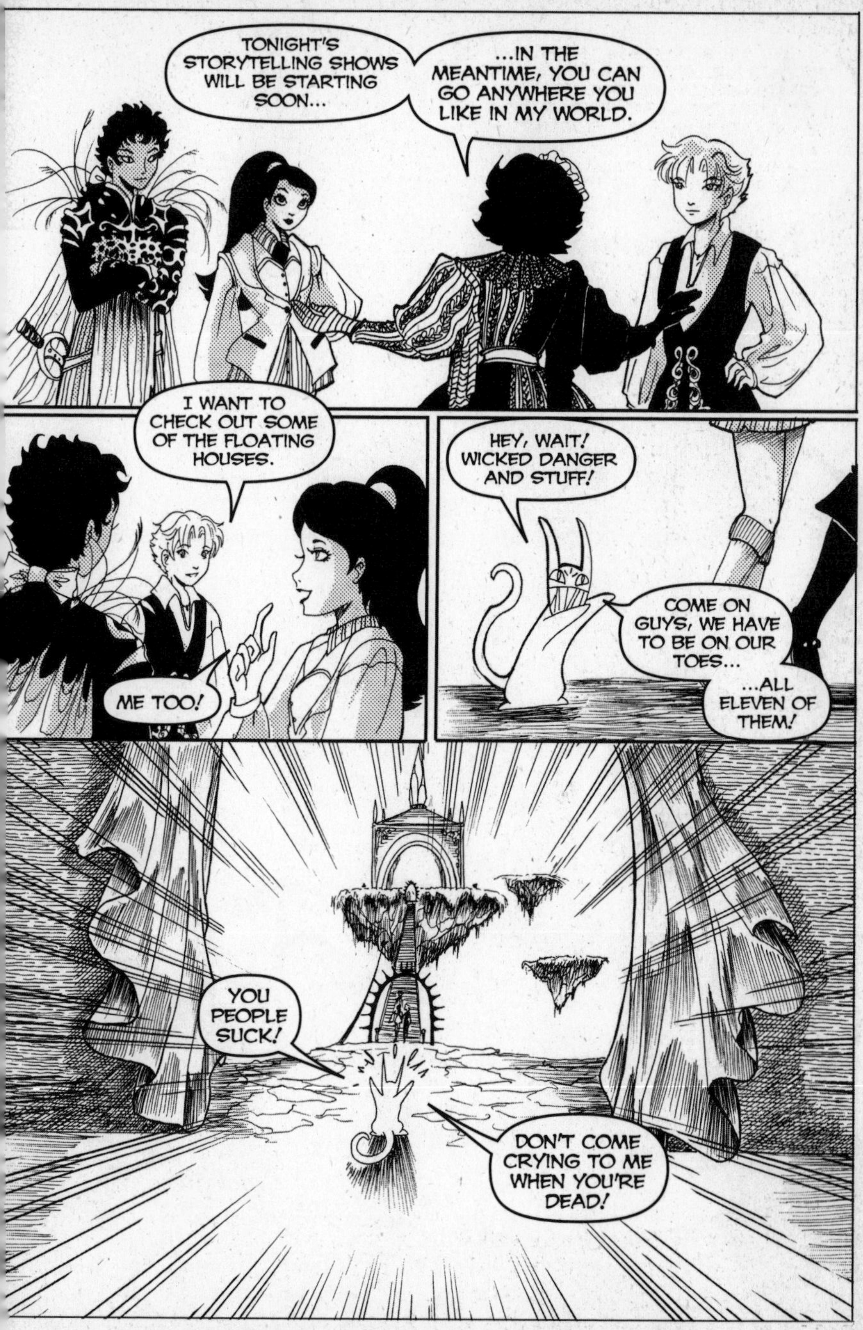
TONIGHT'S STORYTELLING SHOWS WILL BE STARTING SOON...
...IN THE MEANTIME, YOU CAN GO ANYWHERE YOU LIKE IN MY WORLD.
I WANT TO CHECK OUT SOME OF THE FLOATING HOUSES.
ME TOO!
HEY, WAIT! WICKED DANGER AND STUFF!
COME ON GUYS, WE HAVE TO BE ON OUR TOES...
...ALL ELEVEN OF THEM!
YOU PEOPLE SUCK!
DON'T COME CRYING TO ME WHEN YOU'RE DEAD!

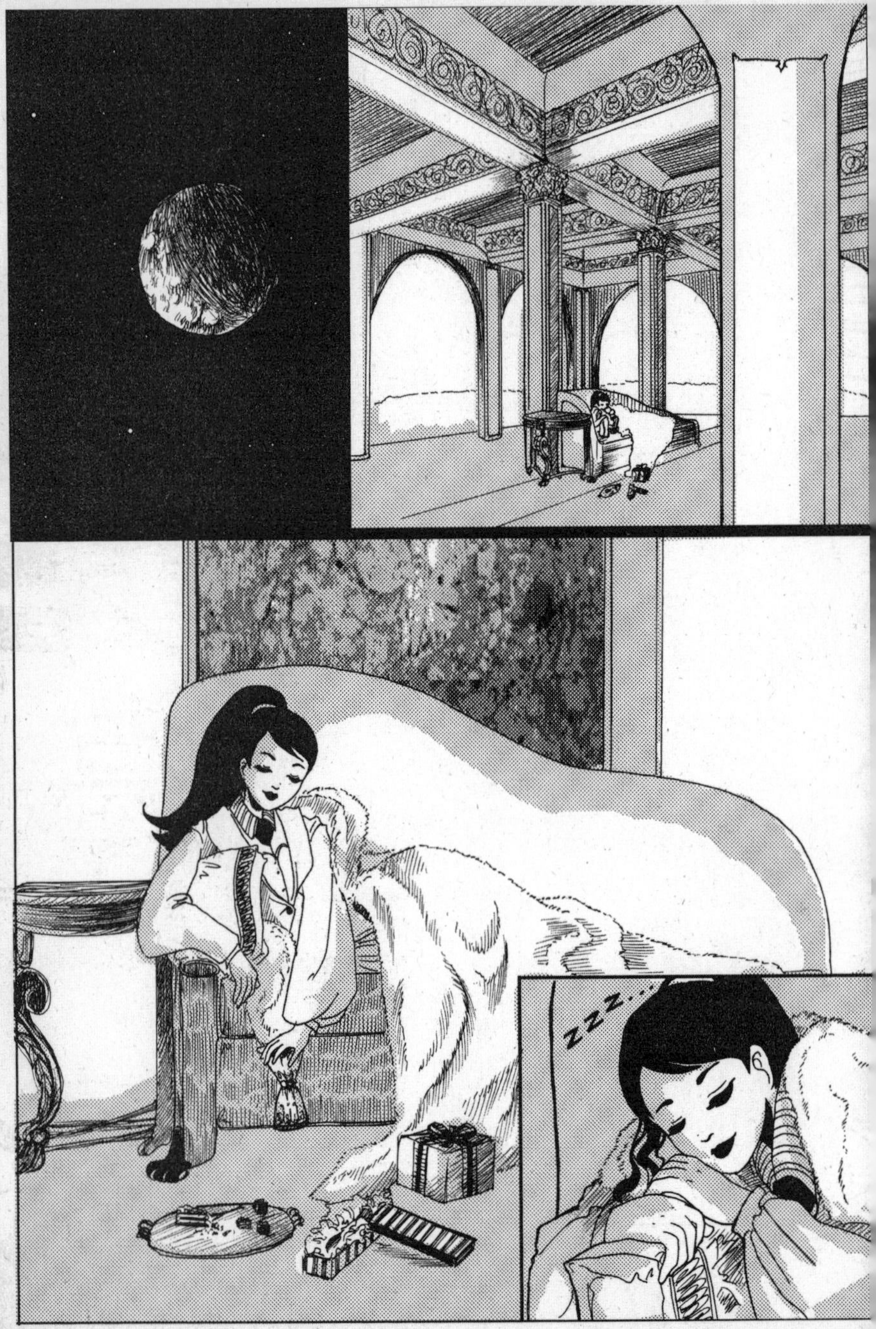
ZZZ...

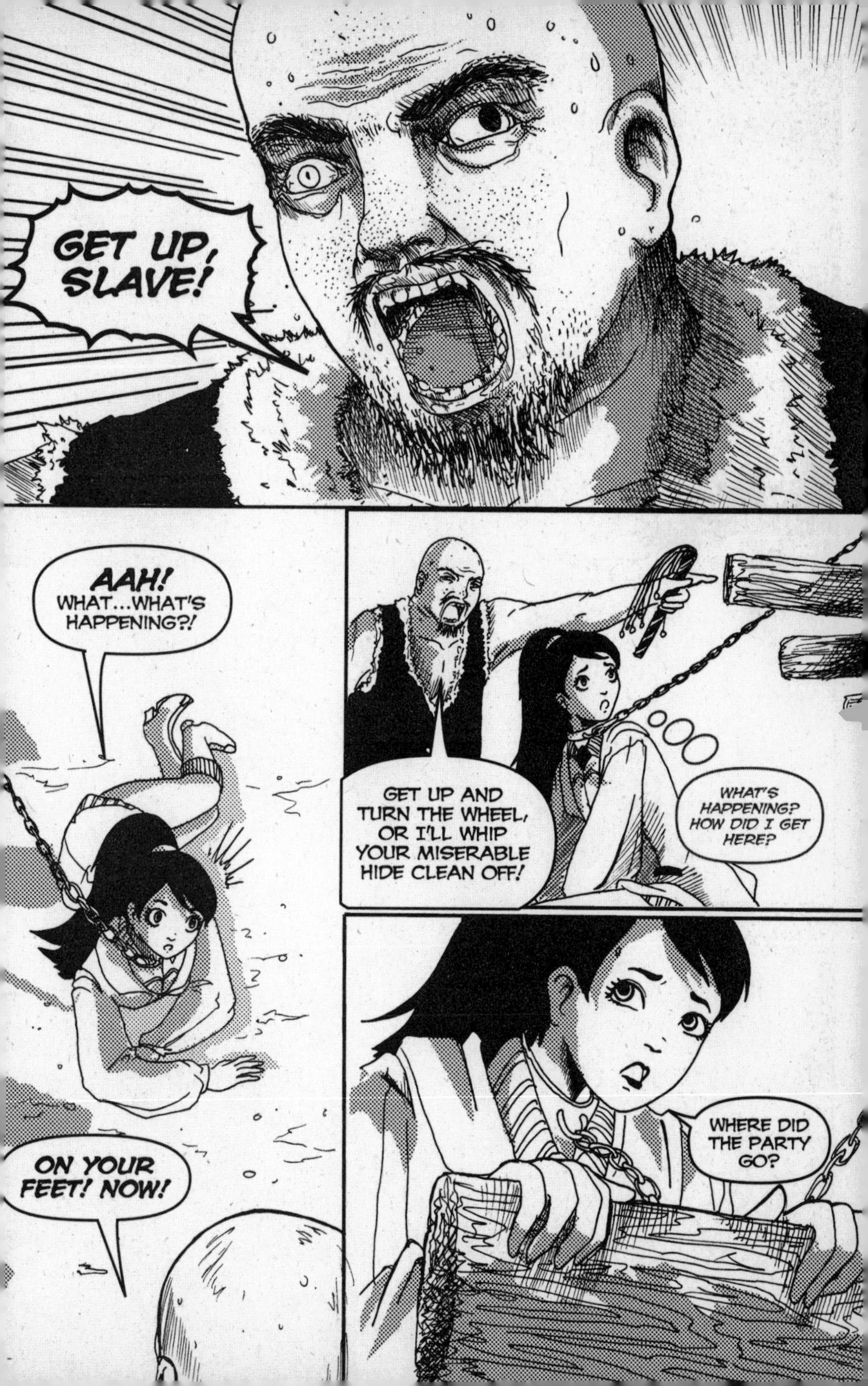
GET UP, SLAVE!
AAH! WHAT...WHAT'S HAPPENING?!
ON YOUR FEET! NOW!
GET UP AND TURN THE WHEEL, OR I'LL WHIP YOUR MISERABLE HIDE CLEAN OFF!
WHAT'S HAPPENING? HOW DID I GET HERE?
WHERE DID THE PARTY GO?

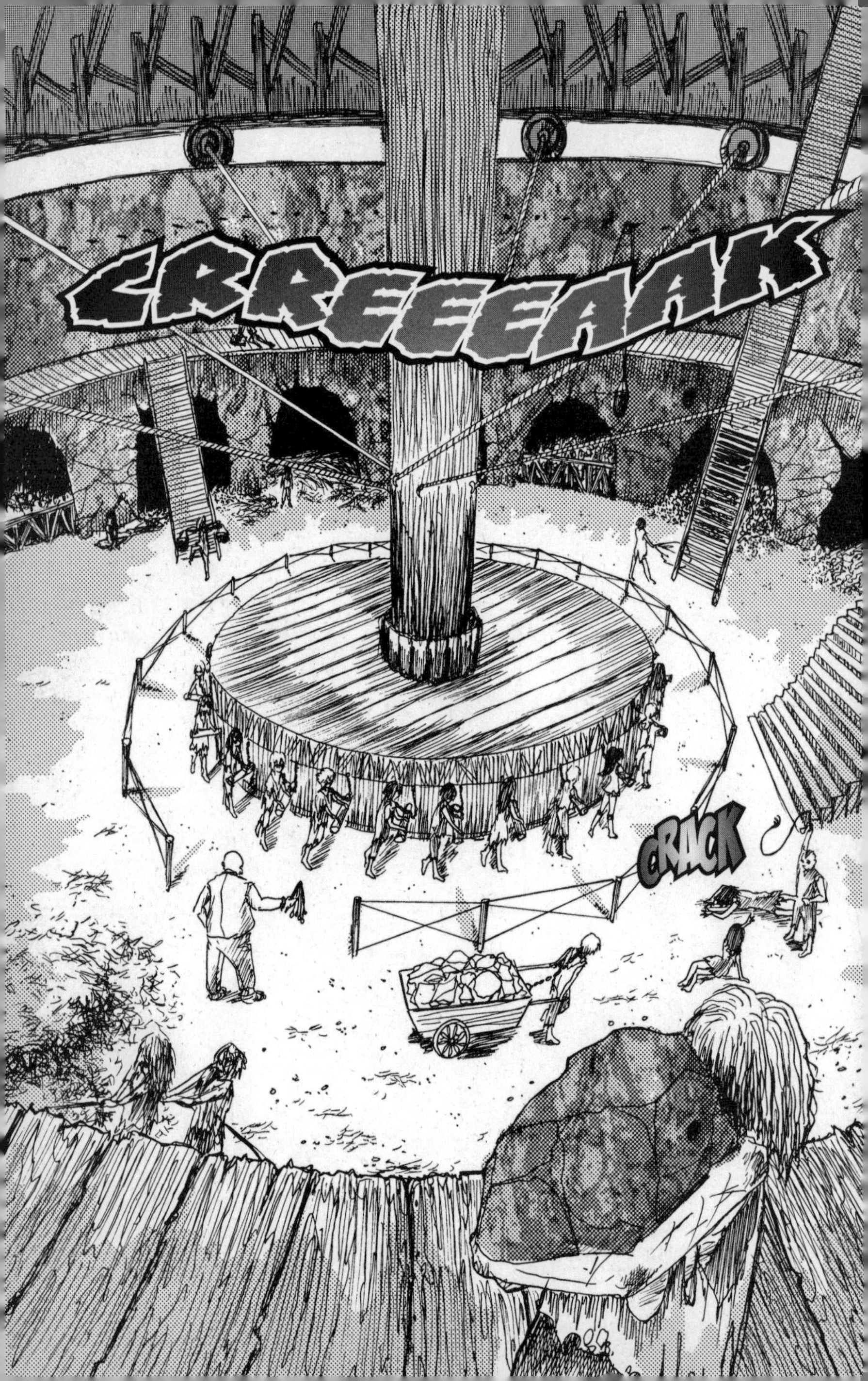
CREEEAAK
CRACK

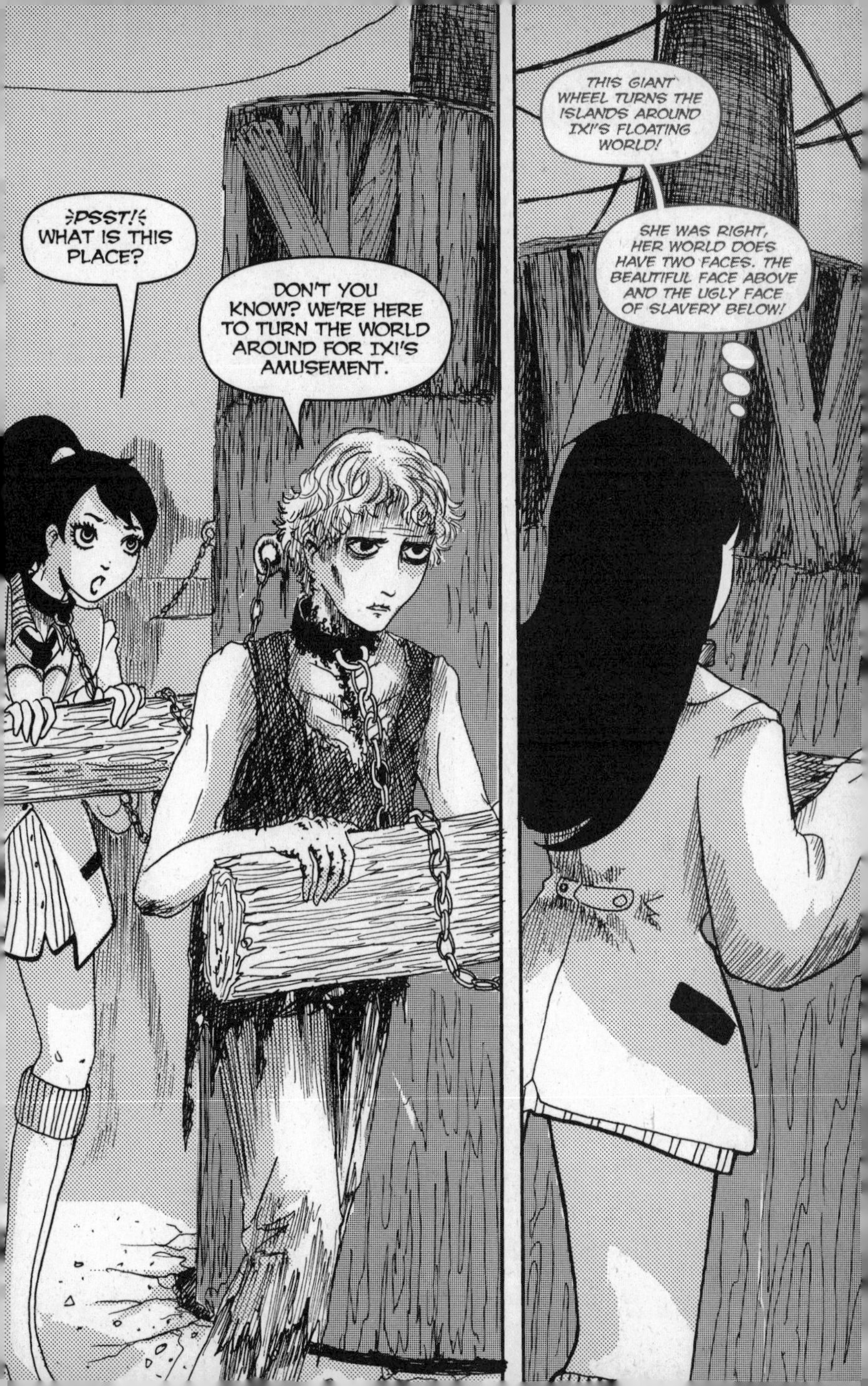

PSST! WHAT IS THIS PLACE?
DON'T YOU KNOW? WE'RE HERE TO TURN THE WORLD AROUND FOR IXI'S AMUSEMENT.
THIS GIANT WHEEL TURNS THE ISLANDS AROUND IXI'S FLOATING WORLD!
SHE WAS RIGHT, HER WORLD DOES HAVE TWO FACES. THE BEAUTIFUL FACE ABOVE AND THE UGLY FACE OF SLAVERY BELOW!

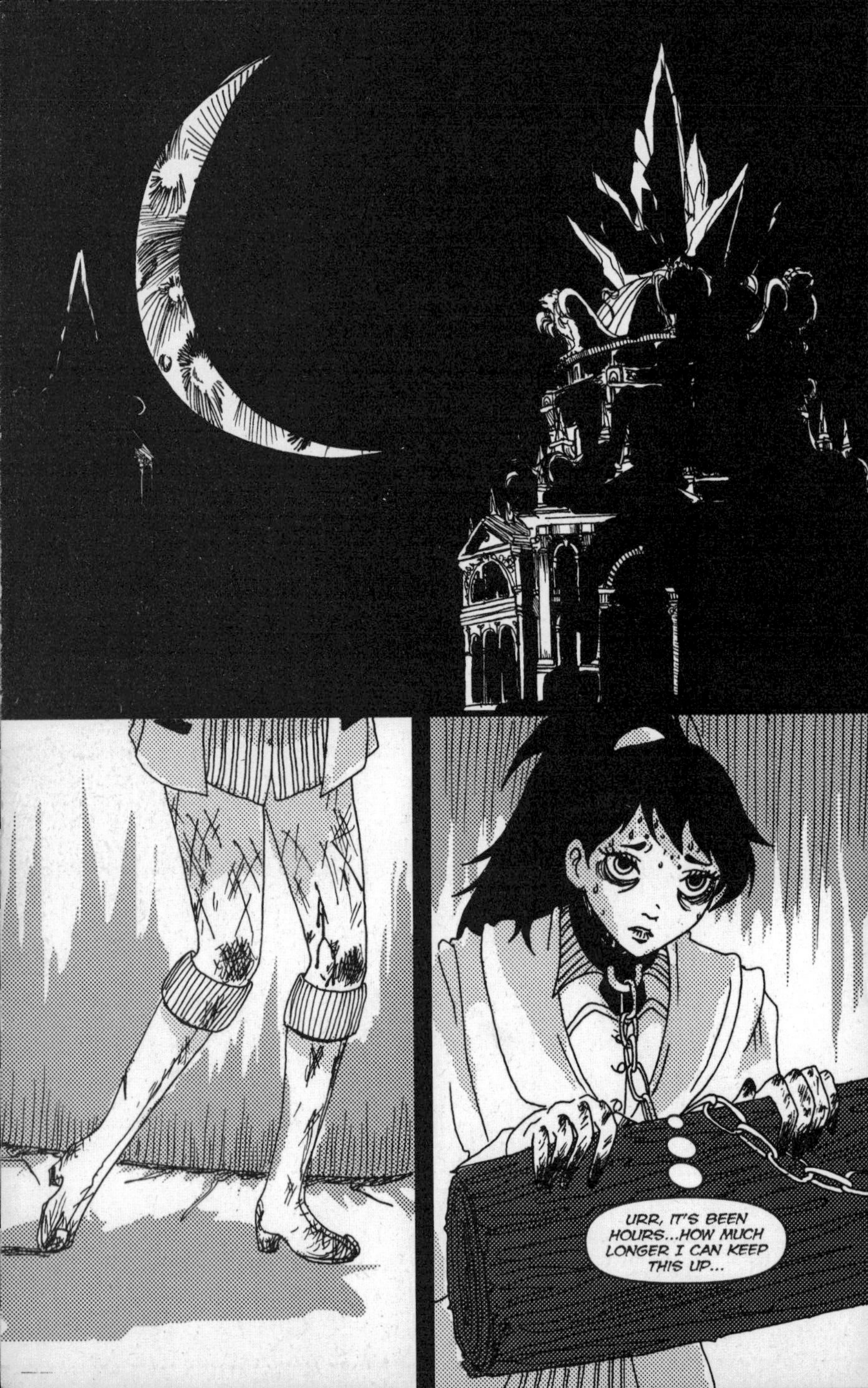
URR, IT'S BEEN HOURS...HOW MUCH LONGER I CAN KEEP THIS UP...

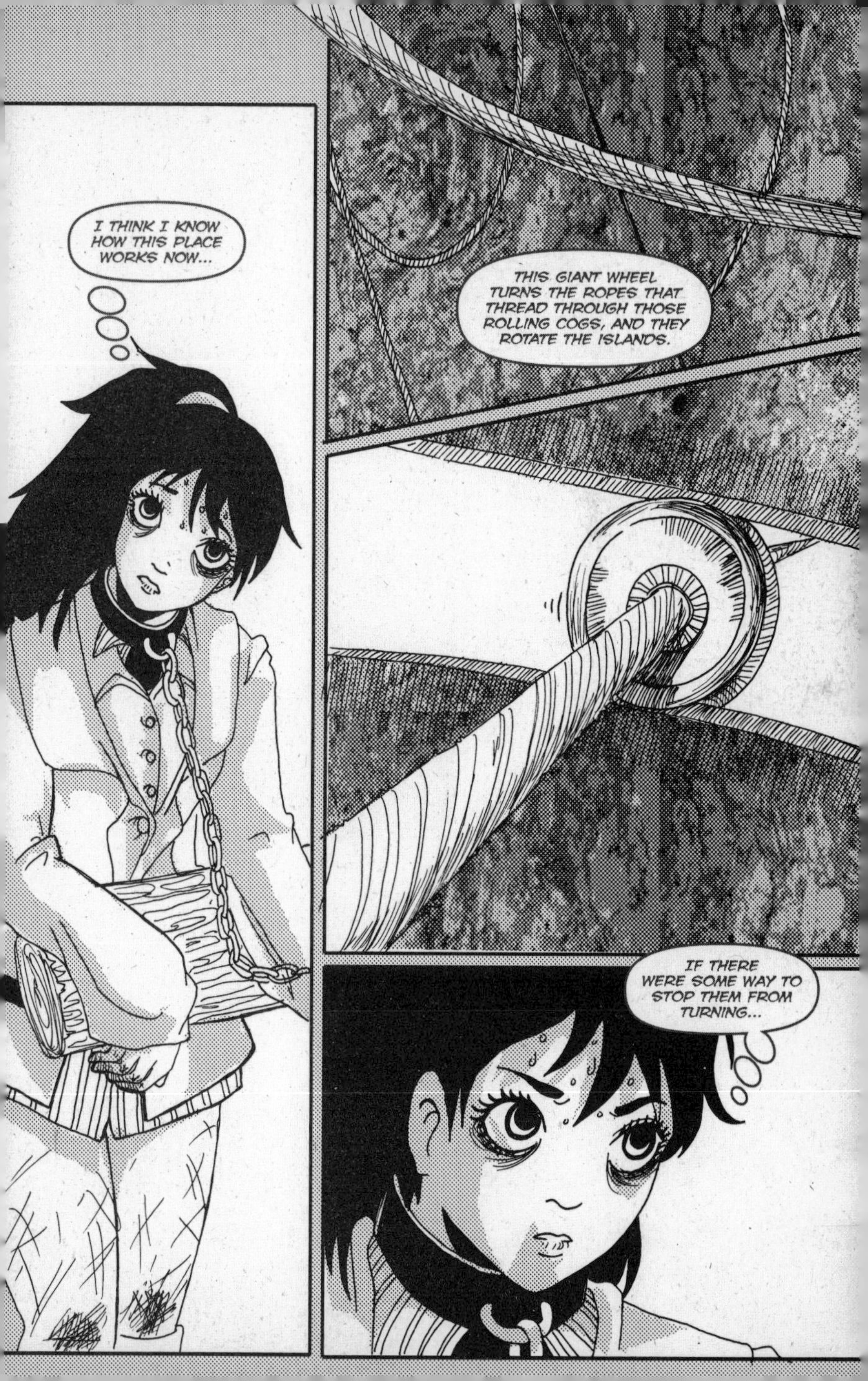
I THINK I KNOW HOW THIS PLACE WORKS NOW...
THIS GIANT WHEEL TURNS THE ROPES THAT THREAD THROUGH THOSE ROLLING COGS, AND THEY ROTATE THE ISLANDS.
IF THERE WERE SOME WAY TO STOP THEM FROM TURNING...

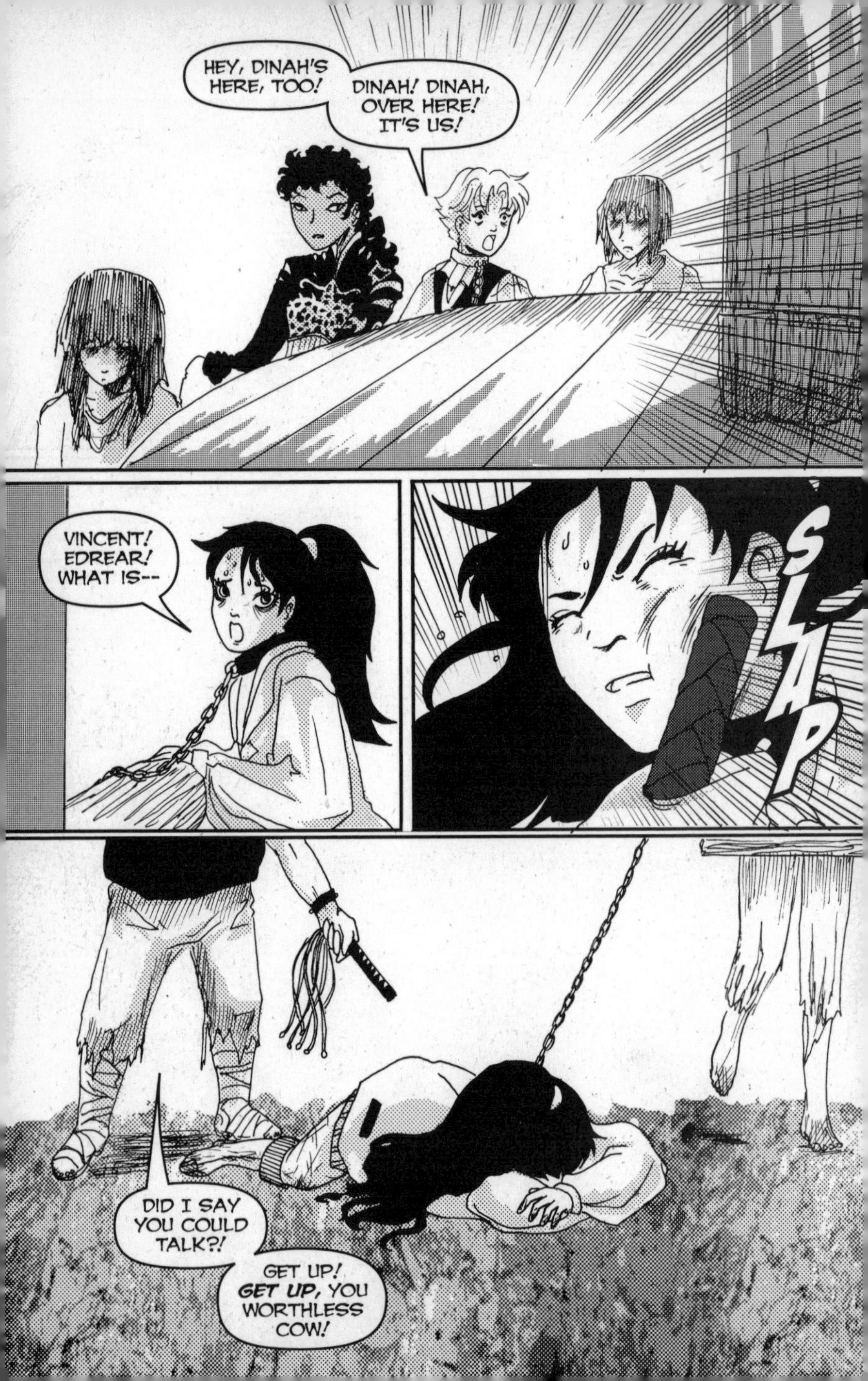
HEY, DINAH'S HERE, TOO!
DINAH! DINAH, OVER HERE! IT'S US!
VINCENT! EDREAR! WHAT IS--
SLAP
DID I SAY YOU COULD TALK?!
GET UP! **GET UP,** YOU WORTHLESS COW!

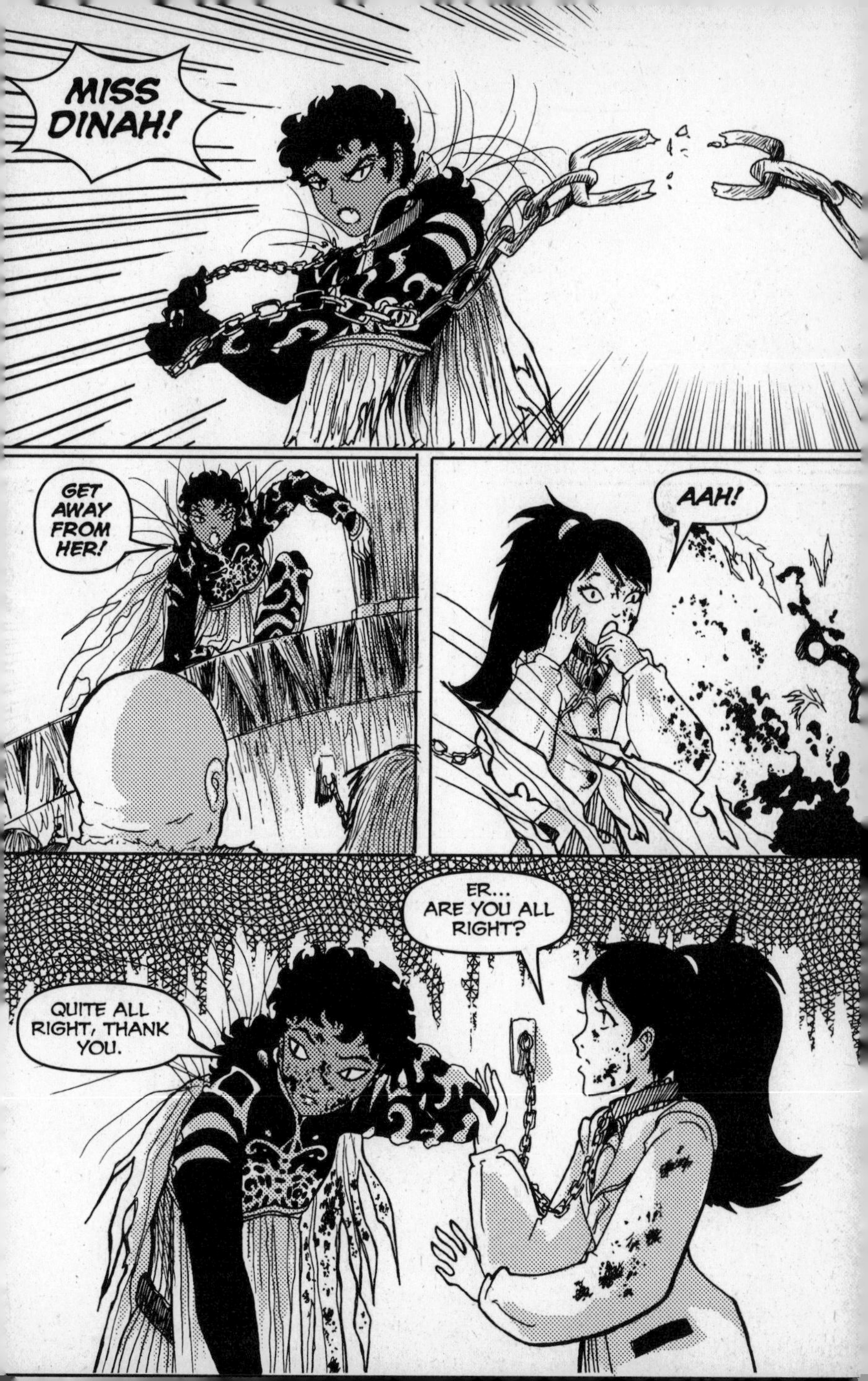
MISS DINAH!
GET AWAY FROM HER!
AAH!
ER... ARE YOU ALL RIGHT?
QUITE ALL RIGHT, THANK YOU.

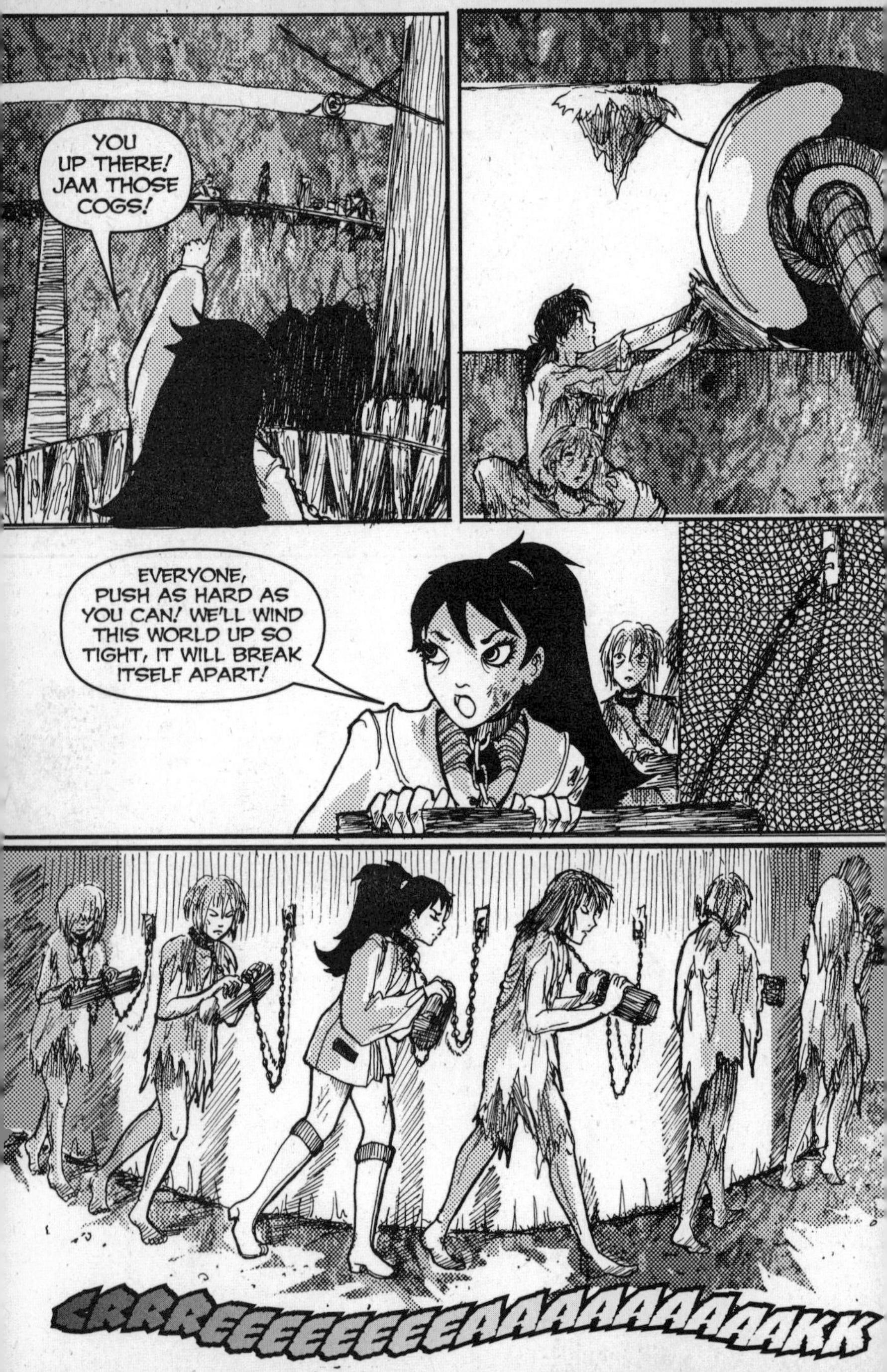
YOU UP THERE! JAM THOSE COGS!
EVERYONE, PUSH AS HARD AS YOU CAN! WE'LL WIND THIS WORLD UP SO TIGHT, IT WILL BREAK ITSELF APART!
CRRREEEEEEEEEEEEAAAAAAAAAAAAKK

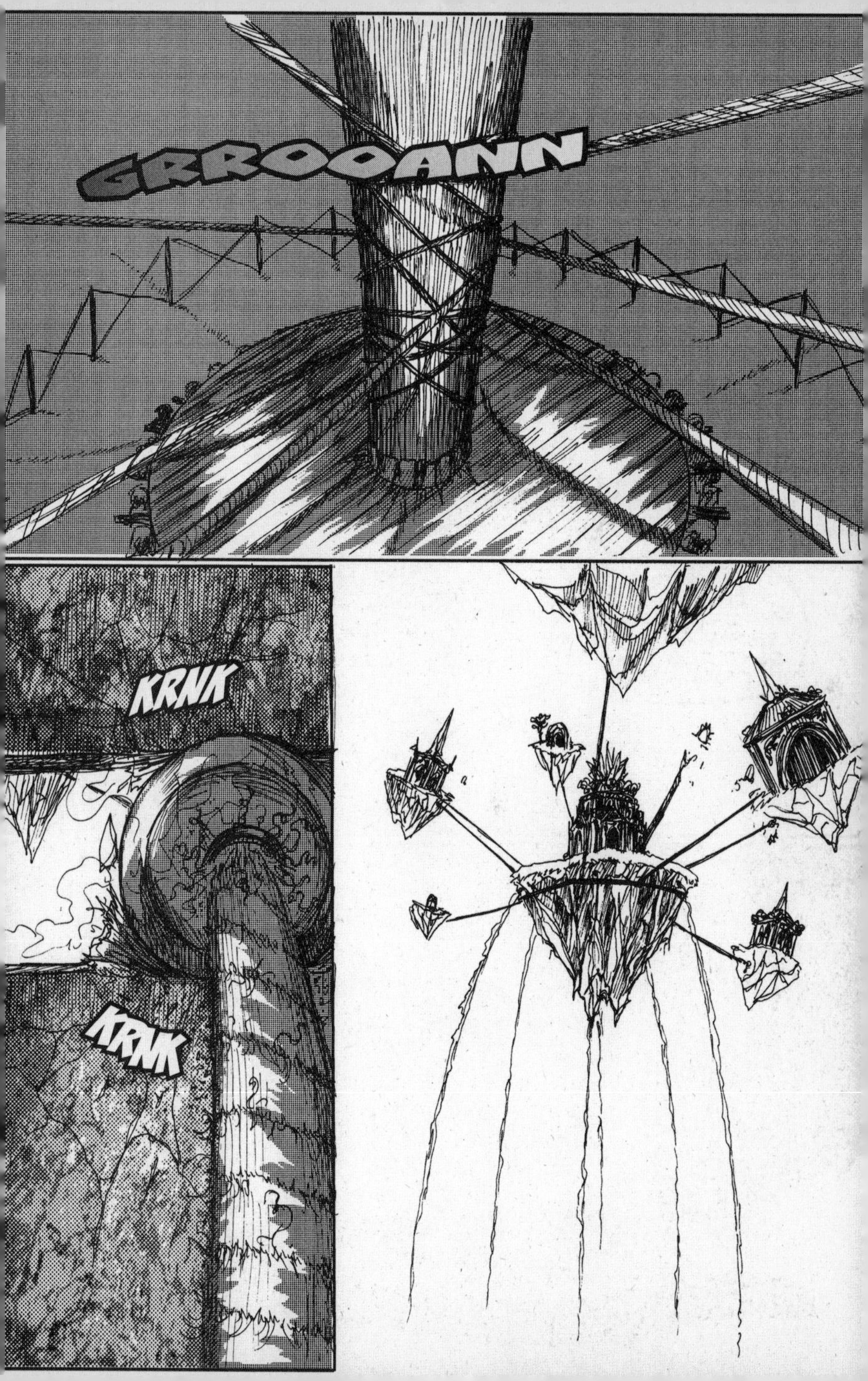
GRROOANN
KRNK
KRNK

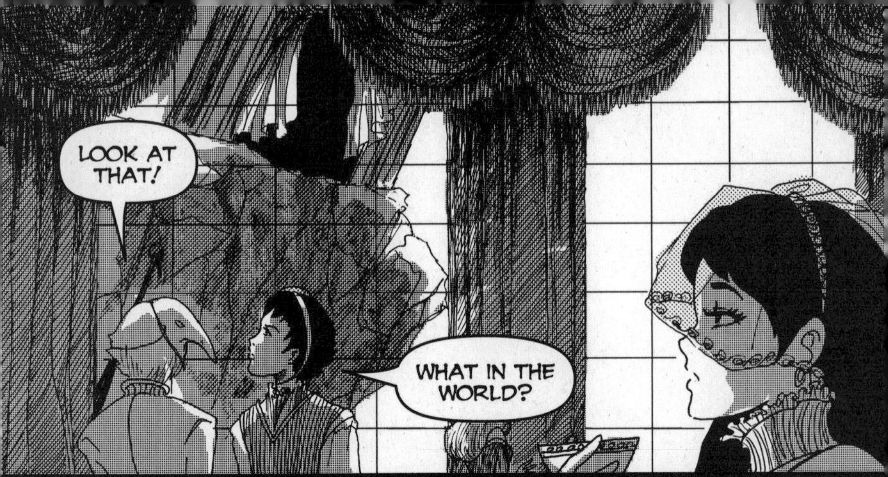
LOOK AT THAT!
WHAT IN THE WORLD?
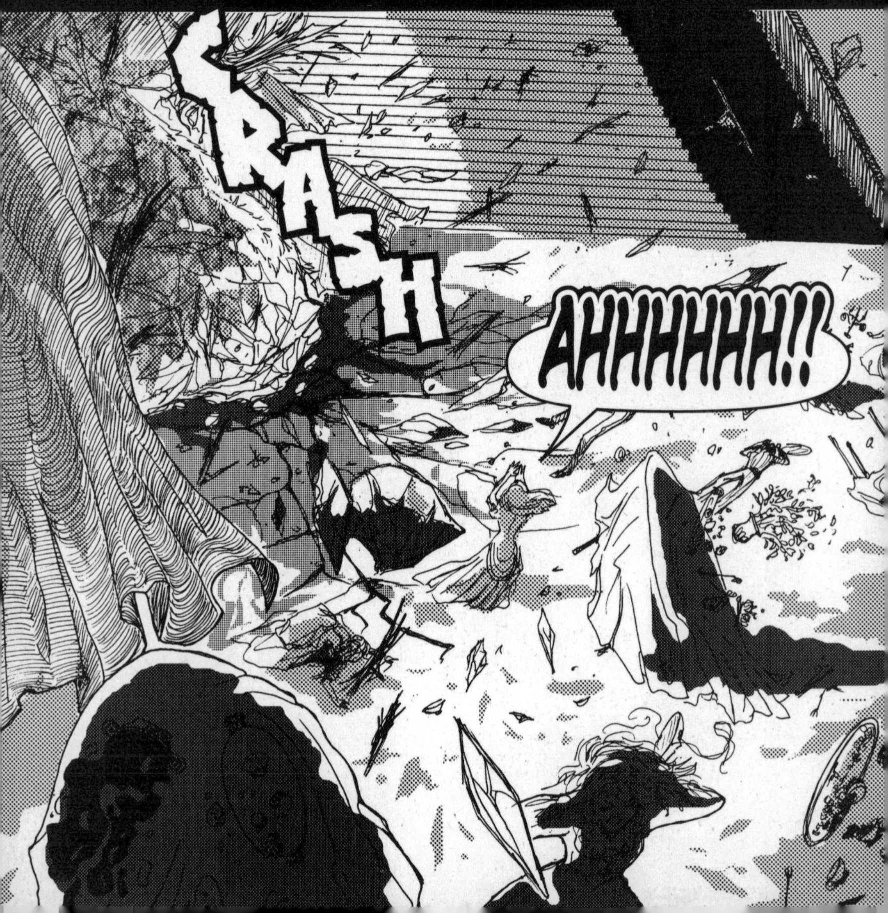
CRASH
AHHHHHH!!

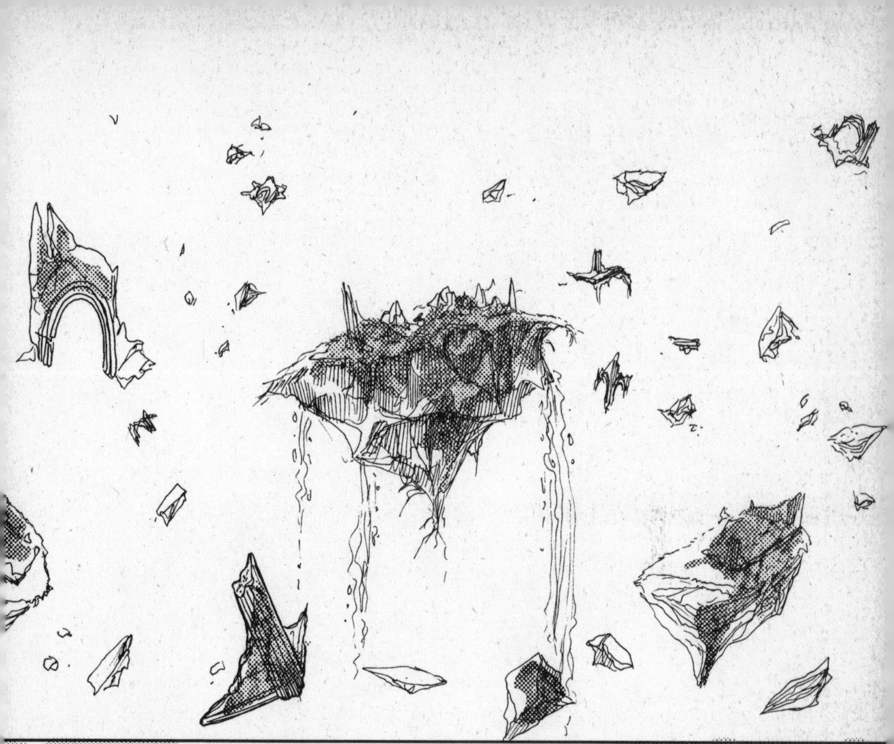

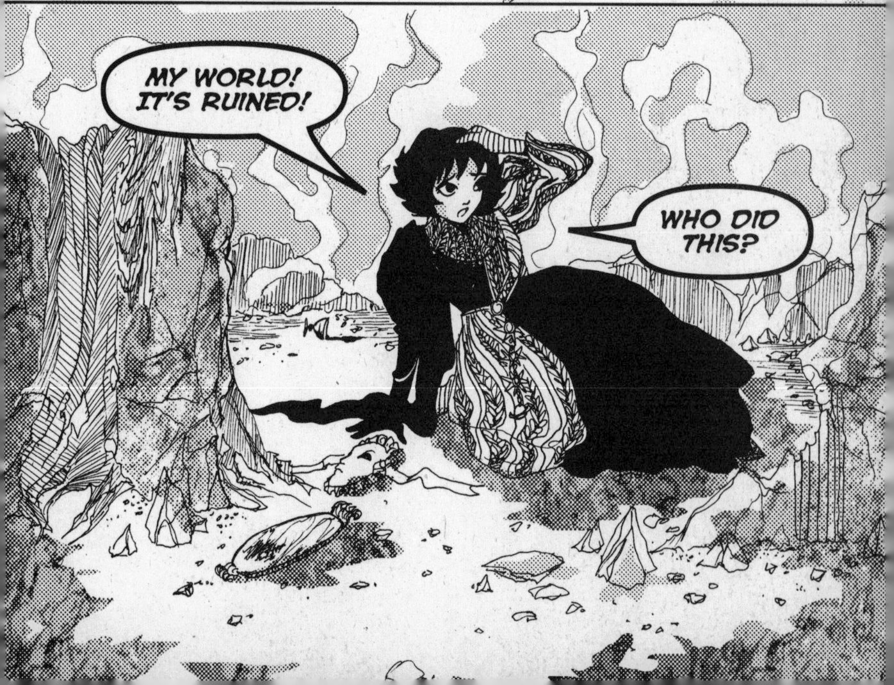
MY WORLD! IT'S RUINED!
WHO DID THIS?

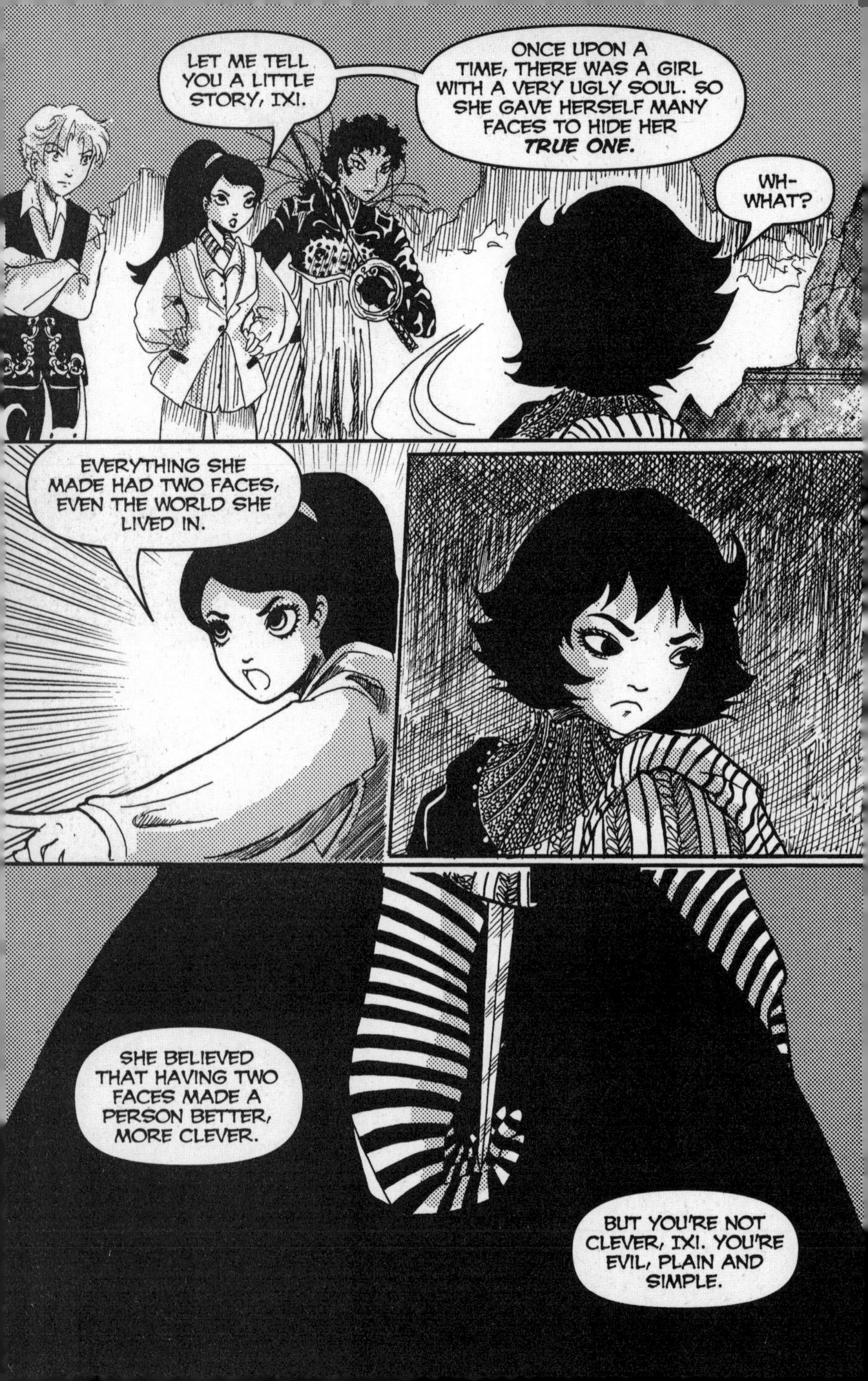
LET ME TELL YOU A LITTLE STORY, IXI.
ONCE UPON A TIME, THERE WAS A GIRL WITH A VERY UGLY SOUL. SO SHE GAVE HERSELF MANY FACES TO HIDE HER *TRUE ONE.*
WH- WHAT?
EVERYTHING SHE MADE HAD TWO FACES, EVEN THE WORLD SHE LIVED IN.
SHE BELIEVED THAT HAVING TWO FACES MADE A PERSON BETTER, MORE CLEVER.
BUT YOU'RE NOT CLEVER, IXI. YOU'RE EVIL, PLAIN AND SIMPLE.

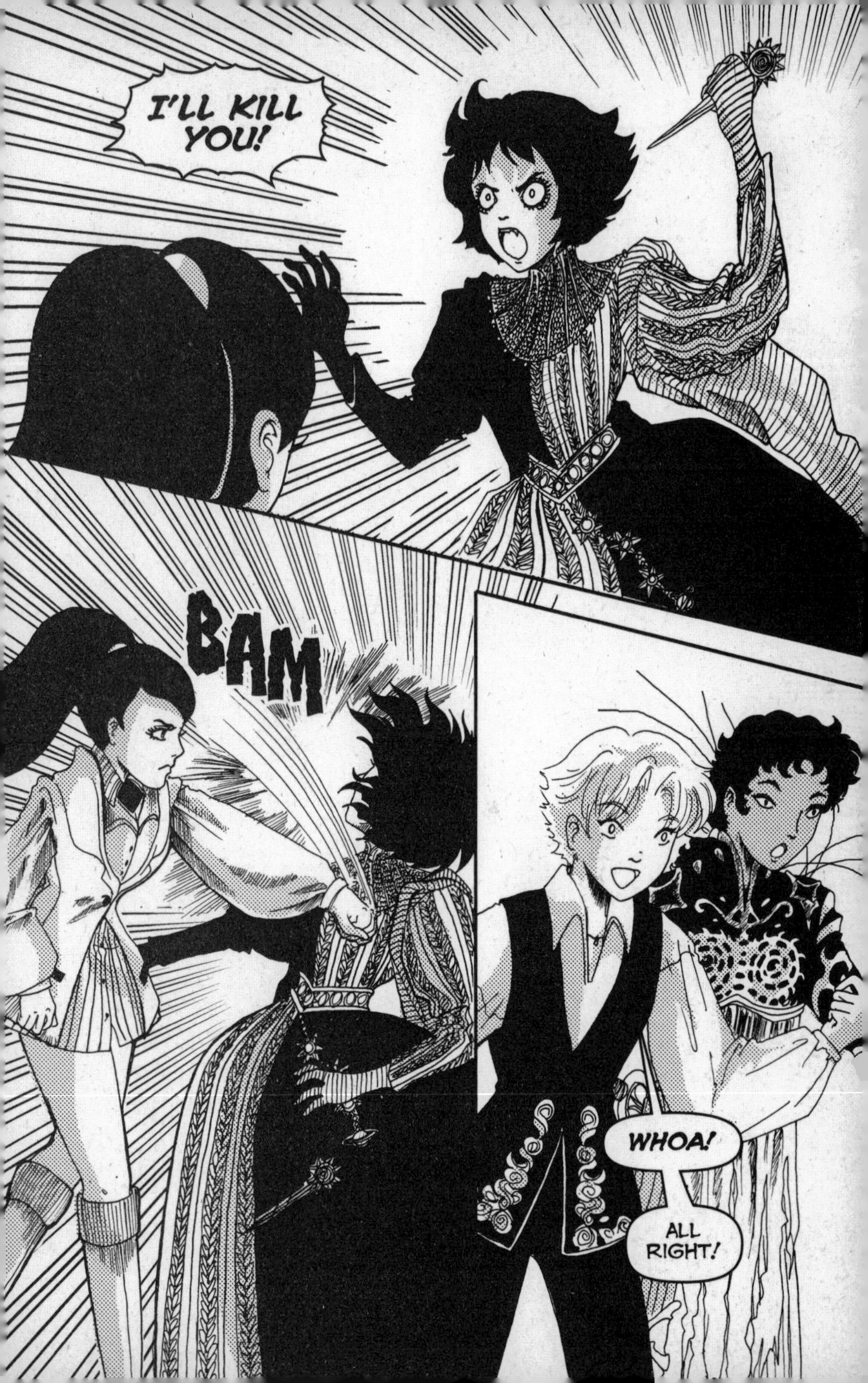
I'LL KILL YOU!
BAM
WHOA!
ALL RIGHT!

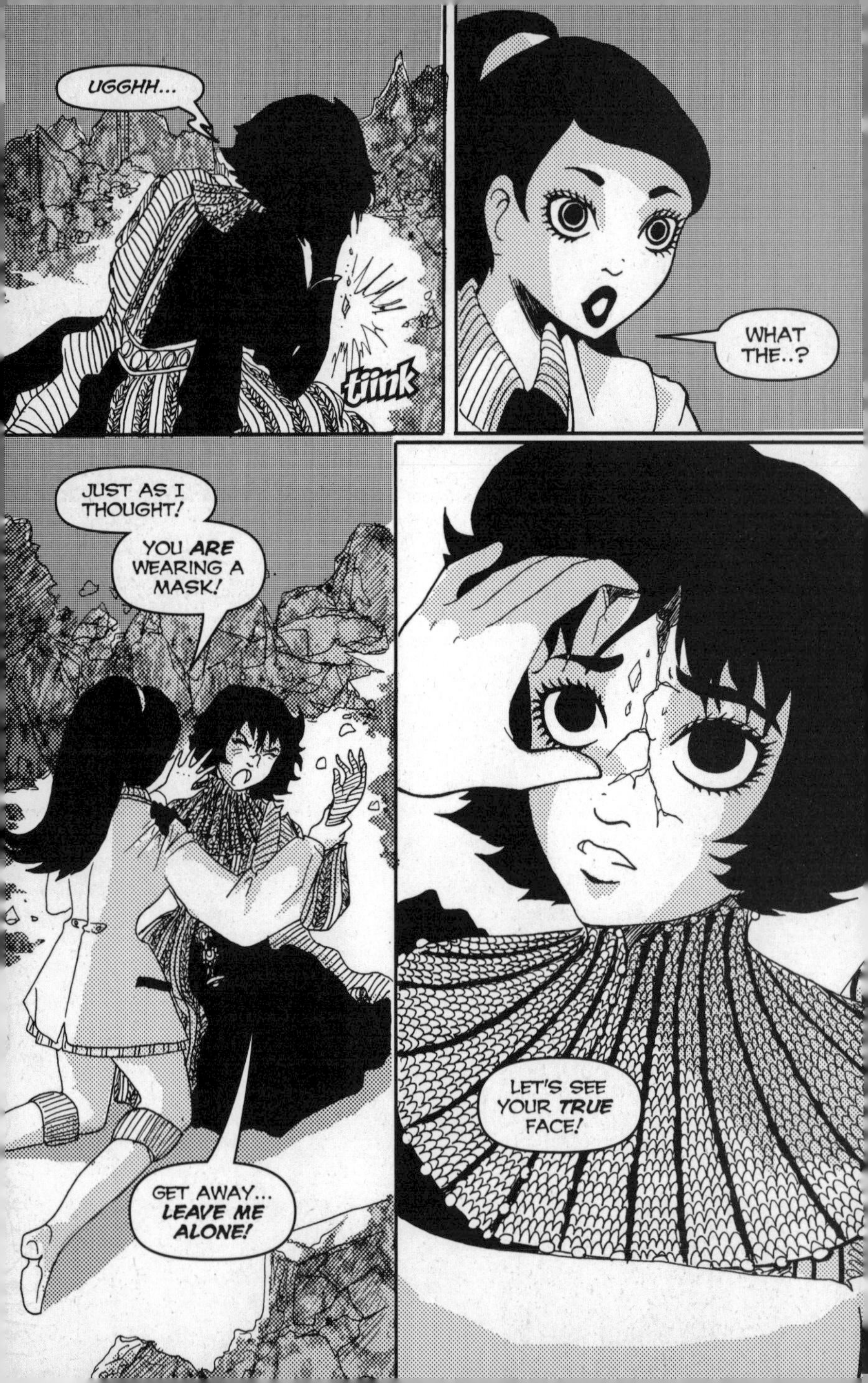
UGGHH...
tiink
WHAT THE..?
JUST AS I THOUGHT!
YOU **ARE** WEARING A MASK!
GET AWAY... ***LEAVE ME ALONE!***
LET'S SEE YOUR ***TRUE*** FACE!

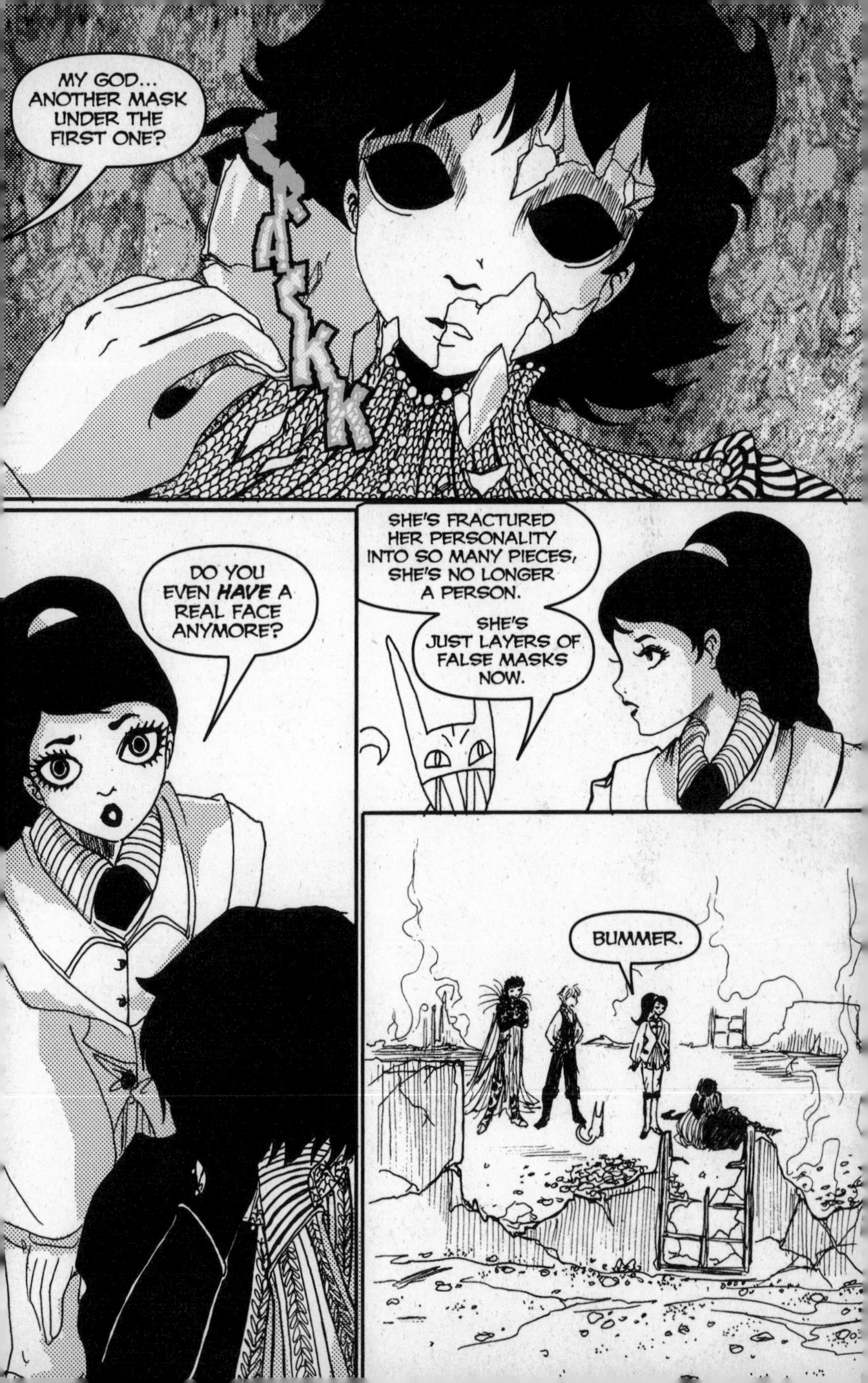
MY GOD... ANOTHER MASK UNDER THE FIRST ONE?
KRASKK
DO YOU EVEN *HAVE* A REAL FACE ANYMORE?
SHE'S FRACTURED HER PERSONALITY INTO SO MANY PIECES, SHE'S NO LONGER A PERSON.
SHE'S JUST LAYERS OF FALSE MASKS NOW.
BUMMER.

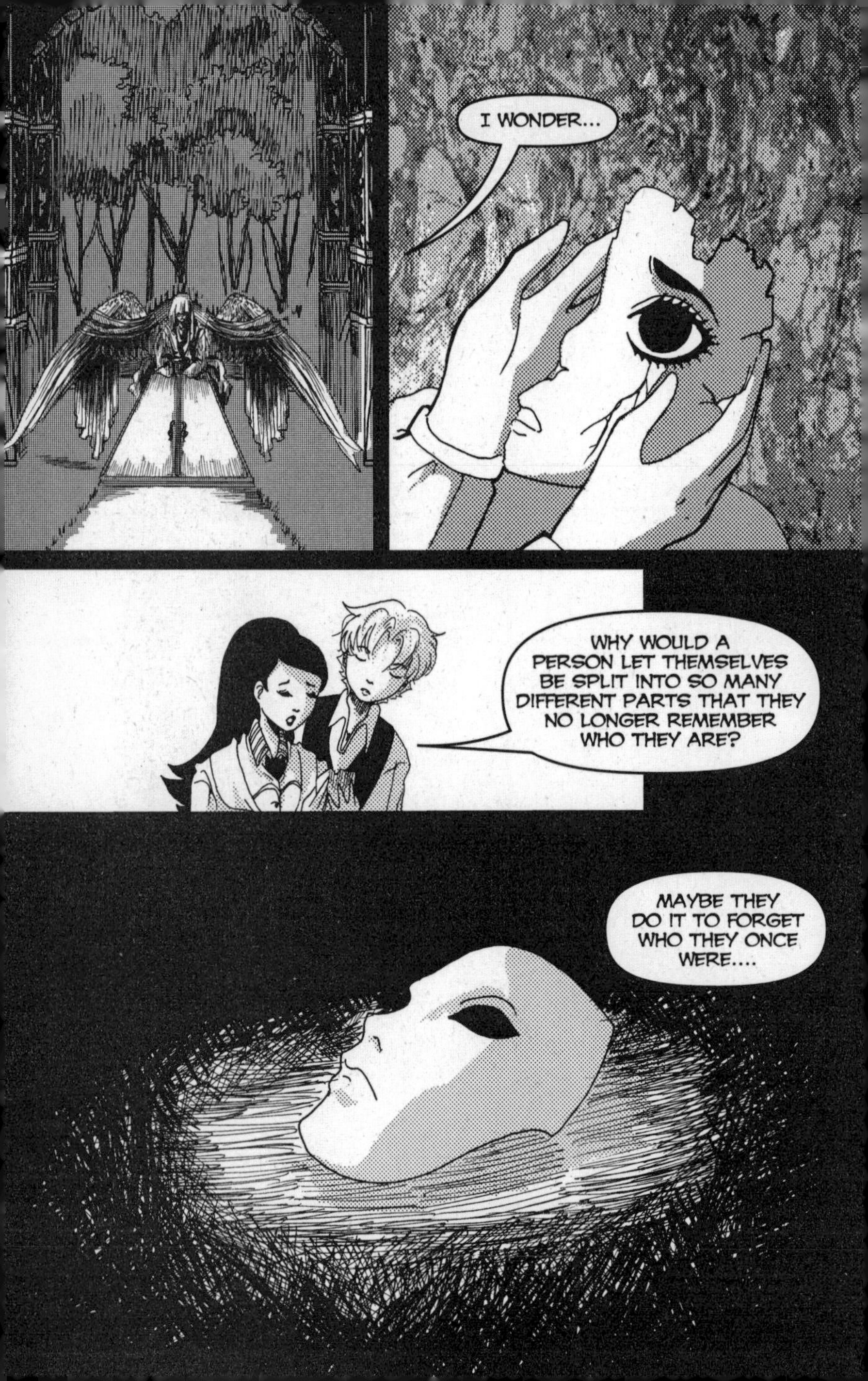
I WONDER...
WHY WOULD A PERSON LET THEMSELVES BE SPLIT INTO SO MANY DIFFERENT PARTS THAT THEY NO LONGER REMEMBER WHO THEY ARE?
MAYBE THEY DO IT TO FORGET WHO THEY ONCE WERE....

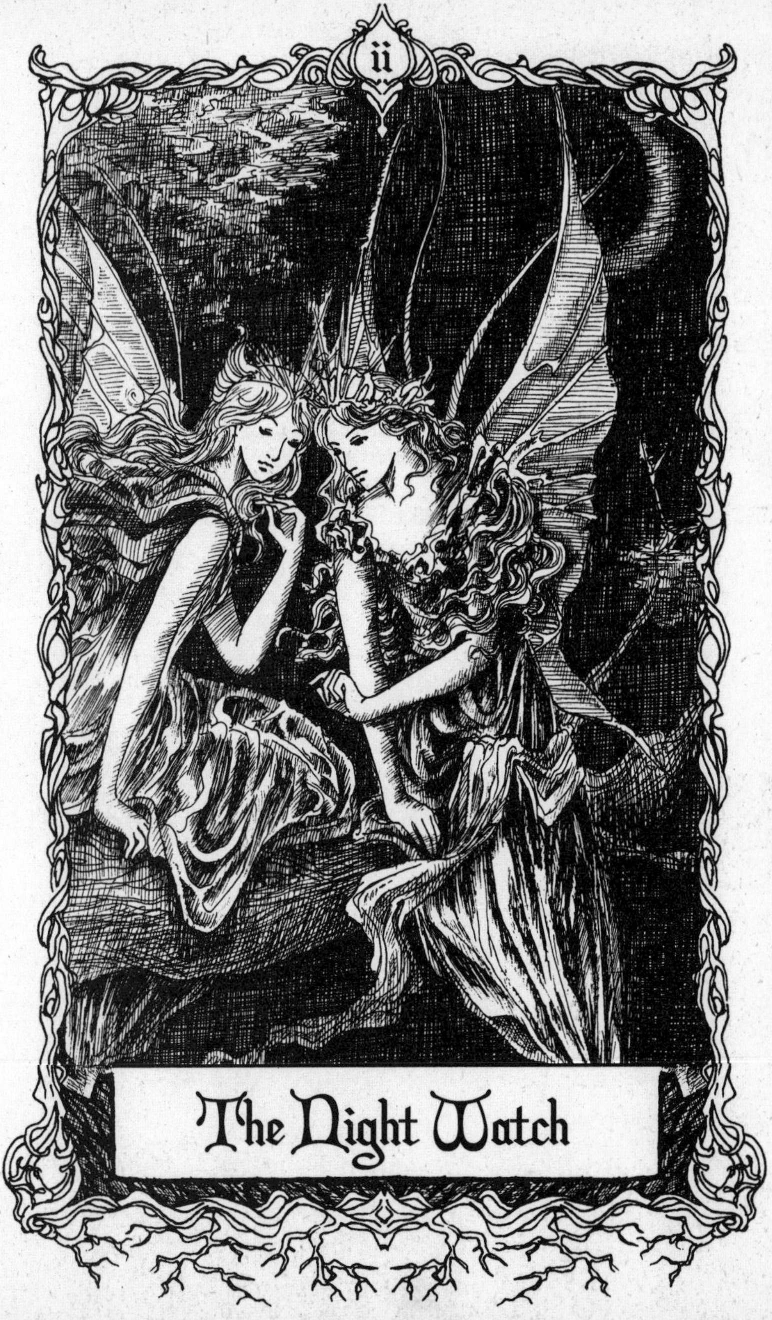
ii
The Night Watch

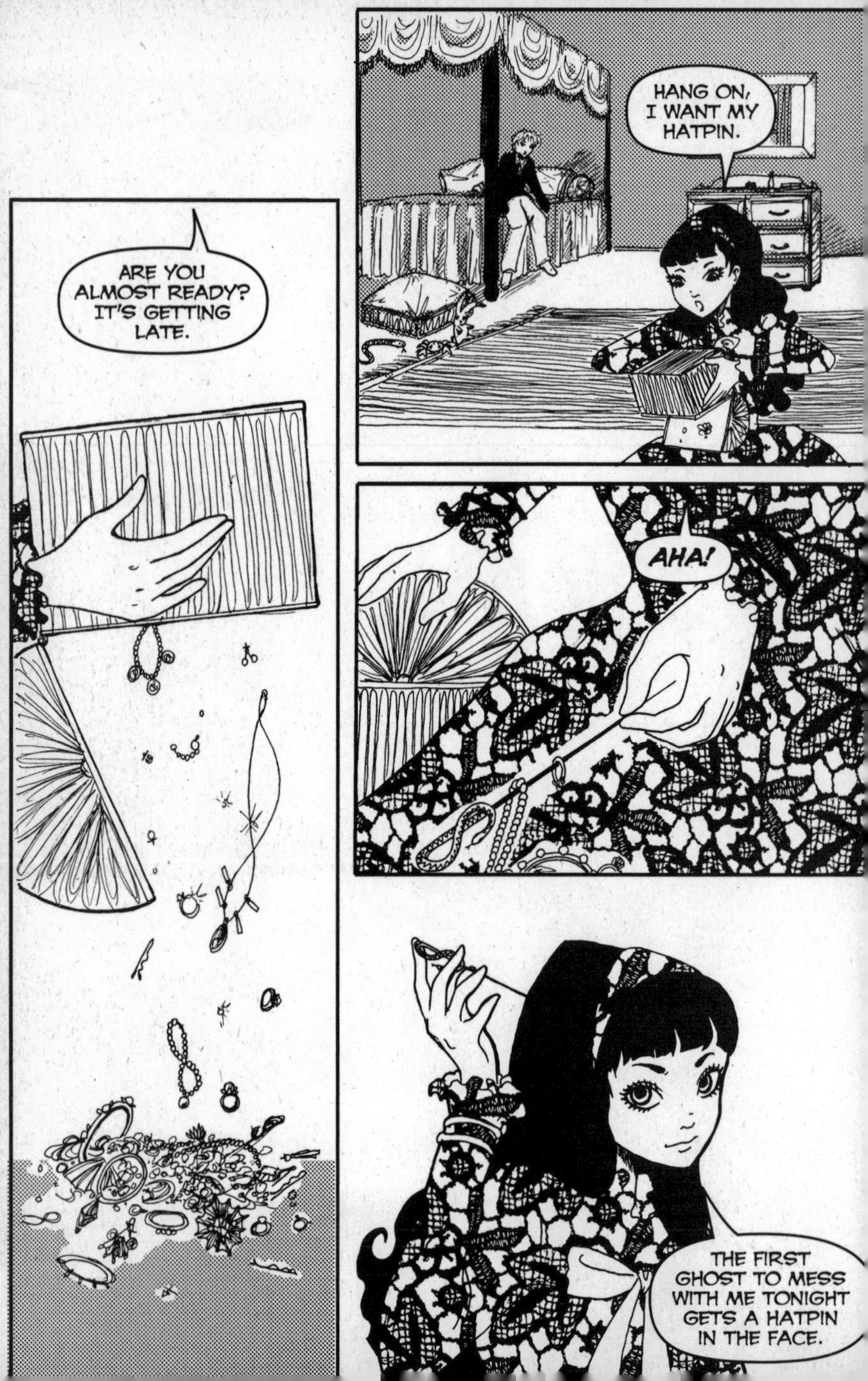
ARE YOU ALMOST READY? IT'S GETTING LATE.
HANG ON, I WANT MY HATPIN.
AHA!
THE FIRST GHOST TO MESS WITH ME TONIGHT GETS A HATPIN IN THE FACE.

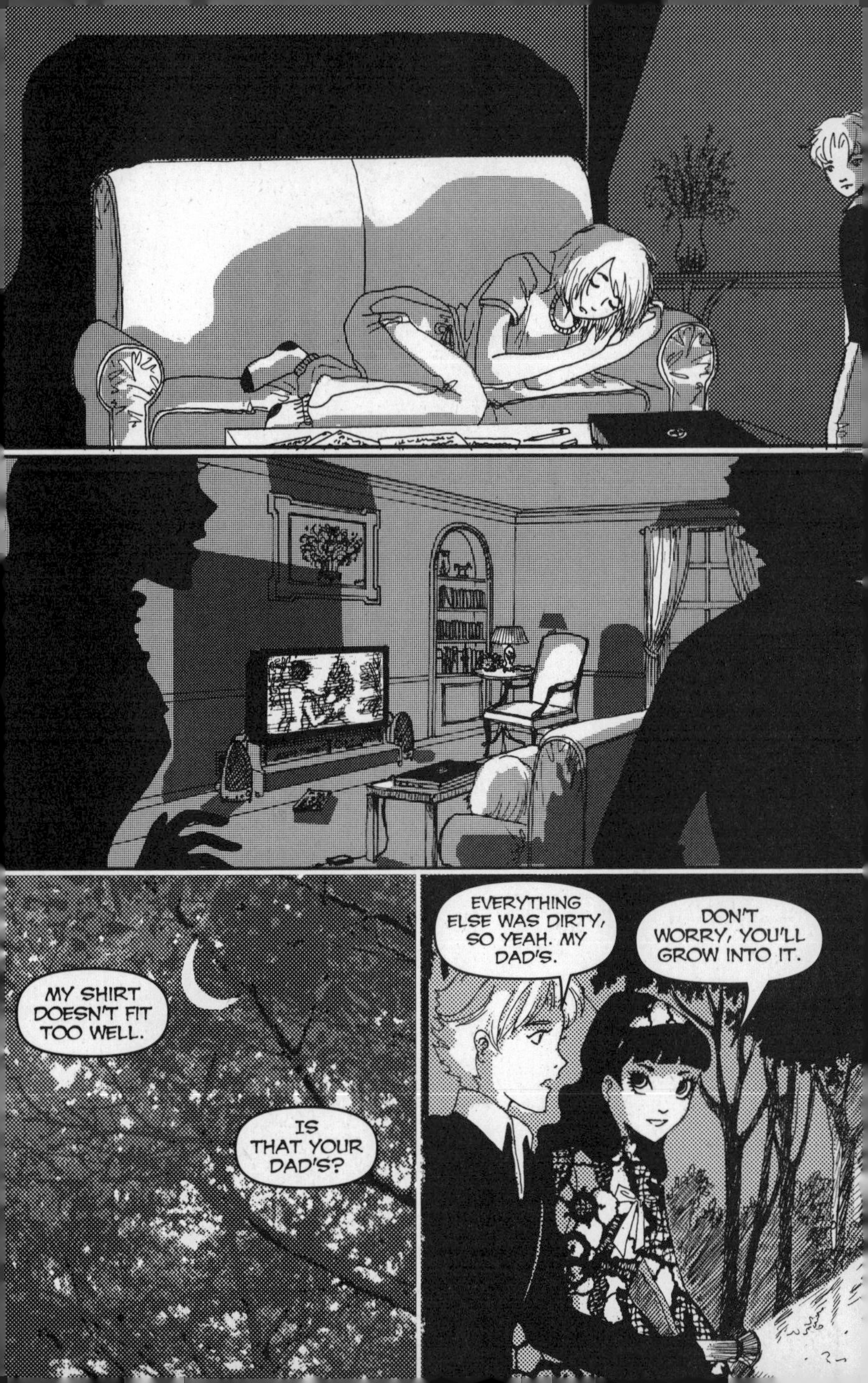
MY SHIRT DOESN'T FIT TOO WELL.
IS THAT YOUR DAD'S?
EVERYTHING ELSE WAS DIRTY, SO YEAH. MY DAD'S.
DON'T WORRY, YOU'LL GROW INTO IT.

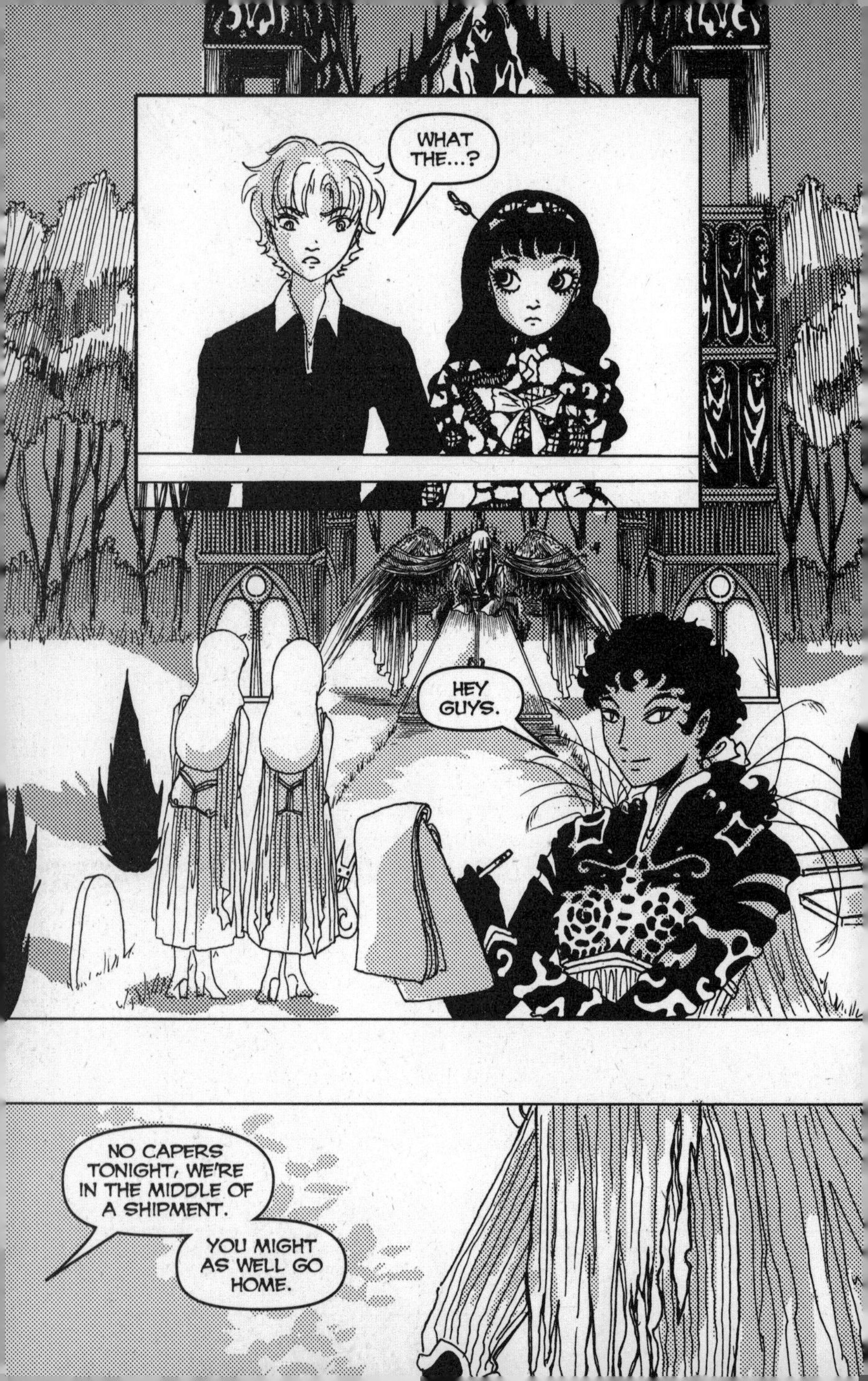
WHAT THE...?
HEY GUYS.
NO CAPERS TONIGHT, WE'RE IN THE MIDDLE OF A SHIPMENT.
YOU MIGHT AS WELL GO HOME.

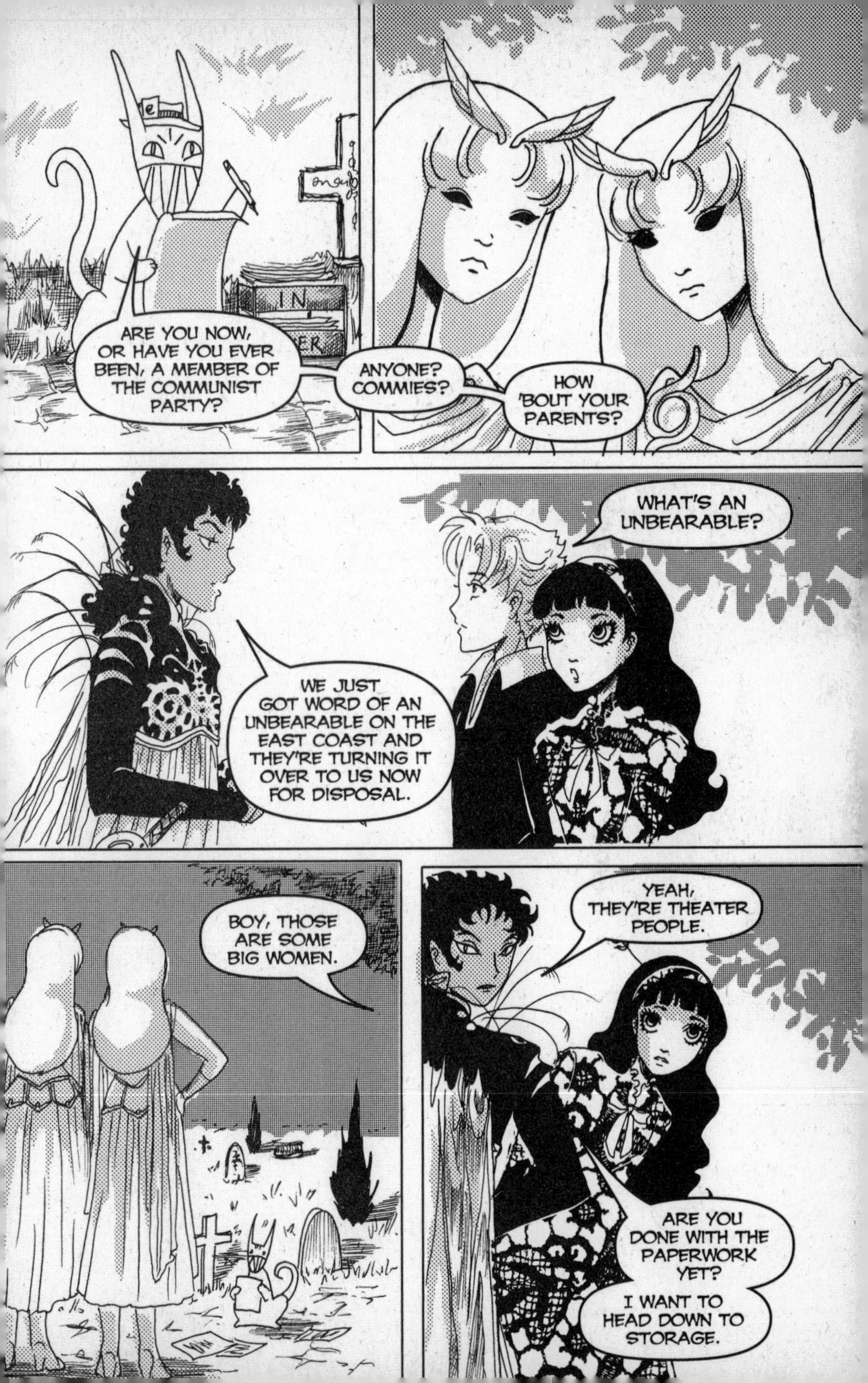
ARE YOU NOW, OR HAVE YOU EVER BEEN, A MEMBER OF THE COMMUNIST PARTY?
ANYONE? COMMIES?
HOW 'BOUT YOUR PARENTS?
WE JUST GOT WORD OF AN UNBEARABLE ON THE EAST COAST AND THEY'RE TURNING IT OVER TO US NOW FOR DISPOSAL.
WHAT'S AN UNBEARABLE?
BOY, THOSE ARE SOME BIG WOMEN.
YEAH, THEY'RE THEATER PEOPLE.
ARE YOU DONE WITH THE PAPERWORK YET?
I WANT TO HEAD DOWN TO STORAGE.

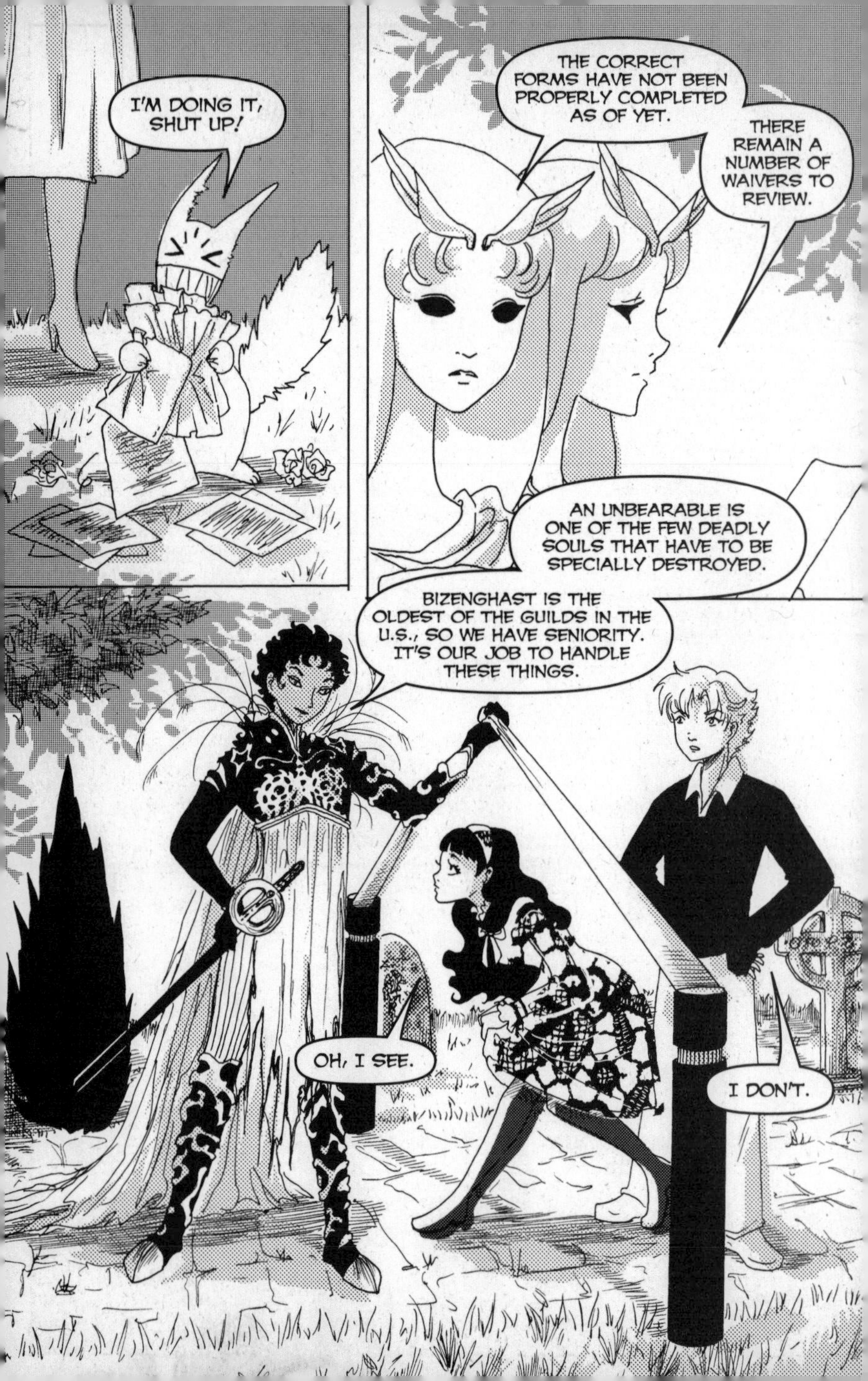
I'M DOING IT, SHUT UP!
THE CORRECT FORMS HAVE NOT BEEN PROPERLY COMPLETED AS OF YET.
THERE REMAIN A NUMBER OF WAIVERS TO REVIEW.
AN UNBEARABLE IS ONE OF THE FEW DEADLY SOULS THAT HAVE TO BE SPECIALLY DESTROYED.
BIZENGHAST IS THE OLDEST OF THE GUILDS IN THE U.S., SO WE HAVE SENIORITY. IT'S OUR JOB TO HANDLE THESE THINGS.
OH, I SEE.
I DON'T.

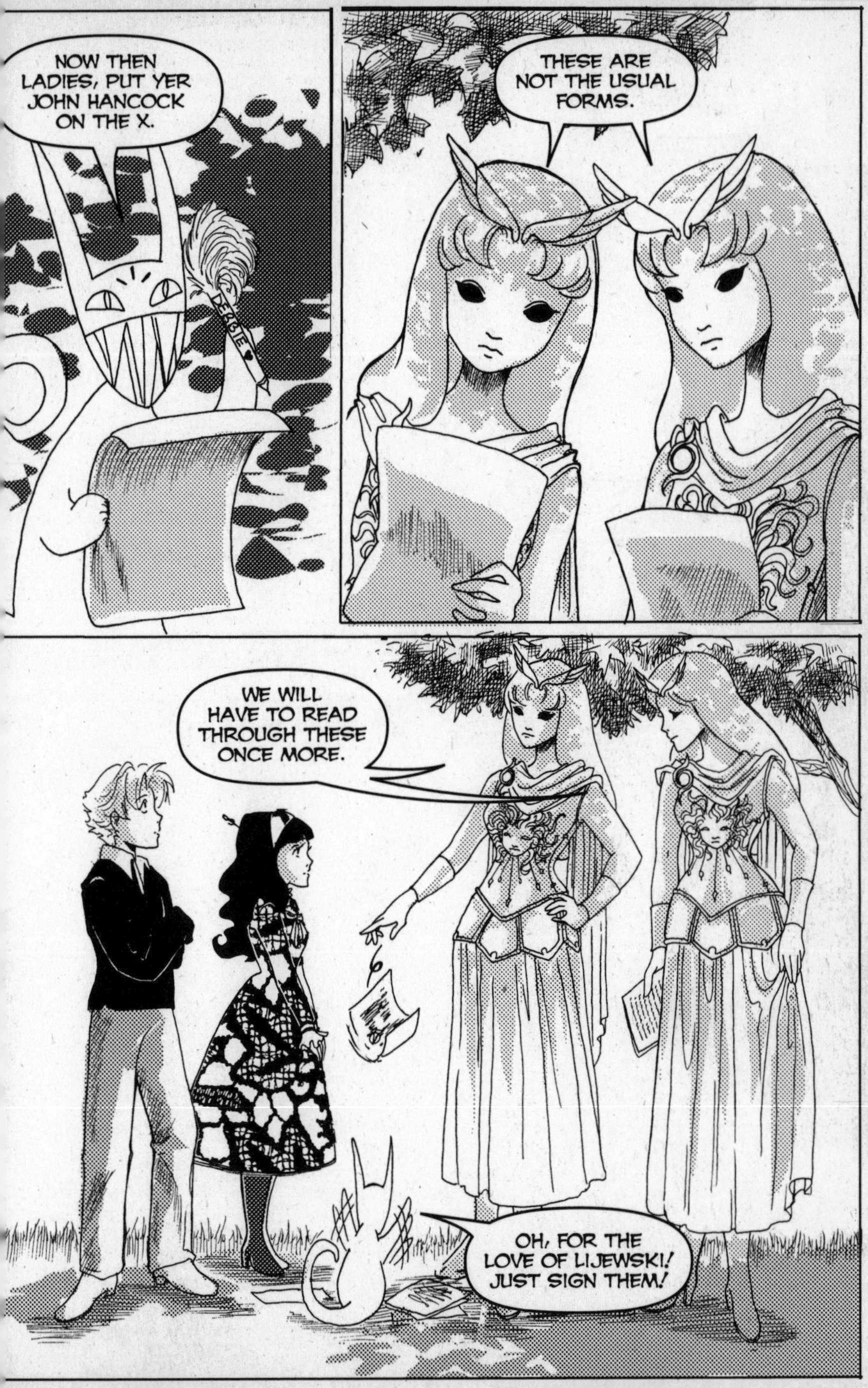
NOW THEN LADIES, PUT YER JOHN HANCOCK ON THE X.
THESE ARE NOT THE USUAL FORMS.
WE WILL HAVE TO READ THROUGH THESE ONCE MORE.
OH, FOR THE LOVE OF LIJEWSKI! JUST SIGN THEM!

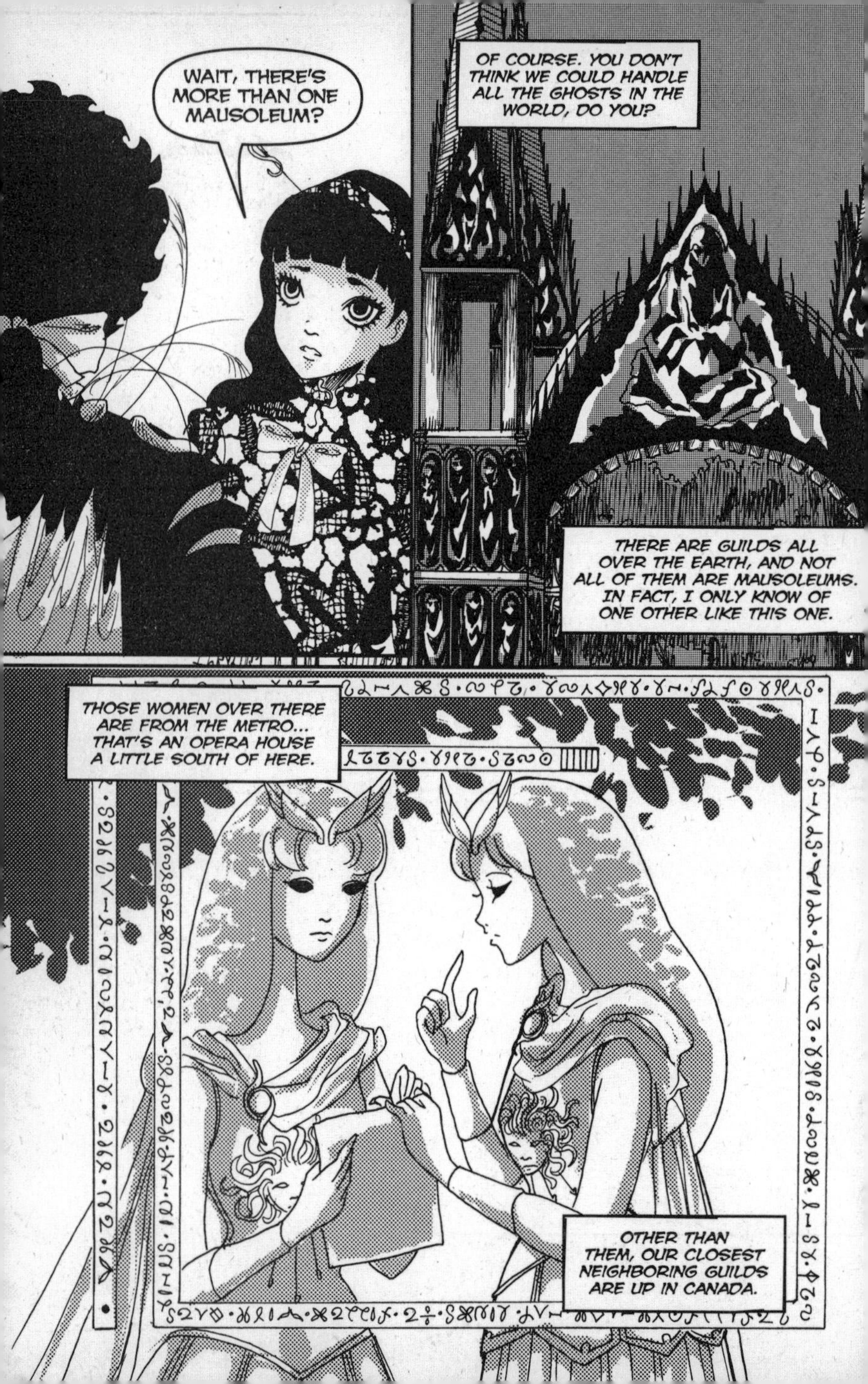

WAIT, THERE'S MORE THAN ONE MAUSOLEUM?
OF COURSE. YOU DON'T THINK WE COULD HANDLE ALL THE GHOSTS IN THE WORLD, DO YOU?
THERE ARE GUILDS ALL OVER THE EARTH, AND NOT ALL OF THEM ARE MAUSOLEUMS. IN FACT, I ONLY KNOW OF ONE OTHER LIKE THIS ONE.
THOSE WOMEN OVER THERE ARE FROM THE METRO... THAT'S AN OPERA HOUSE A LITTLE SOUTH OF HERE.
OTHER THAN THEM, OUR CLOSEST NEIGHBORING GUILDS ARE UP IN CANADA.

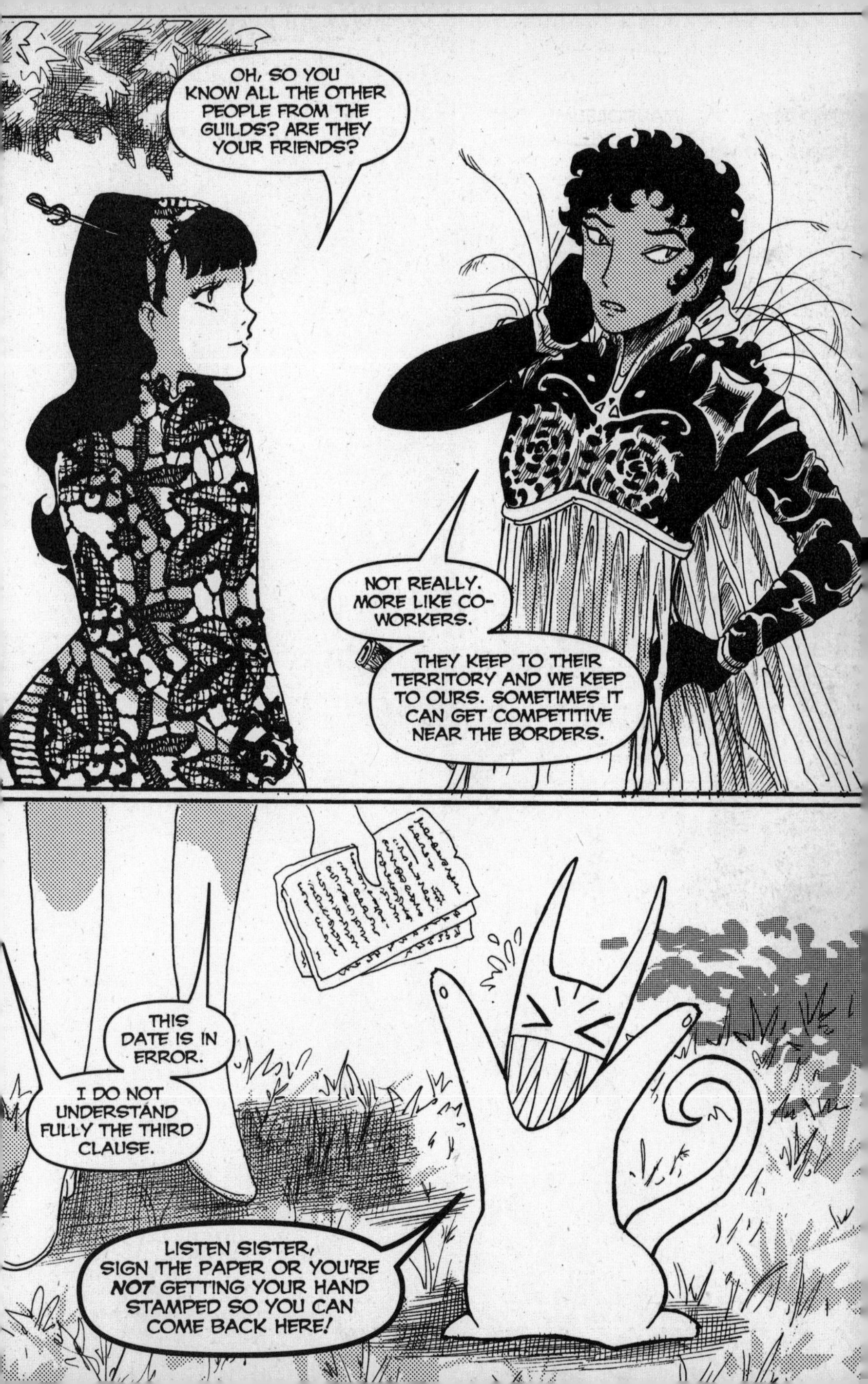
OH, SO YOU KNOW ALL THE OTHER PEOPLE FROM THE GUILDS? ARE THEY YOUR FRIENDS?
NOT REALLY. MORE LIKE CO-WORKERS.
THEY KEEP TO THEIR TERRITORY AND WE KEEP TO OURS. SOMETIMES IT CAN GET COMPETITIVE NEAR THE BORDERS.
THIS DATE IS IN ERROR.
I DO NOT UNDERSTAND FULLY THE THIRD CLAUSE.
LISTEN SISTER, SIGN THE PAPER OR YOU'RE ***NOT*** GETTING YOUR HAND STAMPED SO YOU CAN COME BACK HERE!

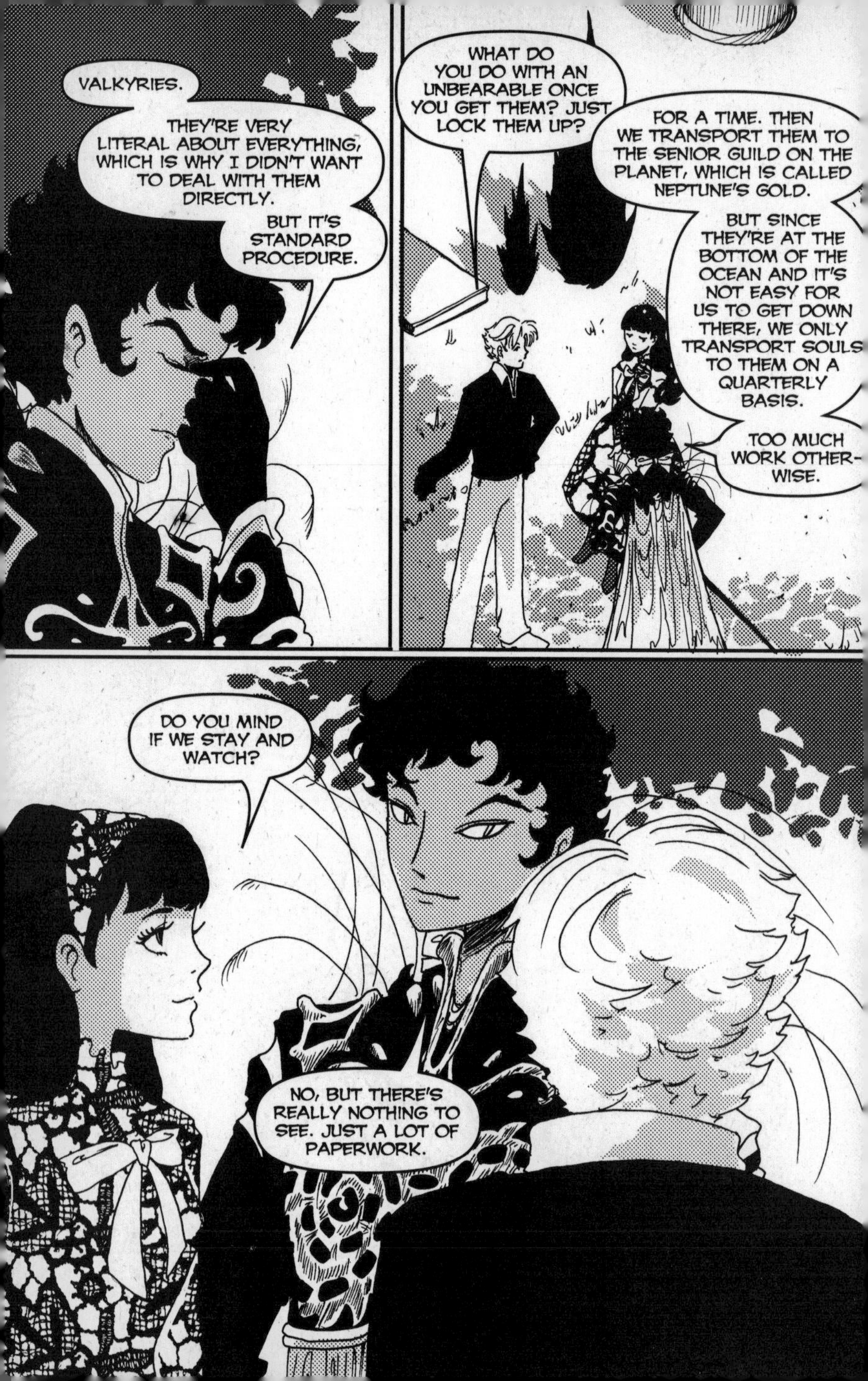
VALKYRIES.
THEY'RE VERY LITERAL ABOUT EVERYTHING, WHICH IS WHY I DIDN'T WANT TO DEAL WITH THEM DIRECTLY.
BUT IT'S STANDARD PROCEDURE.
WHAT DO YOU DO WITH AN UNBEARABLE ONCE YOU GET THEM? JUST LOCK THEM UP?
FOR A TIME. THEN WE TRANSPORT THEM TO THE SENIOR GUILD ON THE PLANET, WHICH IS CALLED NEPTUNE'S GOLD.
BUT SINCE THEY'RE AT THE BOTTOM OF THE OCEAN AND IT'S NOT EASY FOR US TO GET DOWN THERE, WE ONLY TRANSPORT SOULS TO THEM ON A QUARTERLY BASIS.
TOO MUCH WORK OTHER-WISE.
DO YOU MIND IF WE STAY AND WATCH?
NO, BUT THERE'S REALLY NOTHING TO SEE. JUST A LOT OF PAPERWORK.

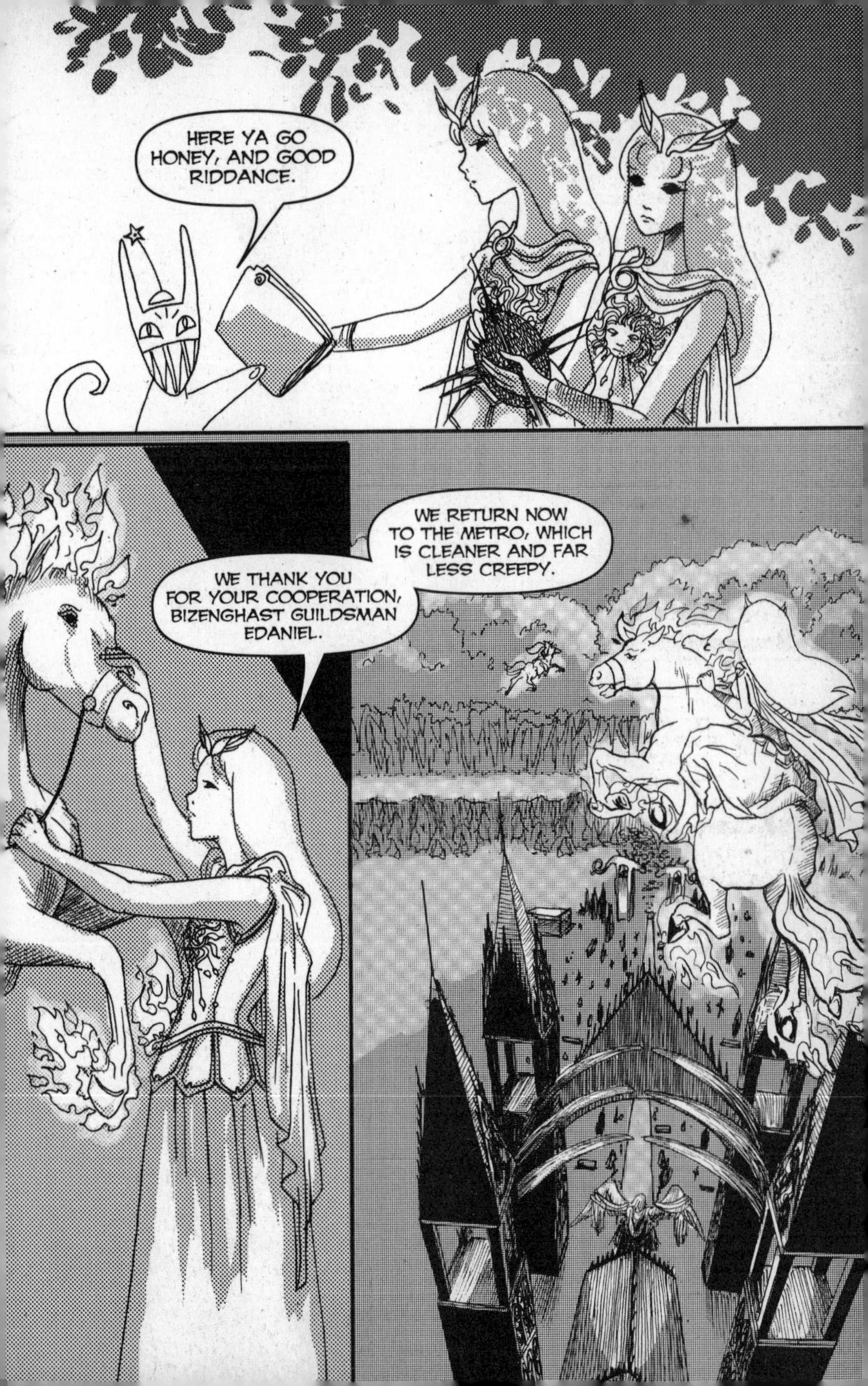
HERE YA GO HONEY, AND GOOD RIDDANCE.
WE THANK YOU FOR YOUR COOPERATION, BIZENGHAST GUILDSMAN EDANIEL.
WE RETURN NOW TO THE METRO, WHICH IS CLEANER AND FAR LESS CREEPY.

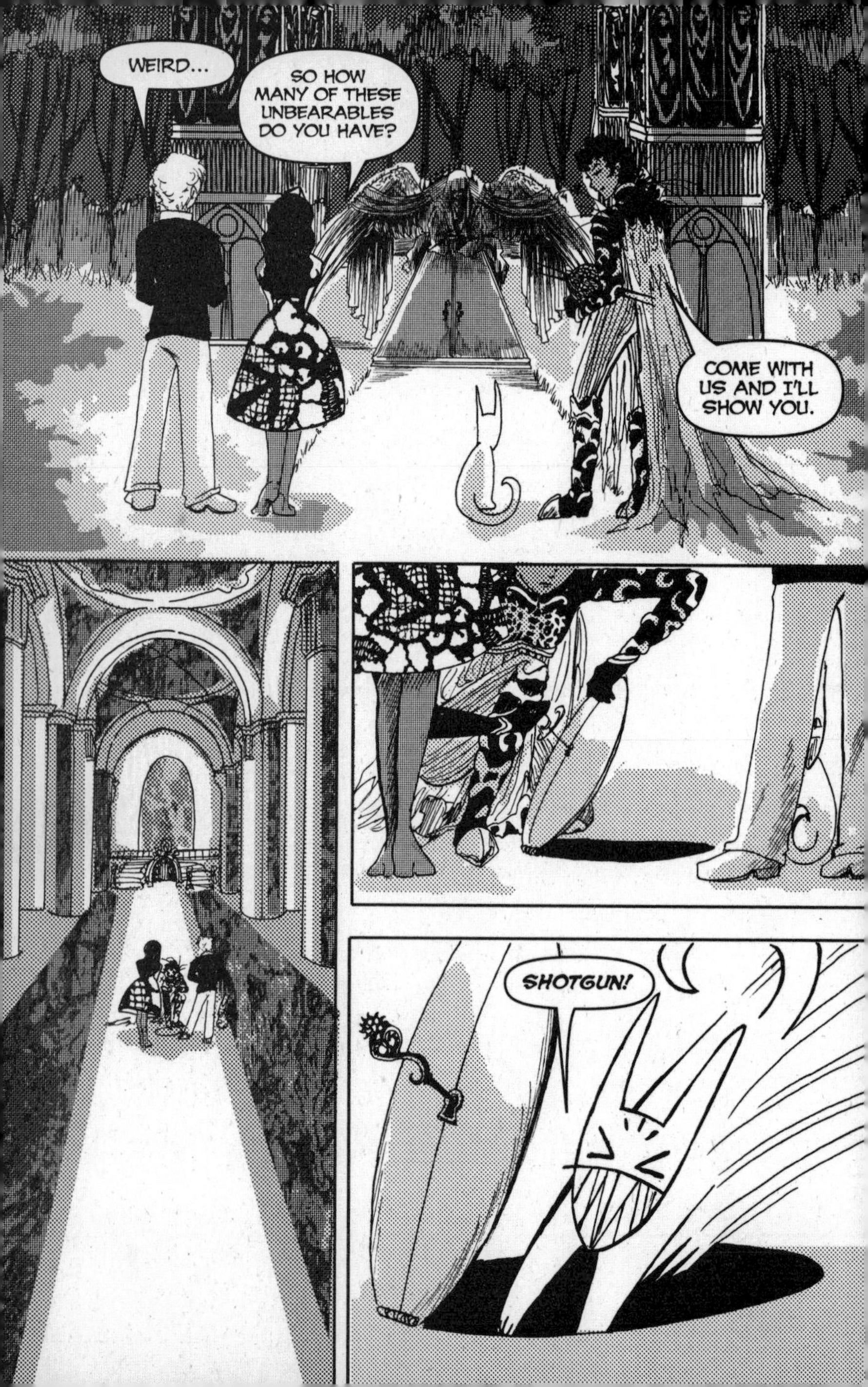

WEIRD...
SO HOW MANY OF THESE UNBEARABLES DO YOU HAVE?
COME WITH US AND I'LL SHOW YOU.
SHOTGUN!

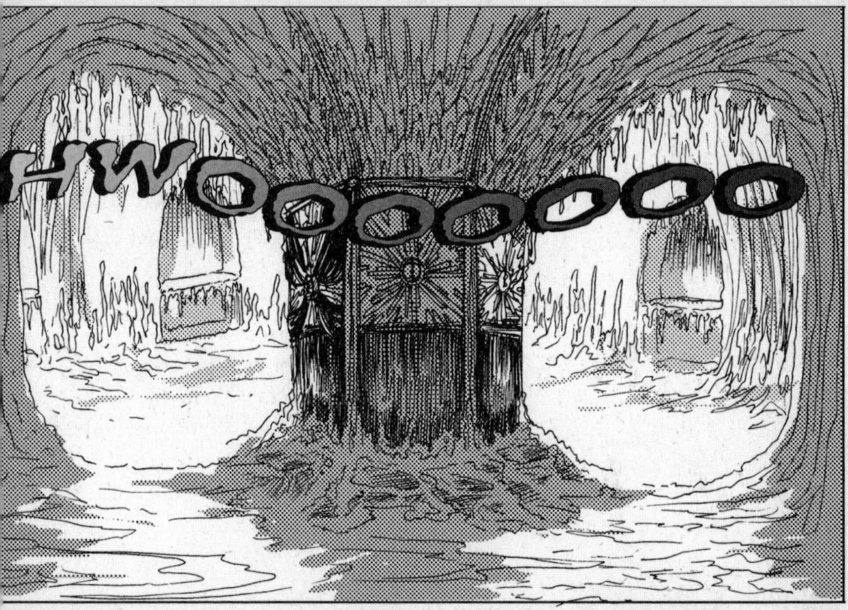
HWOOOOOOOOOO

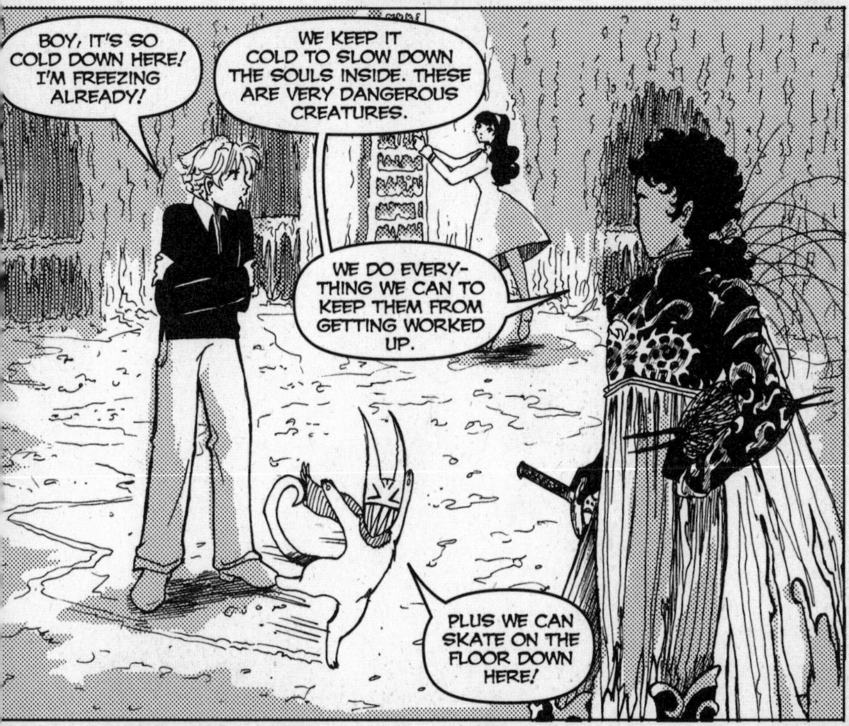
BOY, IT'S SO COLD DOWN HERE! I'M FREEZING ALREADY!
WE KEEP IT COLD TO SLOW DOWN THE SOULS INSIDE. THESE ARE VERY DANGEROUS CREATURES.
WE DO EVERY-THING WE CAN TO KEEP THEM FROM GETTING WORKED UP.
PLUS WE CAN SKATE ON THE FLOOR DOWN HERE!

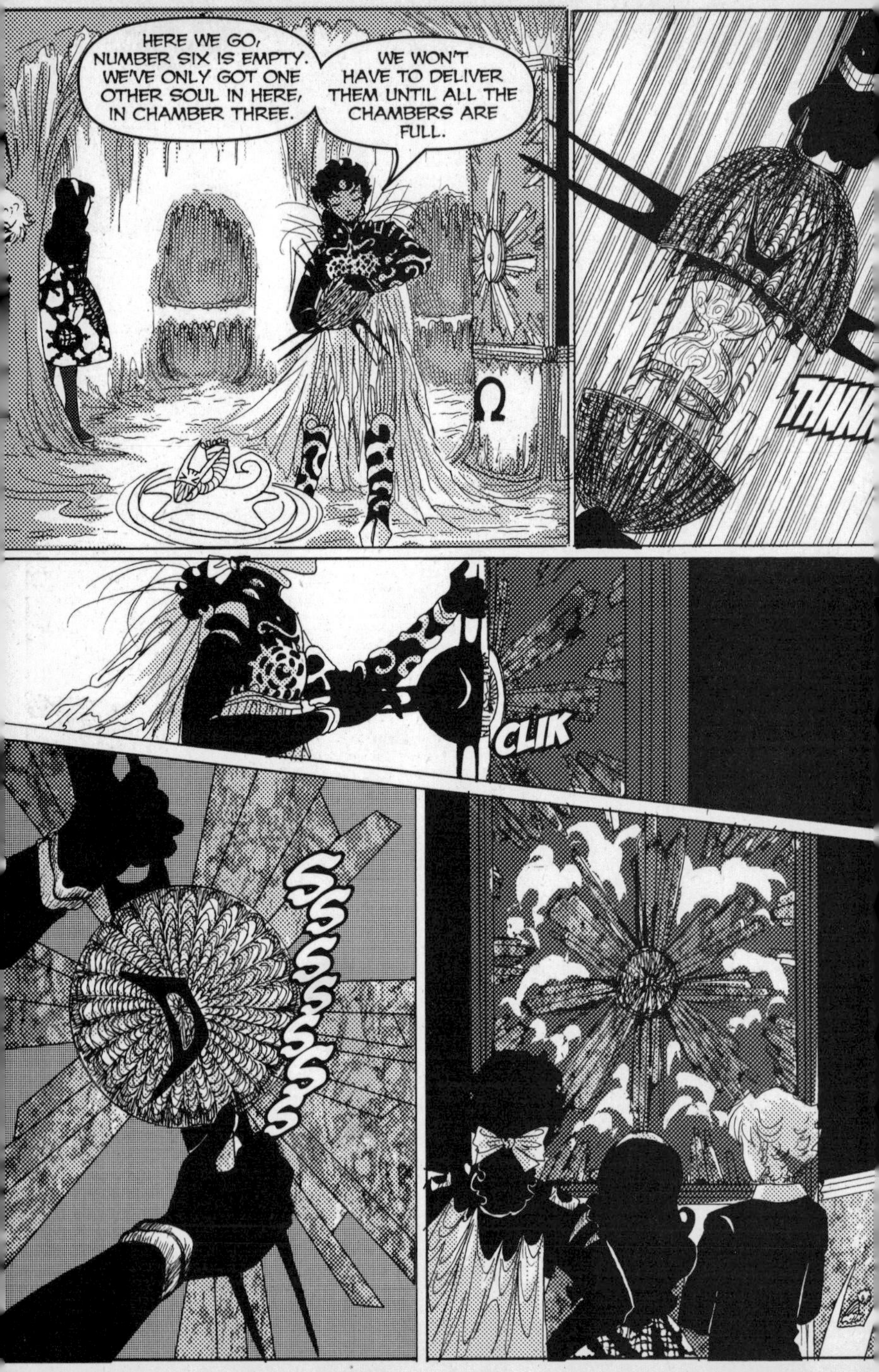
HERE WE GO, NUMBER SIX IS EMPTY. WE'VE ONLY GOT ONE OTHER SOUL IN HERE, IN CHAMBER THREE.
WE WON'T HAVE TO DELIVER THEM UNTIL ALL THE CHAMBERS ARE FULL.
THNN
CLIK
SSSSSSSSS

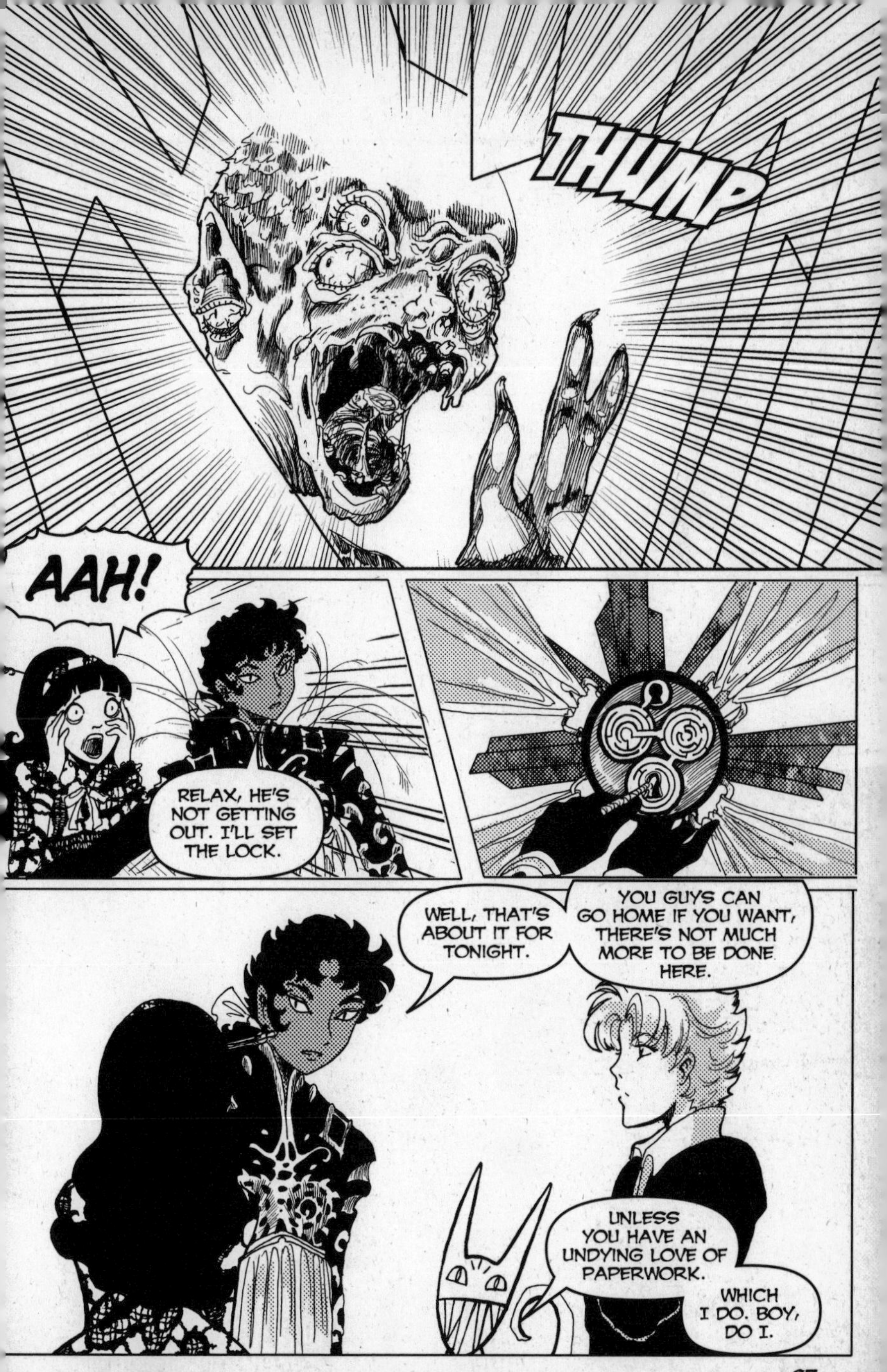
THUMP
AAH!
RELAX, HE'S NOT GETTING OUT. I'LL SET THE LOCK.
WELL, THAT'S ABOUT IT FOR TONIGHT.
YOU GUYS CAN GO HOME IF YOU WANT, THERE'S NOT MUCH MORE TO BE DONE HERE.
UNLESS YOU HAVE AN UNDYING LOVE OF PAPERWORK.
WHICH I DO. BOY, DO I.

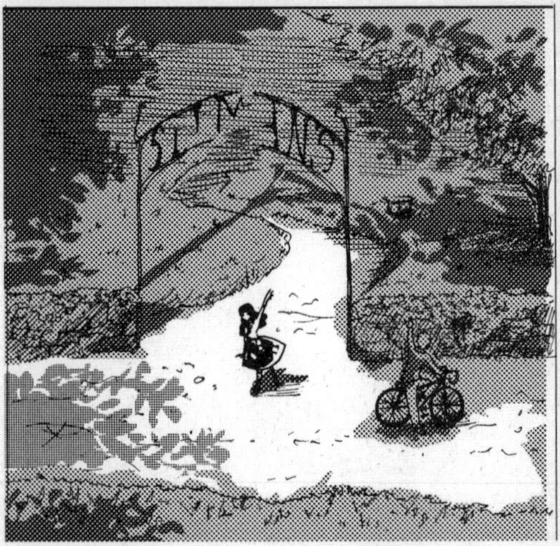

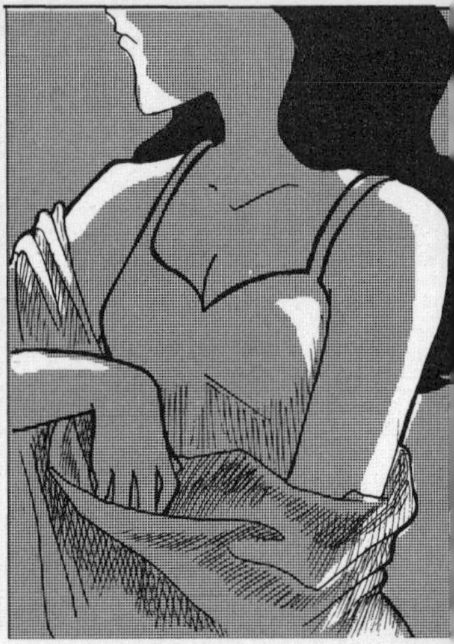

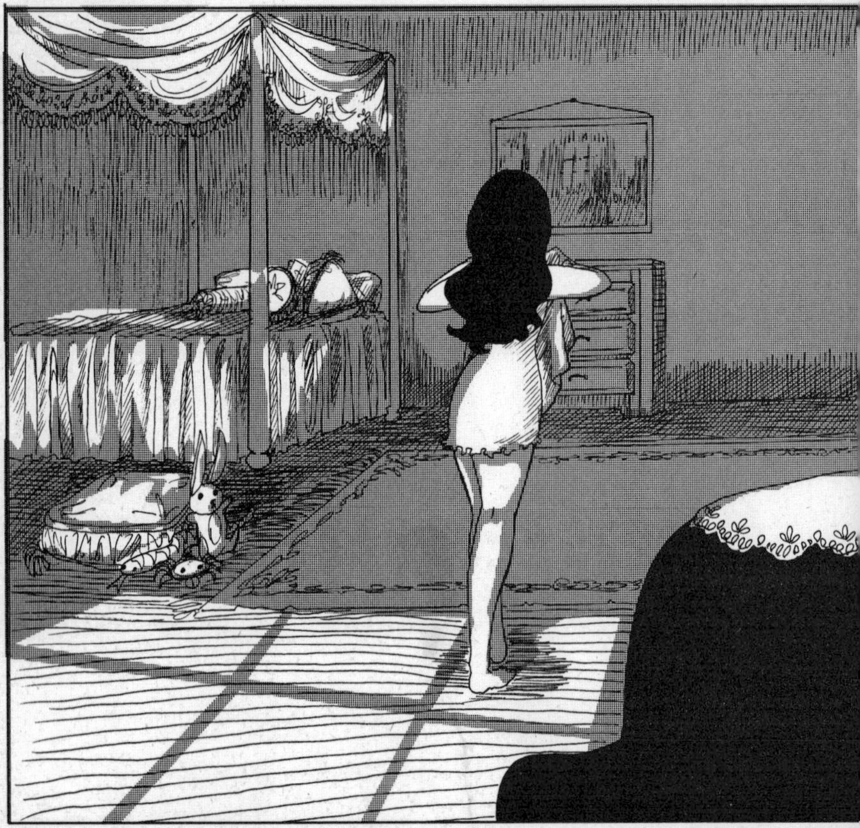

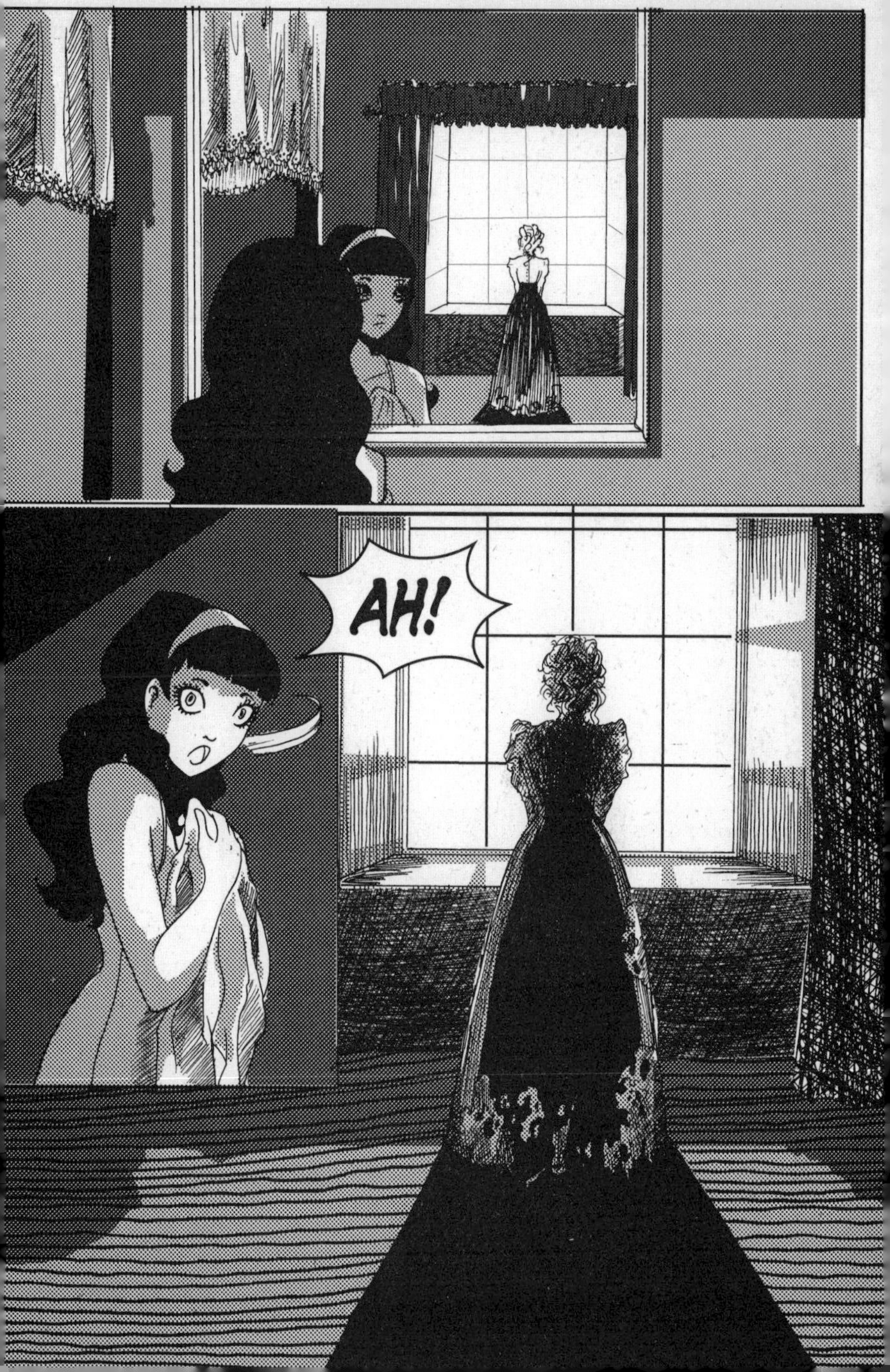
AH!

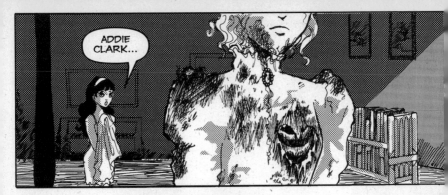

ADDIE CLARK...

ADDIE... ARE YOU AN UNBEARABLE? IS THAT WHY YOU'RE STILL HERE?

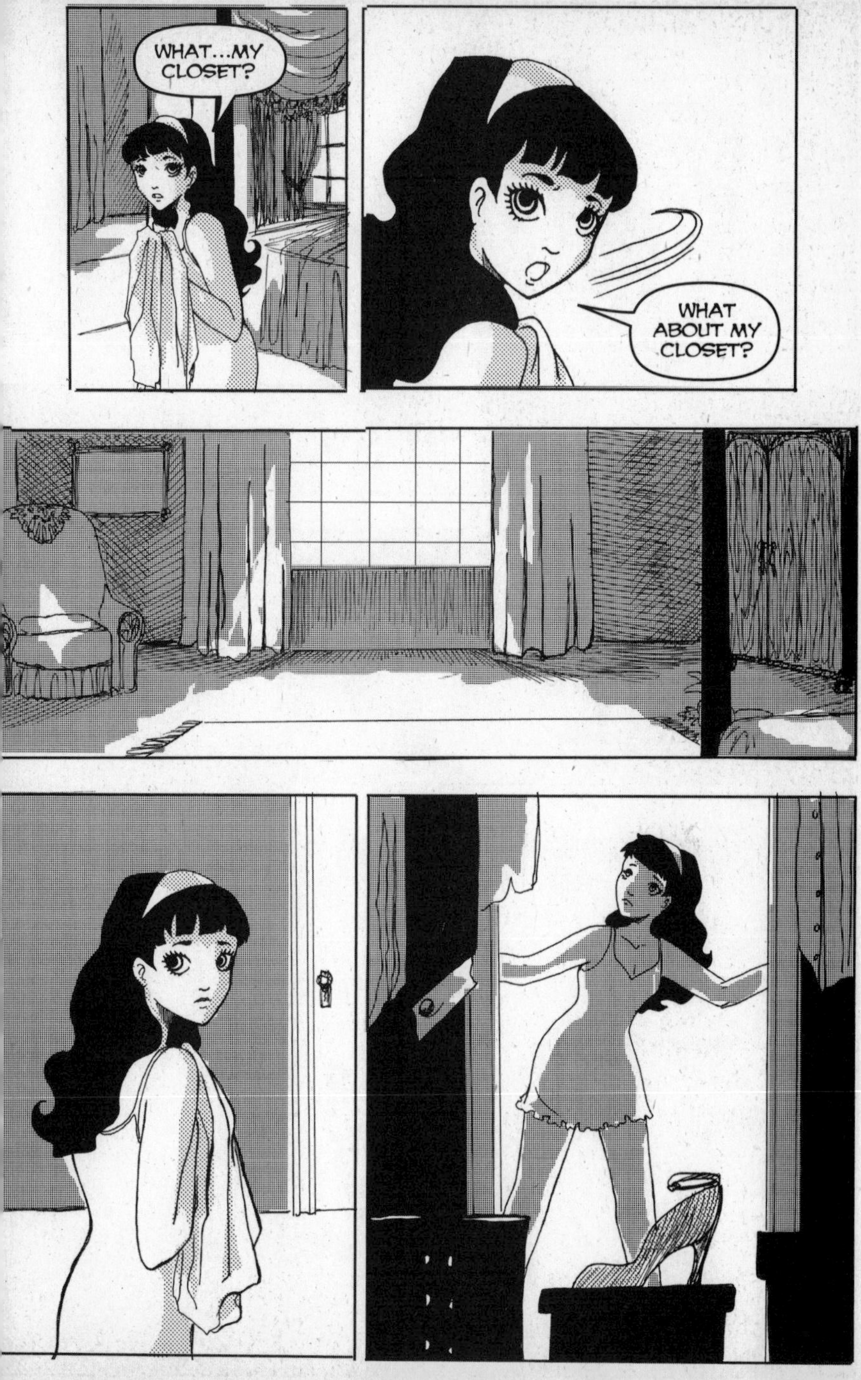
WHAT...MY CLOSET?
WHAT ABOUT MY CLOSET?

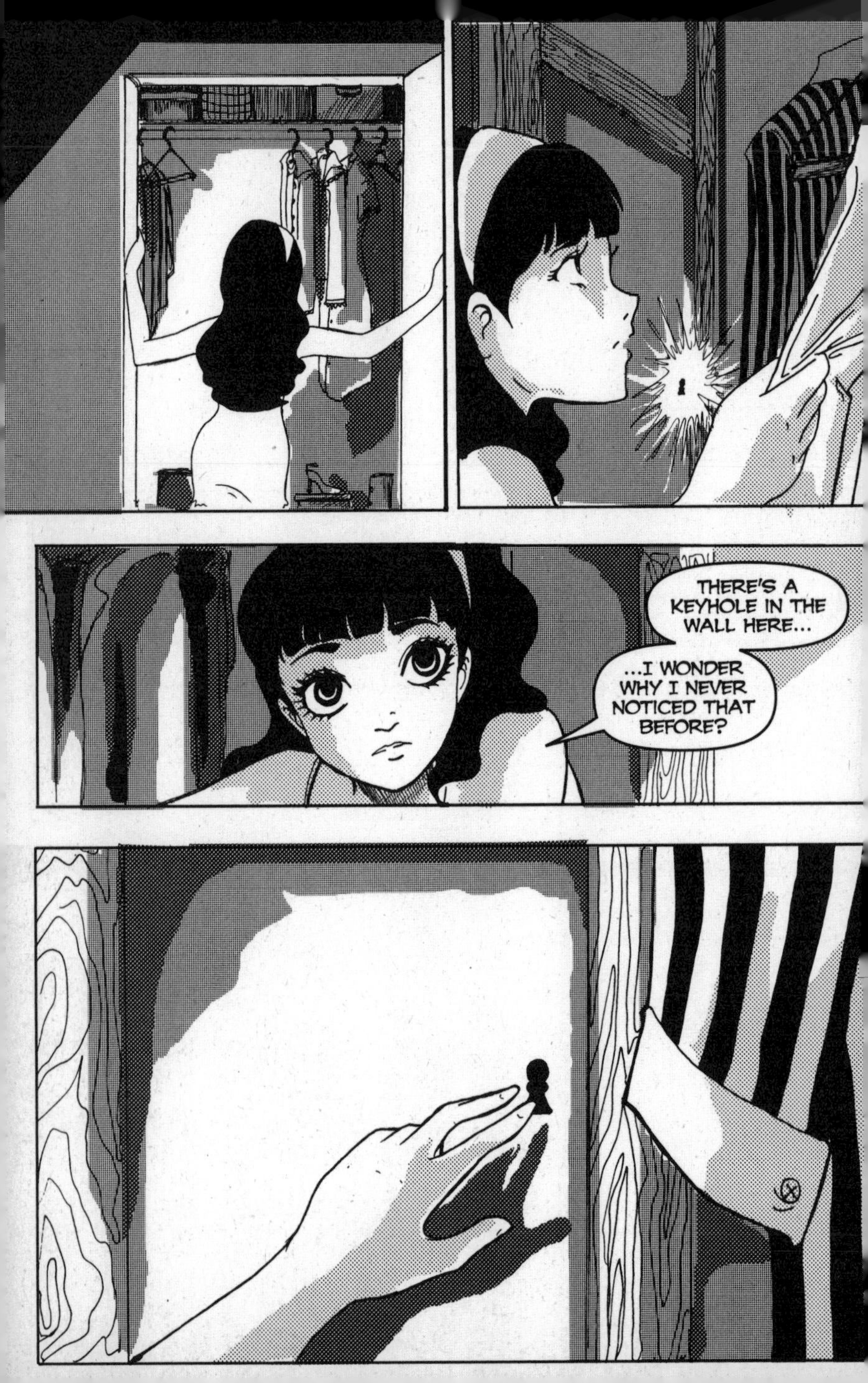
THERE'S A KEYHOLE IN THE WALL HERE...
...I WONDER WHY I NEVER NOTICED THAT BEFORE?

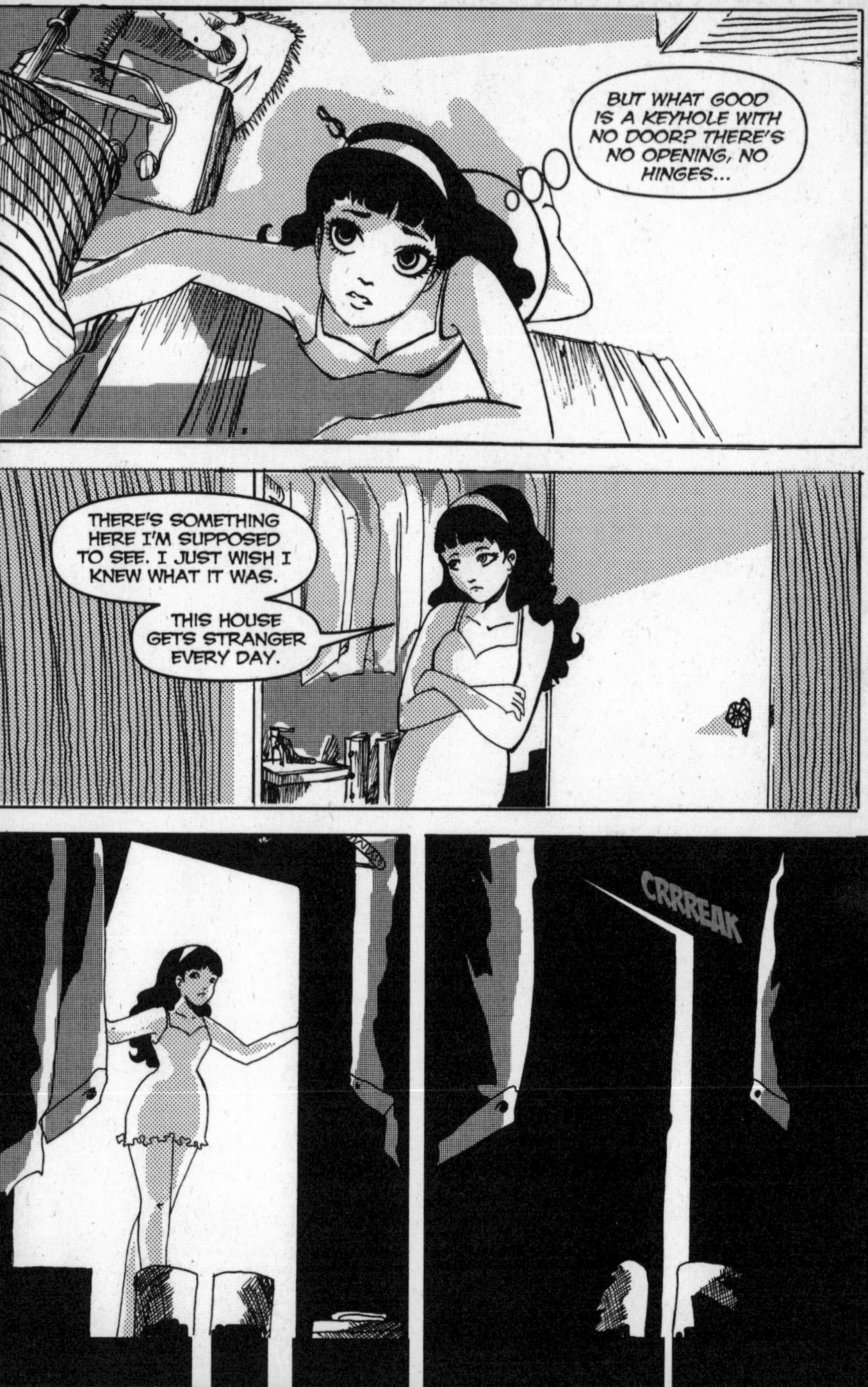
BUT WHAT GOOD IS A KEYHOLE WITH NO DOOR? THERE'S NO OPENING, NO HINGES...
THERE'S SOMETHING HERE I'M SUPPOSED TO SEE. I JUST WISH I KNEW WHAT IT WAS.
THIS HOUSE GETS STRANGER EVERY DAY.
CRRREAK

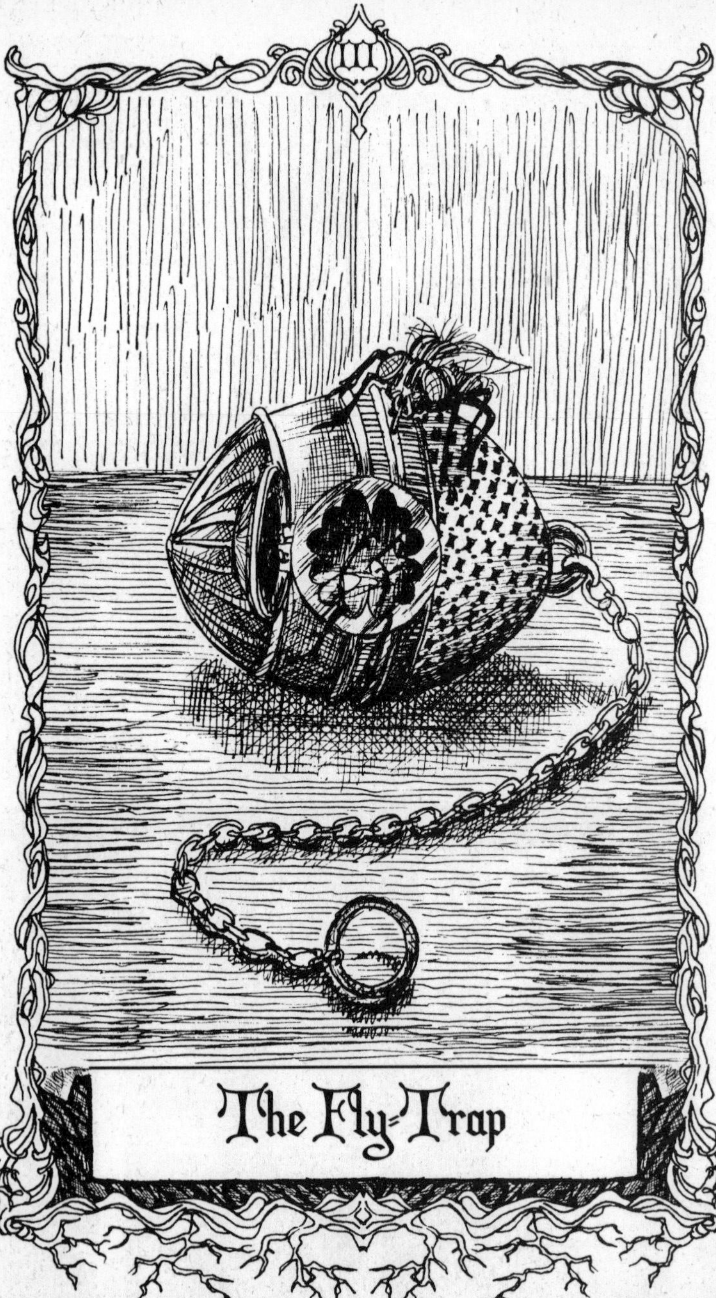
III
The Fly-Trap

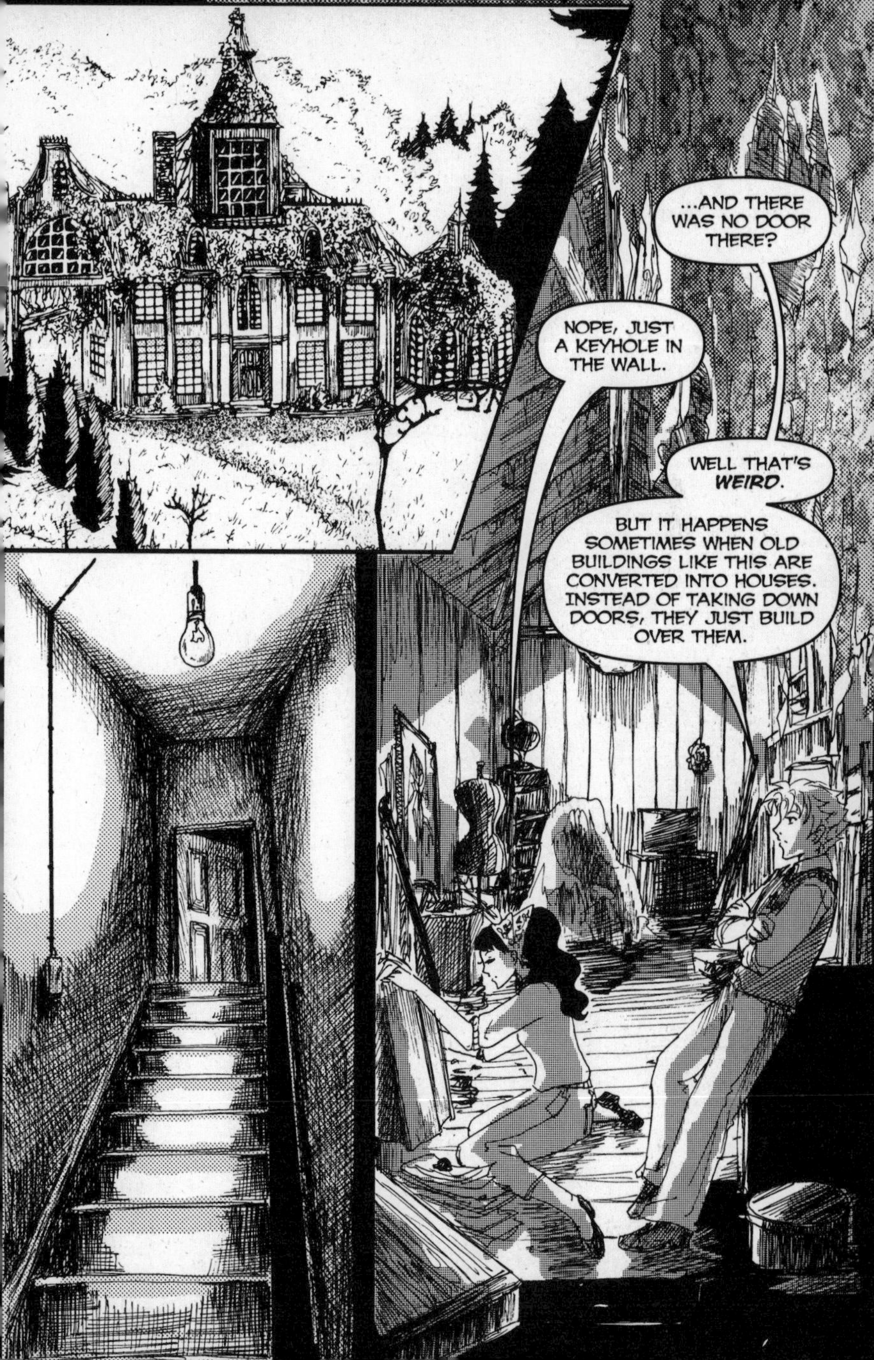
...AND THERE WAS NO DOOR THERE?
NOPE, JUST A KEYHOLE IN THE WALL.
WELL THAT'S ***WEIRD***.
BUT IT HAPPENS SOMETIMES WHEN OLD BUILDINGS LIKE THIS ARE CONVERTED INTO HOUSES. INSTEAD OF TAKING DOWN DOORS, THEY JUST BUILD OVER THEM.

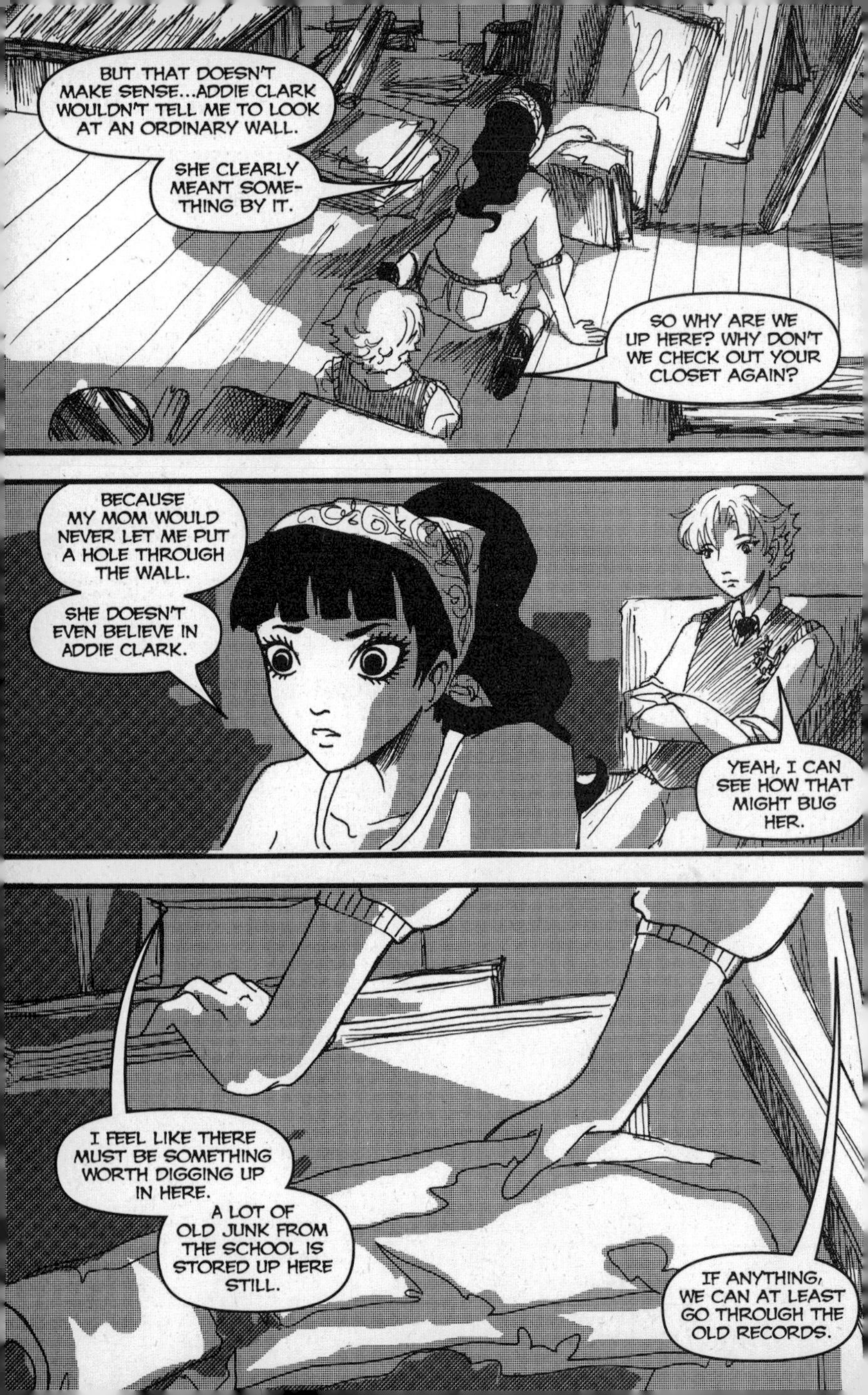
BUT THAT DOESN'T MAKE SENSE...ADDIE CLARK WOULDN'T TELL ME TO LOOK AT AN ORDINARY WALL.
SHE CLEARLY MEANT SOME-THING BY IT.
SO WHY ARE WE UP HERE? WHY DON'T WE CHECK OUT YOUR CLOSET AGAIN?
BECAUSE MY MOM WOULD NEVER LET ME PUT A HOLE THROUGH THE WALL.
SHE DOESN'T EVEN BELIEVE IN ADDIE CLARK.
YEAH, I CAN SEE HOW THAT MIGHT BUG HER.
I FEEL LIKE THERE MUST BE SOMETHING WORTH DIGGING UP IN HERE.
A LOT OF OLD JUNK FROM THE SCHOOL IS STORED UP HERE STILL.
IF ANYTHING, WE CAN AT LEAST GO THROUGH THE OLD RECORDS.

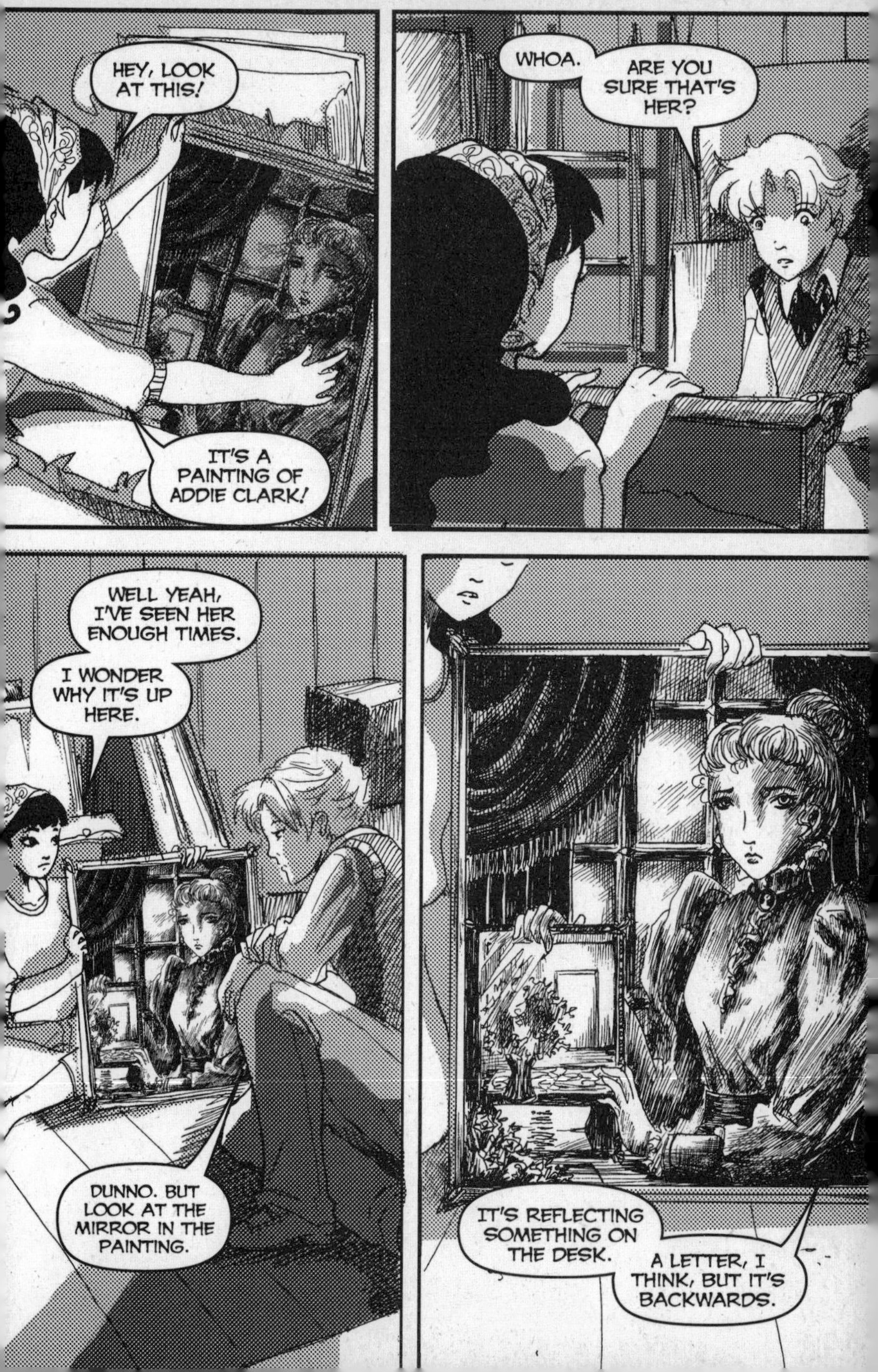
HEY, LOOK AT THIS!
IT'S A PAINTING OF ADDIE CLARK!
WHOA.
ARE YOU SURE THAT'S HER?
WELL YEAH, I'VE SEEN HER ENOUGH TIMES.
I WONDER WHY IT'S UP HERE.
DUNNO. BUT LOOK AT THE MIRROR IN THE PAINTING.
IT'S REFLECTING SOMETHING ON THE DESK.
A LETTER, I THINK, BUT IT'S BACKWARDS.

HANG ON.

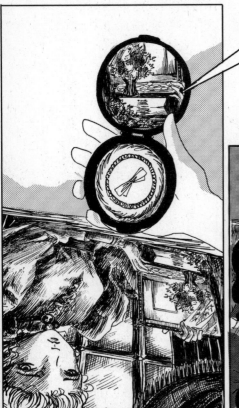

Small harbors can calm a mighty sea,
Small waves can bring us safely home.
Small arbors can tame the wilderness,
Wild undergrowth fills a world all my own.

Dark corners can hide a larger room,
Dark stairways can fill a big home.
Dark secrets are kept and accepted,
Whilst understood by a world all my own.

Heaven can call back its angels,
Heaven can bring them all home.
Heaven can hide us all safely,
While underneath, in a world all our own.

HUH. I'VE NEVER HEARD THAT POEM BEFORE.

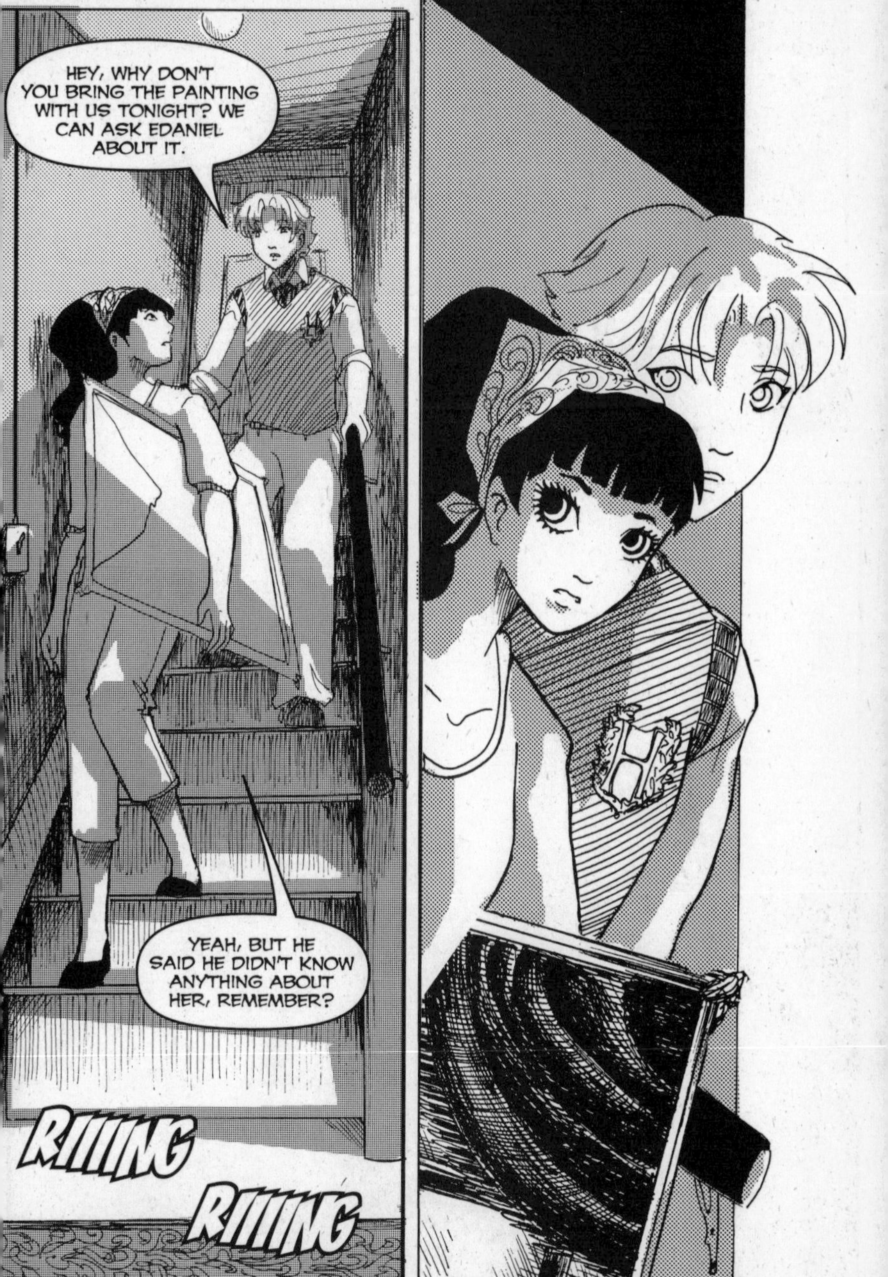
HEY, WHY DON'T YOU BRING THE PAINTING WITH US TONIGHT? WE CAN ASK EDANIEL ABOUT IT.
YEAH, BUT HE SAID HE DIDN'T KNOW ANYTHING ABOUT HER, REMEMBER?
RIIIING
RIIIING

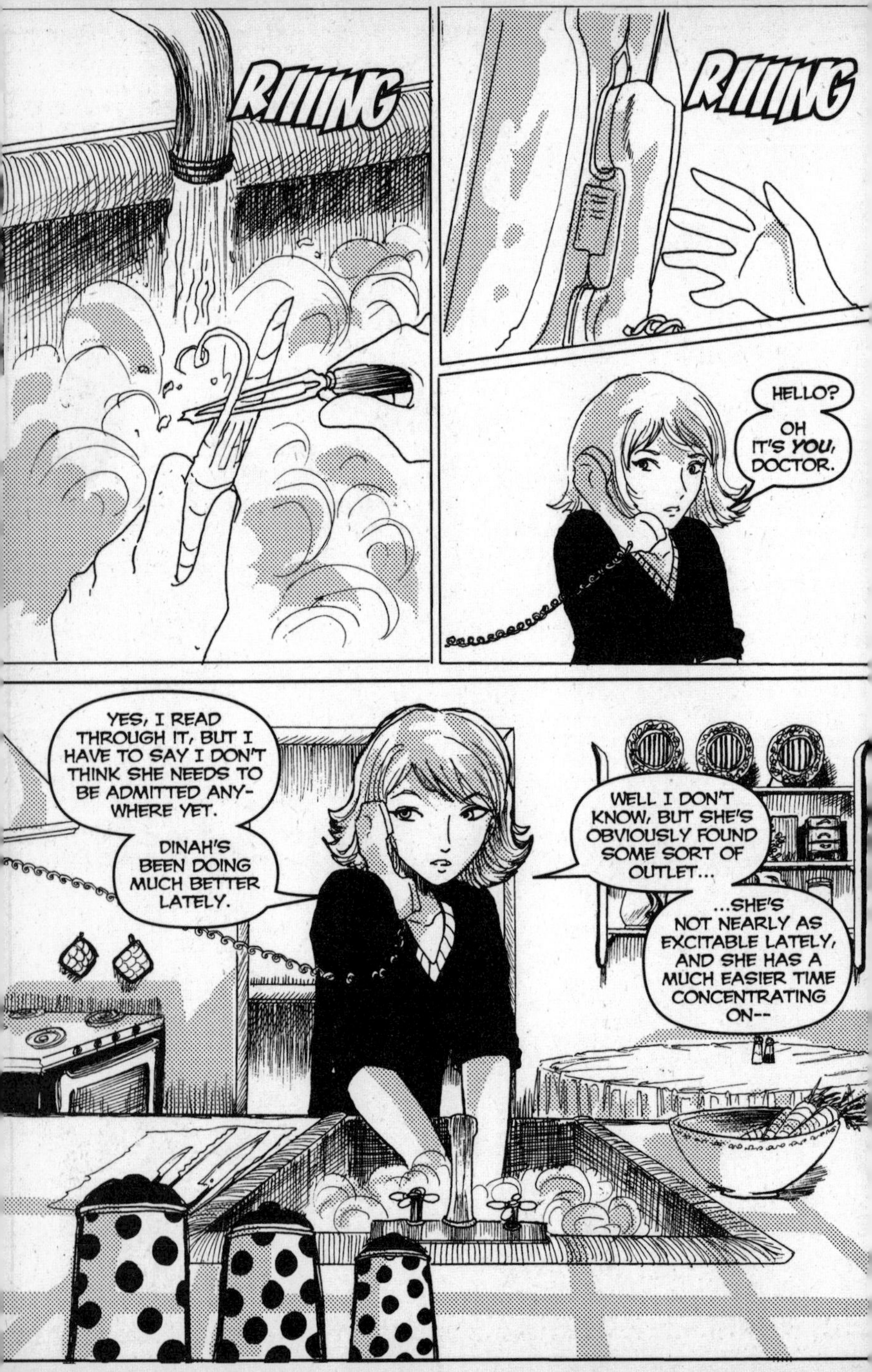
RIIIING
RIIIING
HELLO?
OH IT'S *YOU*, DOCTOR.
YES, I READ THROUGH IT, BUT I HAVE TO SAY I DON'T THINK SHE NEEDS TO BE ADMITTED ANY-WHERE YET.
DINAH'S BEEN DOING MUCH BETTER LATELY.
WELL I DON'T KNOW, BUT SHE'S OBVIOUSLY FOUND SOME SORT OF OUTLET...
...SHE'S NOT NEARLY AS EXCITABLE LATELY, AND SHE HAS A MUCH EASIER TIME CONCENTRATING ON--

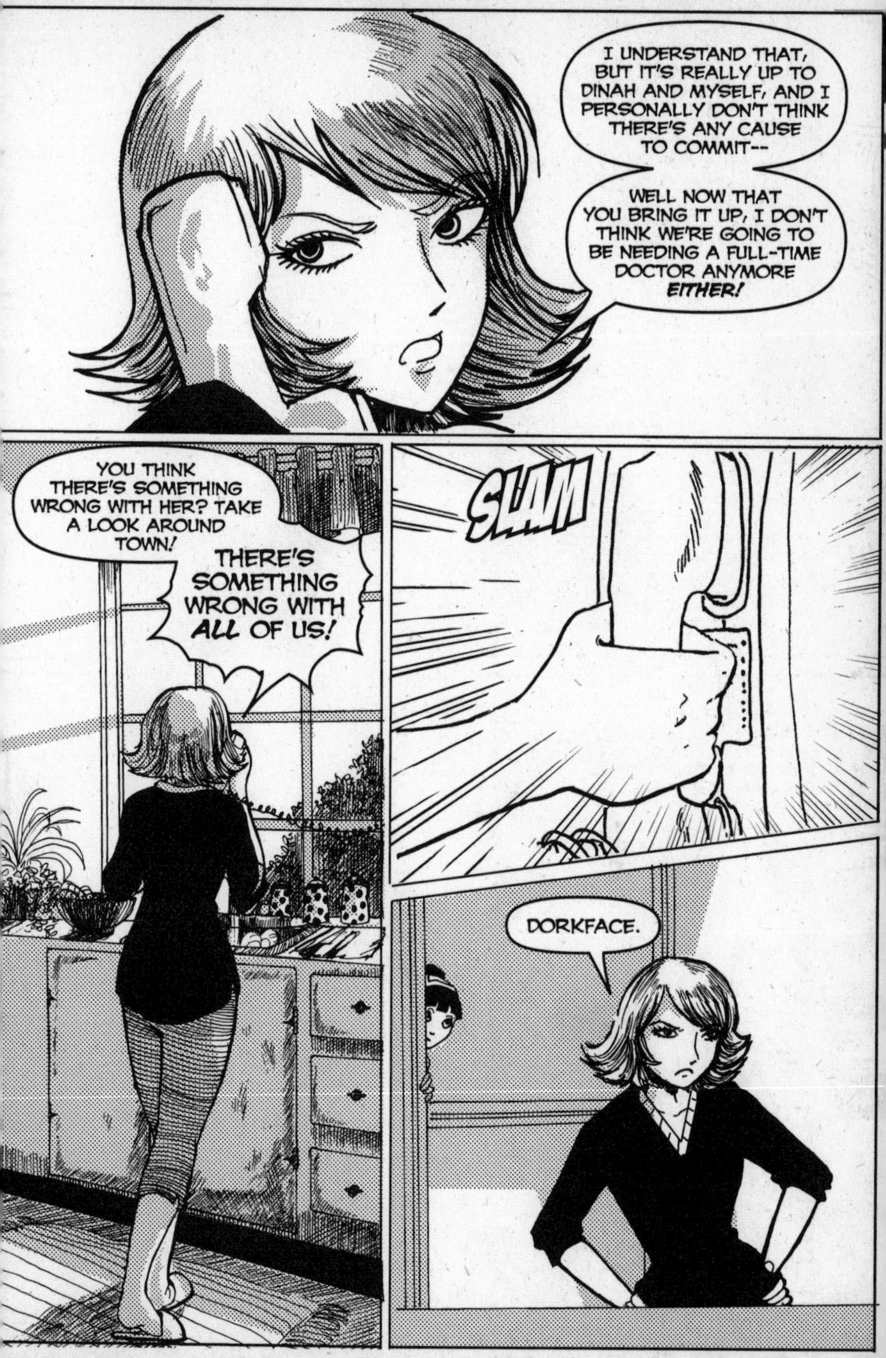
I UNDERSTAND THAT, BUT IT'S REALLY UP TO DINAH AND MYSELF, AND I PERSONALLY DON'T THINK THERE'S ANY CAUSE TO COMMIT--
WELL NOW THAT YOU BRING IT UP, I DON'T THINK WE'RE GOING TO BE NEEDING A FULL-TIME DOCTOR ANYMORE *EITHER!*
YOU THINK THERE'S SOMETHING WRONG WITH HER? TAKE A LOOK AROUND TOWN!
THERE'S SOMETHING WRONG WITH *ALL* OF US!
SLAM
DORKFACE.

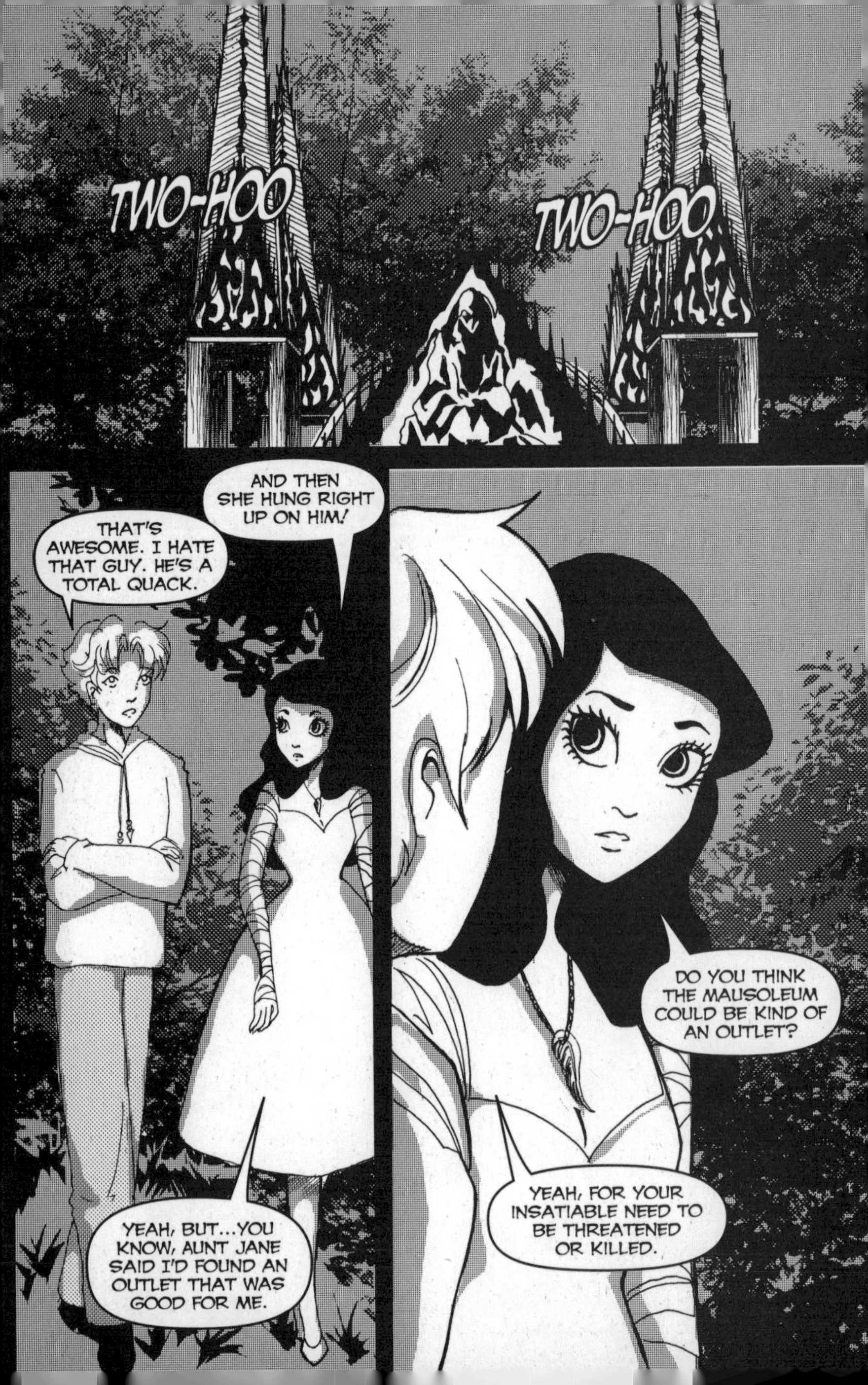
TWO-HOO
TWO-HOO
THAT'S AWESOME. I HATE THAT GUY. HE'S A TOTAL QUACK.
AND THEN SHE HUNG RIGHT UP ON HIM!
YEAH, BUT...YOU KNOW, AUNT JANE SAID I'D FOUND AN OUTLET THAT WAS GOOD FOR ME.
DO YOU THINK THE MAUSOLEUM COULD BE KIND OF AN OUTLET?
YEAH, FOR YOUR INSATIABLE NEED TO BE THREATENED OR KILLED.

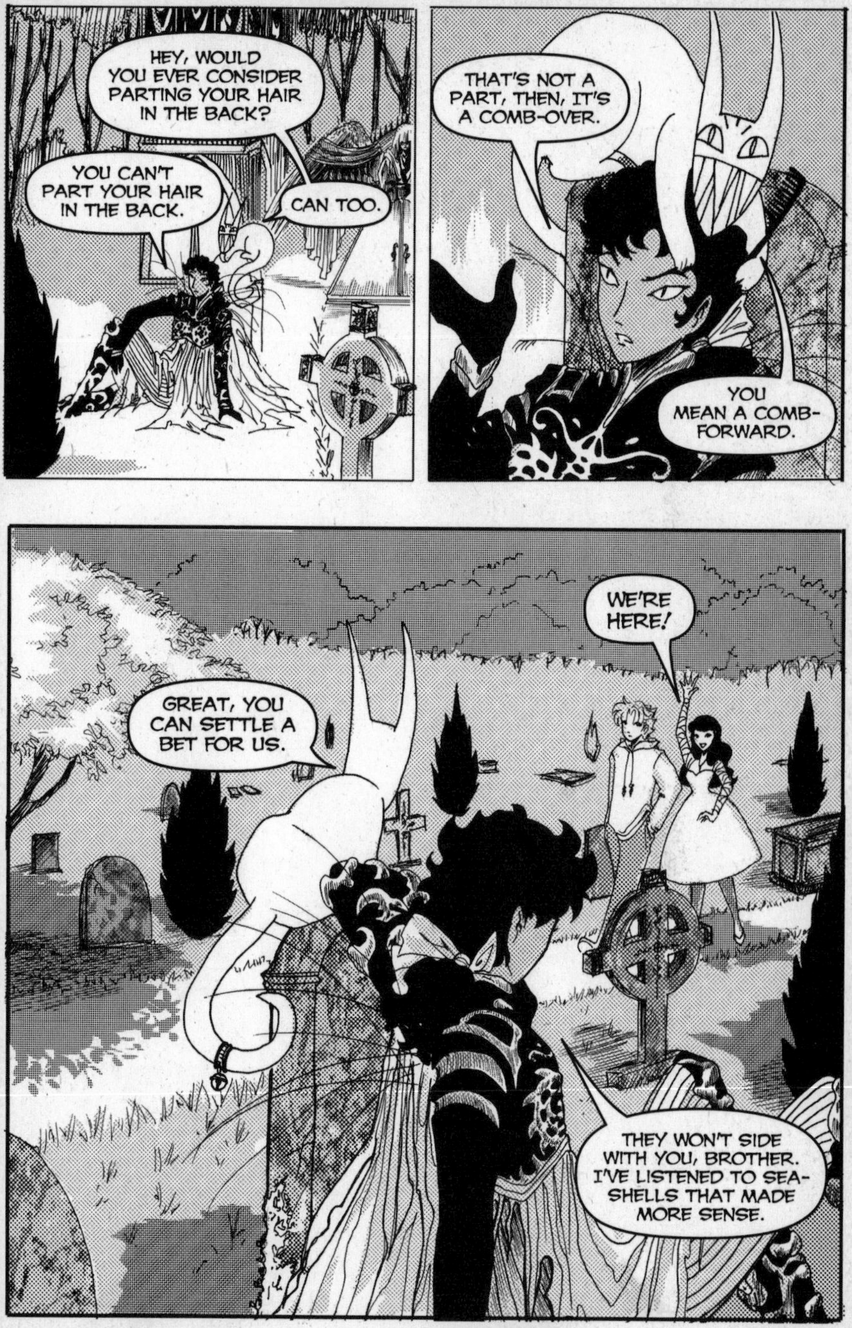
HEY, WOULD YOU EVER CONSIDER PARTING YOUR HAIR IN THE BACK?
YOU CAN'T PART YOUR HAIR IN THE BACK.
CAN TOO.
THAT'S NOT A PART, THEN, IT'S A COMB-OVER.
YOU MEAN A COMB-FORWARD.
WE'RE HERE!
GREAT, YOU CAN SETTLE A BET FOR US.
THEY WON'T SIDE WITH YOU, BROTHER. I'VE LISTENED TO SEA-SHELLS THAT MADE MORE SENSE.

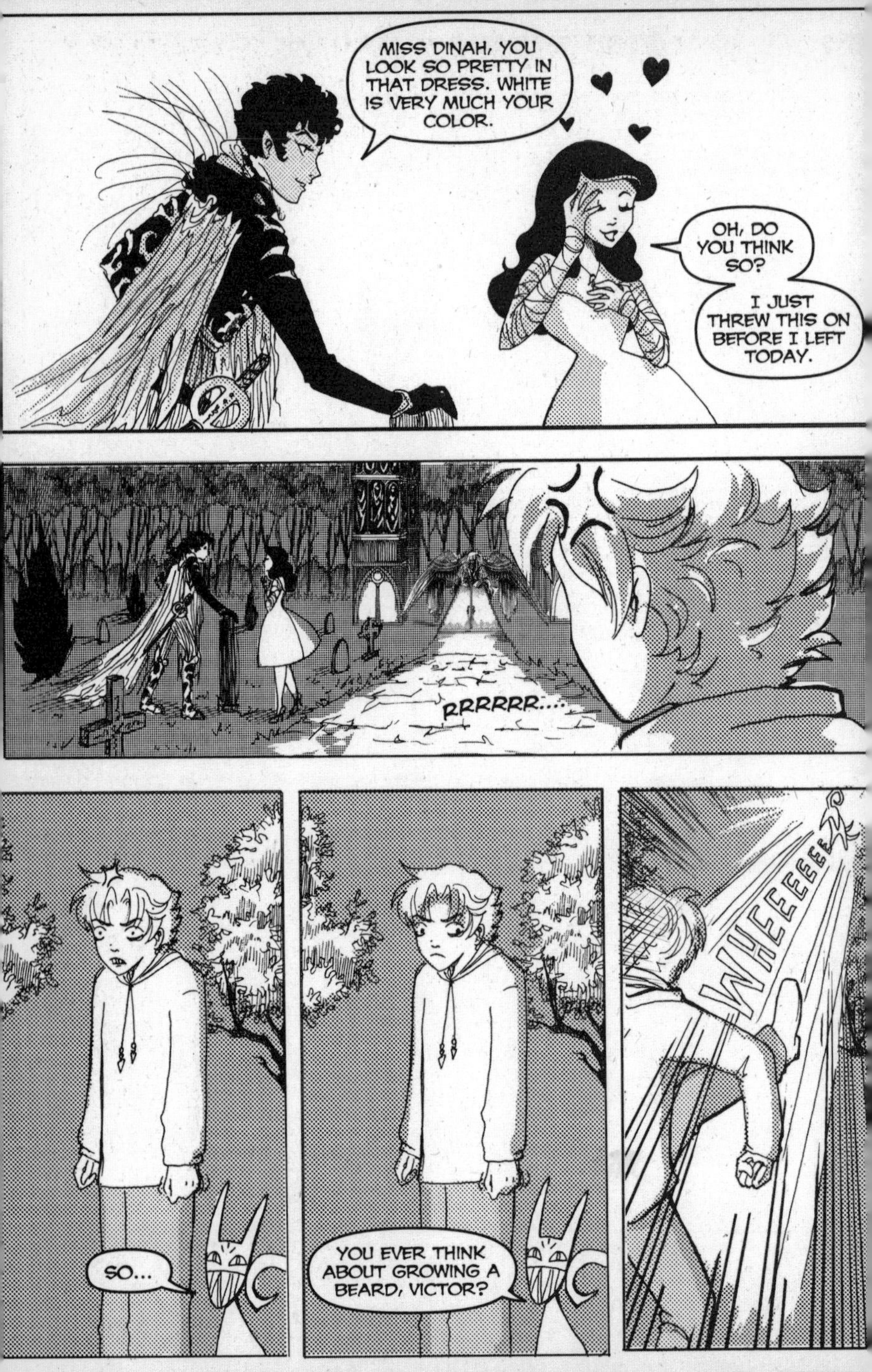
MISS DINAH, YOU LOOK SO PRETTY IN THAT DRESS. WHITE IS VERY MUCH YOUR COLOR.
OH, DO YOU THINK SO?
I JUST THREW THIS ON BEFORE I LEFT TODAY.
RRRRRR....
SO...
YOU EVER THINK ABOUT GROWING A BEARD, VICTOR?
WHEEEEEEE

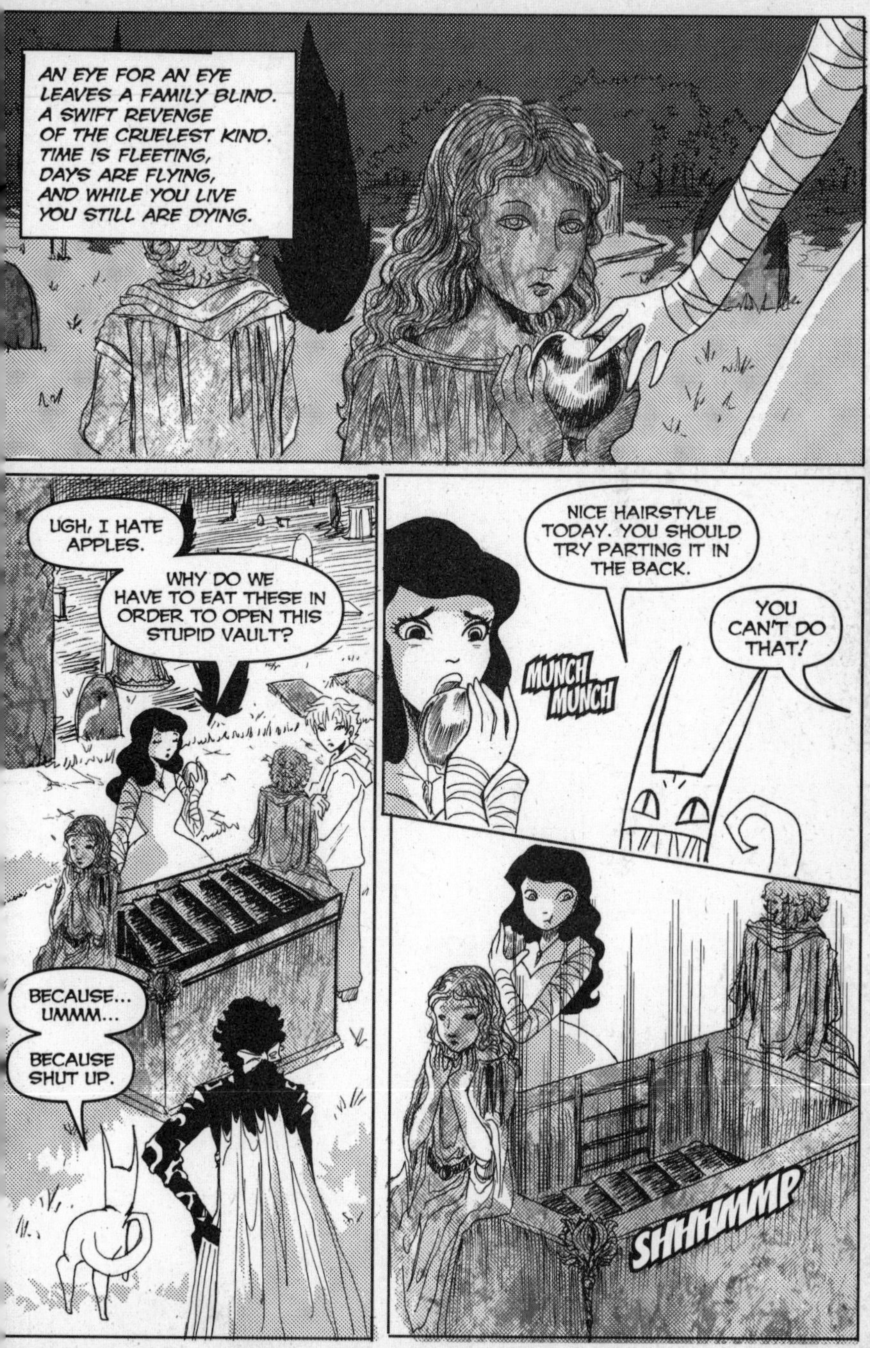
AN EYE FOR AN EYE LEAVES A FAMILY BLIND. A SWIFT REVENGE OF THE CRUELEST KIND. TIME IS FLEETING, DAYS ARE FLYING, AND WHILE YOU LIVE YOU STILL ARE DYING.
UGH, I HATE APPLES.
WHY DO WE HAVE TO EAT THESE IN ORDER TO OPEN THIS STUPID VAULT?
BECAUSE... UMMM...
BECAUSE SHUT UP.
NICE HAIRSTYLE TODAY. YOU SHOULD TRY PARTING IT IN THE BACK.
MUNCH MUNCH
YOU CAN'T DO THAT!
SHHHMMMP

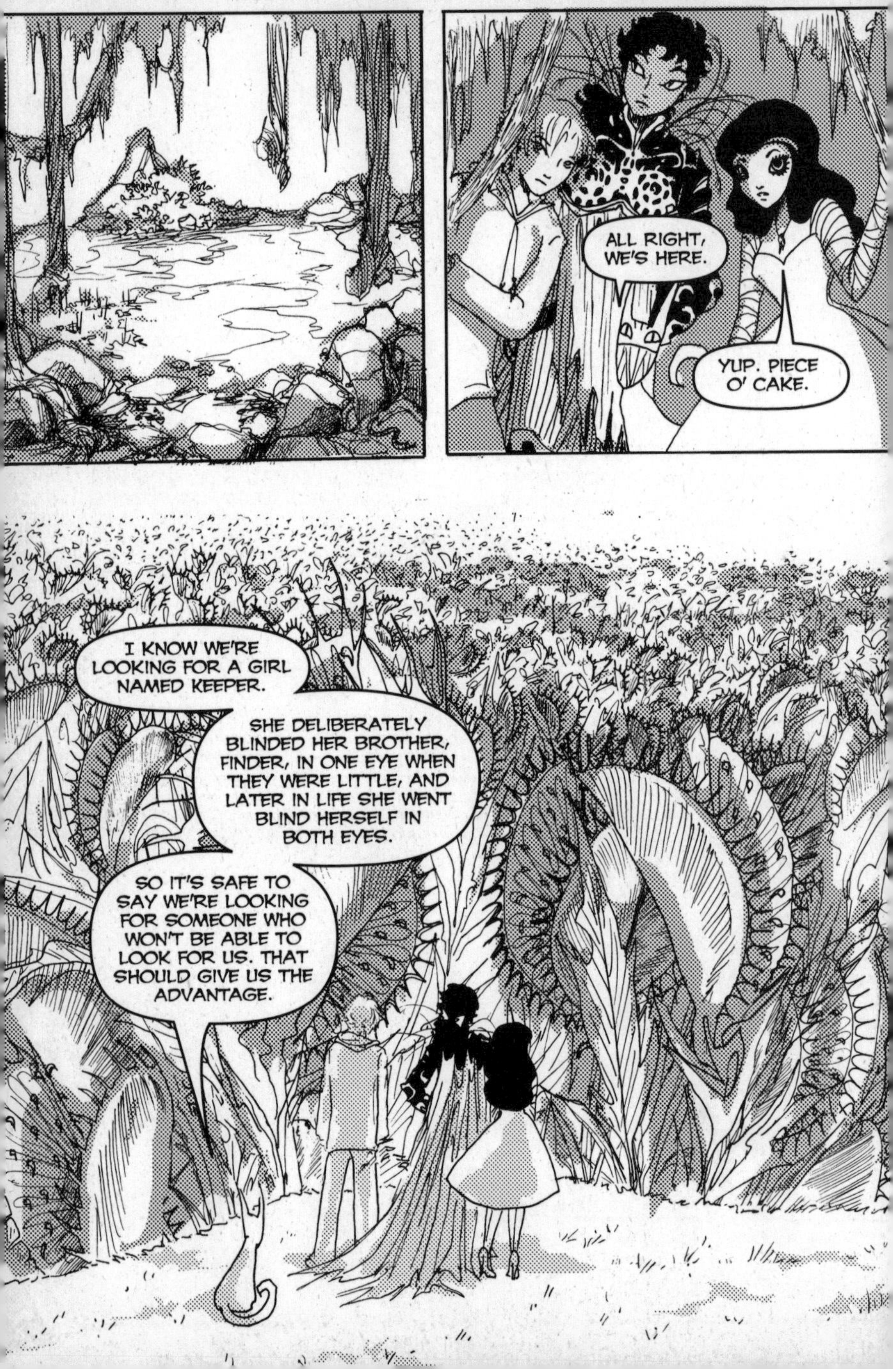
ALL RIGHT, WE'S HERE.
YUP. PIECE O' CAKE.
I KNOW WE'RE LOOKING FOR A GIRL NAMED KEEPER.
SHE DELIBERATELY BLINDED HER BROTHER, FINDER, IN ONE EYE WHEN THEY WERE LITTLE, AND LATER IN LIFE SHE WENT BLIND HERSELF IN BOTH EYES.
SO IT'S SAFE TO SAY WE'RE LOOKING FOR SOMEONE WHO WON'T BE ABLE TO LOOK FOR US. THAT SHOULD GIVE US THE ADVANTAGE.

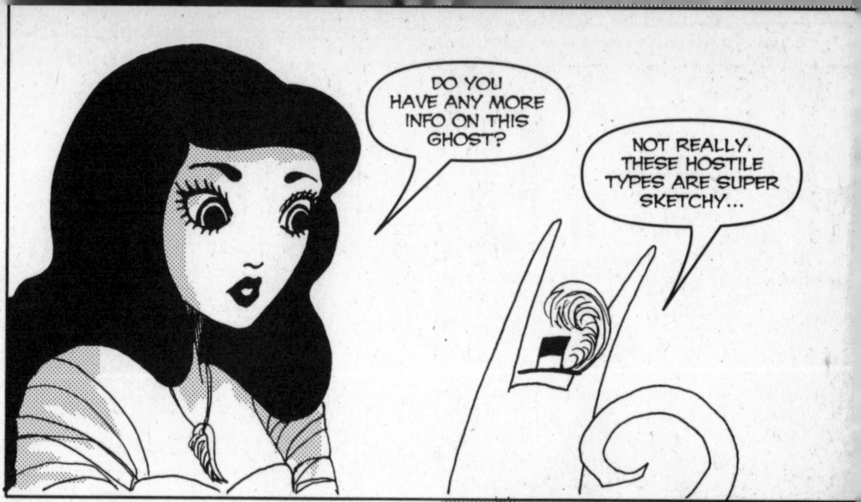
DO YOU HAVE ANY MORE INFO ON THIS GHOST?
NOT REALLY. THESE HOSTILE TYPES ARE SUPER SKETCHY...

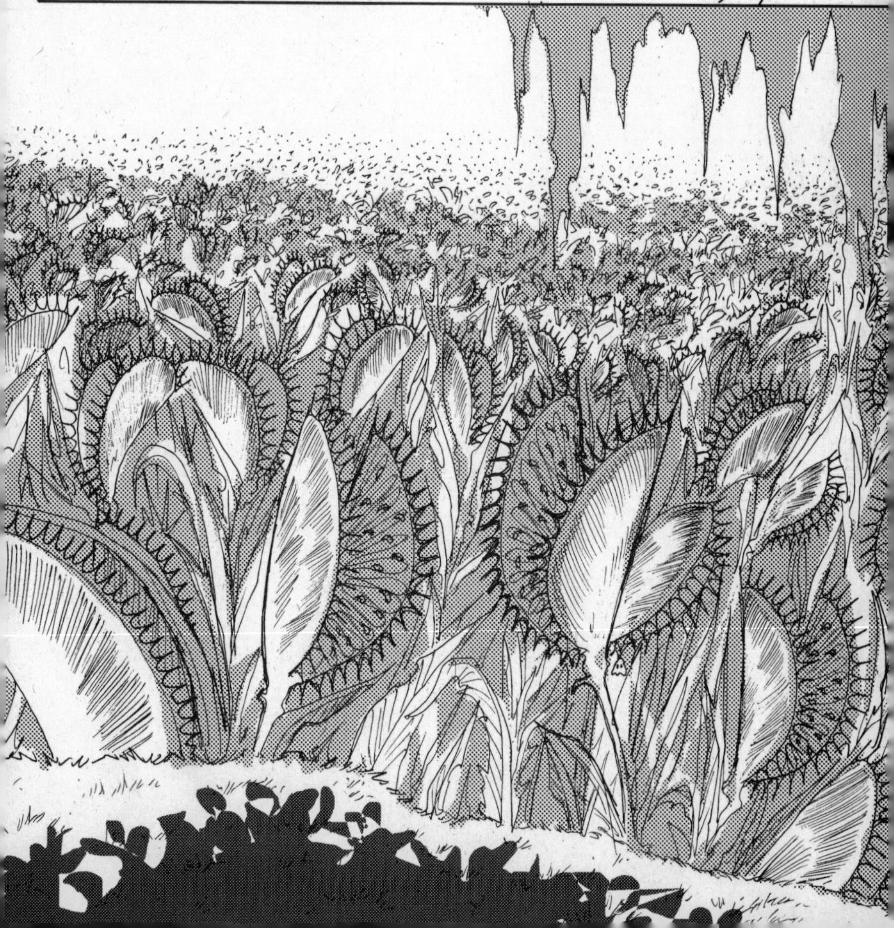

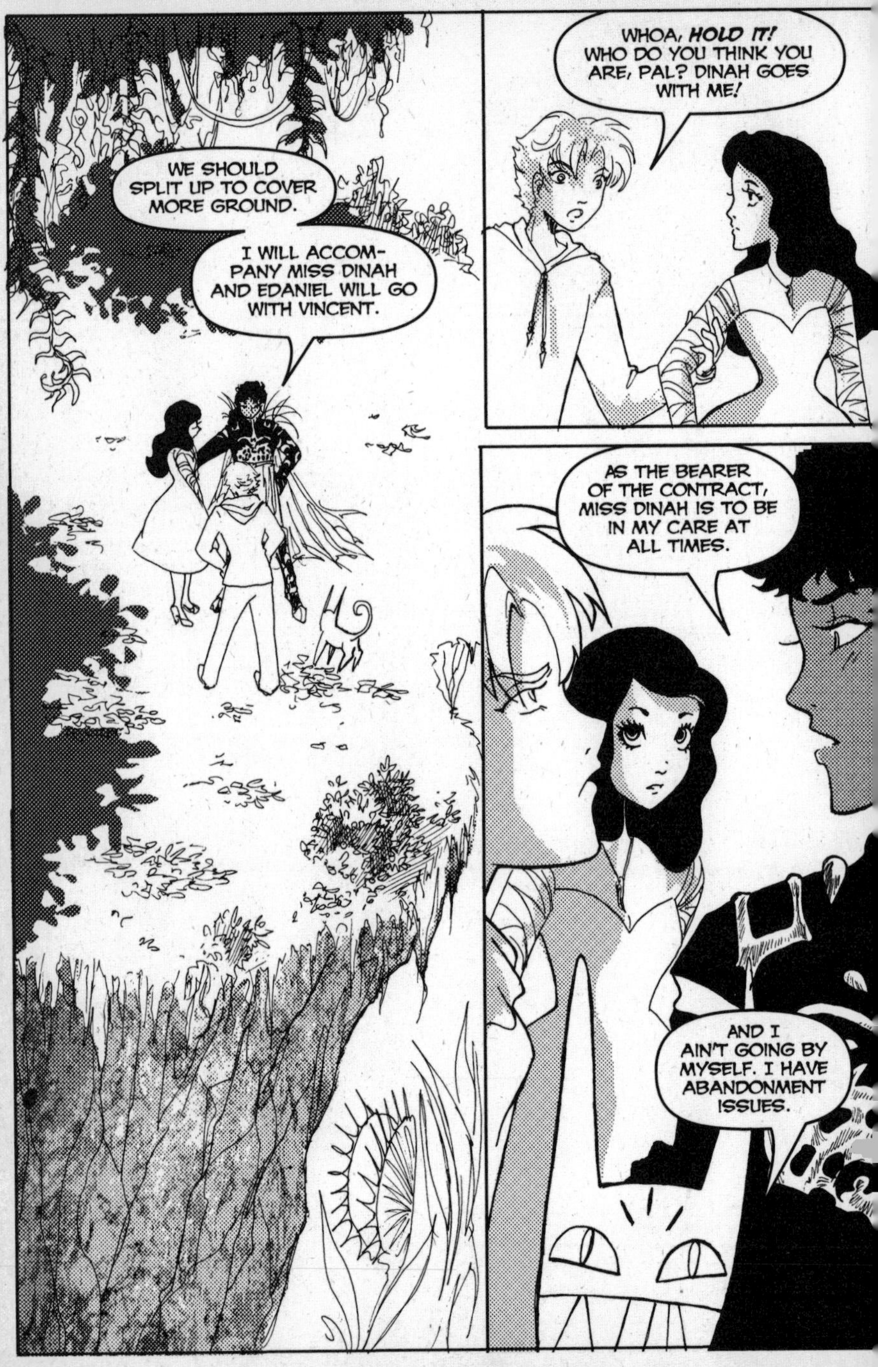
WE SHOULD SPLIT UP TO COVER MORE GROUND.
I WILL ACCOMPANY MISS DINAH AND EDANIEL WILL GO WITH VINCENT.
WHOA, ***HOLD IT!*** WHO DO YOU THINK YOU ARE, PAL? DINAH GOES WITH ME*!*
AS THE BEARER OF THE CONTRACT, MISS DINAH IS TO BE IN MY CARE AT ALL TIMES.
AND I AIN'T GOING BY MYSELF. I HAVE ABANDONMENT ISSUES.

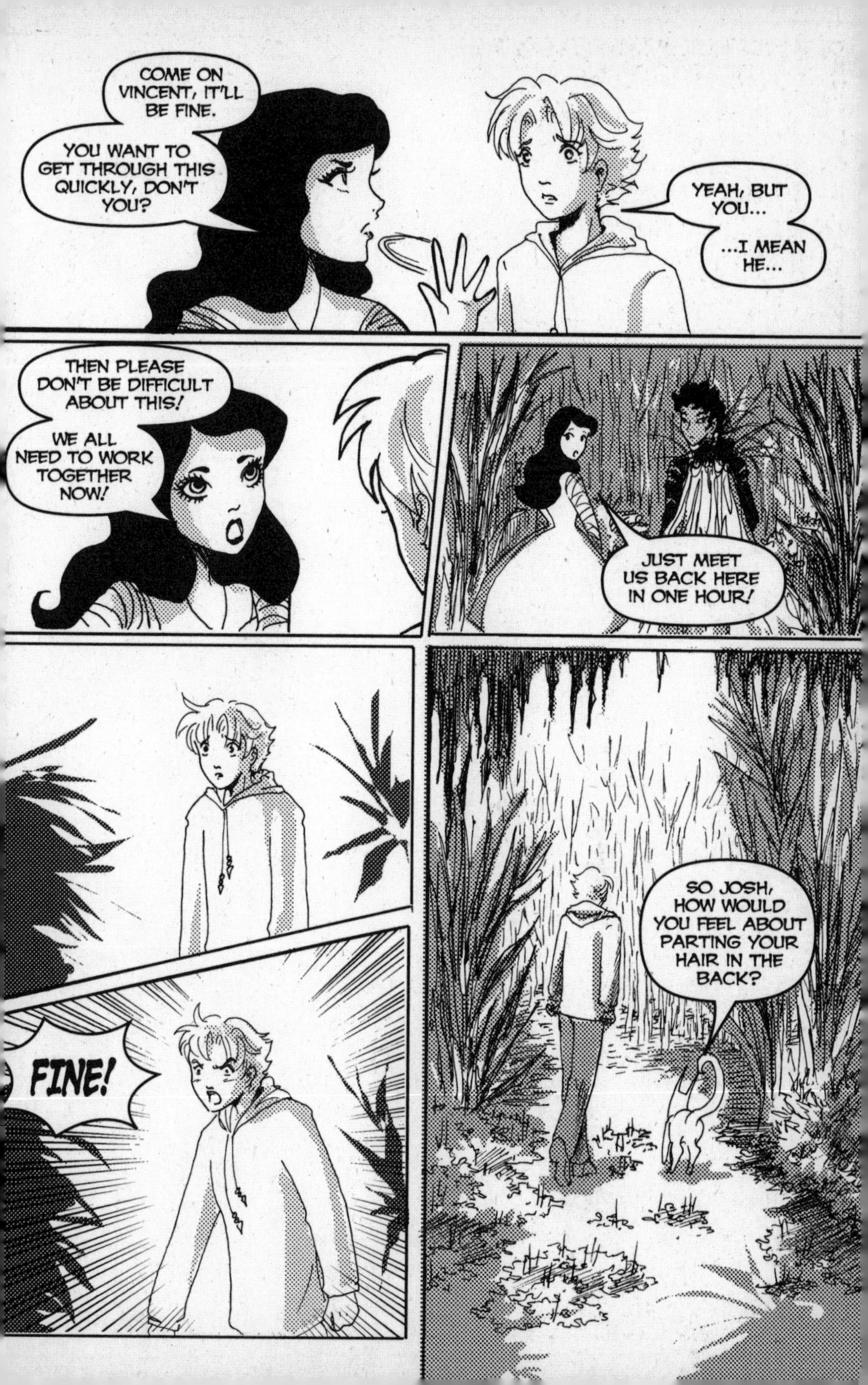
COME ON VINCENT, IT'LL BE FINE.
YOU WANT TO GET THROUGH THIS QUICKLY, DON'T YOU?
YEAH, BUT YOU...
...I MEAN HE...
THEN PLEASE DON'T BE DIFFICULT ABOUT THIS!
WE ALL NEED TO WORK TOGETHER NOW!
JUST MEET US BACK HERE IN ONE HOUR!
FINE!
SO JOSH, HOW WOULD YOU FEEL ABOUT PARTING YOUR HAIR IN THE BACK?

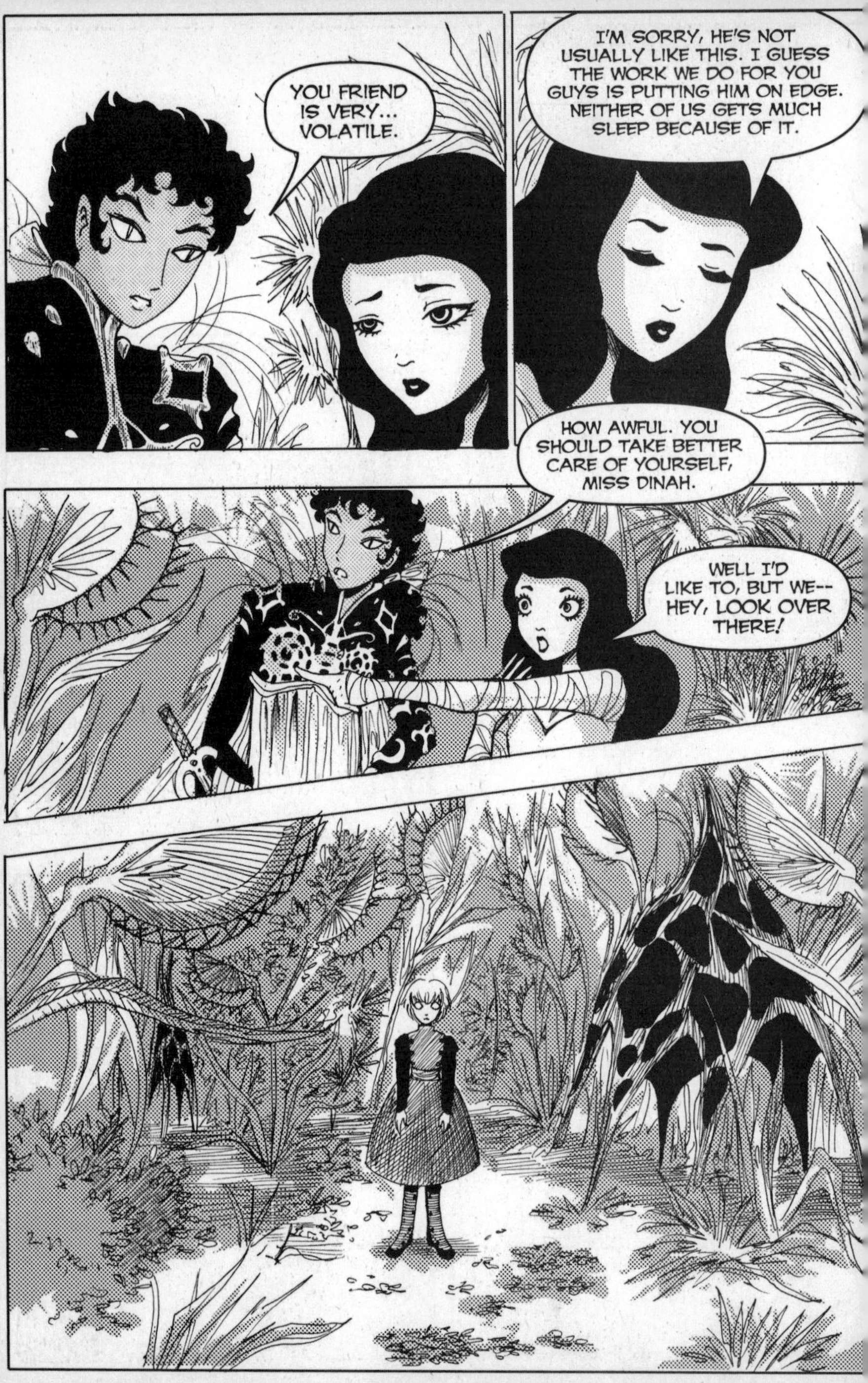
YOU FRIEND IS VERY... VOLATILE.
I'M SORRY, HE'S NOT USUALLY LIKE THIS. I GUESS THE WORK WE DO FOR YOU GUYS IS PUTTING HIM ON EDGE. NEITHER OF US GETS MUCH SLEEP BECAUSE OF IT.
HOW AWFUL. YOU SHOULD TAKE BETTER CARE OF YOURSELF, MISS DINAH.
WELL I'D LIKE TO, BUT WE-- HEY, LOOK OVER THERE!

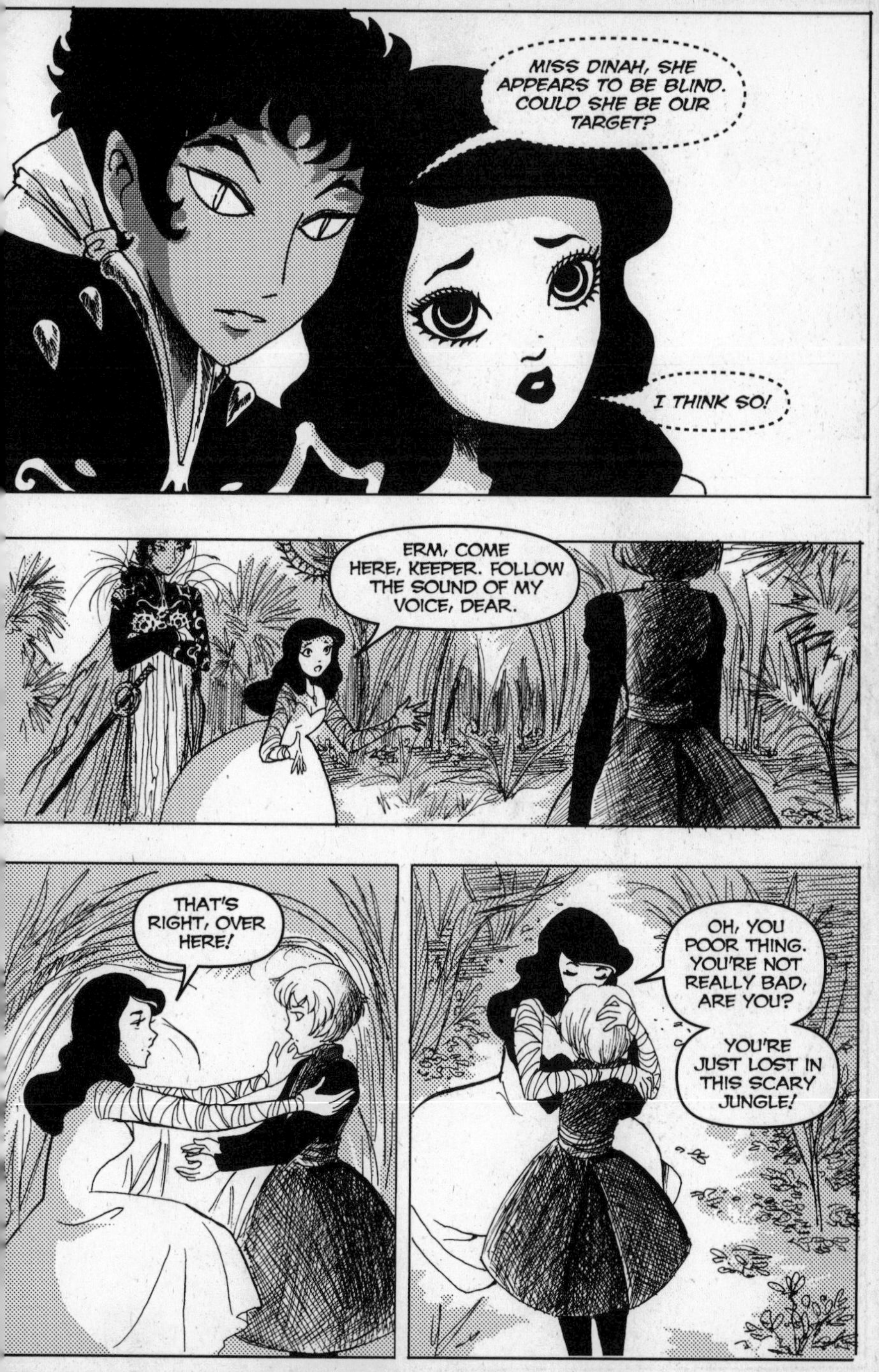
MISS DINAH, SHE APPEARS TO BE BLIND. COULD SHE BE OUR TARGET?
I THINK SO!
ERM, COME HERE, KEEPER. FOLLOW THE SOUND OF MY VOICE, DEAR.
THAT'S RIGHT, OVER HERE!
OH, YOU POOR THING. YOU'RE NOT REALLY BAD, ARE YOU?
YOU'RE JUST LOST IN THIS SCARY JUNGLE!

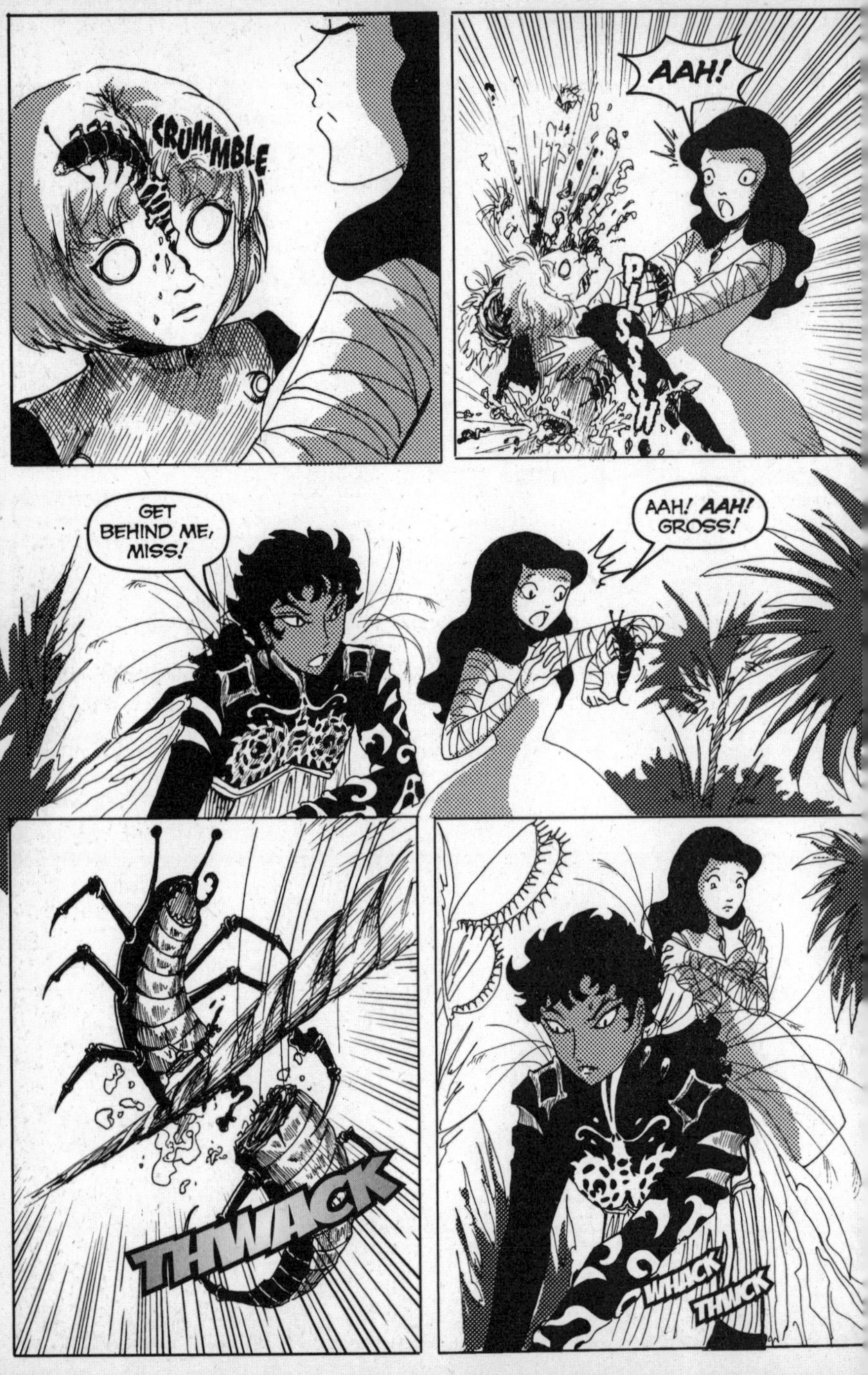
CRUMMBLE
AAH!
PLSSSH
GET BEHIND ME, MISS!
AAH! AAH! GROSS!
THWACK
WHACK
THWCK

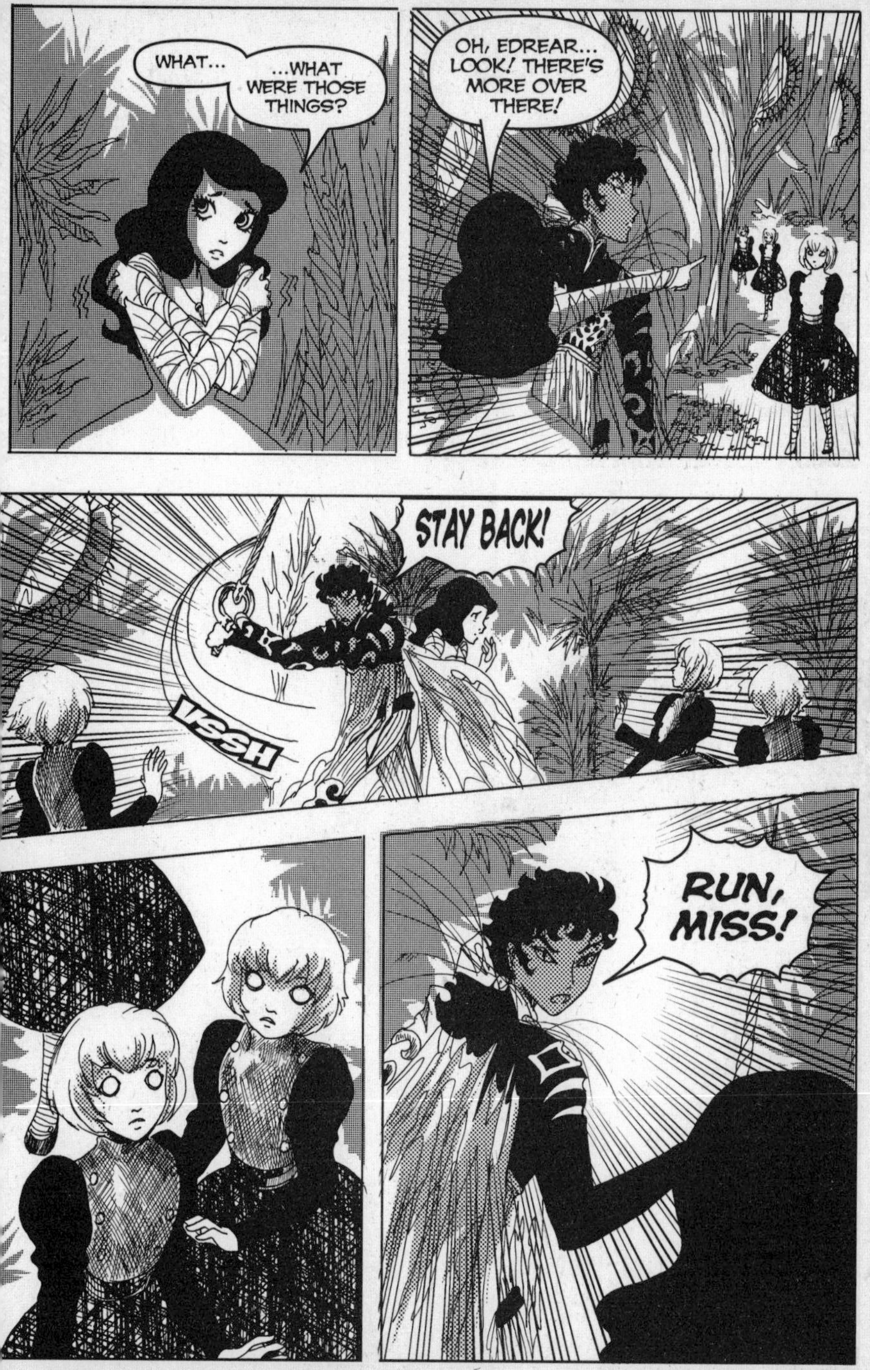
WHAT...
...WHAT WERE THOSE THINGS?
OH, EDREAR... LOOK! THERE'S MORE OVER THERE!
STAY BACK!
VSSH
RUN, MISS!

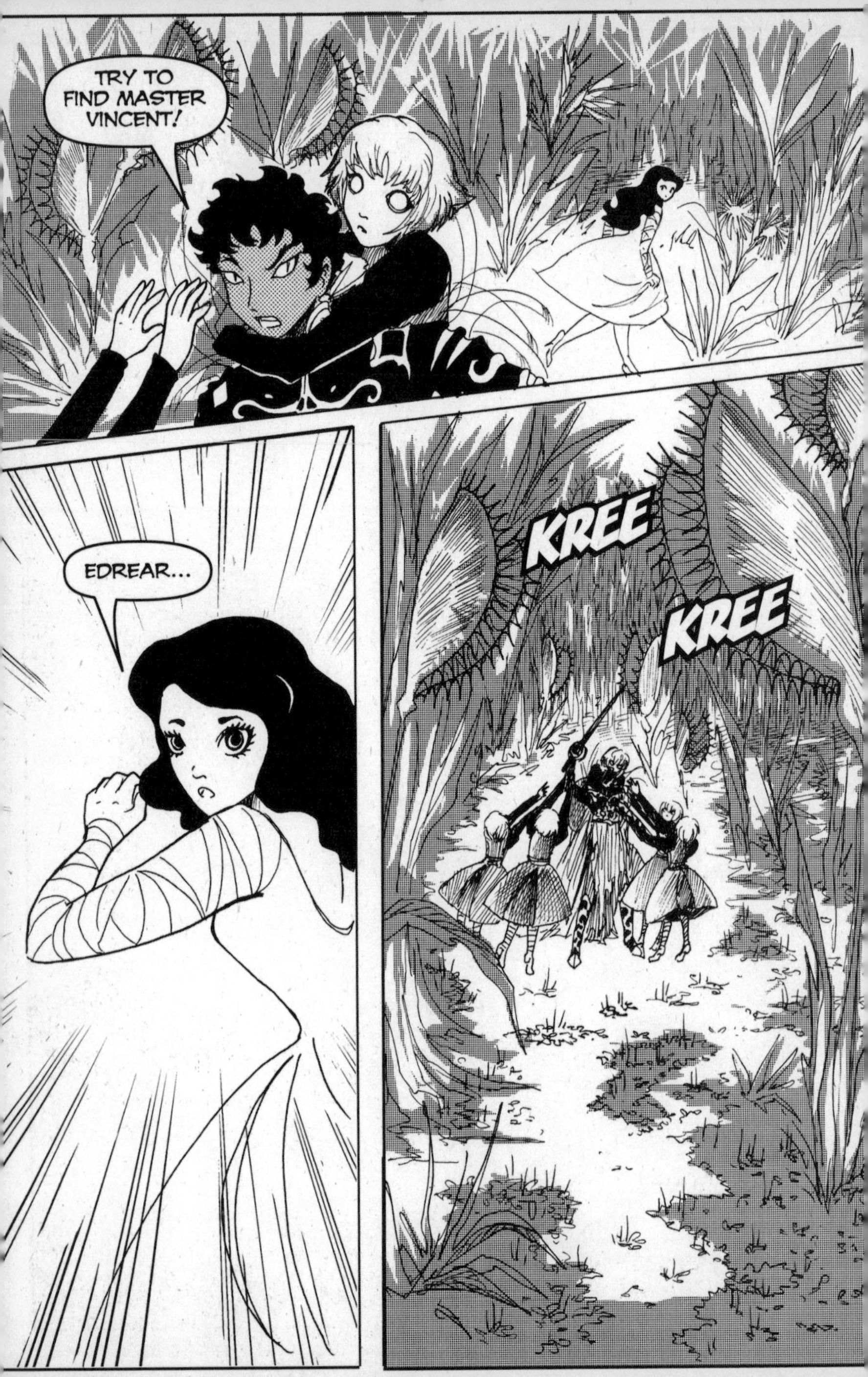
TRY TO FIND MASTER VINCENT!
EDREAR...
KREE
KREE

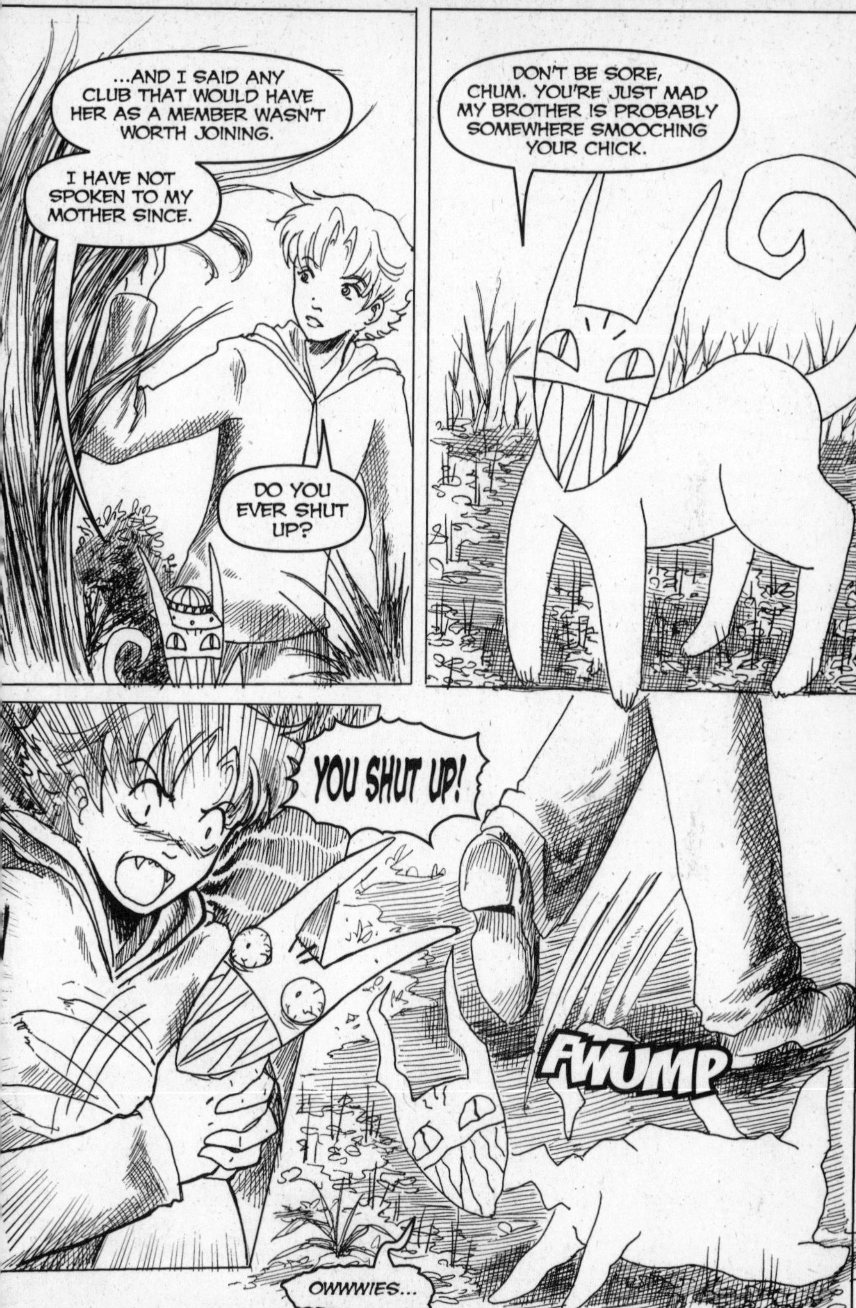
...AND I SAID ANY CLUB THAT WOULD HAVE HER AS A MEMBER WASN'T WORTH JOINING.
I HAVE NOT SPOKEN TO MY MOTHER SINCE.
DO YOU EVER SHUT UP?
DON'T BE SORE, CHUM. YOU'RE JUST MAD MY BROTHER IS PROBABLY SOMEWHERE SMOOCHING YOUR CHICK.
YOU SHUT UP!
FWUMP
OWWWIES...

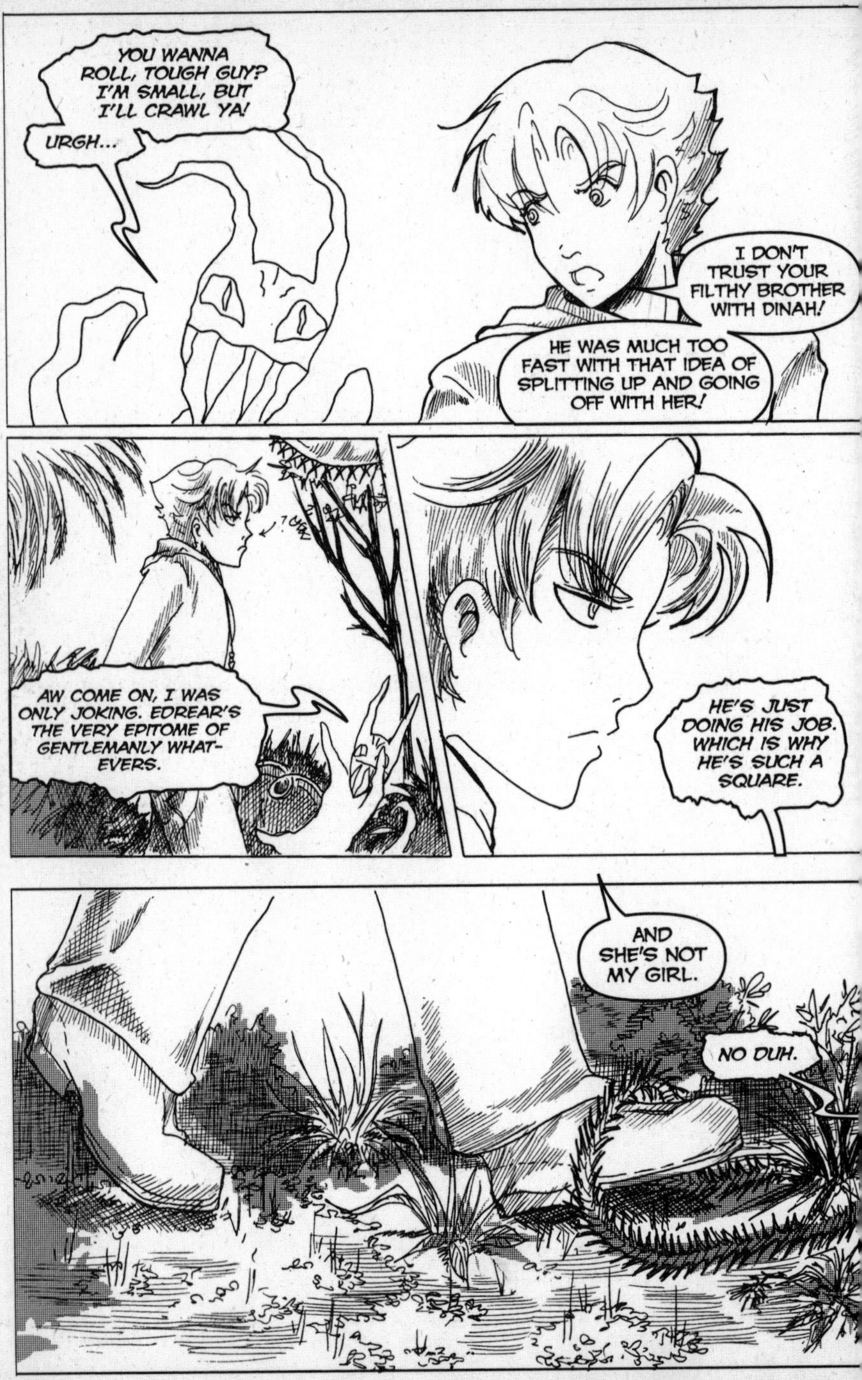
YOU WANNA ROLL, TOUGH GUY? I'M SMALL, BUT I'LL CRAWL YA!
URGH...
I DON'T TRUST YOUR FILTHY BROTHER WITH DINAH!
HE WAS MUCH TOO FAST WITH THAT IDEA OF SPLITTING UP AND GOING OFF WITH HER!
AW COME ON, I WAS ONLY JOKING. EDREAR'S THE VERY EPITOME OF GENTLEMANLY WHAT-EVERS.
HE'S JUST DOING HIS JOB. WHICH IS WHY HE'S SUCH A SQUARE.
AND SHE'S NOT MY GIRL.
NO DUH.

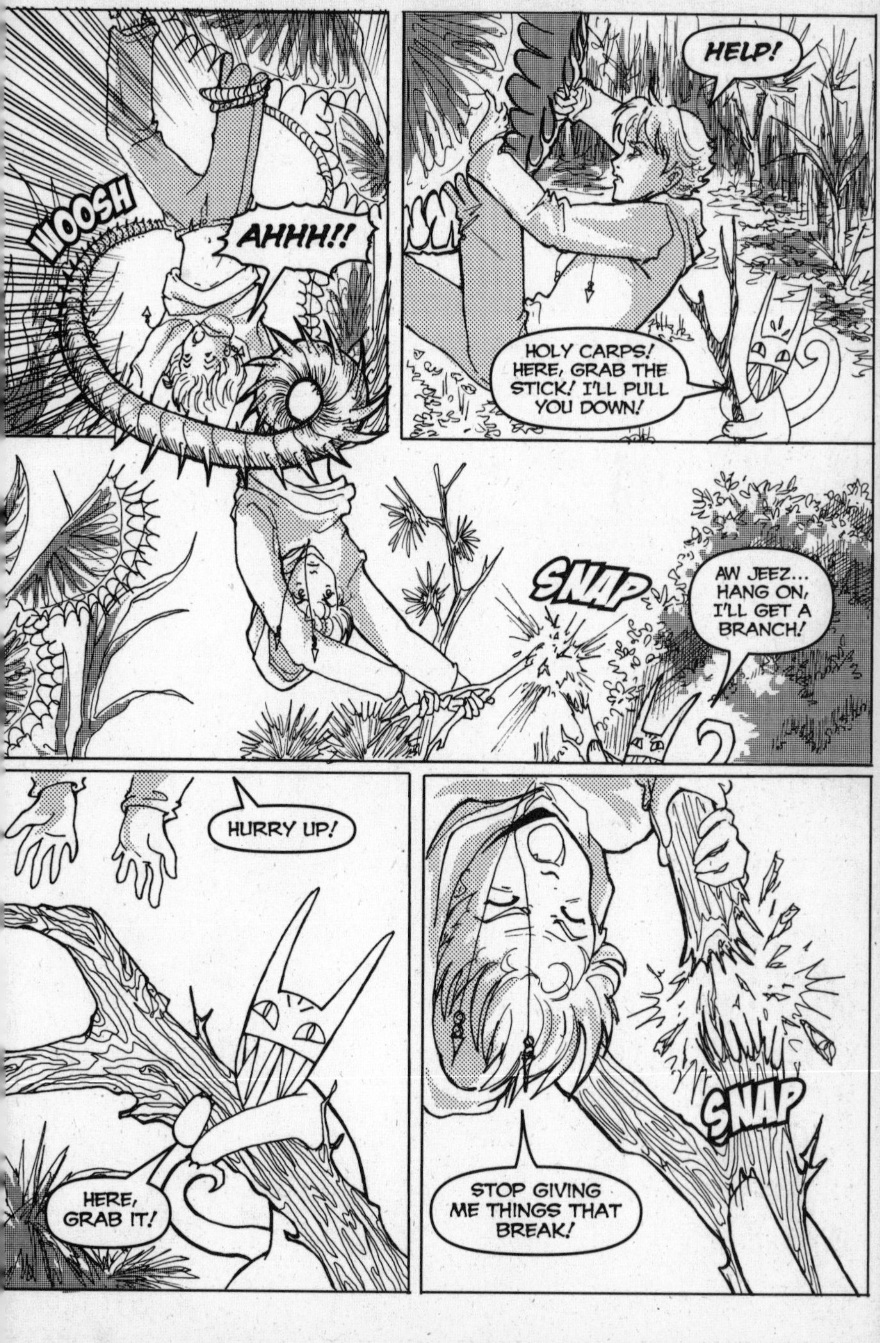
WOOSH
AHHH!!
HELP!
HOLY CARPS! HERE, GRAB THE STICK! I'LL PULL YOU DOWN!
SNAP
AW JEEZ... HANG ON, I'LL GET A BRANCH!
HURRY UP!
HERE, GRAB IT!
SNAP
STOP GIVING ME THINGS THAT BREAK!

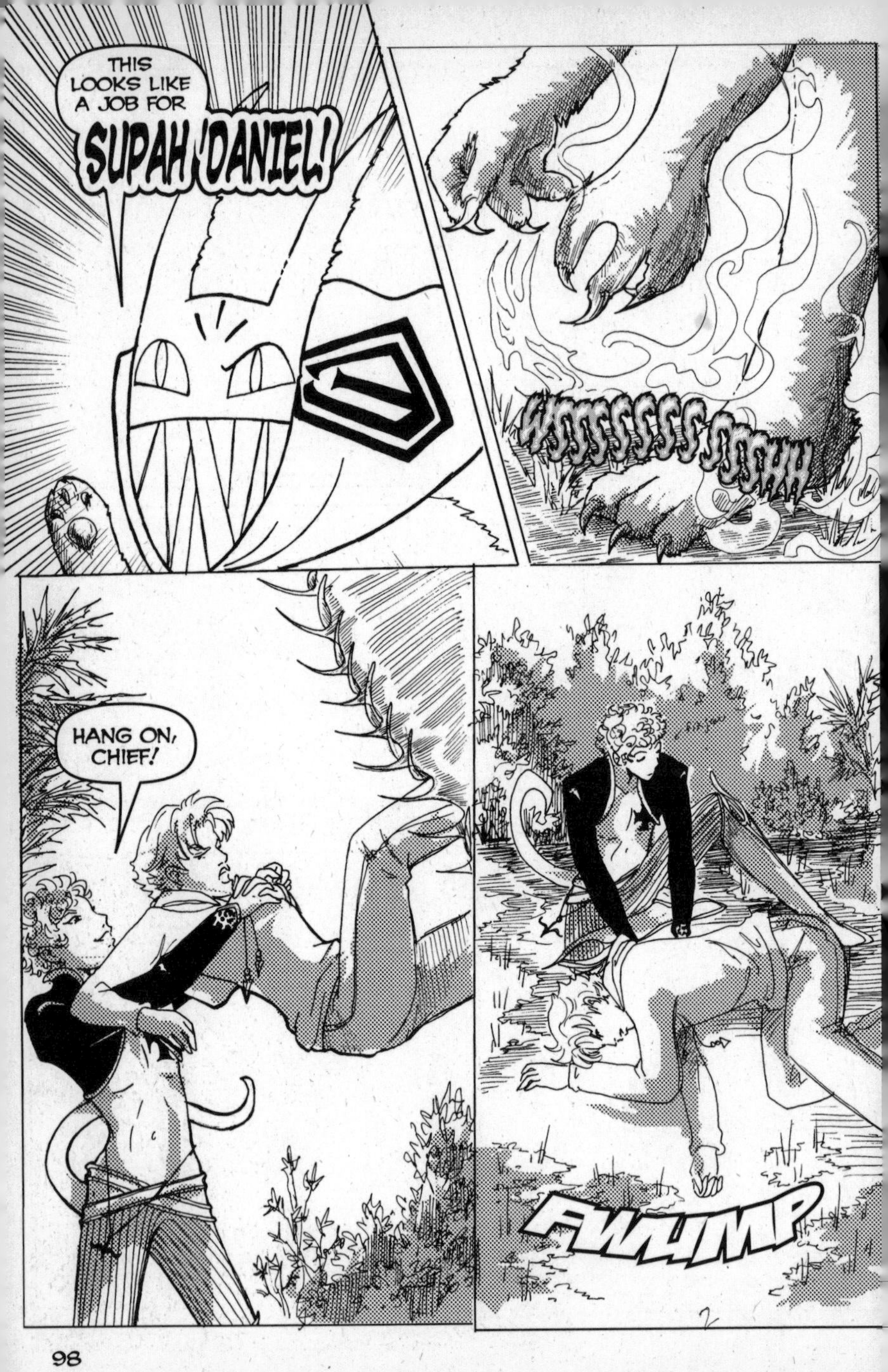
THIS LOOKS LIKE A JOB FOR SUPAH 'DANIEL!
HSSSSSSSSSSSHH
HANG ON, CHIEF!
FWUMP

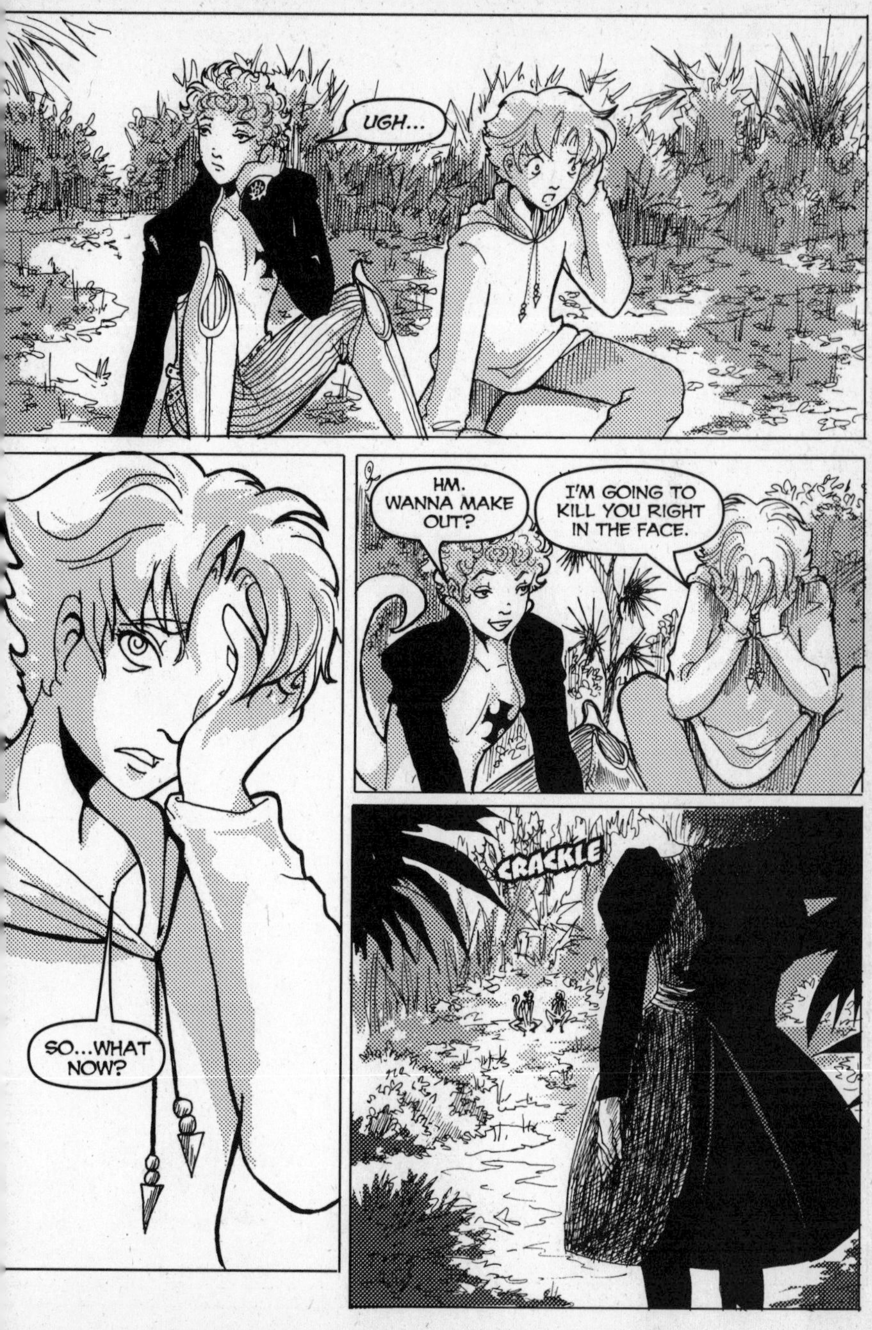
UGH...
SO...WHAT NOW?
HM. WANNA MAKE OUT?
I'M GOING TO KILL YOU RIGHT IN THE FACE.
CRACKLE

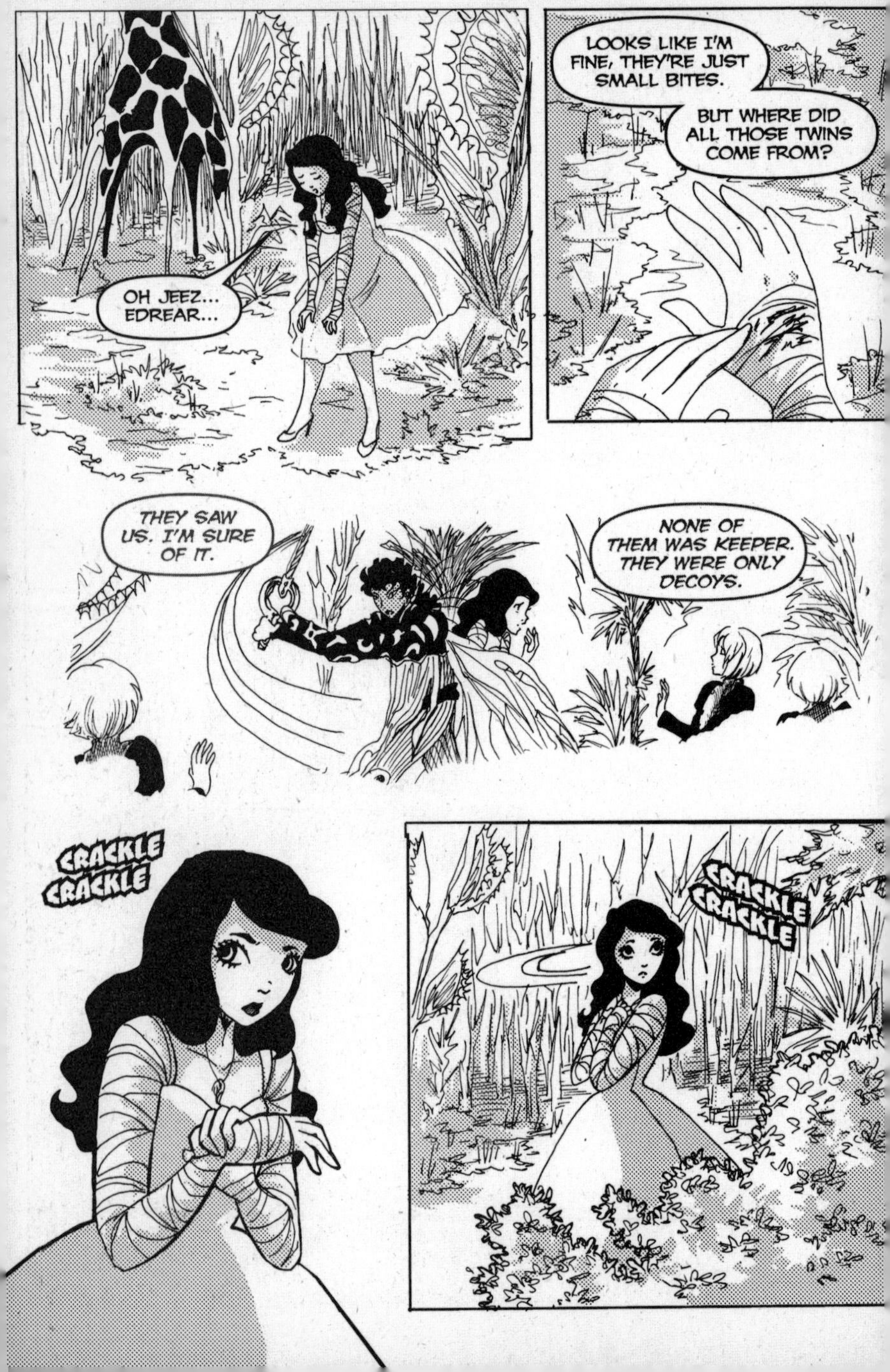
OH JEEZ... EDREAR...
LOOKS LIKE I'M FINE, THEY'RE JUST SMALL BITES.
BUT WHERE DID ALL THOSE TWINS COME FROM?
THEY SAW US. I'M SURE OF IT.
NONE OF THEM WAS KEEPER. THEY WERE ONLY DECOYS.
CRACKLE CRACKLE
CRACKLE CRACKLE

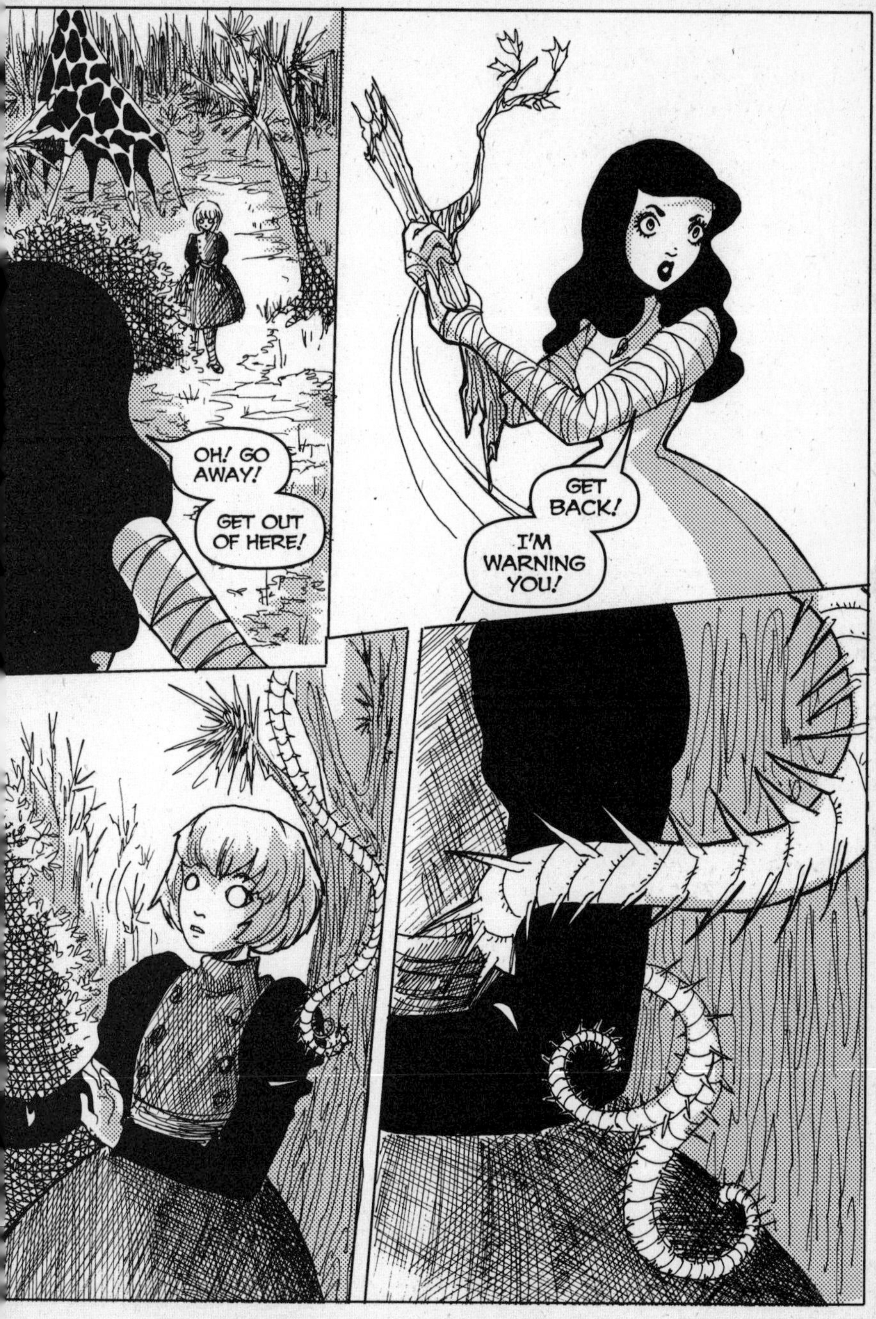
OH! GO AWAY!
GET OUT OF HERE!
GET BACK!
I'M WARNING YOU!

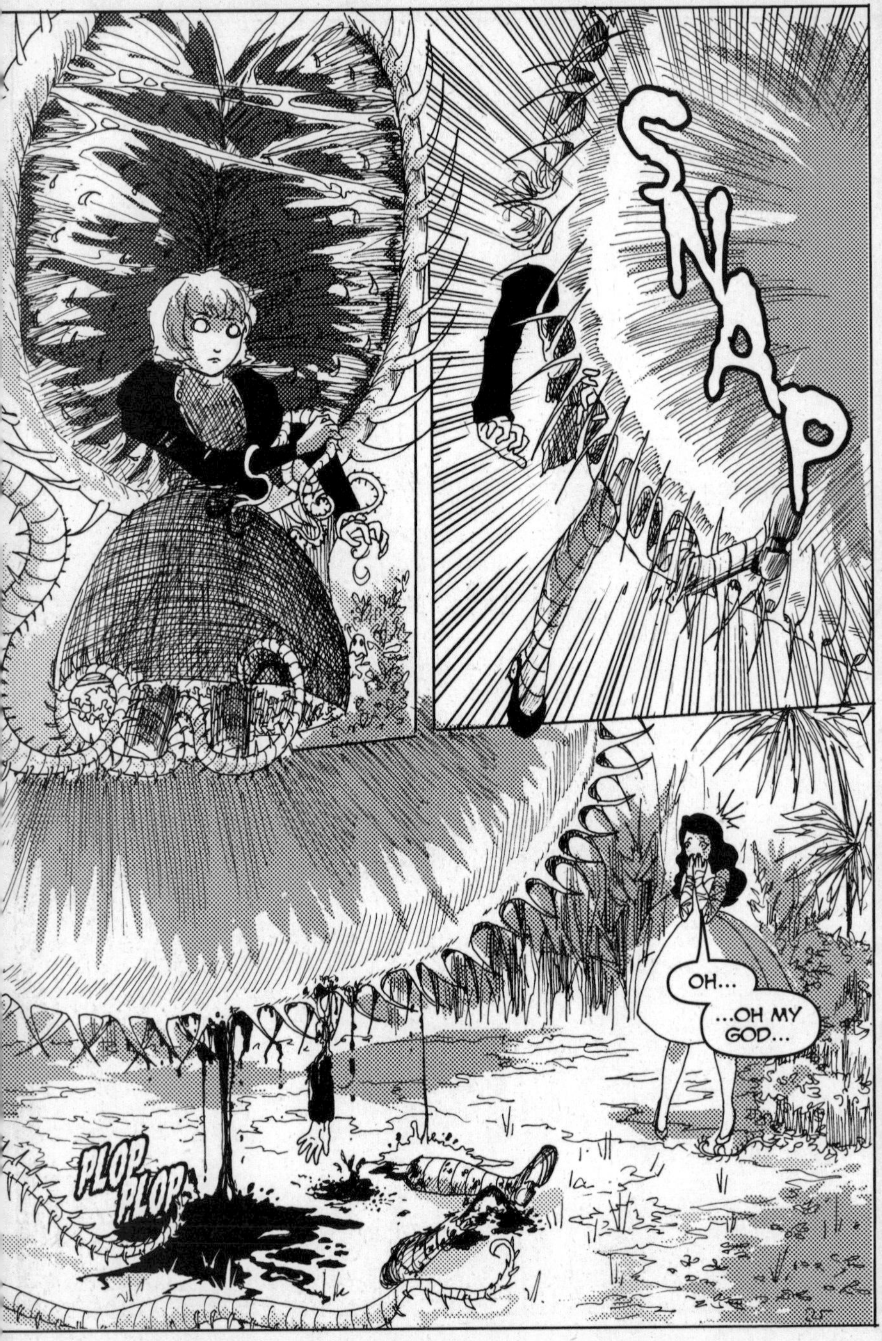
SNAP
PLOP
PLOP
OH...
...OH MY GOD...

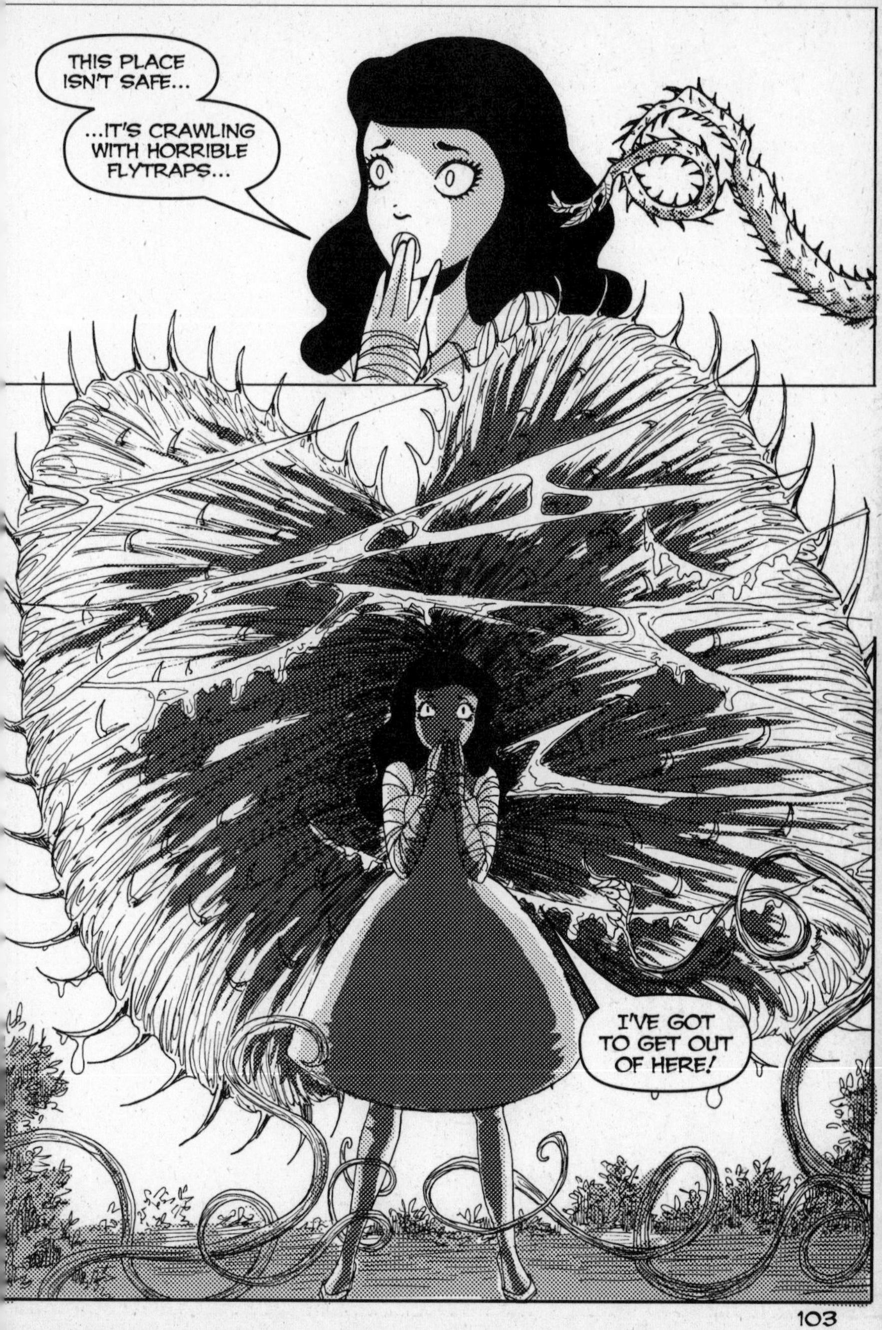
THIS PLACE ISN'T SAFE...
...IT'S CRAWLING WITH HORRIBLE FLYTRAPS...
I'VE GOT TO GET OUT OF HERE!

IV
The Blind

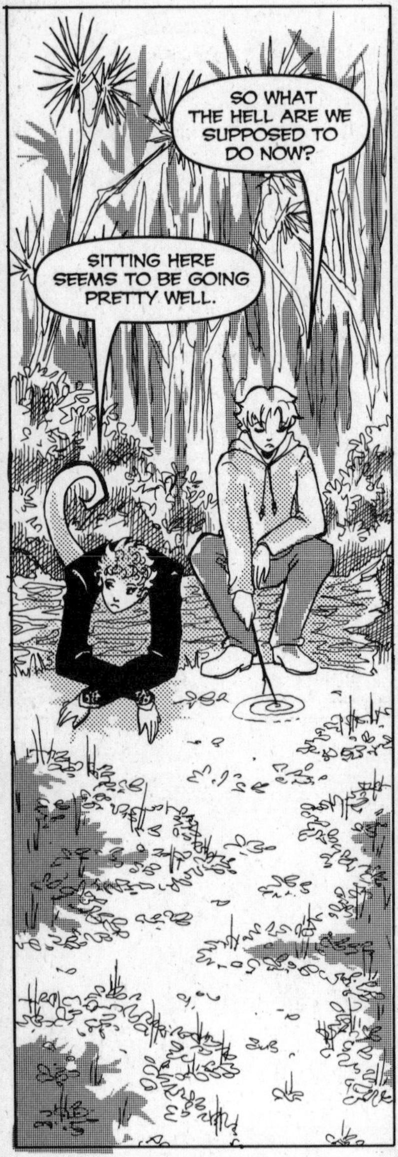
SO WHAT THE HELL ARE WE SUPPOSED TO DO NOW?
SITTING HERE SEEMS TO BE GOING PRETTY WELL.
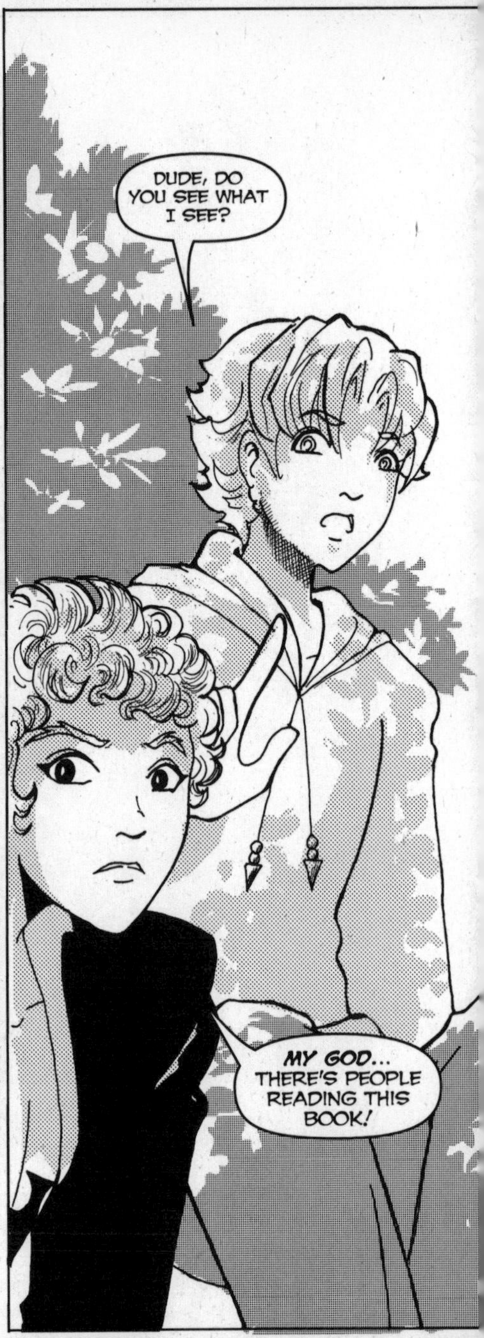
DUDE, DO YOU SEE WHAT I SEE?
MY GOD... THERE'S PEOPLE READING THIS BOOK!

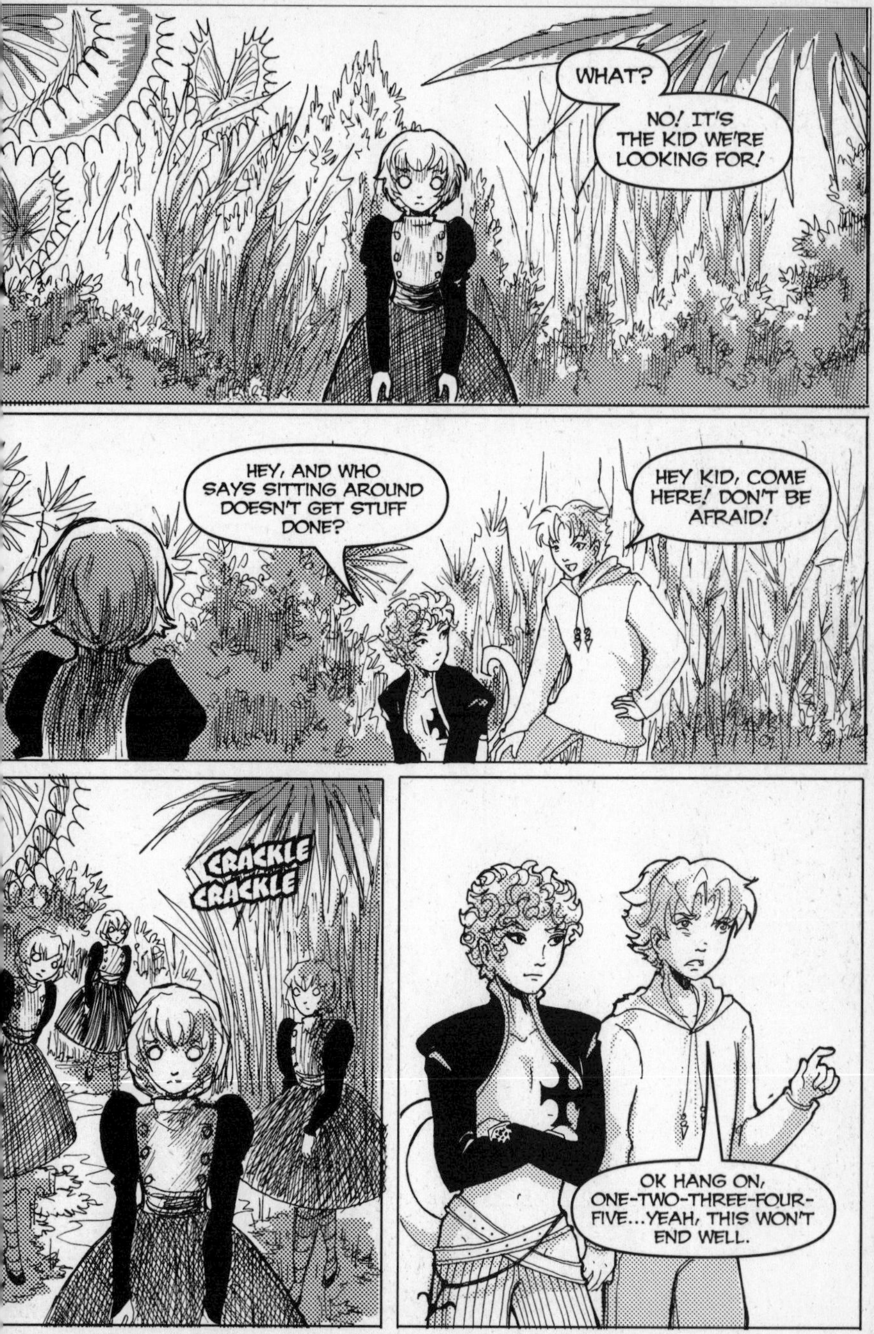
WHAT?
NO! IT'S THE KID WE'RE LOOKING FOR!
HEY, AND WHO SAYS SITTING AROUND DOESN'T GET STUFF DONE?
HEY KID, COME HERE! DON'T BE AFRAID!
CRACKLE CRACKLE
OK HANG ON, ONE-TWO-THREE-FOUR-FIVE...YEAH, THIS WON'T END WELL.

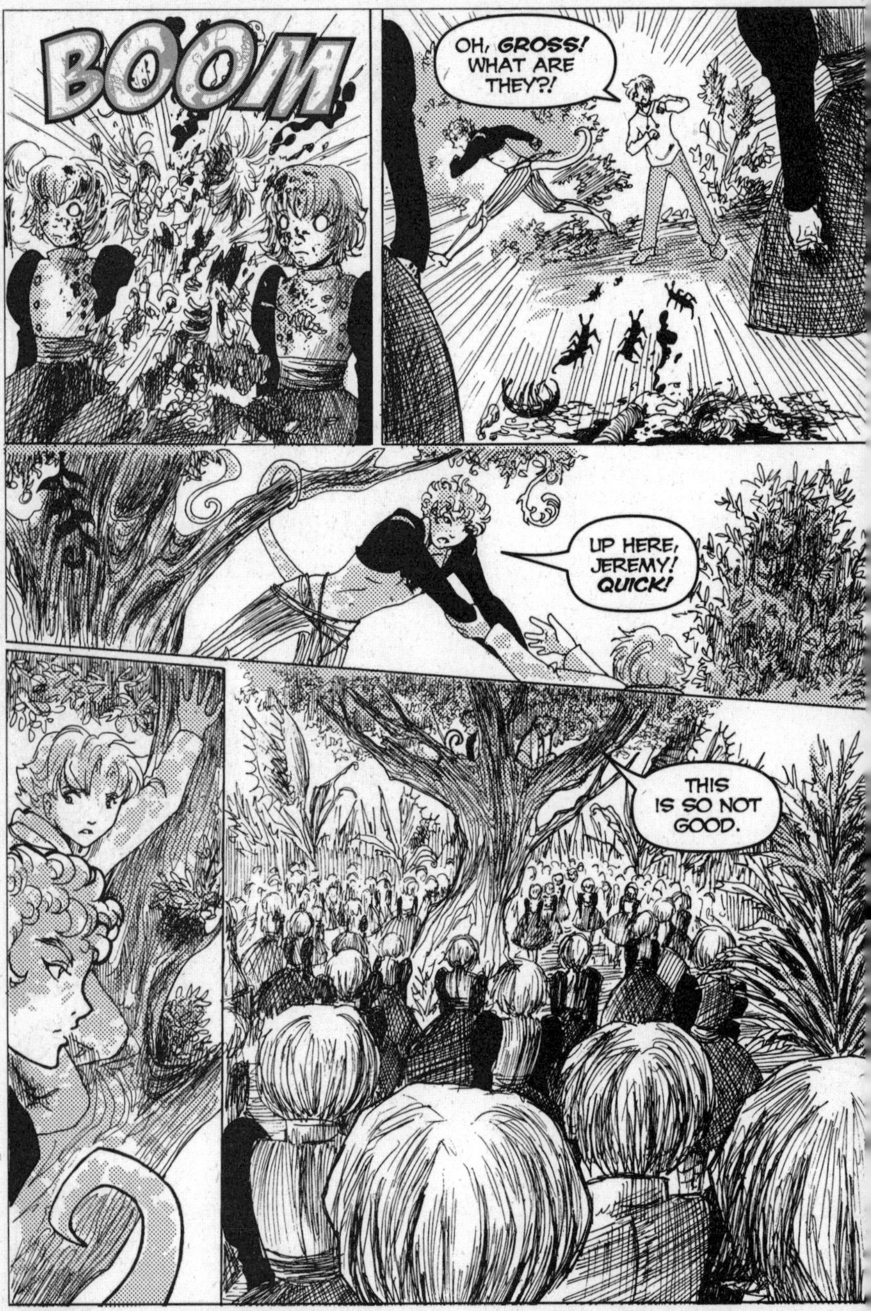
BOOM
OH, GROSS! WHAT ARE THEY?!
UP HERE, JEREMY! QUICK!
THIS IS SO NOT GOOD.

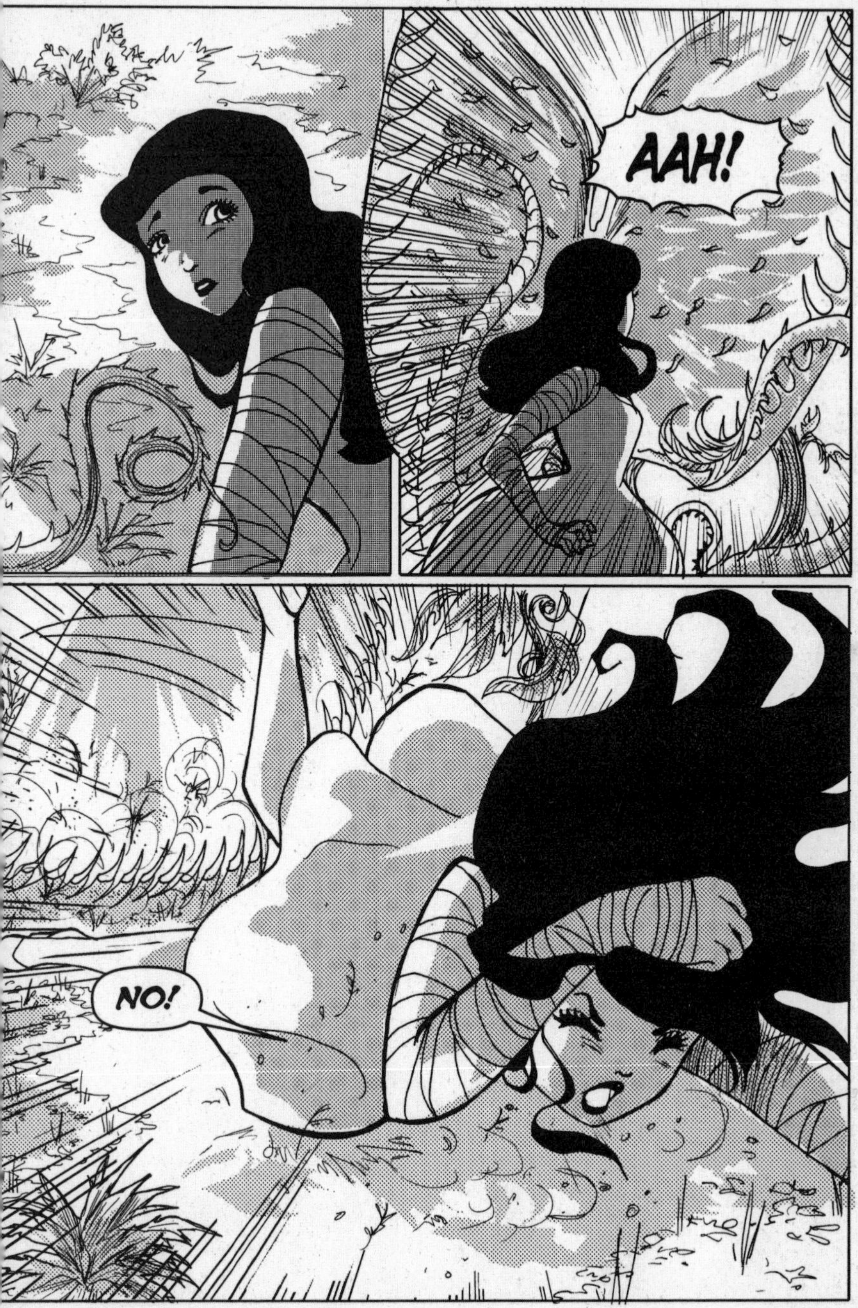
AAH!
NO!

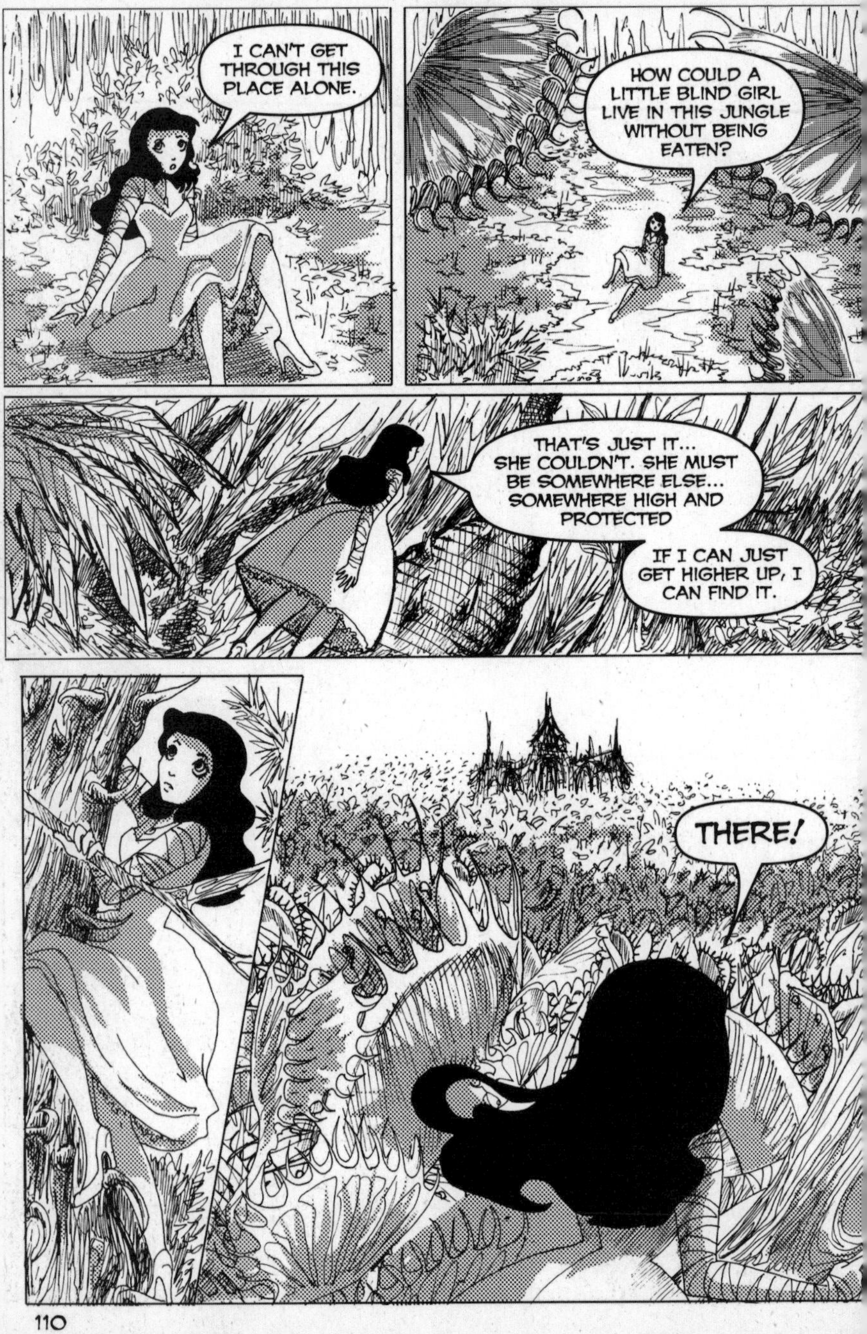
I CAN'T GET THROUGH THIS PLACE ALONE.
HOW COULD A LITTLE BLIND GIRL LIVE IN THIS JUNGLE WITHOUT BEING EATEN?
THAT'S JUST IT... SHE COULDN'T. SHE MUST BE SOMEWHERE ELSE... SOMEWHERE HIGH AND PROTECTED
IF I CAN JUST GET HIGHER UP, I CAN FIND IT.
THERE!

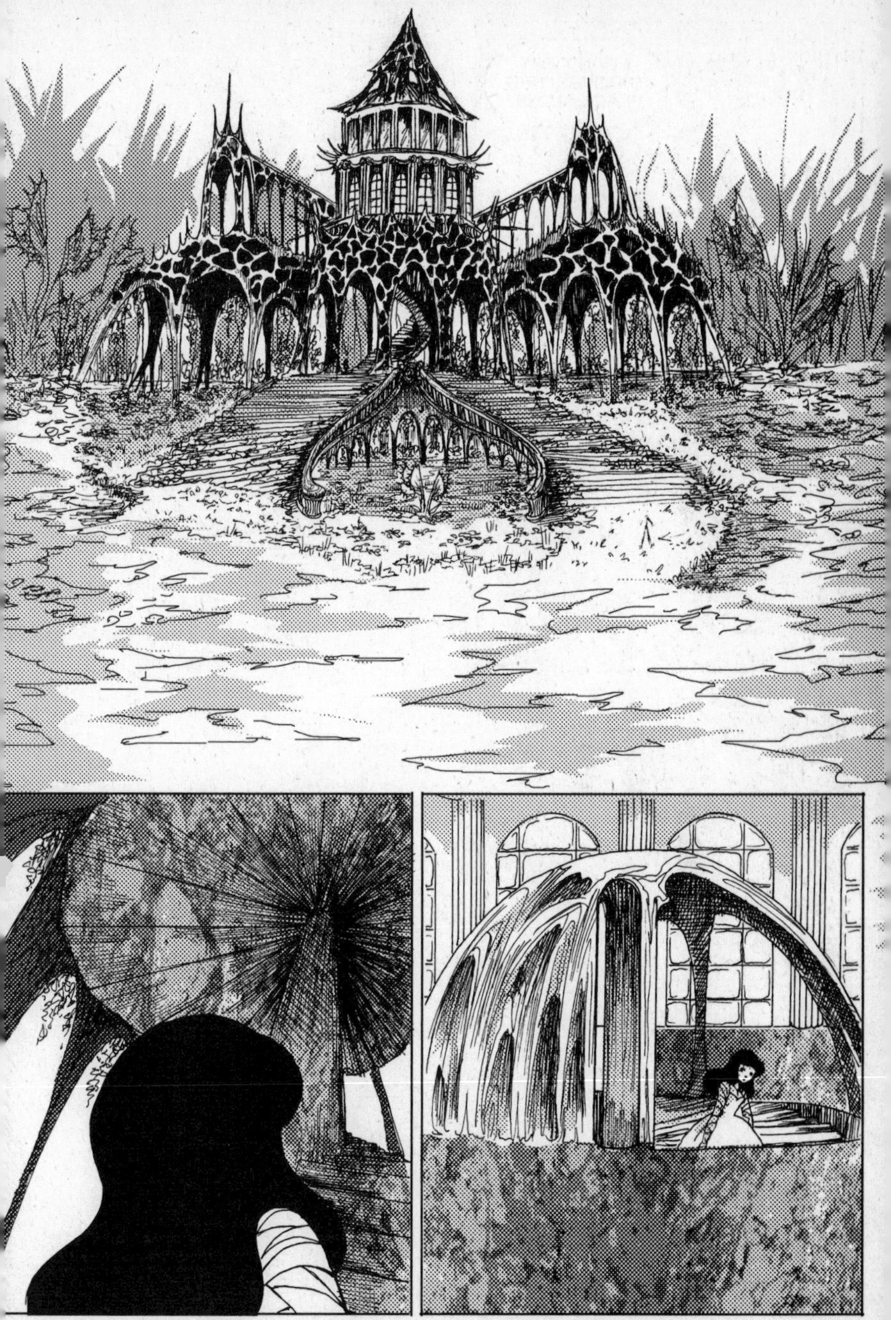

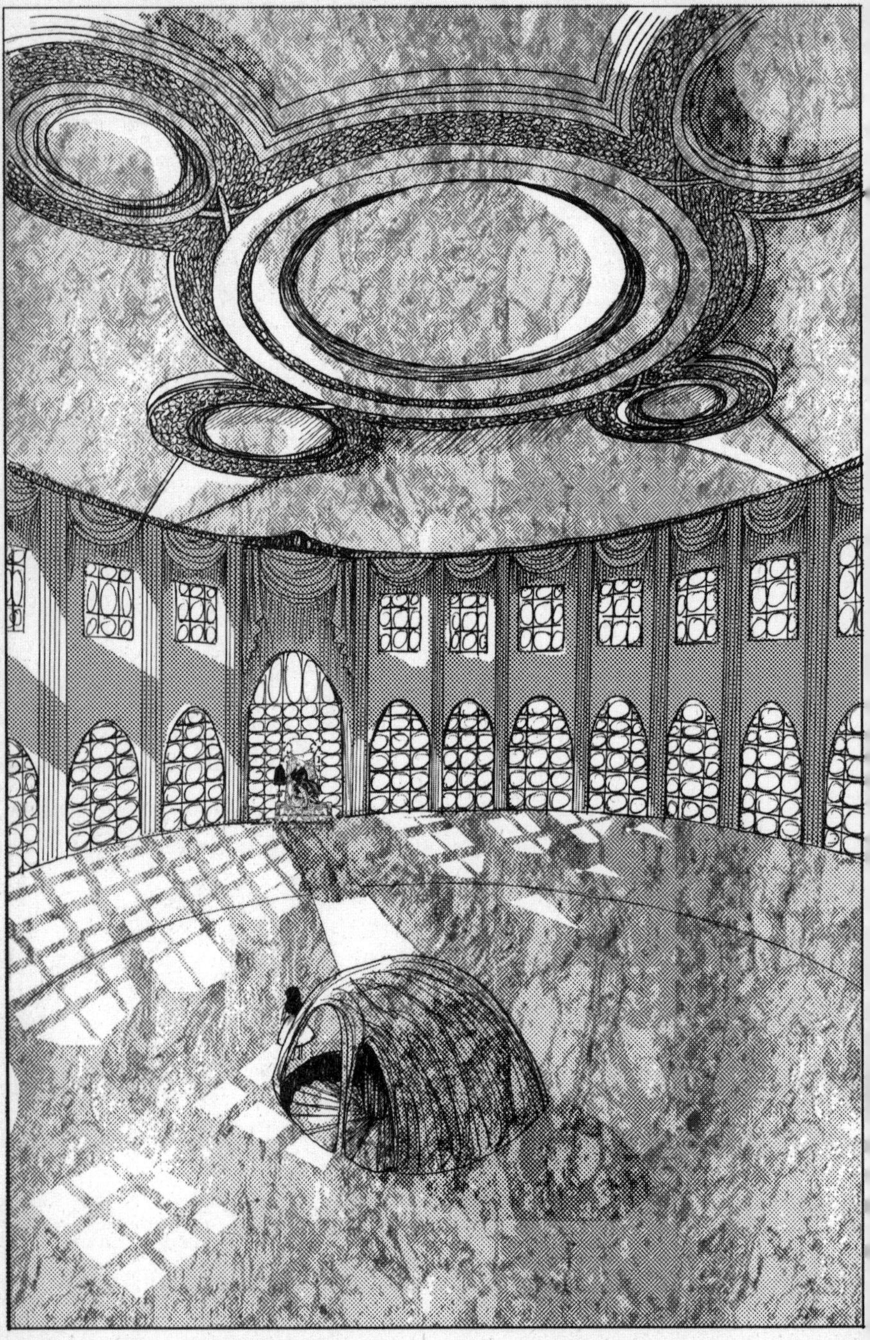

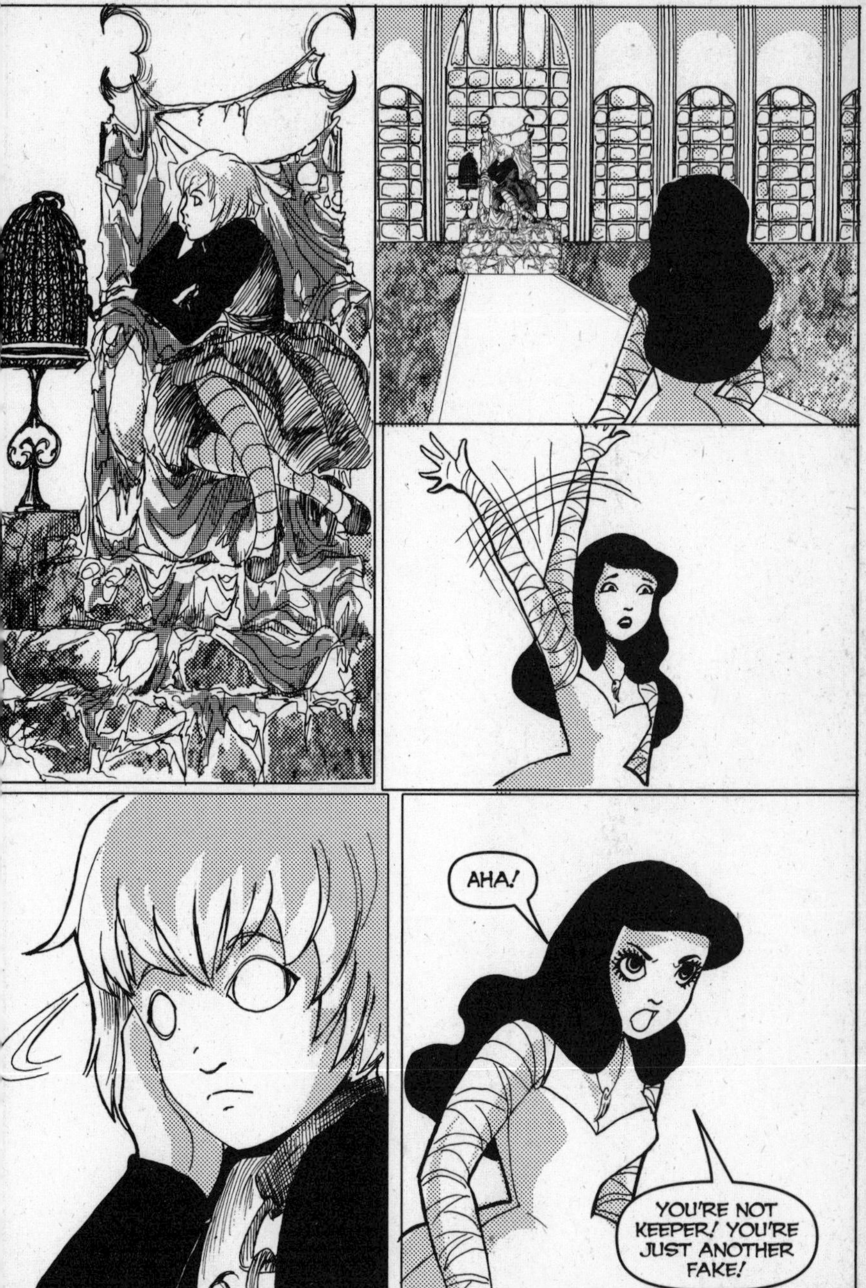
AHA!
YOU'RE NOT KEEPER! YOU'RE JUST ANOTHER FAKE!

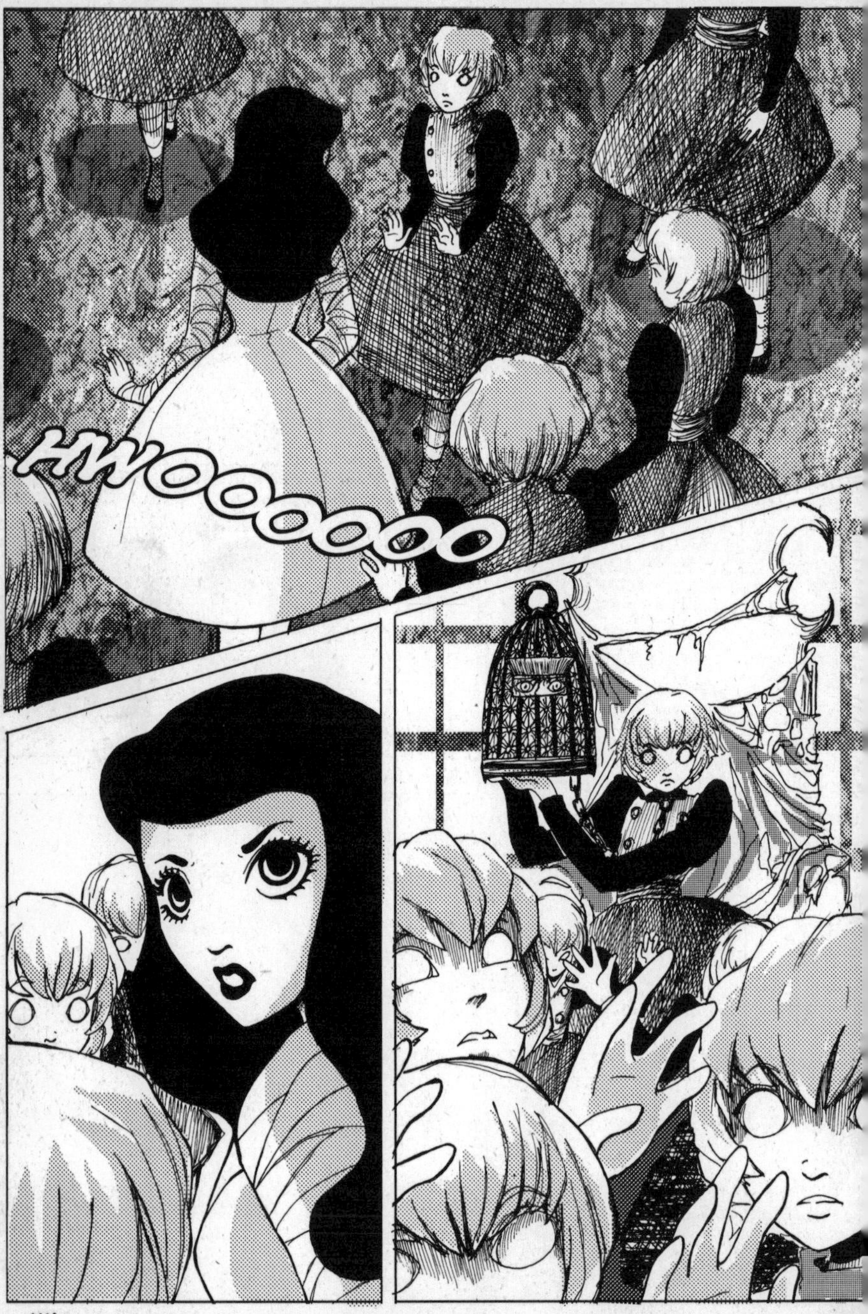
HWOOOOOO

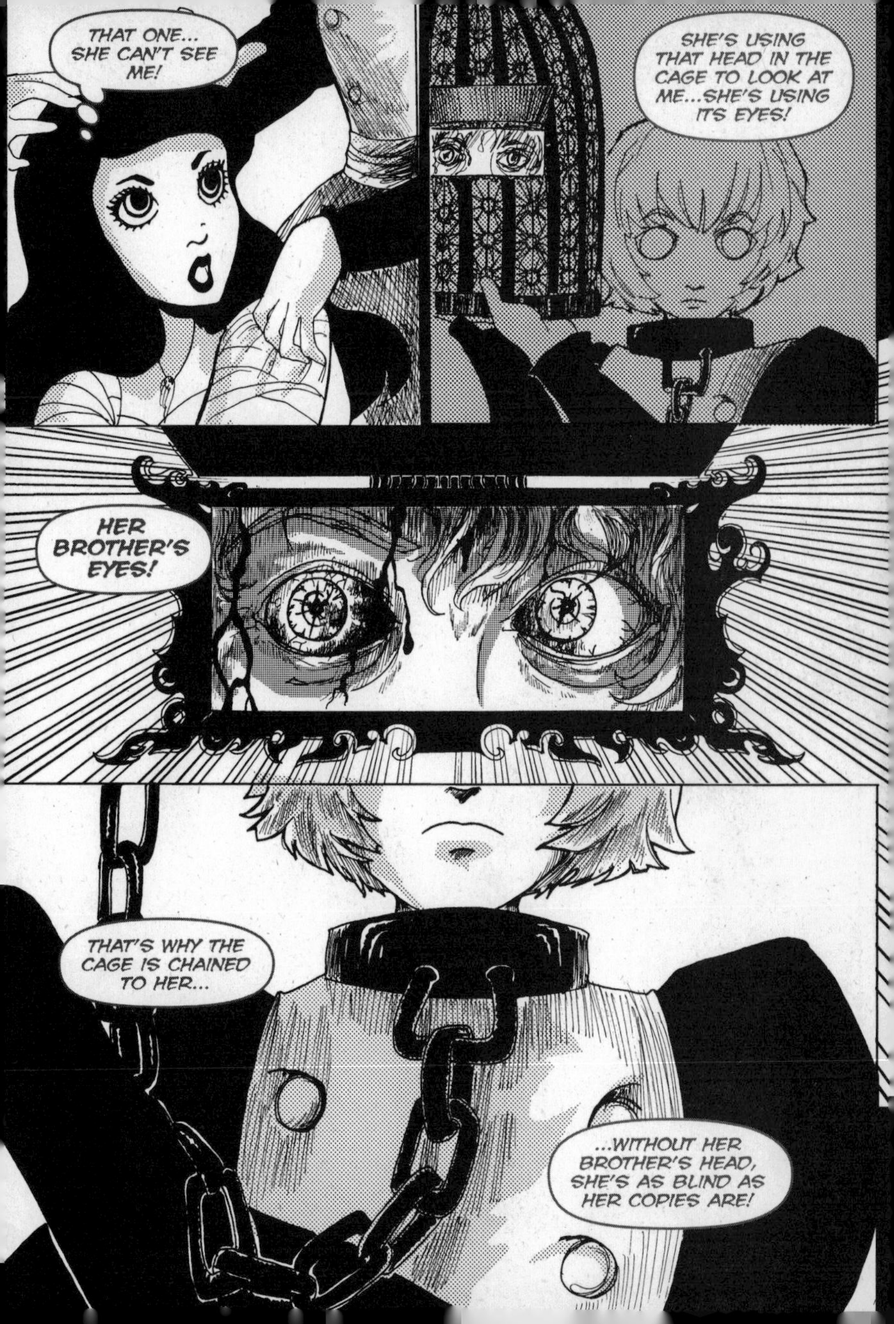
THAT ONE... SHE CAN'T SEE ME!
SHE'S USING THAT HEAD IN THE CAGE TO LOOK AT ME...SHE'S USING ITS EYES!
HER BROTHER'S EYES!
THAT'S WHY THE CAGE IS CHAINED TO HER...
...WITHOUT HER BROTHER'S HEAD, SHE'S AS BLIND AS HER COPIES ARE!

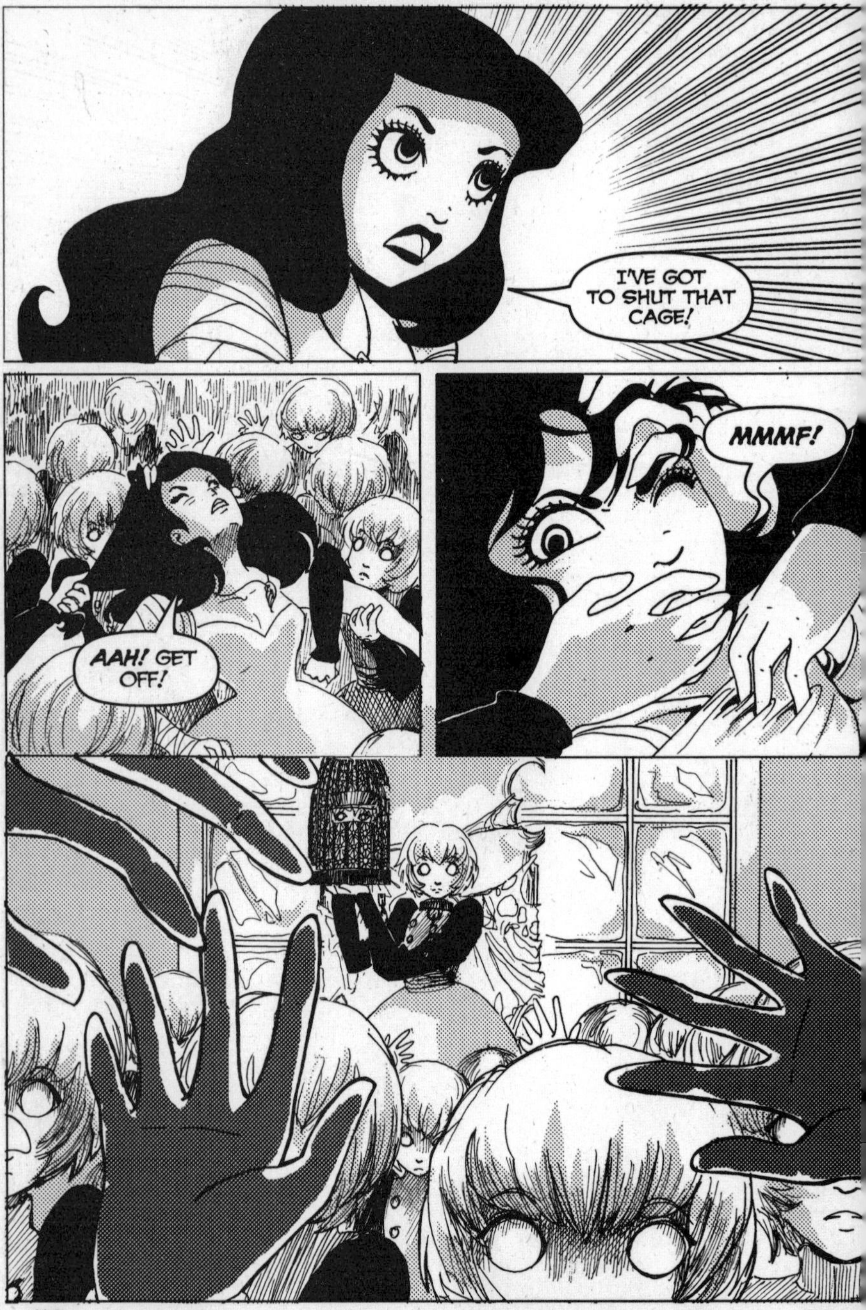
I'VE GOT TO SHUT THAT CAGE!
AAH! GET OFF!
MMMF!

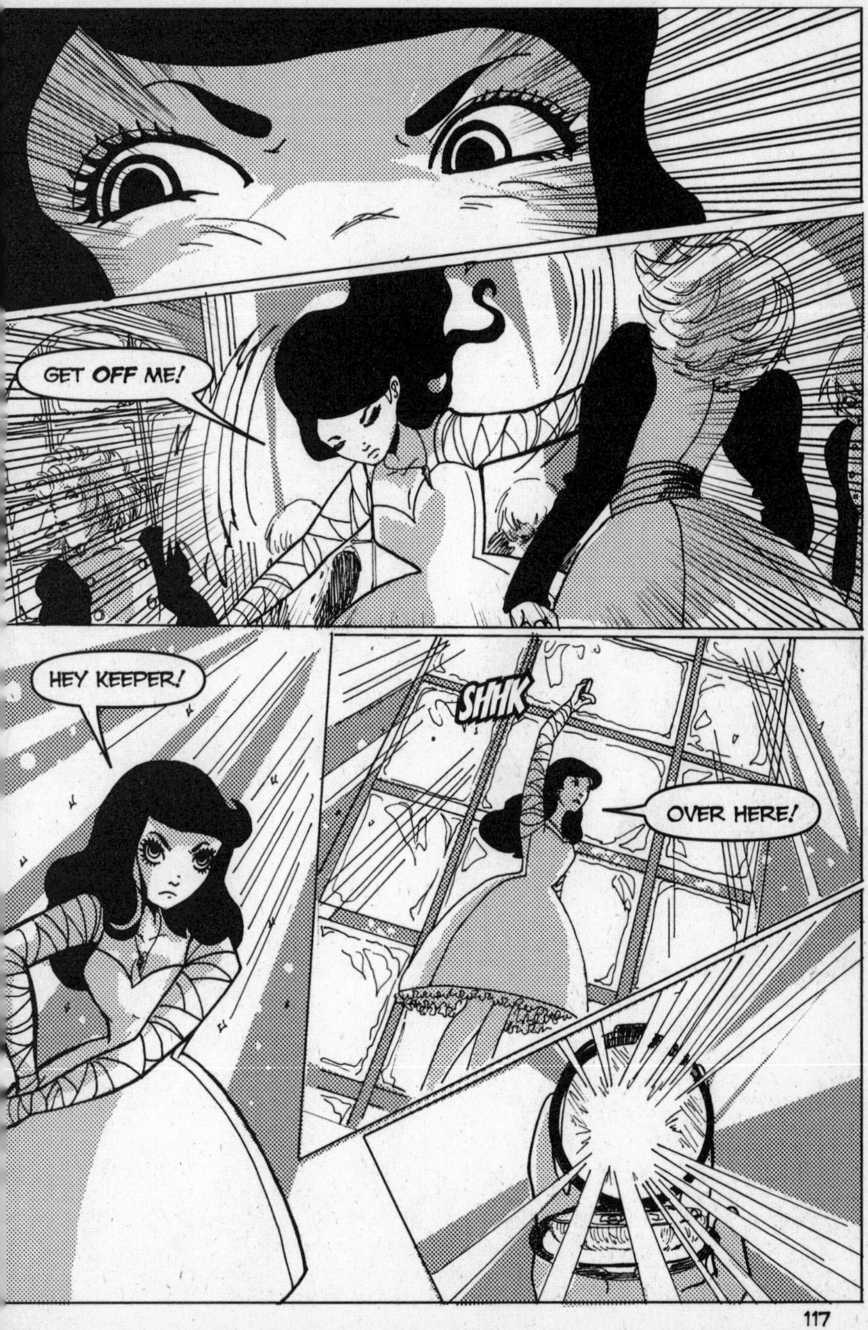

GET OFF ME!
HEY KEEPER!
SHHK
OVER HERE!

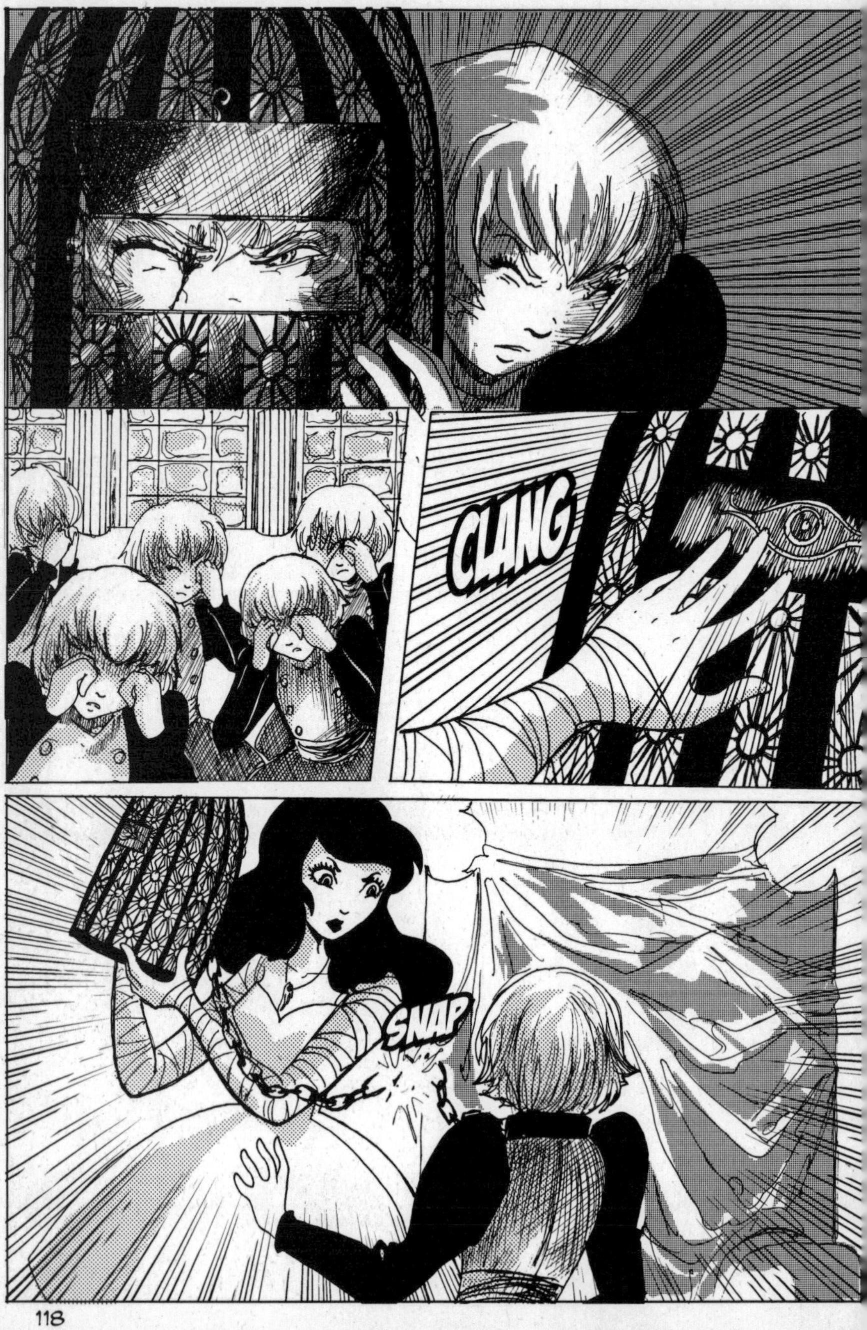
CLANG
SNAP

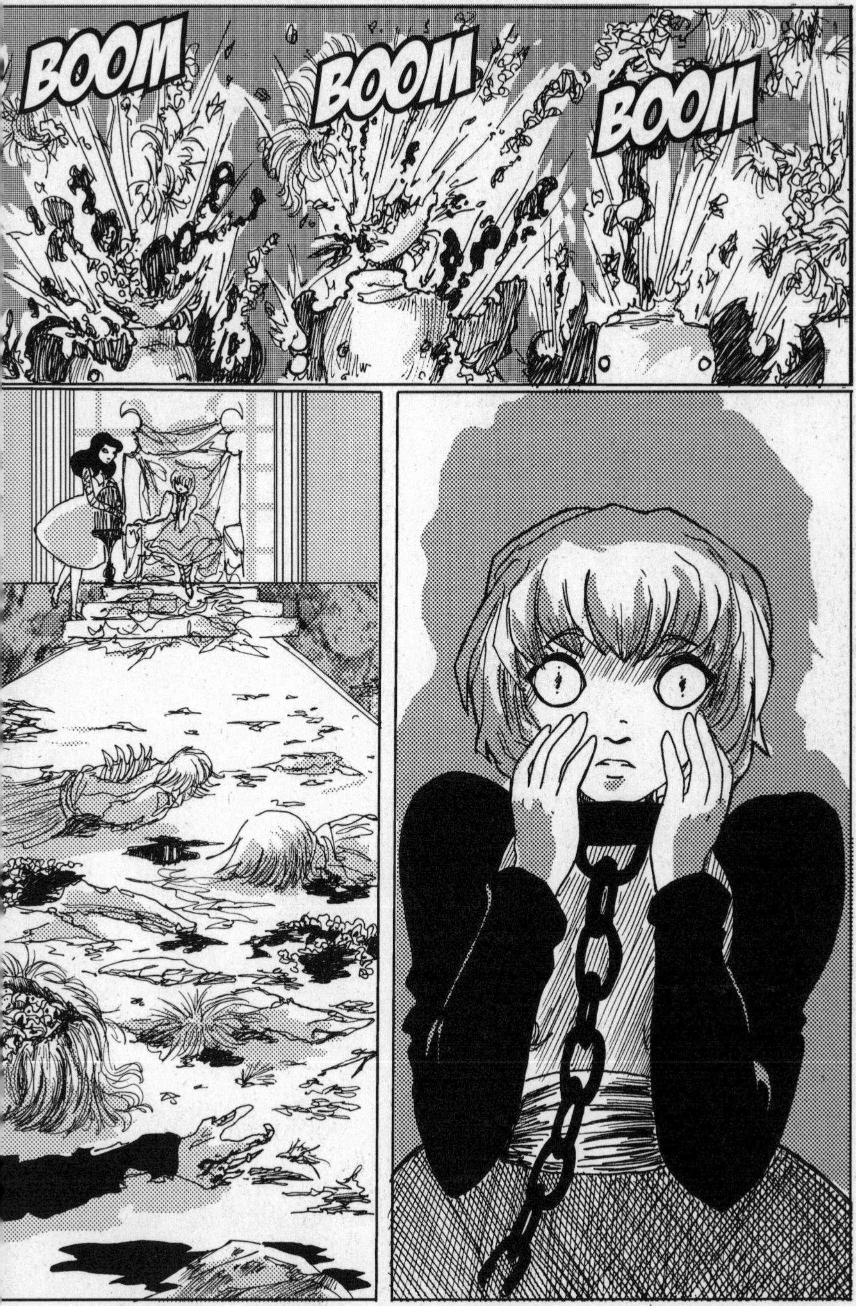
BOOM
BOOM
BOOM

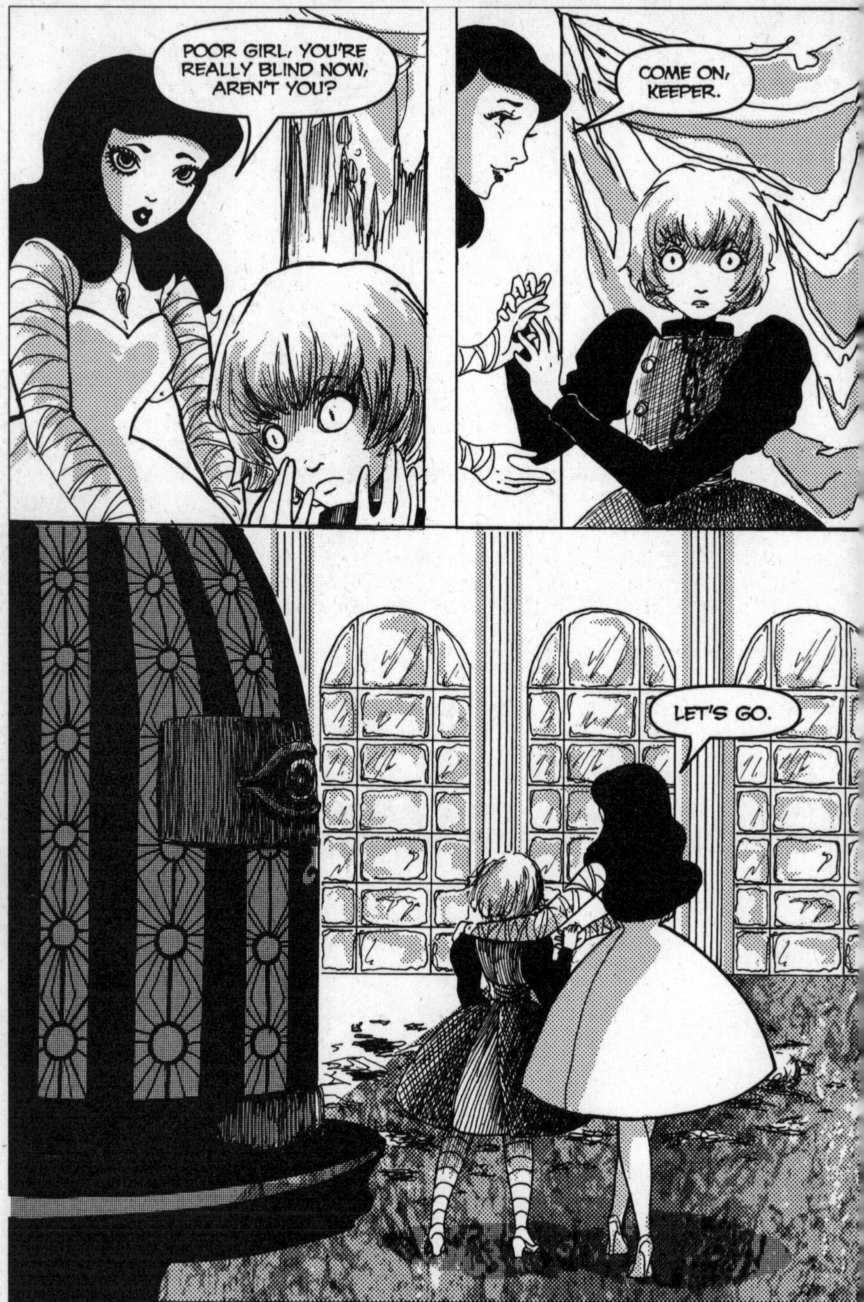
POOR GIRL, YOU'RE REALLY BLIND NOW, AREN'T YOU?
COME ON, KEEPER.
LET'S GO.

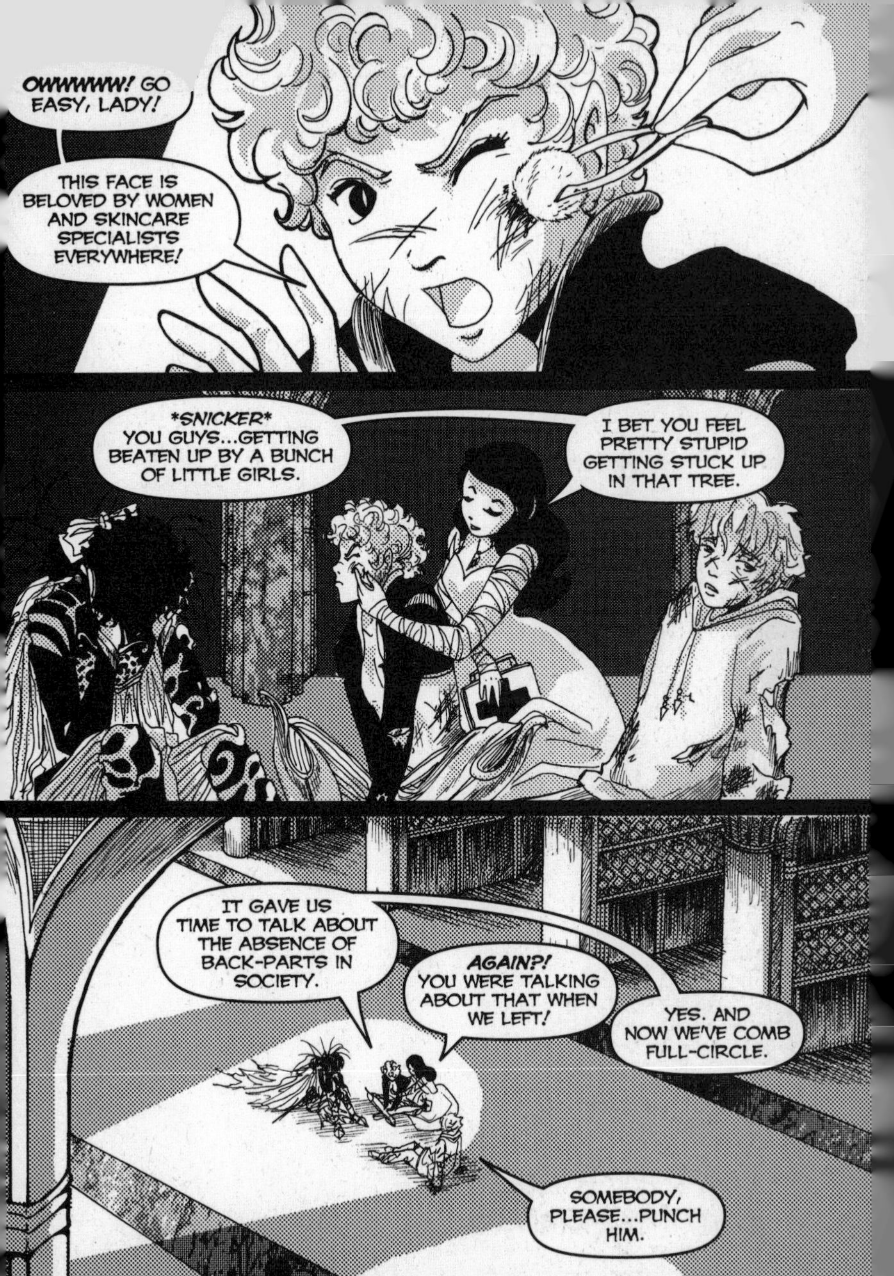
OWWWWW! GO EASY, LADY!
THIS FACE IS BELOVED BY WOMEN AND SKINCARE SPECIALISTS EVERYWHERE!
SNICKER YOU GUYS...GETTING BEATEN UP BY A BUNCH OF LITTLE GIRLS.
I BET YOU FEEL PRETTY STUPID GETTING STUCK UP IN THAT TREE.
IT GAVE US TIME TO TALK ABOUT THE ABSENCE OF BACK-PARTS IN SOCIETY.
AGAIN?! YOU WERE TALKING ABOUT THAT WHEN WE LEFT!
YES. AND NOW WE'VE COMB FULL-CIRCLE.
SOMEBODY, PLEASE...PUNCH HIM.

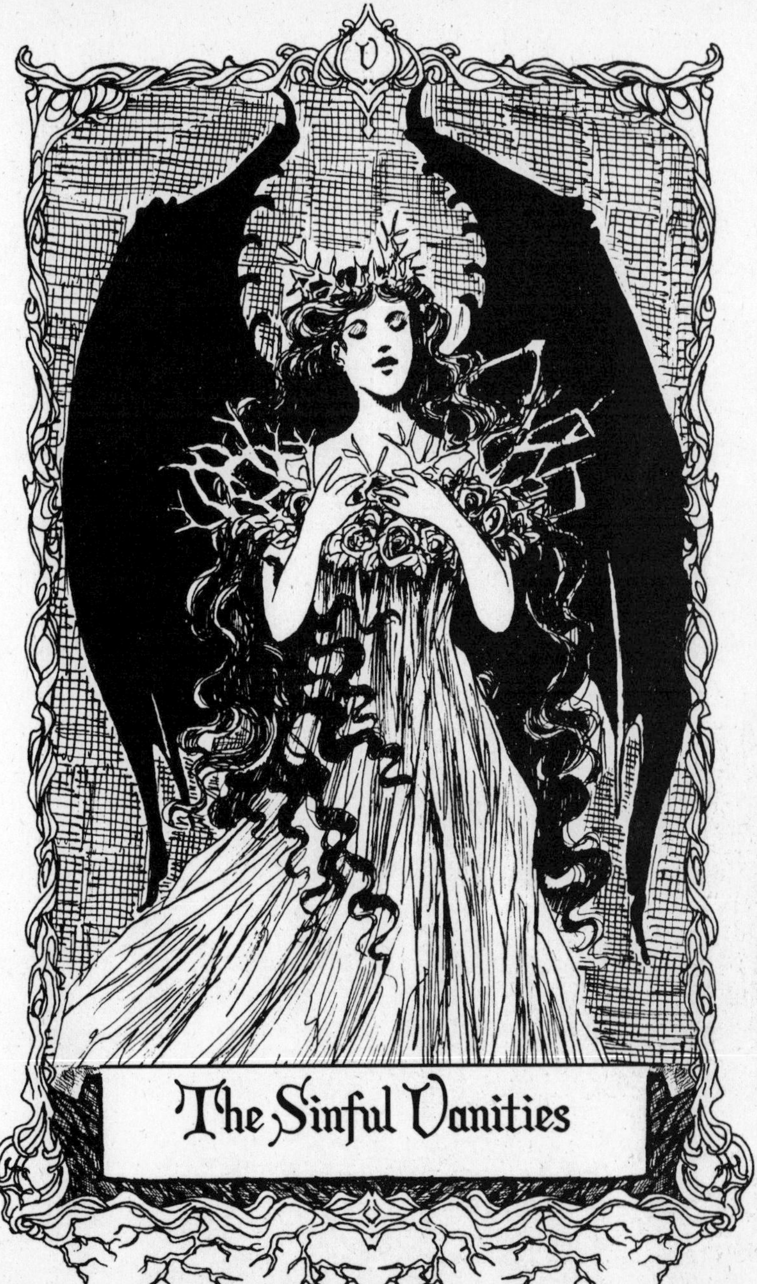
V
The Sinful Vanities

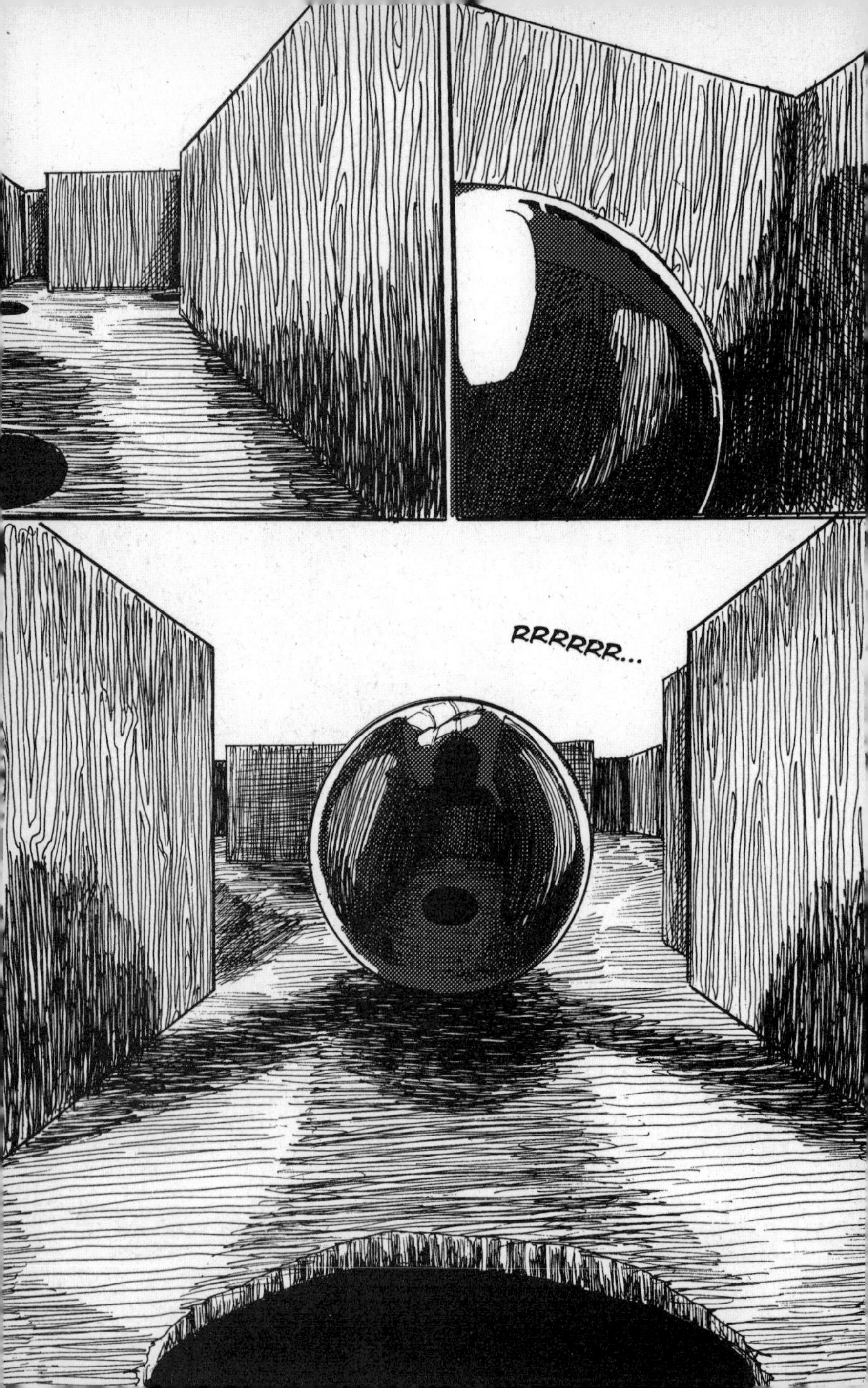
RRRRRR...

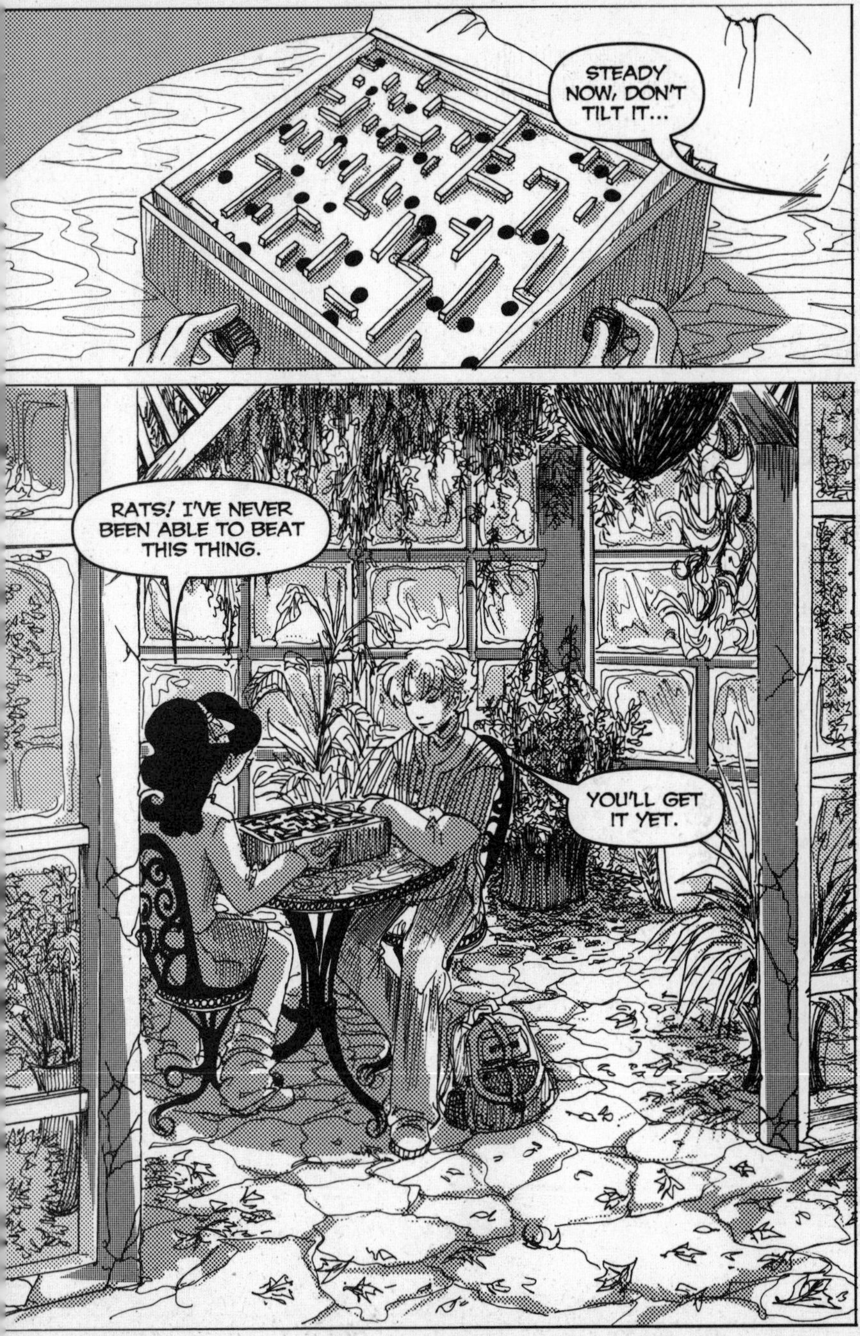
STEADY NOW, DON'T TILT IT...
RATS! I'VE NEVER BEEN ABLE TO BEAT THIS THING.
YOU'LL GET IT YET.

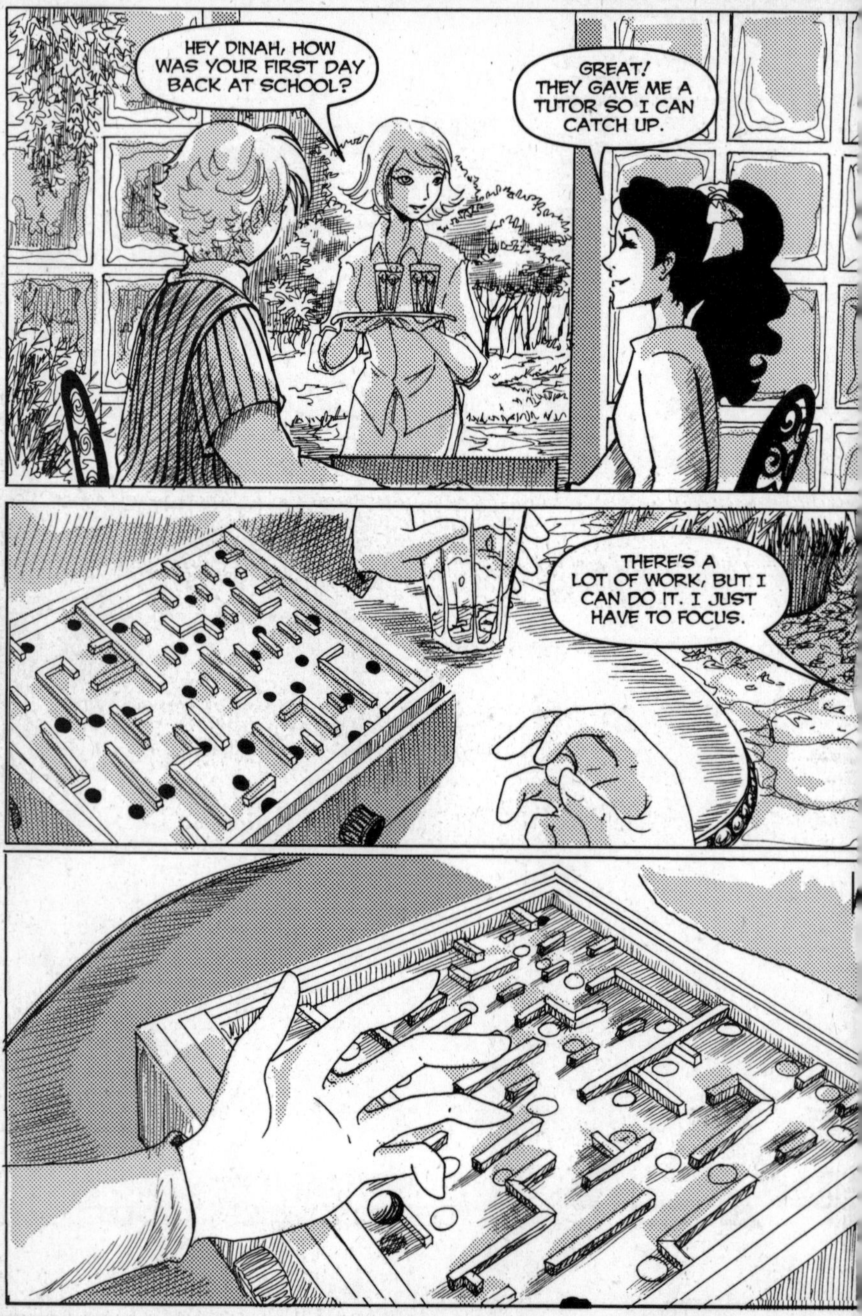
HEY DINAH, HOW WAS YOUR FIRST DAY BACK AT SCHOOL?
GREAT! THEY GAVE ME A TUTOR SO I CAN CATCH UP.
THERE'S A LOT OF WORK, BUT I CAN DO IT. I JUST HAVE TO FOCUS.

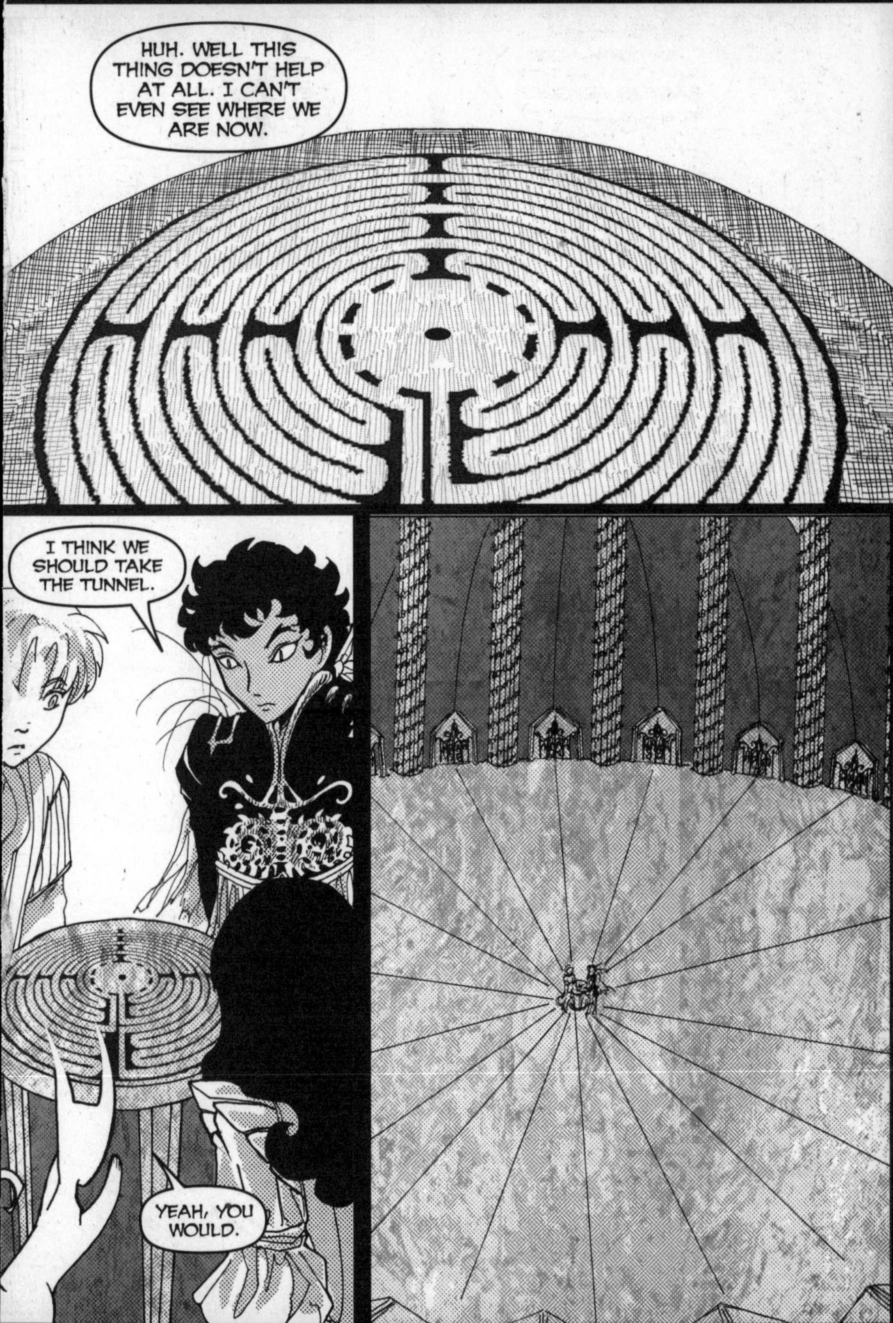
HUH. WELL THIS THING DOESN'T HELP AT ALL. I CAN'T EVEN SEE WHERE WE ARE NOW.
I THINK WE SHOULD TAKE THE TUNNEL.
YEAH, YOU WOULD.

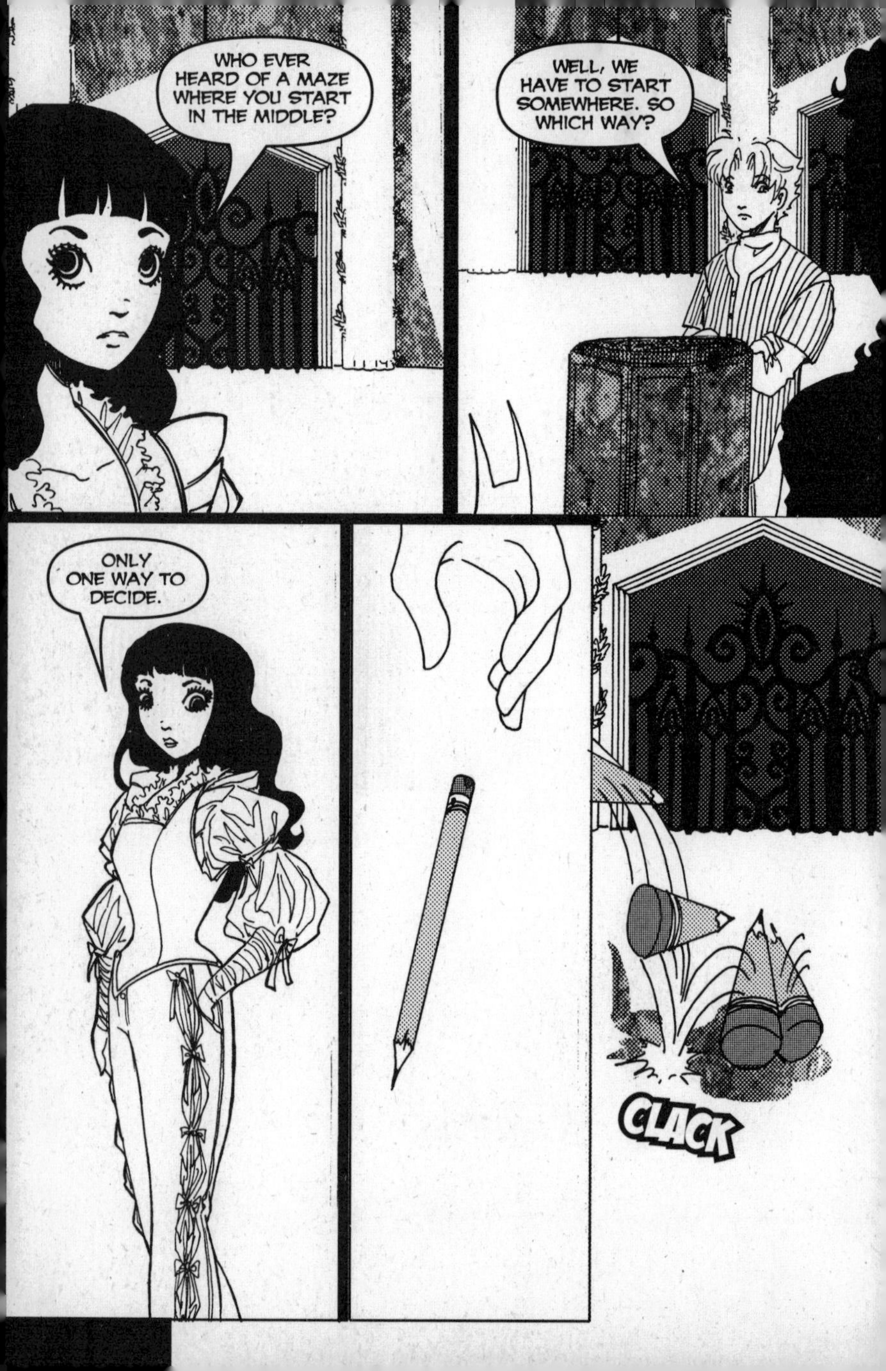
WHO EVER HEARD OF A MAZE WHERE YOU START IN THE MIDDLE?
WELL, WE HAVE TO START SOMEWHERE. SO WHICH WAY?
ONLY ONE WAY TO DECIDE.
CLACK

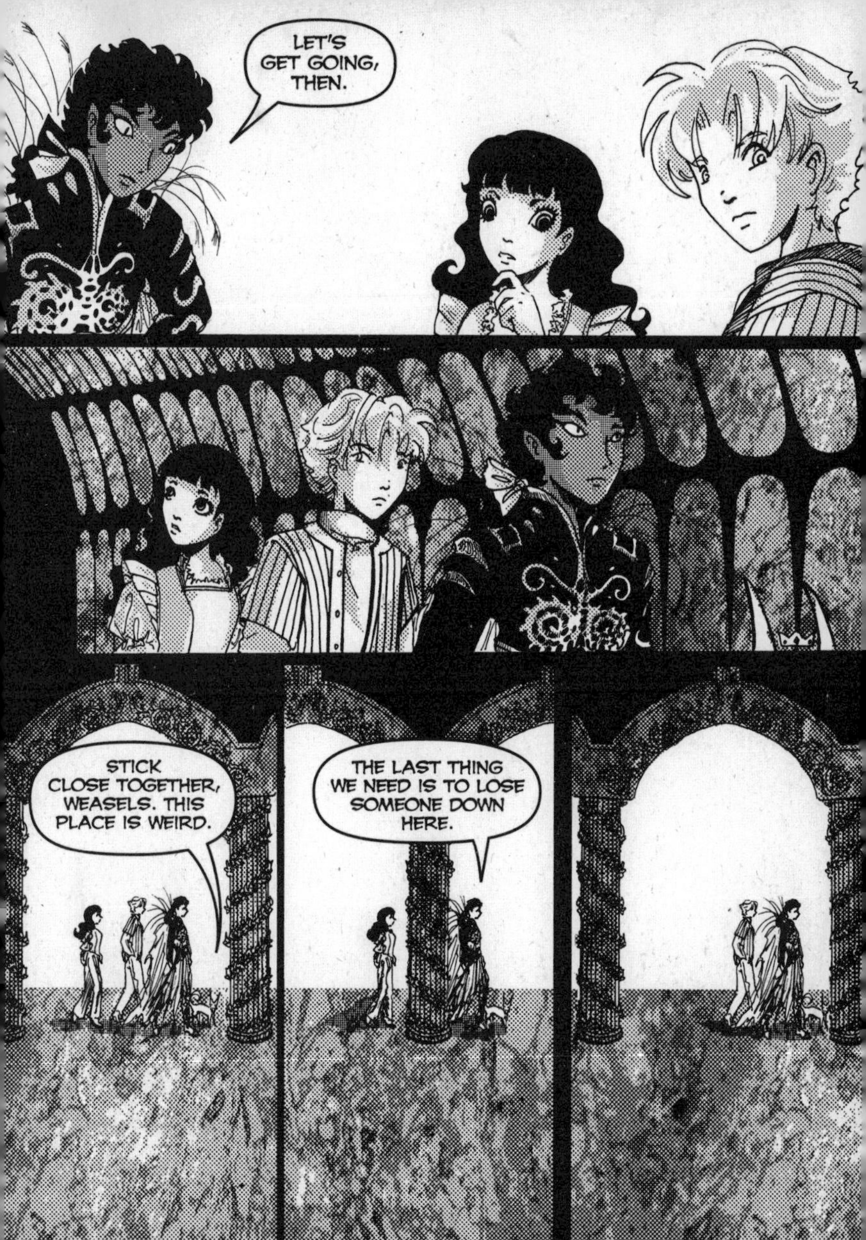
LET'S GET GOING, THEN.
STICK CLOSE TOGETHER, WEASELS. THIS PLACE IS WEIRD.
THE LAST THING WE NEED IS TO LOSE SOMEONE DOWN HERE.

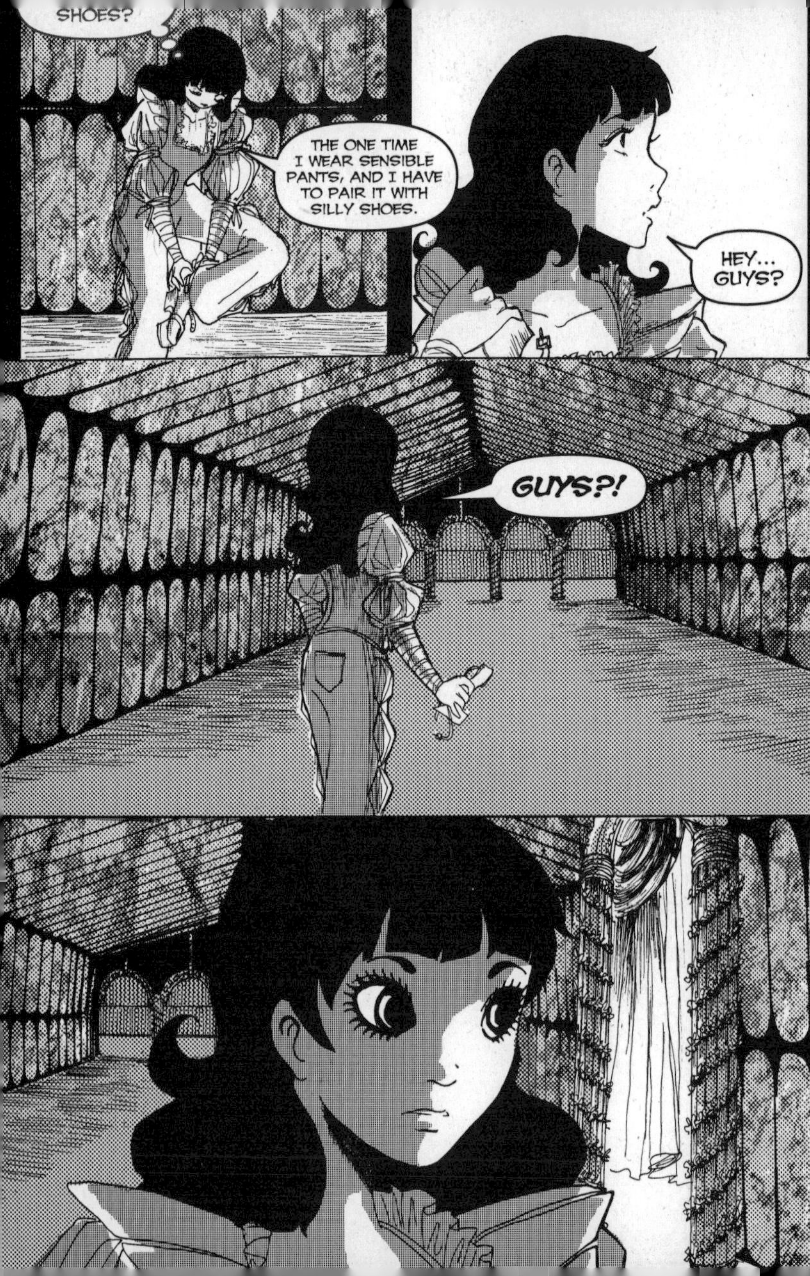
SHOES?
THE ONE TIME I WEAR SENSIBLE PANTS, AND I HAVE TO PAIR IT WITH SILLY SHOES.
HEY... GUYS?
GUYS?!

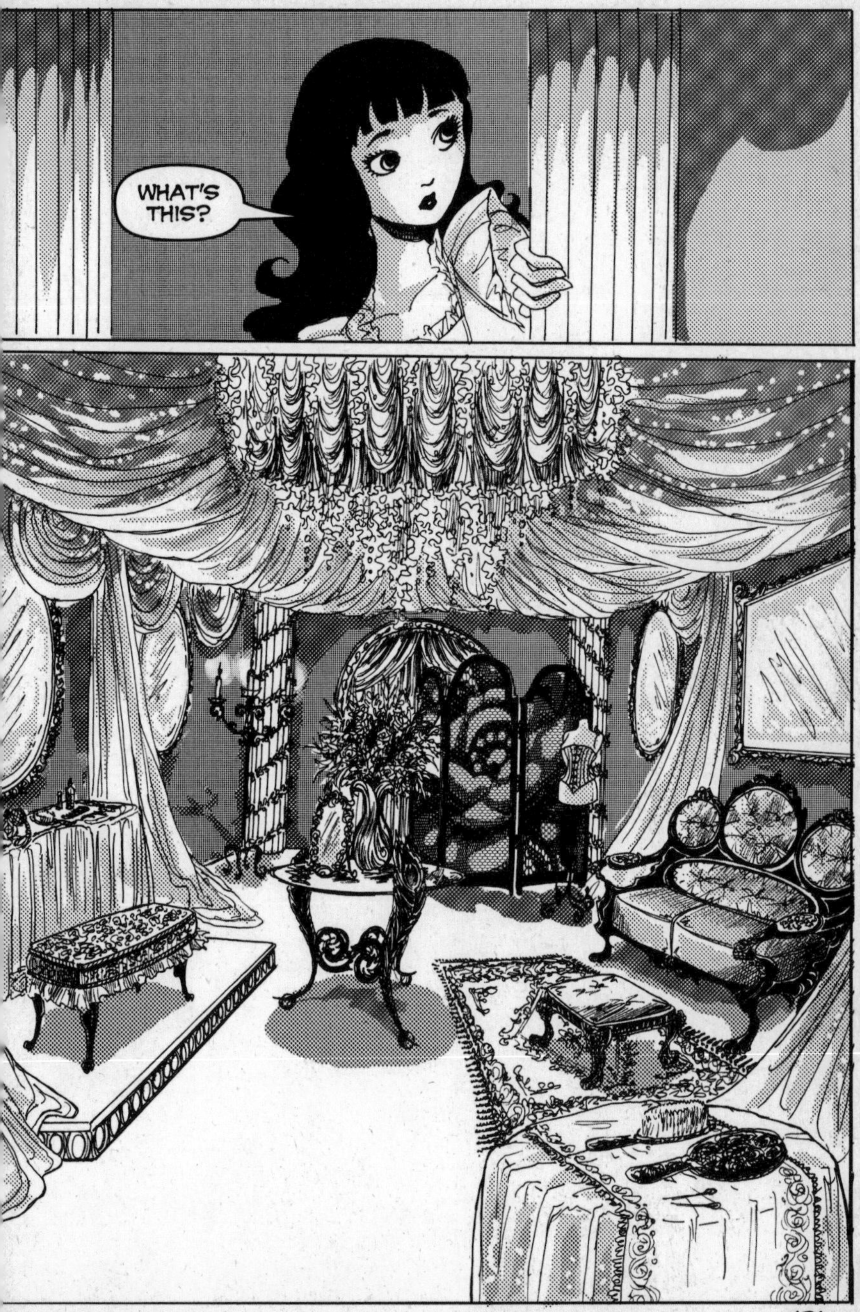
WHAT'S THIS?

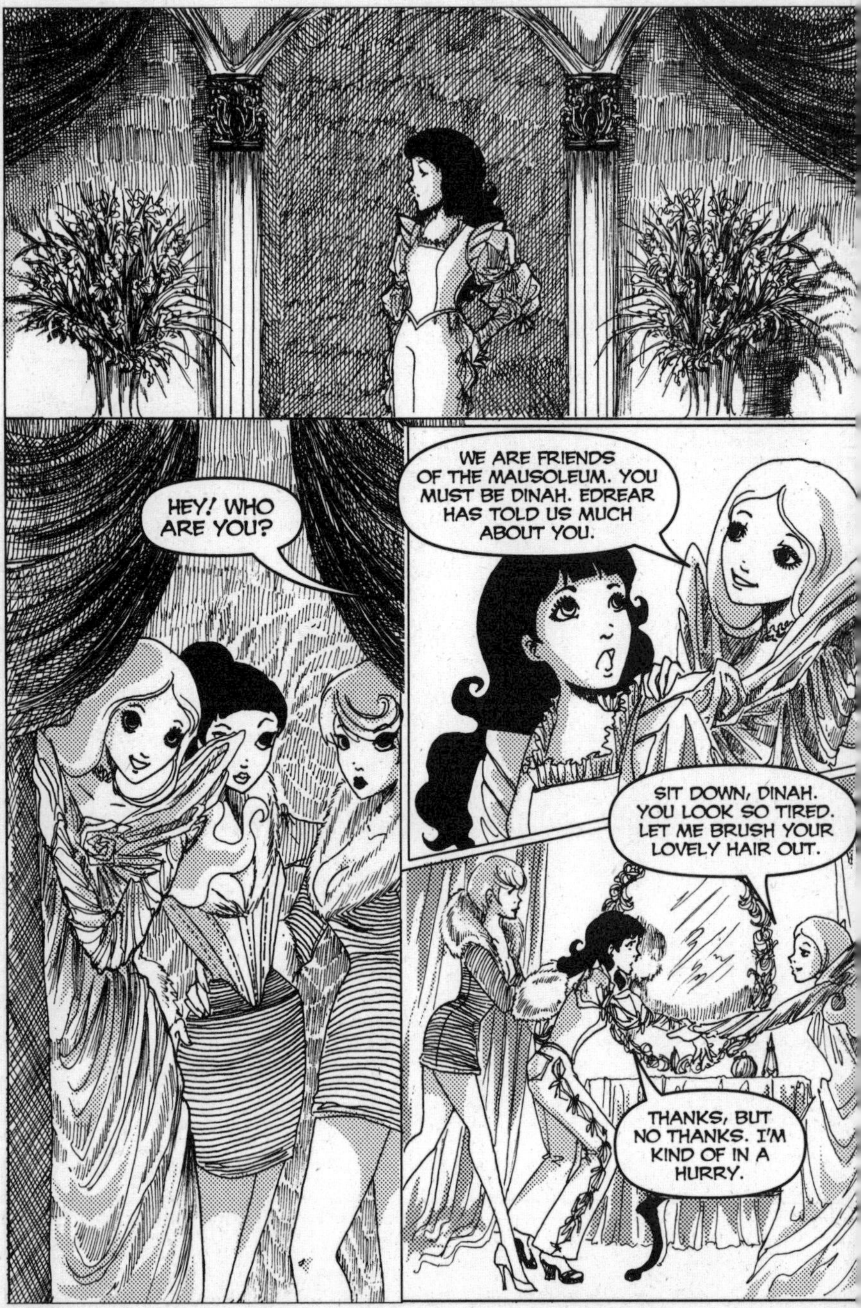
HEY! WHO ARE YOU?
WE ARE FRIENDS OF THE MAUSOLEUM. YOU MUST BE DINAH. EDREAR HAS TOLD US MUCH ABOUT YOU.
SIT DOWN, DINAH. YOU LOOK SO TIRED. LET ME BRUSH YOUR LOVELY HAIR OUT.
THANKS, BUT NO THANKS. I'M KIND OF IN A HURRY.

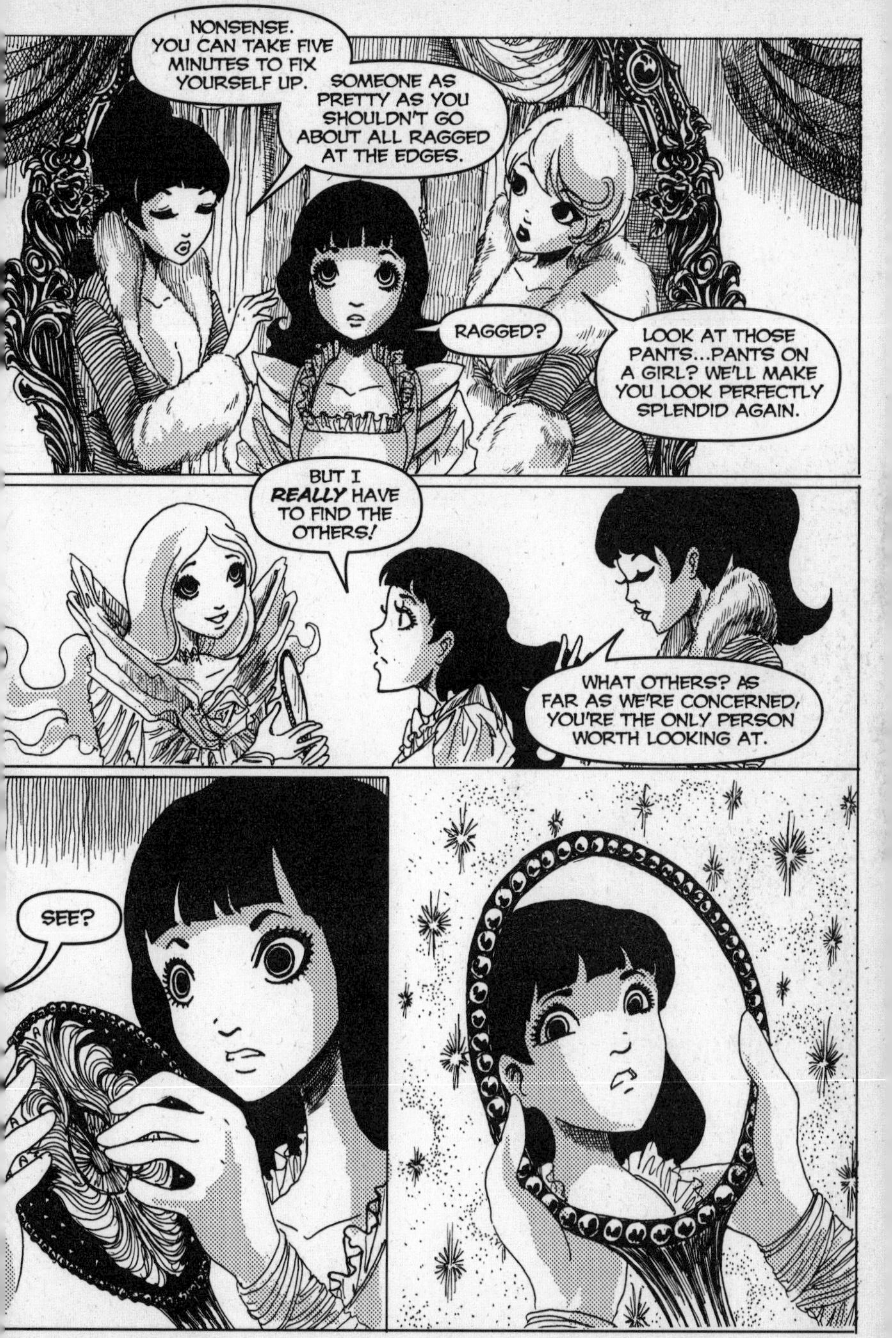
NONSENSE. YOU CAN TAKE FIVE MINUTES TO FIX YOURSELF UP.
SOMEONE AS PRETTY AS YOU SHOULDN'T GO ABOUT ALL RAGGED AT THE EDGES.
RAGGED?
LOOK AT THOSE PANTS...PANTS ON A GIRL? WE'LL MAKE YOU LOOK PERFECTLY SPLENDID AGAIN.
BUT I ***REALLY*** HAVE TO FIND THE OTHERS!
WHAT OTHERS? AS FAR AS WE'RE CONCERNED, YOU'RE THE ONLY PERSON WORTH LOOKING AT.
SEE?

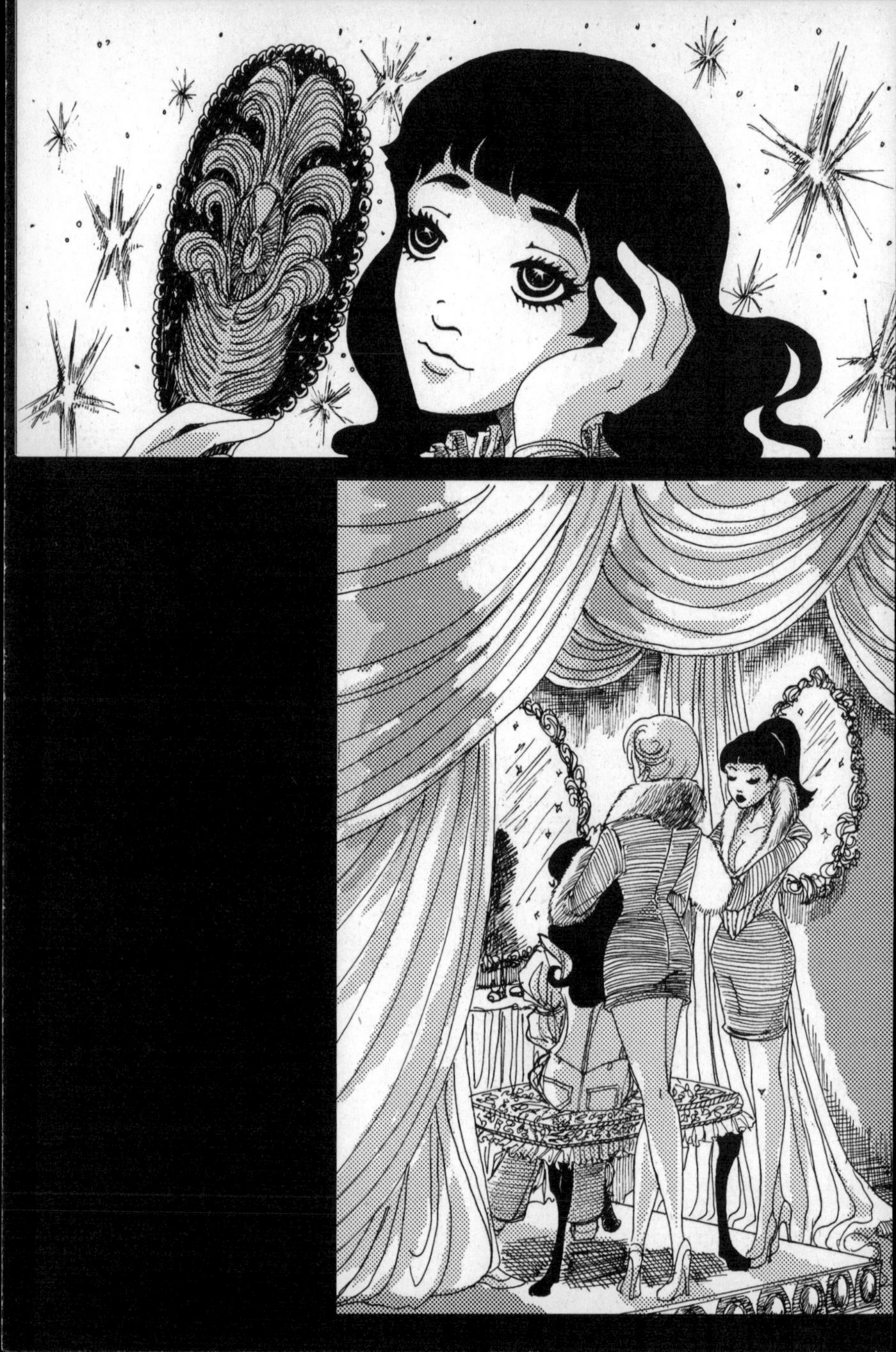

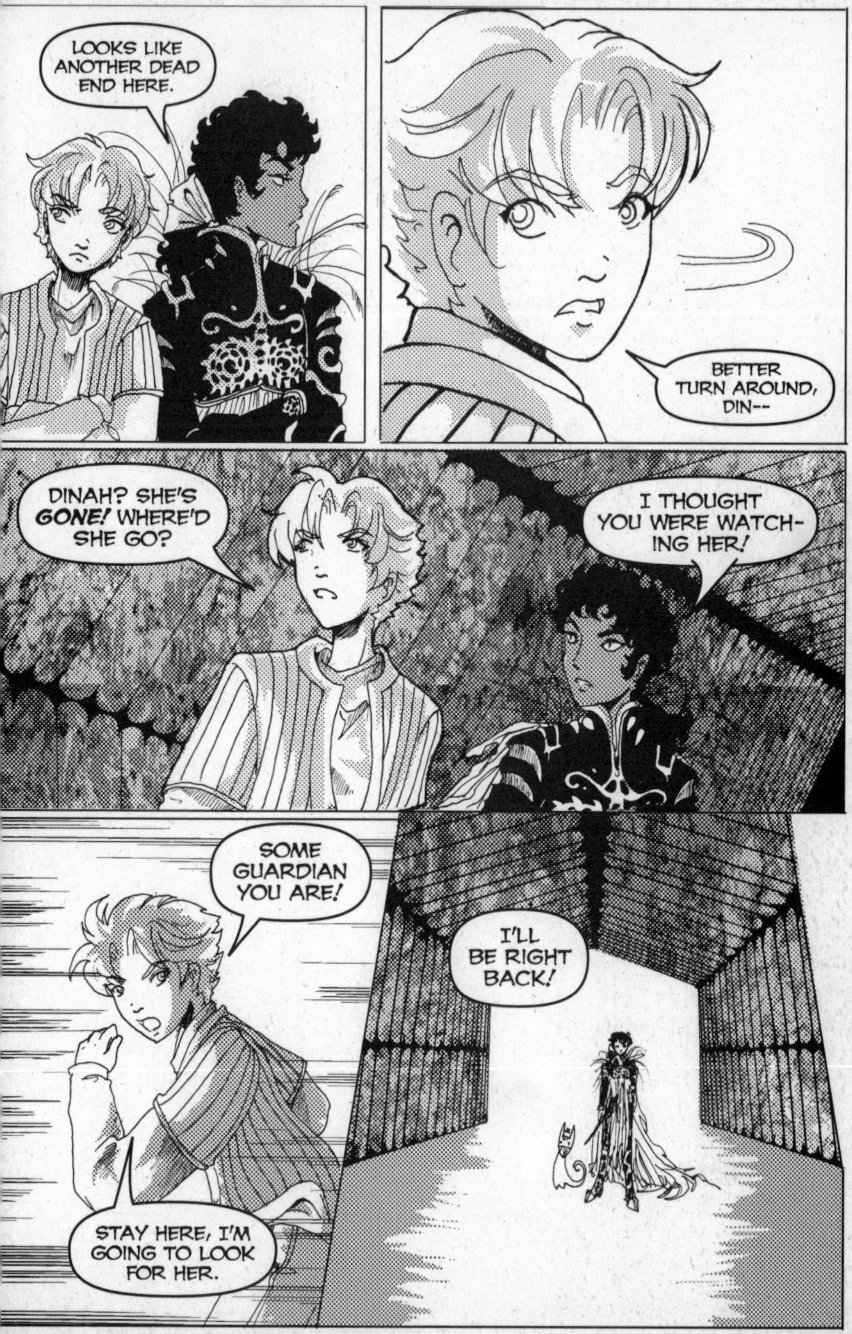
LOOKS LIKE ANOTHER DEAD END HERE.
BETTER TURN AROUND, DIN--
DINAH? SHE'S *GONE!* WHERE'D SHE GO?
I THOUGHT YOU WERE WATCHING HER!
SOME GUARDIAN YOU ARE!
STAY HERE, I'M GOING TO LOOK FOR HER.
I'LL BE RIGHT BACK!

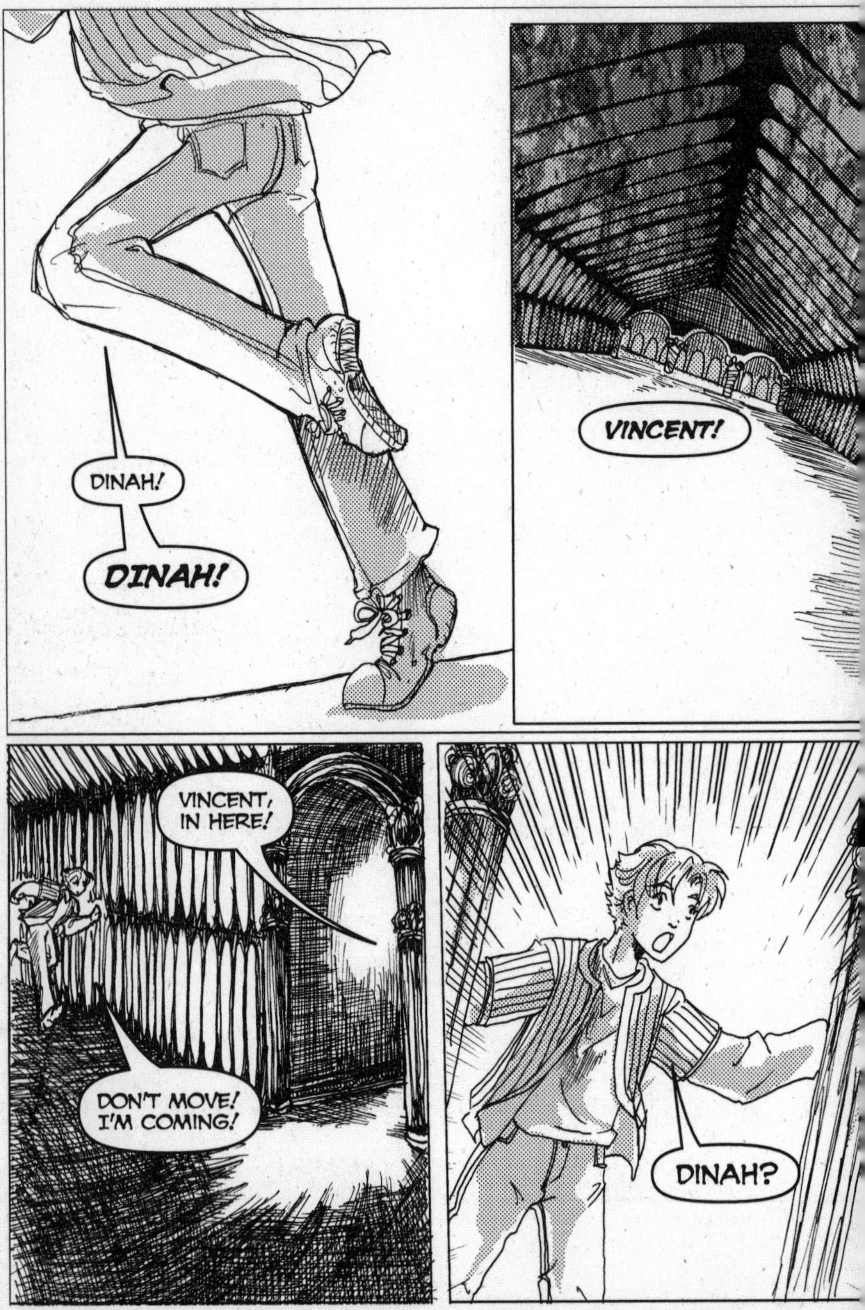
DINAH!
DINAH!
VINCENT!
VINCENT, IN HERE!
DON'T MOVE! I'M COMING!
DINAH?

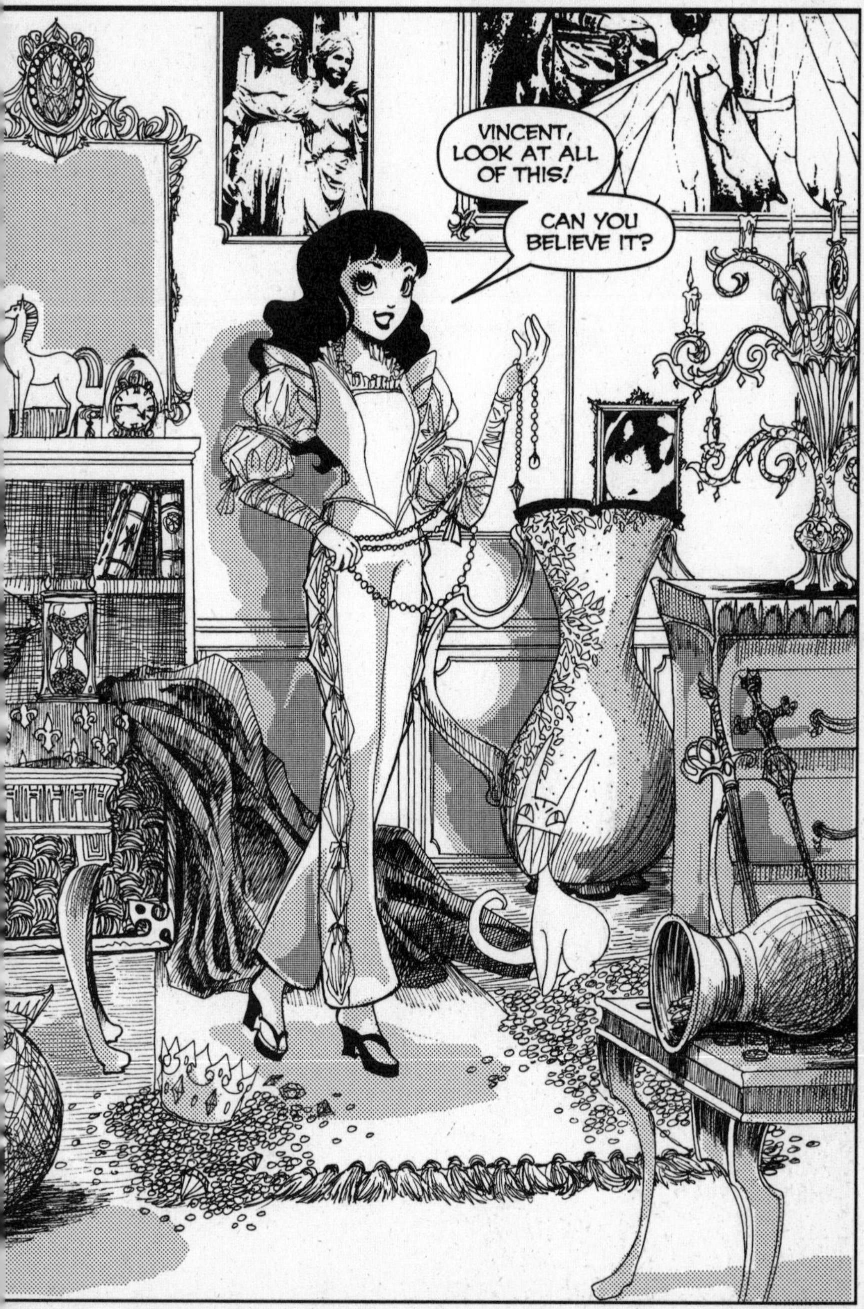
VINCENT, LOOK AT ALL OF THIS!
CAN YOU BELIEVE IT?

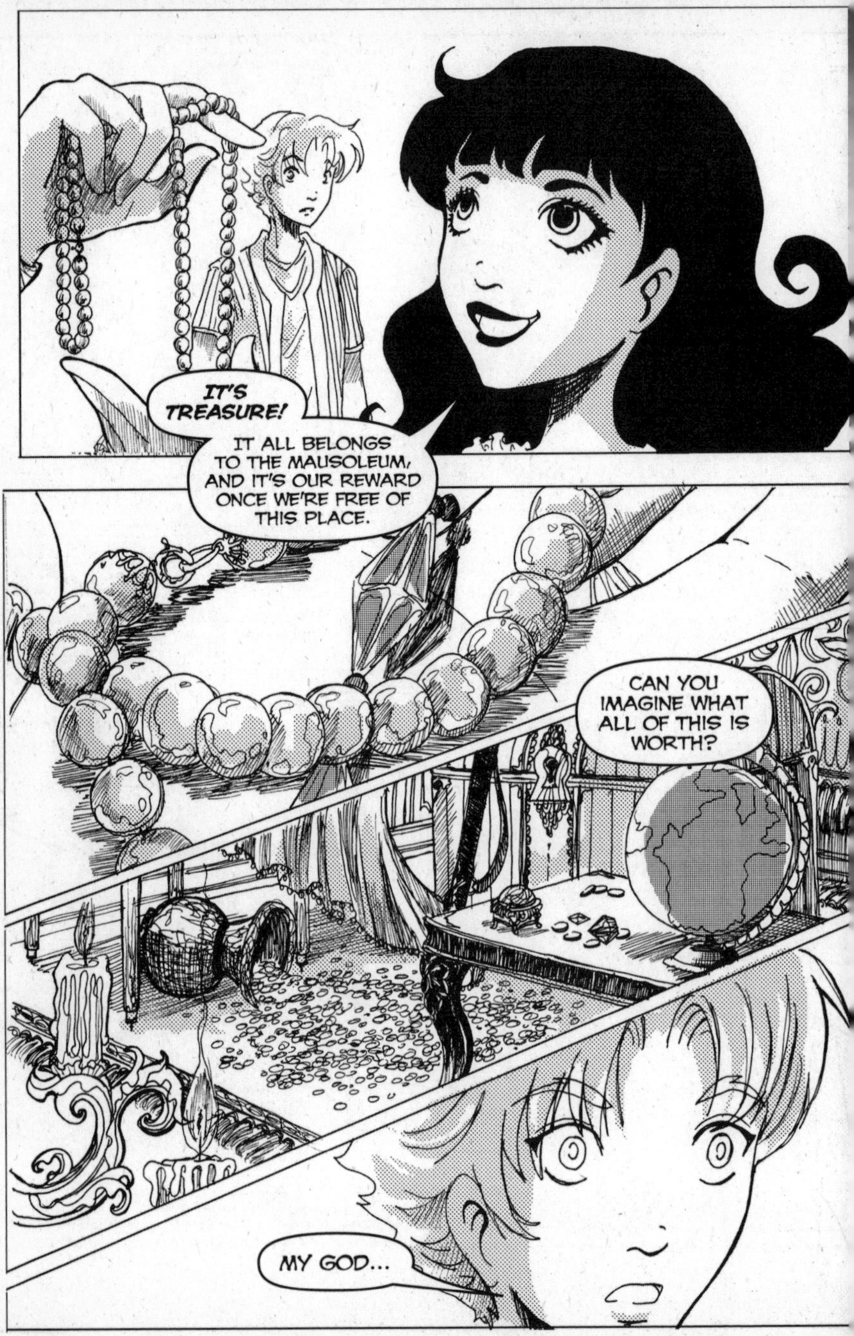
IT'S TREASURE!
IT ALL BELONGS TO THE MAUSOLEUM, AND IT'S OUR REWARD ONCE WE'RE FREE OF THIS PLACE.
CAN YOU IMAGINE WHAT ALL OF THIS IS WORTH?
MY GOD...

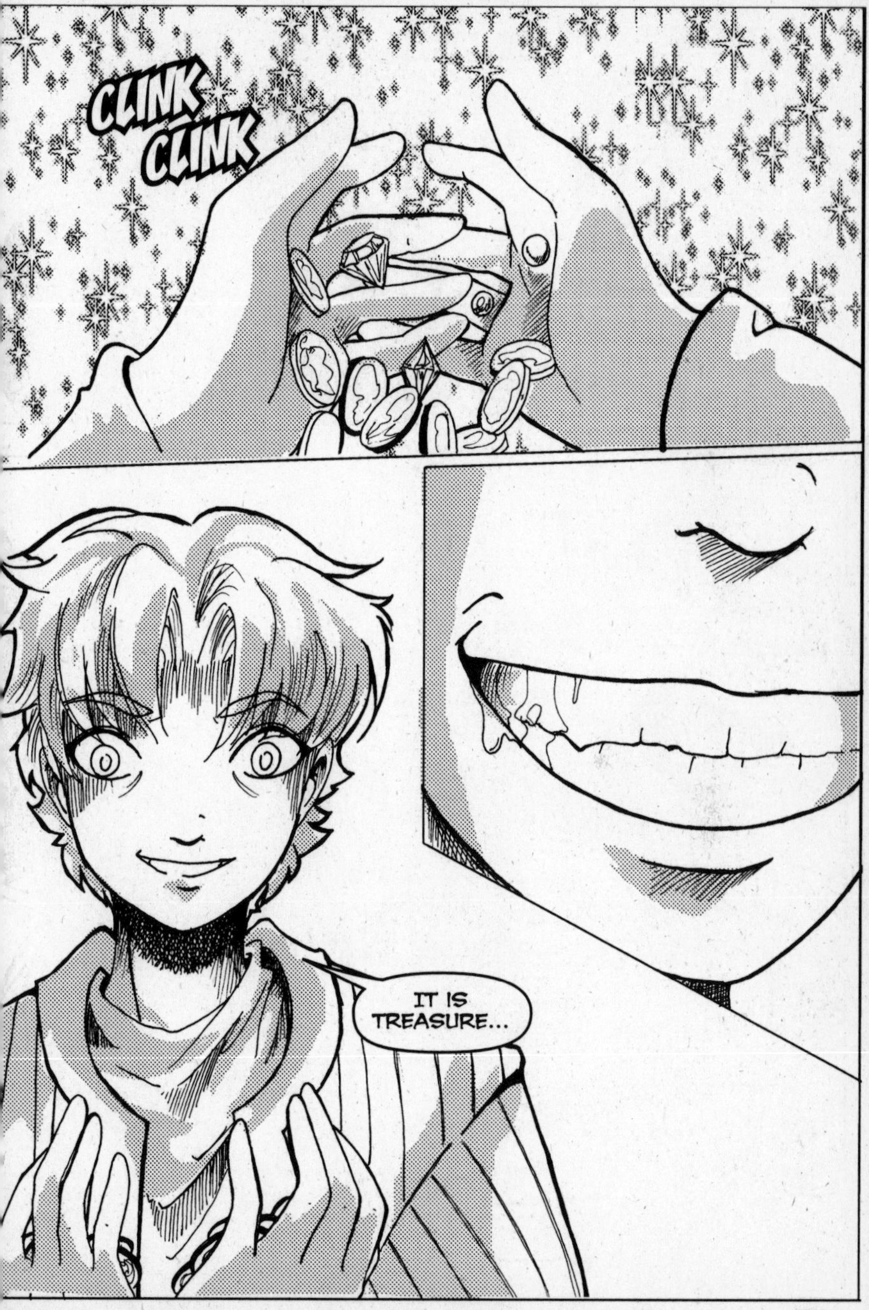
CLINK CLINK
IT IS TREASURE...

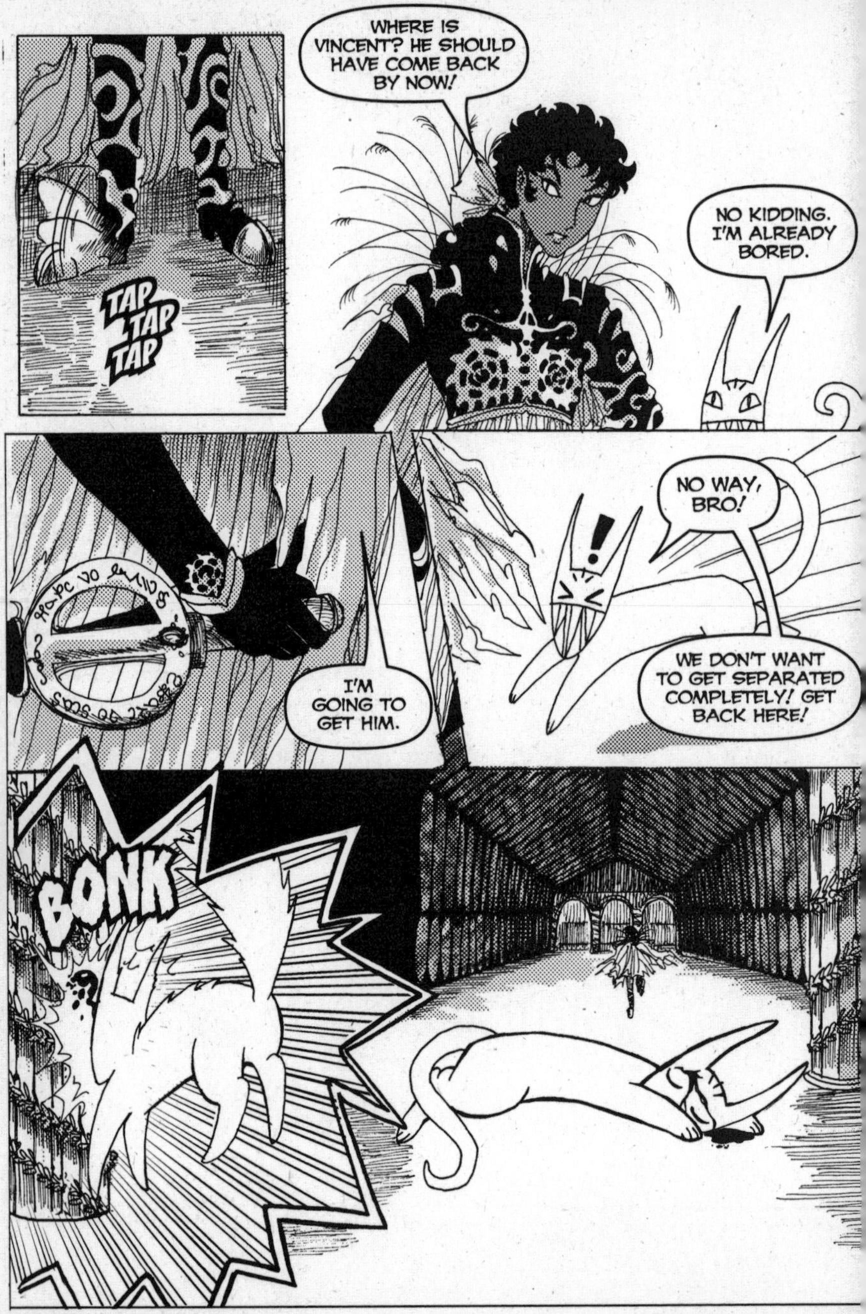

TAP TAP TAP
WHERE IS VINCENT? HE SHOULD HAVE COME BACK BY NOW!
NO KIDDING. I'M ALREADY BORED.
I'M GOING TO GET HIM.
!
NO WAY, BRO!
WE DON'T WANT TO GET SEPARATED COMPLETELY! GET BACK HERE!
BONK

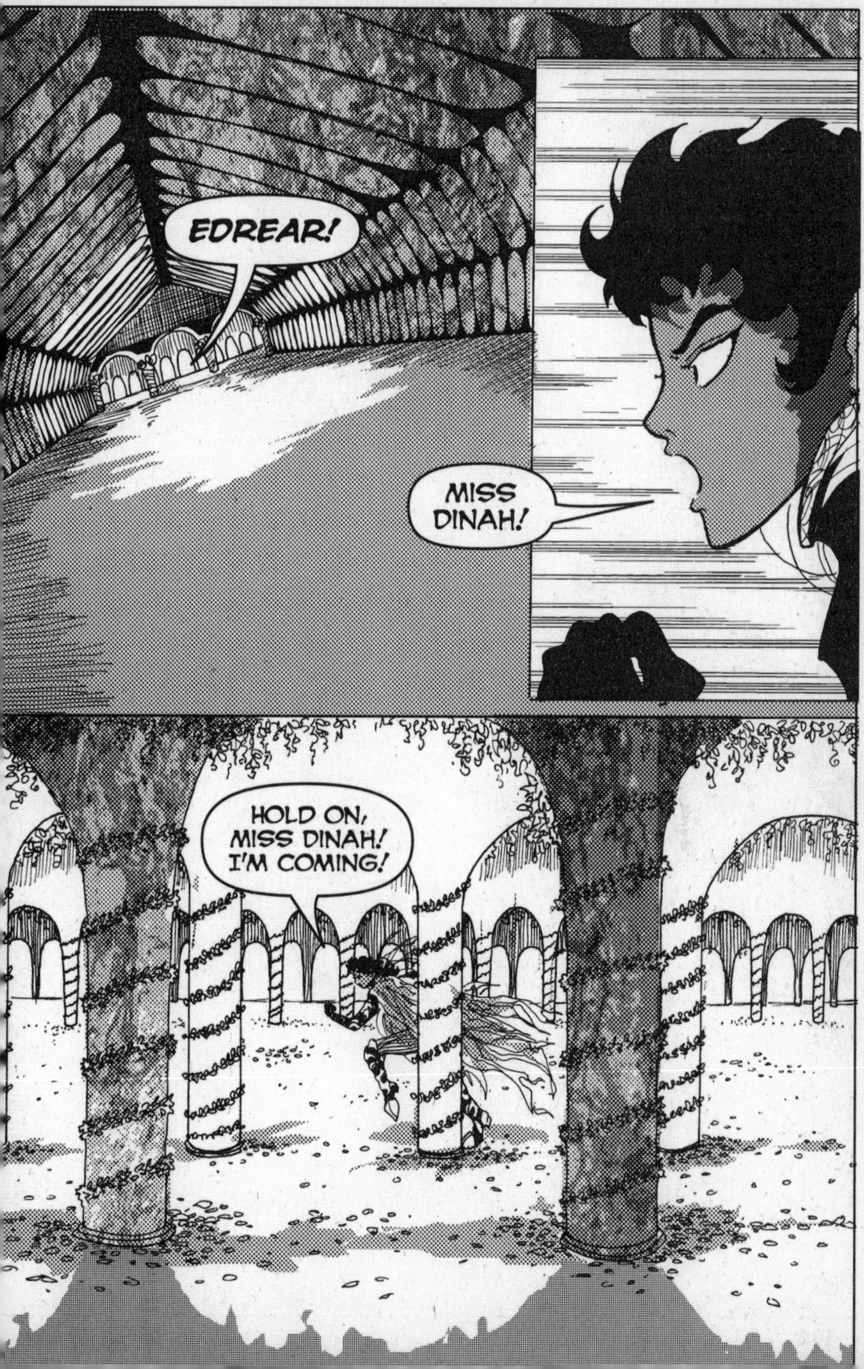
MISS DINAH!
EDREAR!
HOLD ON, MISS DINAH! I'M COMING!

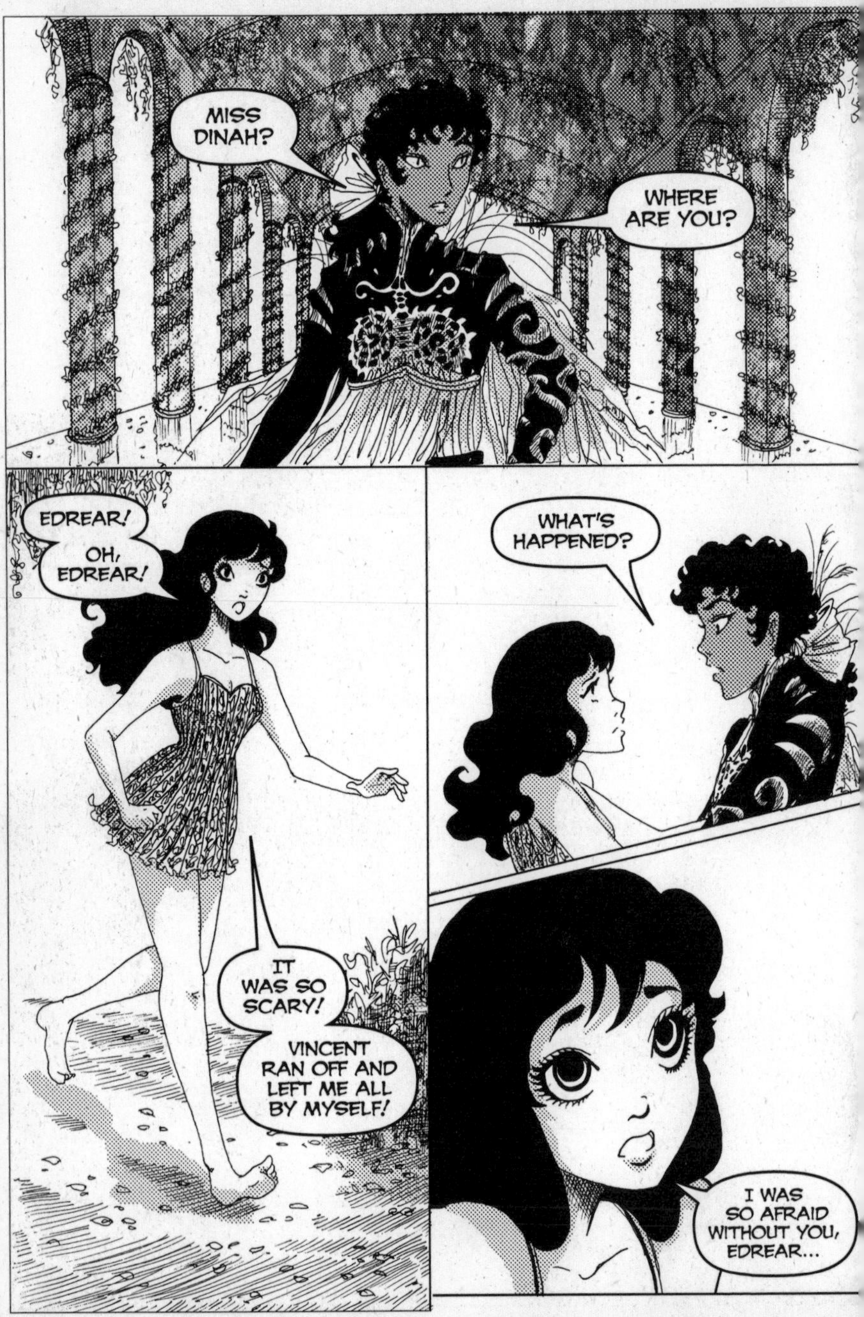
MISS DINAH?
WHERE ARE YOU?
EDREAR!
OH, EDREAR!
IT WAS SO SCARY!
VINCENT RAN OFF AND LEFT ME ALL BY MYSELF!
WHAT'S HAPPENED?
I WAS SO AFRAID WITHOUT YOU, EDREAR...

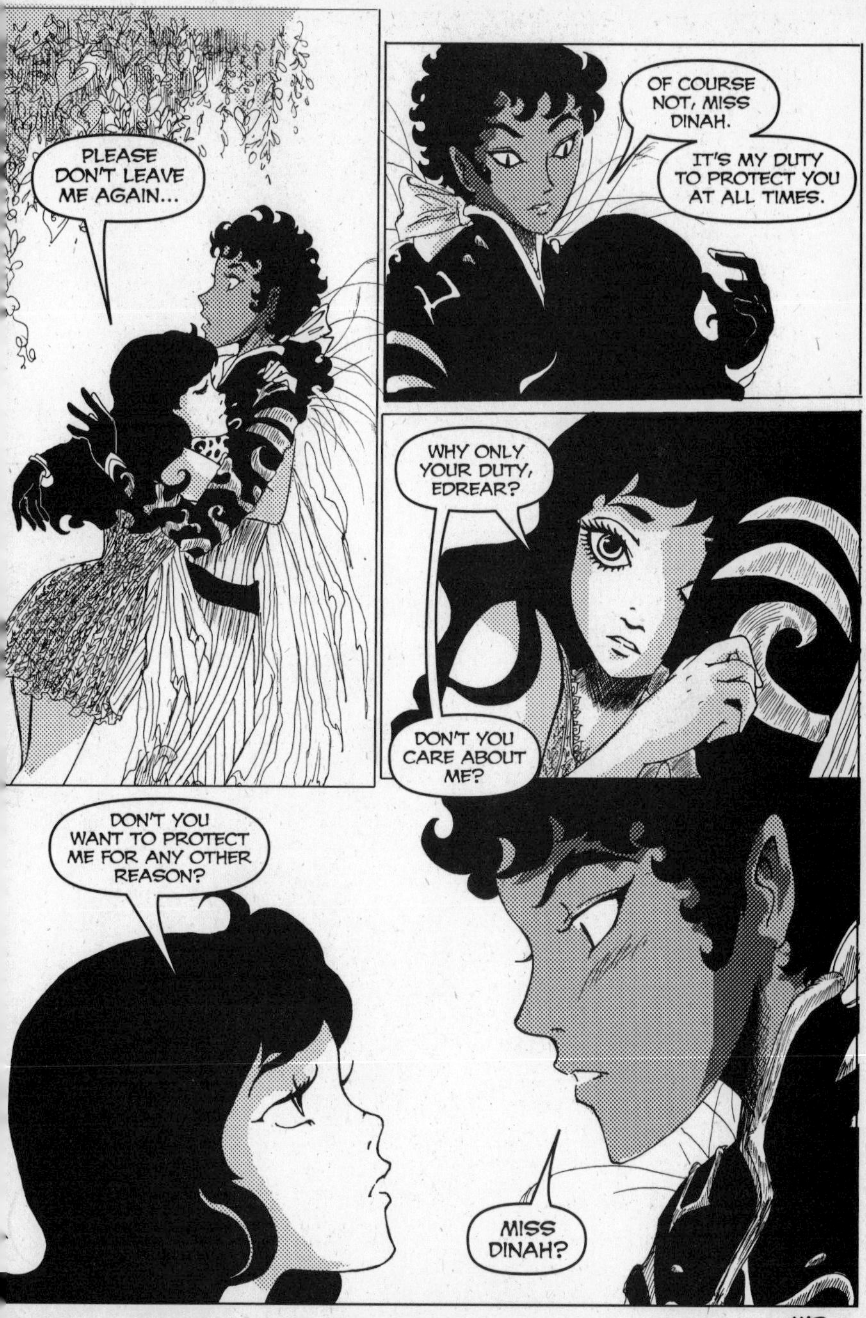
PLEASE DON'T LEAVE ME AGAIN...
OF COURSE NOT, MISS DINAH.
IT'S MY DUTY TO PROTECT YOU AT ALL TIMES.
WHY ONLY YOUR DUTY, EDREAR?
DON'T YOU CARE ABOUT ME?
DON'T YOU WANT TO PROTECT ME FOR ANY OTHER REASON?
MISS DINAH?

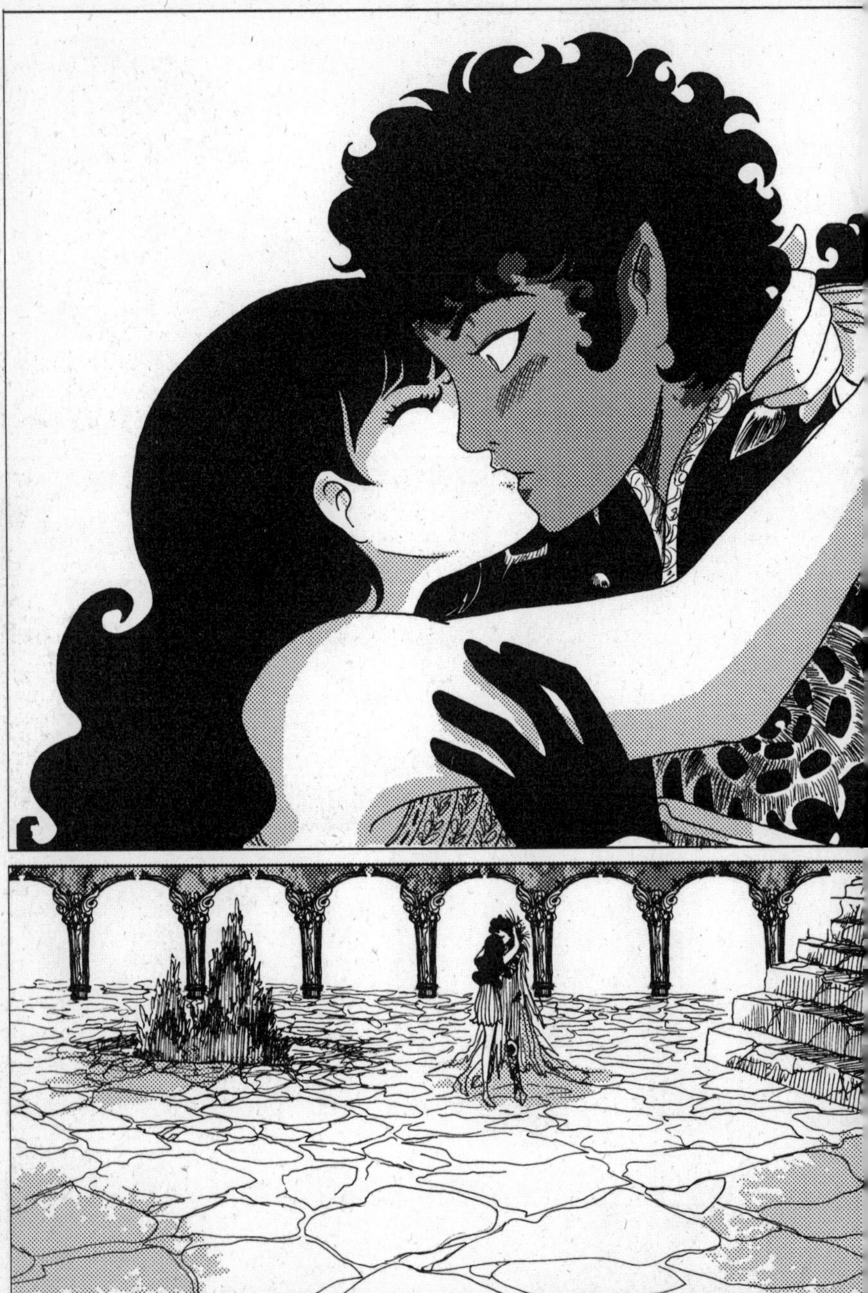

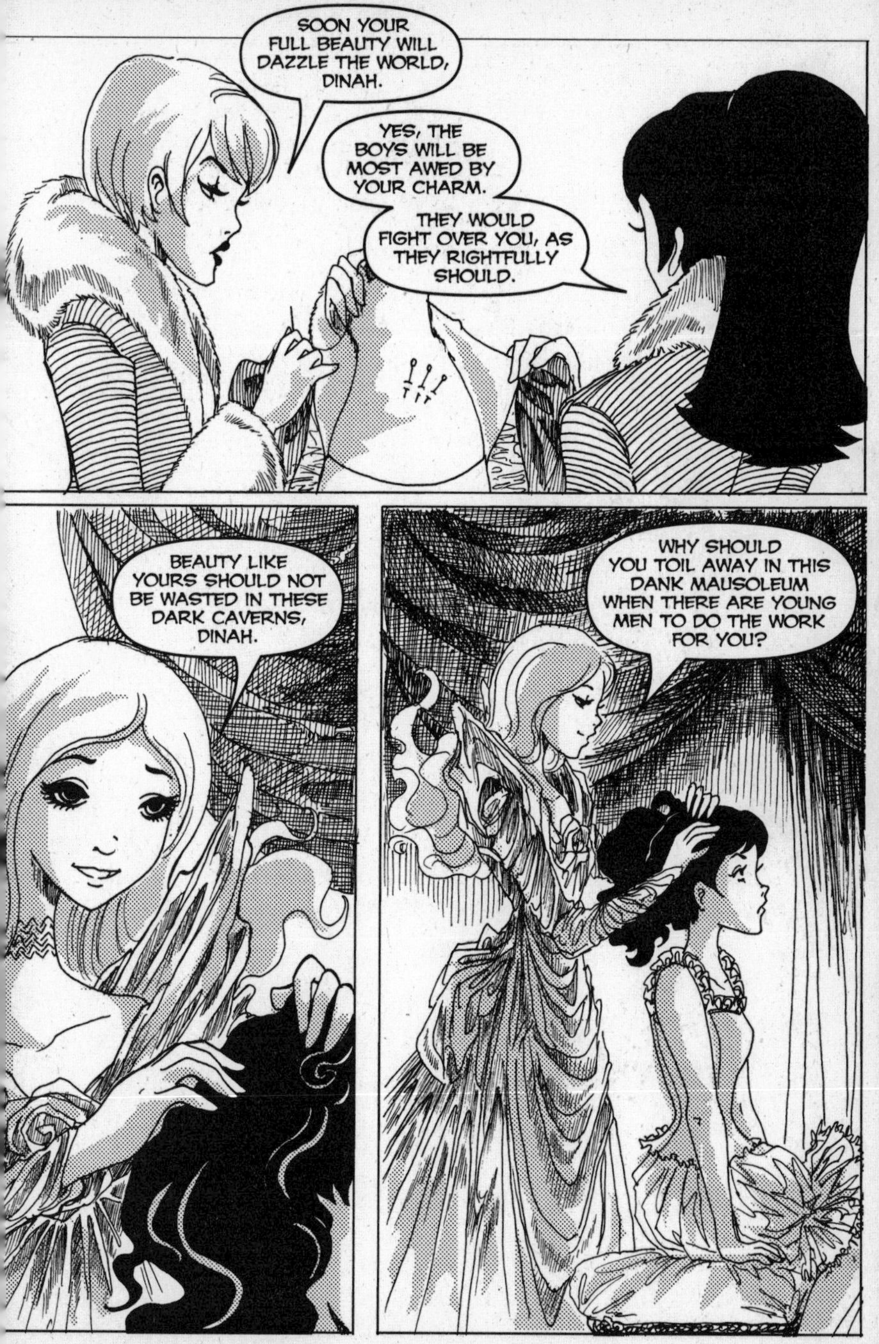
SOON YOUR FULL BEAUTY WILL DAZZLE THE WORLD, DINAH.
YES, THE BOYS WILL BE MOST AWED BY YOUR CHARM.
THEY WOULD FIGHT OVER YOU, AS THEY RIGHTFULLY SHOULD.
BEAUTY LIKE YOURS SHOULD NOT BE WASTED IN THESE DARK CAVERNS, DINAH.
WHY SHOULD YOU TOIL AWAY IN THIS DANK MAUSOLEUM WHEN THERE ARE YOUNG MEN TO DO THE WORK FOR YOU?

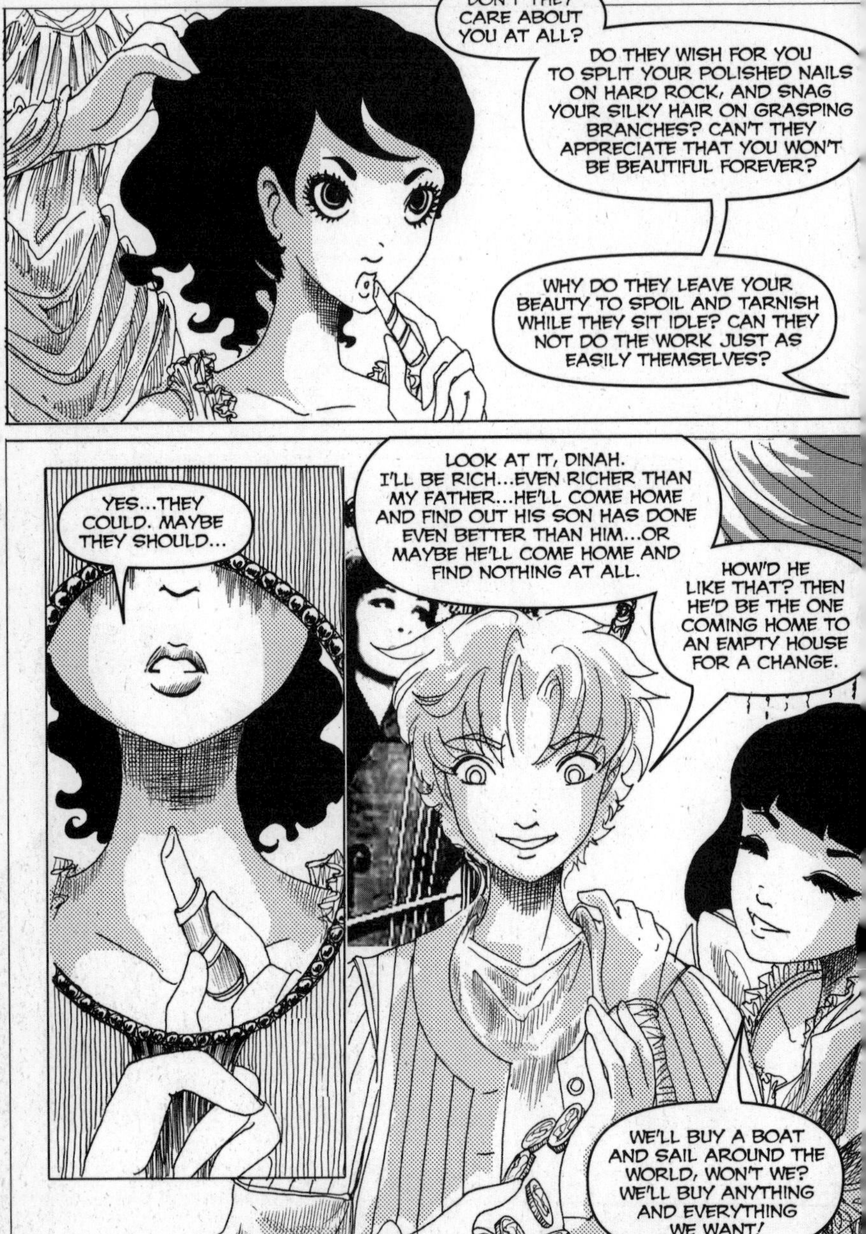
DON'T THEY CARE ABOUT YOU AT ALL?
DO THEY WISH FOR YOU TO SPLIT YOUR POLISHED NAILS ON HARD ROCK, AND SNAG YOUR SILKY HAIR ON GRASPING BRANCHES? CAN'T THEY APPRECIATE THAT YOU WON'T BE BEAUTIFUL FOREVER?
WHY DO THEY LEAVE YOUR BEAUTY TO SPOIL AND TARNISH WHILE THEY SIT IDLE? CAN THEY NOT DO THE WORK JUST AS EASILY THEMSELVES?
YES...THEY COULD. MAYBE THEY SHOULD...
LOOK AT IT, DINAH. I'LL BE RICH...EVEN RICHER THAN MY FATHER...HE'LL COME HOME AND FIND OUT HIS SON HAS DONE EVEN BETTER THAN HIM...OR MAYBE HE'LL COME HOME AND FIND NOTHING AT ALL.
HOW'D HE LIKE THAT? THEN HE'D BE THE ONE COMING HOME TO AN EMPTY HOUSE FOR A CHANGE.
WE'LL BUY A BOAT AND SAIL AROUND THE WORLD, WON'T WE? WE'LL BUY ANYTHING AND EVERYTHING WE WANT!

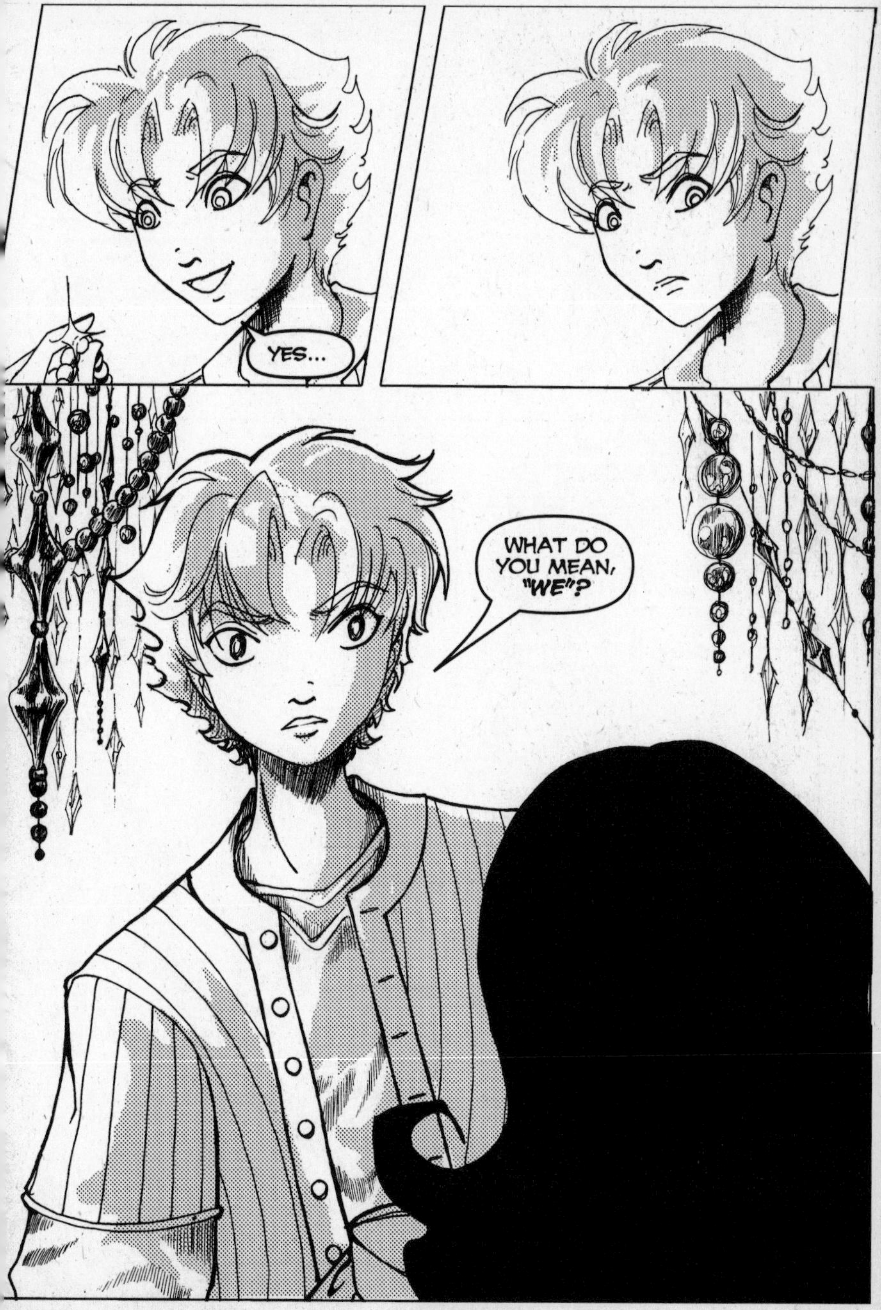
YES...
WHAT DO YOU MEAN, "WE"?

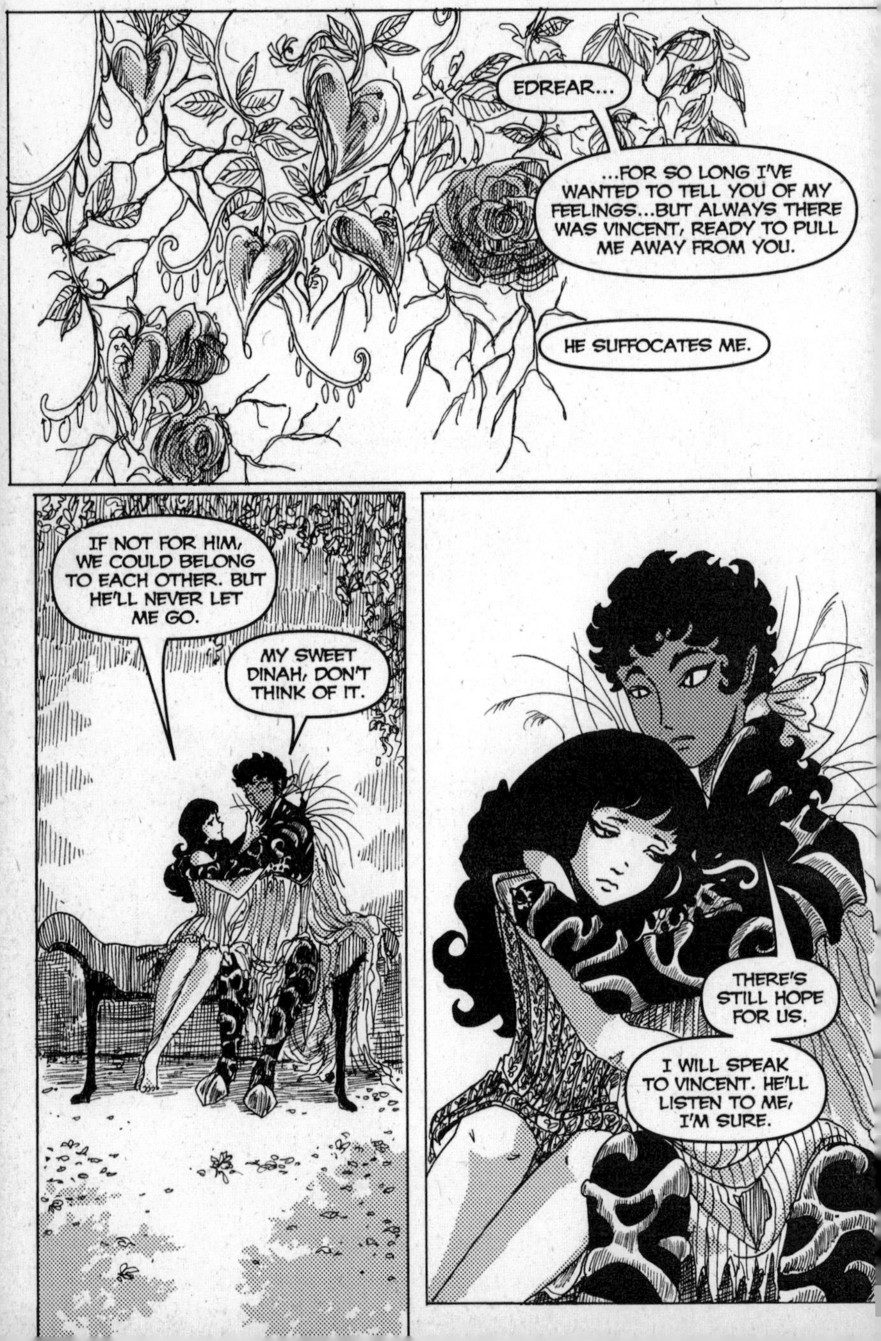
EDREAR...
...FOR SO LONG I'VE WANTED TO TELL YOU OF MY FEELINGS...BUT ALWAYS THERE WAS VINCENT, READY TO PULL ME AWAY FROM YOU.
HE SUFFOCATES ME.
IF NOT FOR HIM, WE COULD BELONG TO EACH OTHER. BUT HE'LL NEVER LET ME GO.
MY SWEET DINAH, DON'T THINK OF IT.
THERE'S STILL HOPE FOR US.
I WILL SPEAK TO VINCENT. HE'LL LISTEN TO ME, I'M SURE.

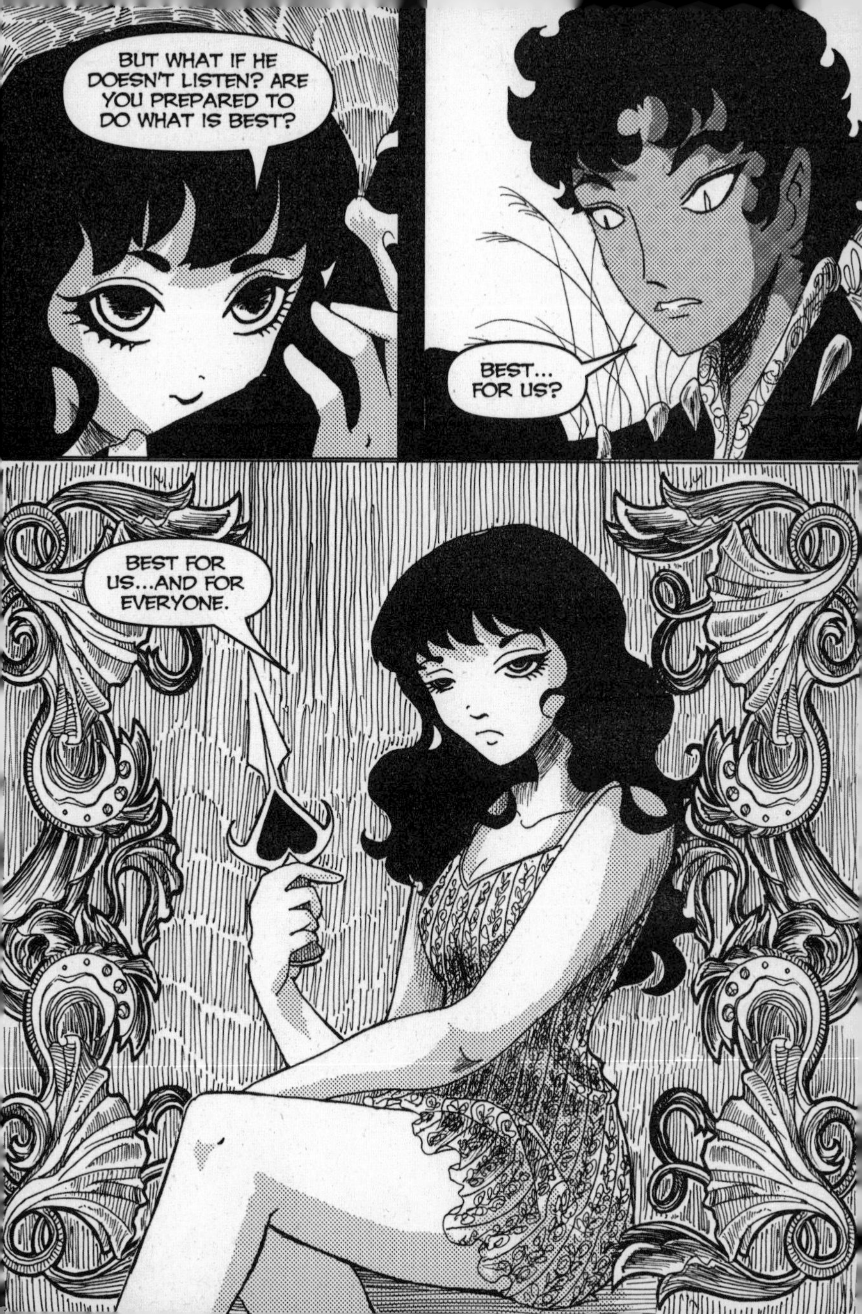
BUT WHAT IF HE DOESN'T LISTEN? ARE YOU PREPARED TO DO WHAT IS BEST?
BEST... FOR US?
BEST FOR US...AND FOR EVERYONE.

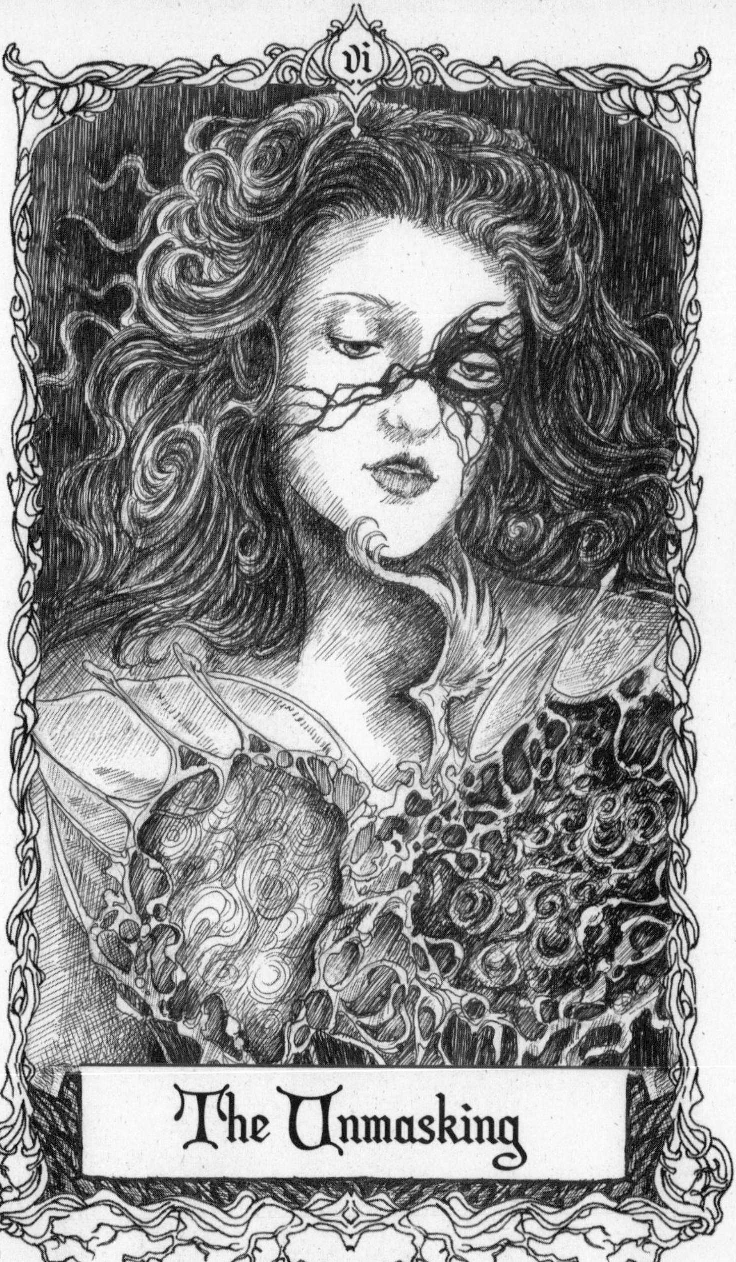
vi
The Unmasking

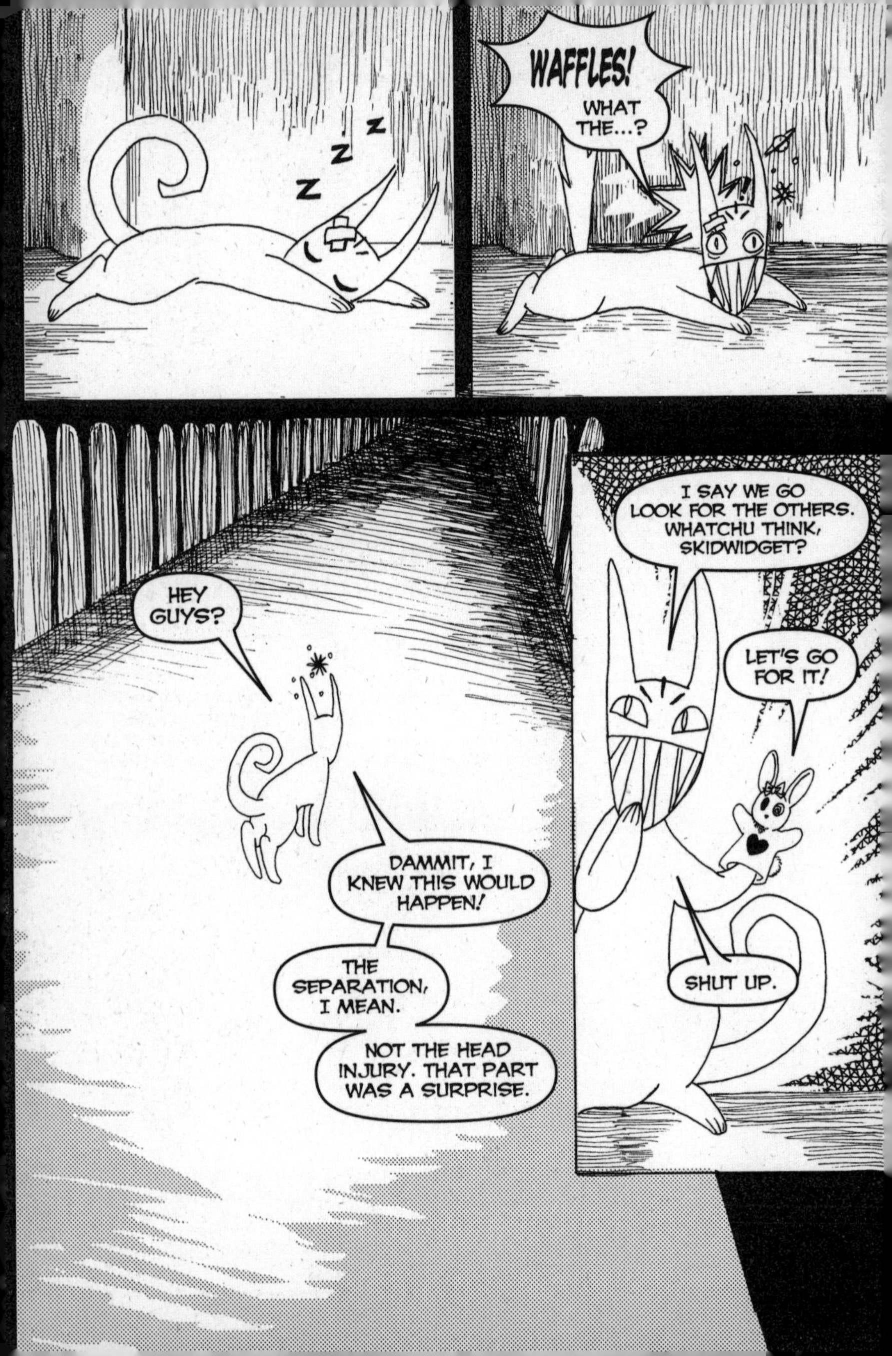
Z Z Z
WAFFLES!
WHAT THE...?
HEY GUYS?
DAMMIT, I KNEW THIS WOULD HAPPEN!
THE SEPARATION, I MEAN.
NOT THE HEAD INJURY. THAT PART WAS A SURPRISE.
I SAY WE GO LOOK FOR THE OTHERS. WHATCHU THINK, SKIDWIDGET?
LET'S GO FOR IT!
SHUT UP.

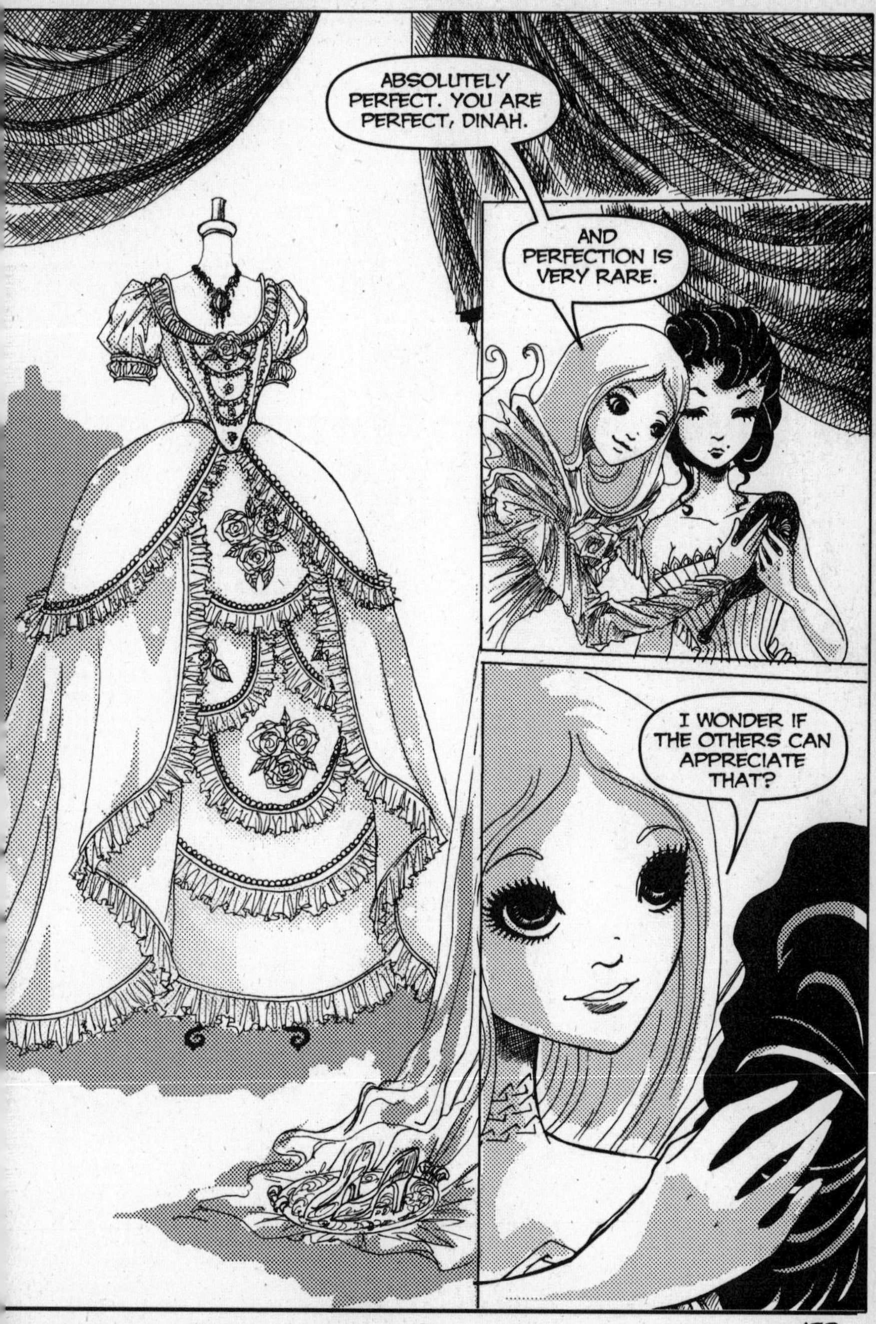
ABSOLUTELY PERFECT. YOU ARE PERFECT, DINAH.
AND PERFECTION IS VERY RARE.
I WONDER IF THE OTHERS CAN APPRECIATE THAT?

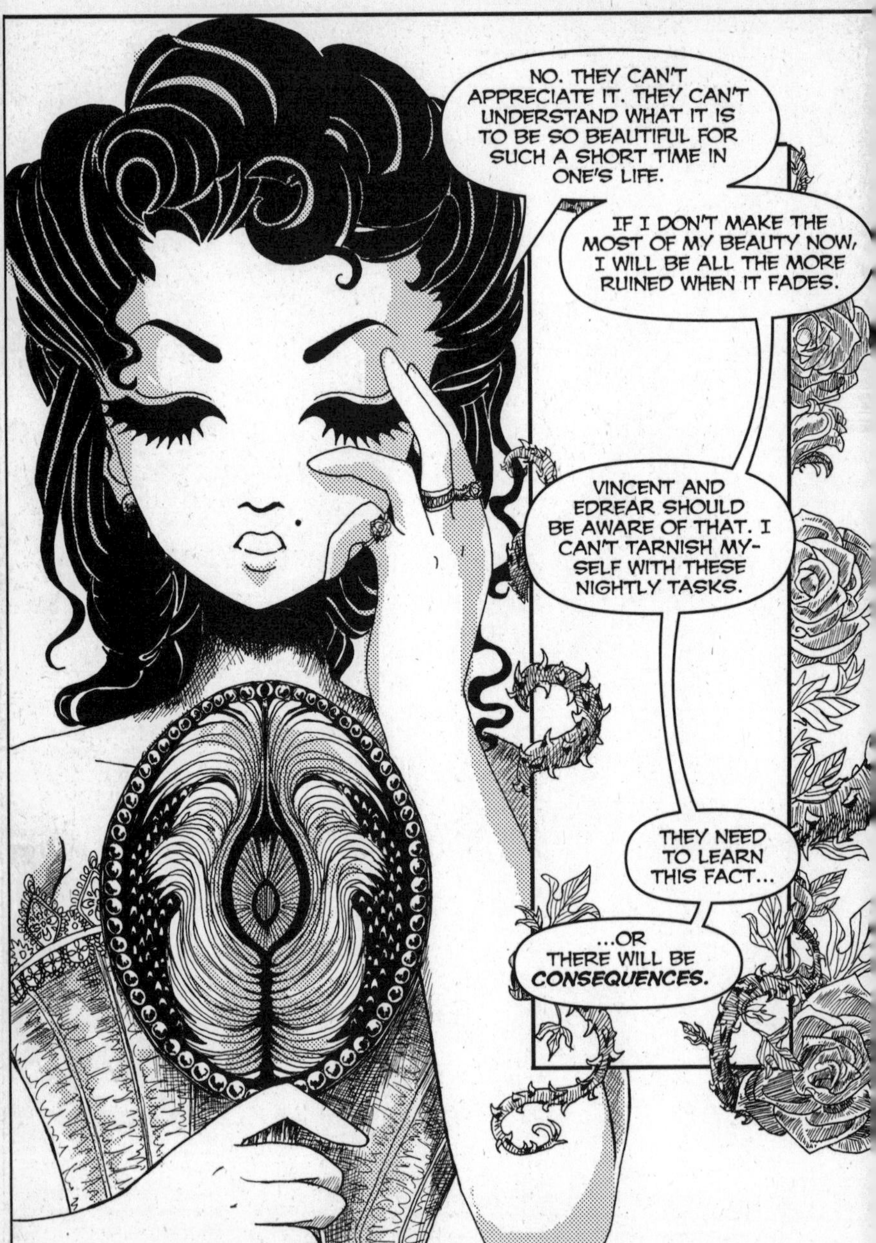
NO. THEY CAN'T APPRECIATE IT. THEY CAN'T UNDERSTAND WHAT IT IS TO BE SO BEAUTIFUL FOR SUCH A SHORT TIME IN ONE'S LIFE.
IF I DON'T MAKE THE MOST OF MY BEAUTY NOW, I WILL BE ALL THE MORE RUINED WHEN IT FADES.
VINCENT AND EDREAR SHOULD BE AWARE OF THAT. I CAN'T TARNISH MY-SELF WITH THESE NIGHTLY TASKS.
THEY NEED TO LEARN THIS FACT...
...OR THERE WILL BE *CONSEQUENCES.*

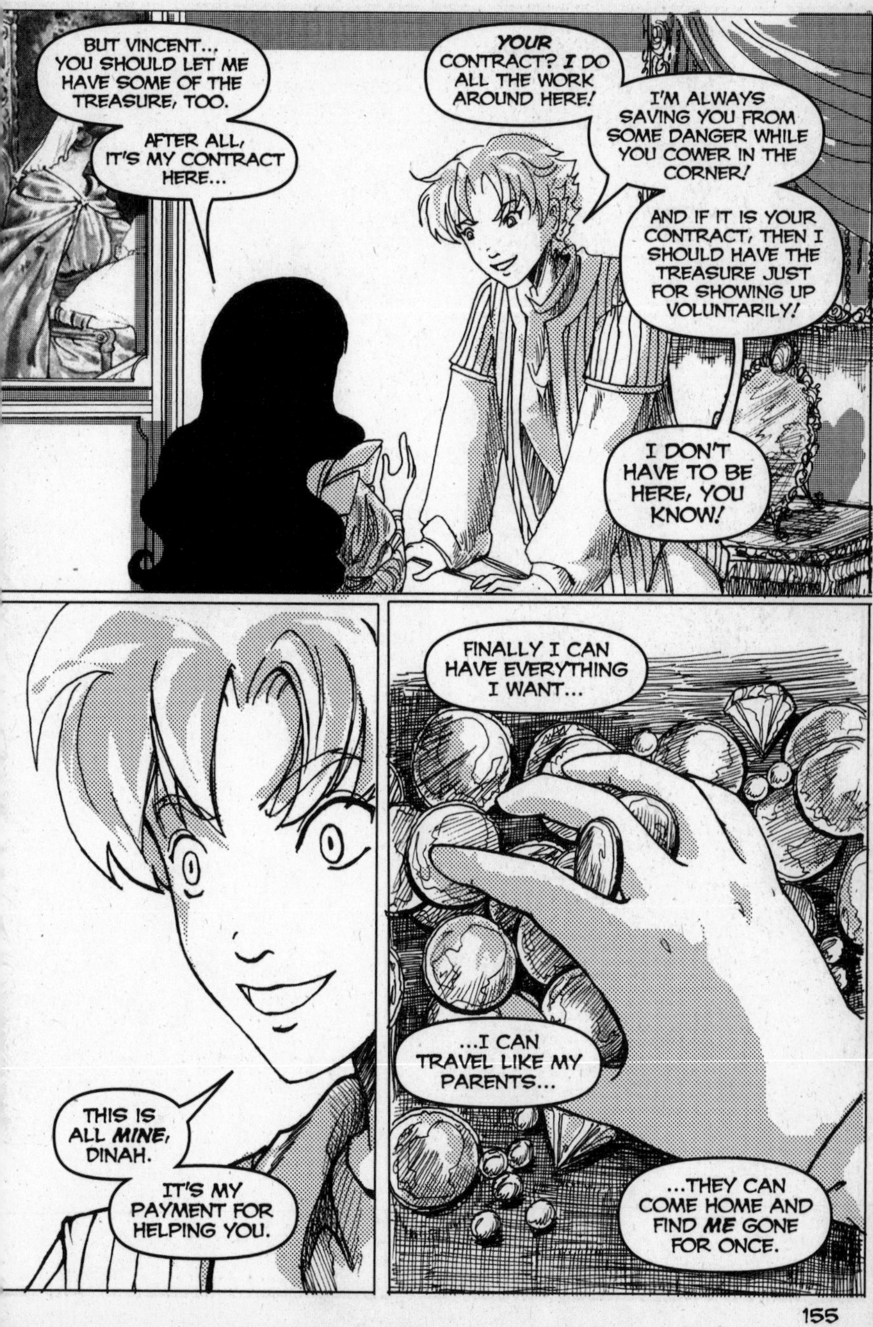
BUT VINCENT... YOU SHOULD LET ME HAVE SOME OF THE TREASURE, TOO.
AFTER ALL, IT'S MY CONTRACT HERE...
YOUR CONTRACT? *I* DO ALL THE WORK AROUND HERE!
I'M ALWAYS SAVING YOU FROM SOME DANGER WHILE YOU COWER IN THE CORNER!
AND IF IT IS YOUR CONTRACT, THEN I SHOULD HAVE THE TREASURE JUST FOR SHOWING UP VOLUNTARILY!
I DON'T HAVE TO BE HERE, YOU KNOW!
THIS IS ALL *MINE*, DINAH.
IT'S MY PAYMENT FOR HELPING YOU.
FINALLY I CAN HAVE EVERYTHING I WANT...
...I CAN TRAVEL LIKE MY PARENTS...
...THEY CAN COME HOME AND FIND *ME* GONE FOR ONCE.

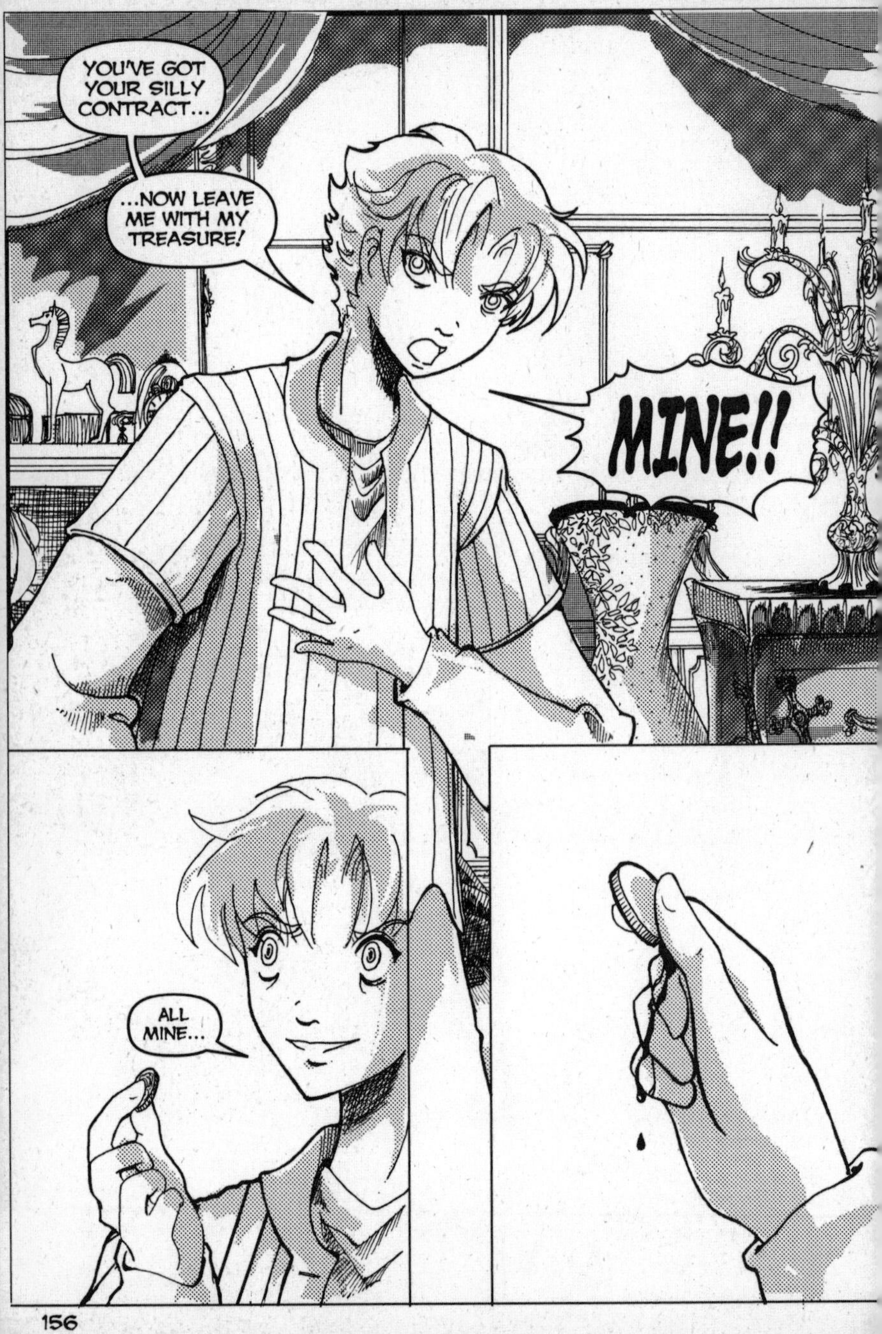
YOU'VE GOT YOUR SILLY CONTRACT...
...NOW LEAVE ME WITH MY TREASURE!
MINE!!
ALL MINE...

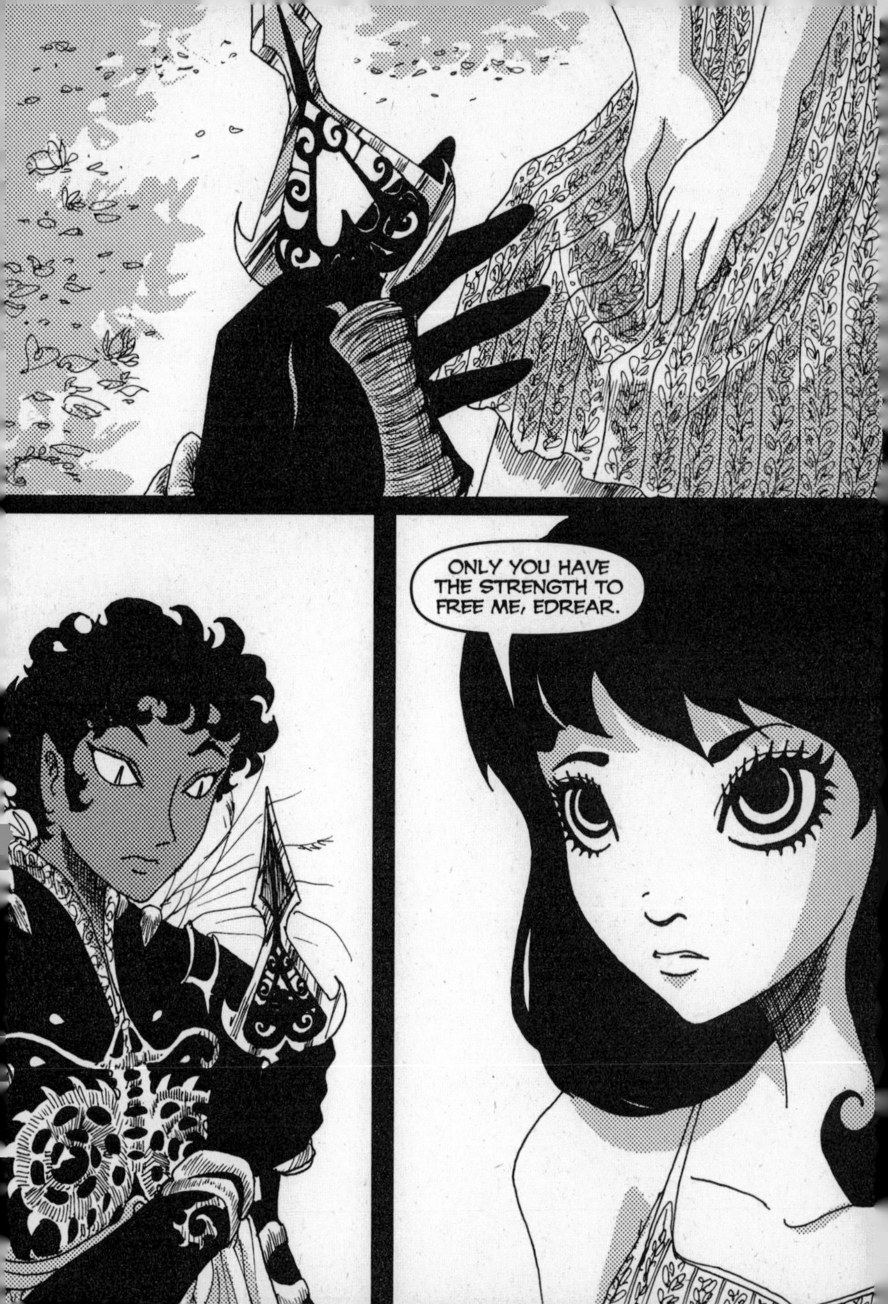
ONLY YOU HAVE THE STRENGTH TO FREE ME, EDREAR.

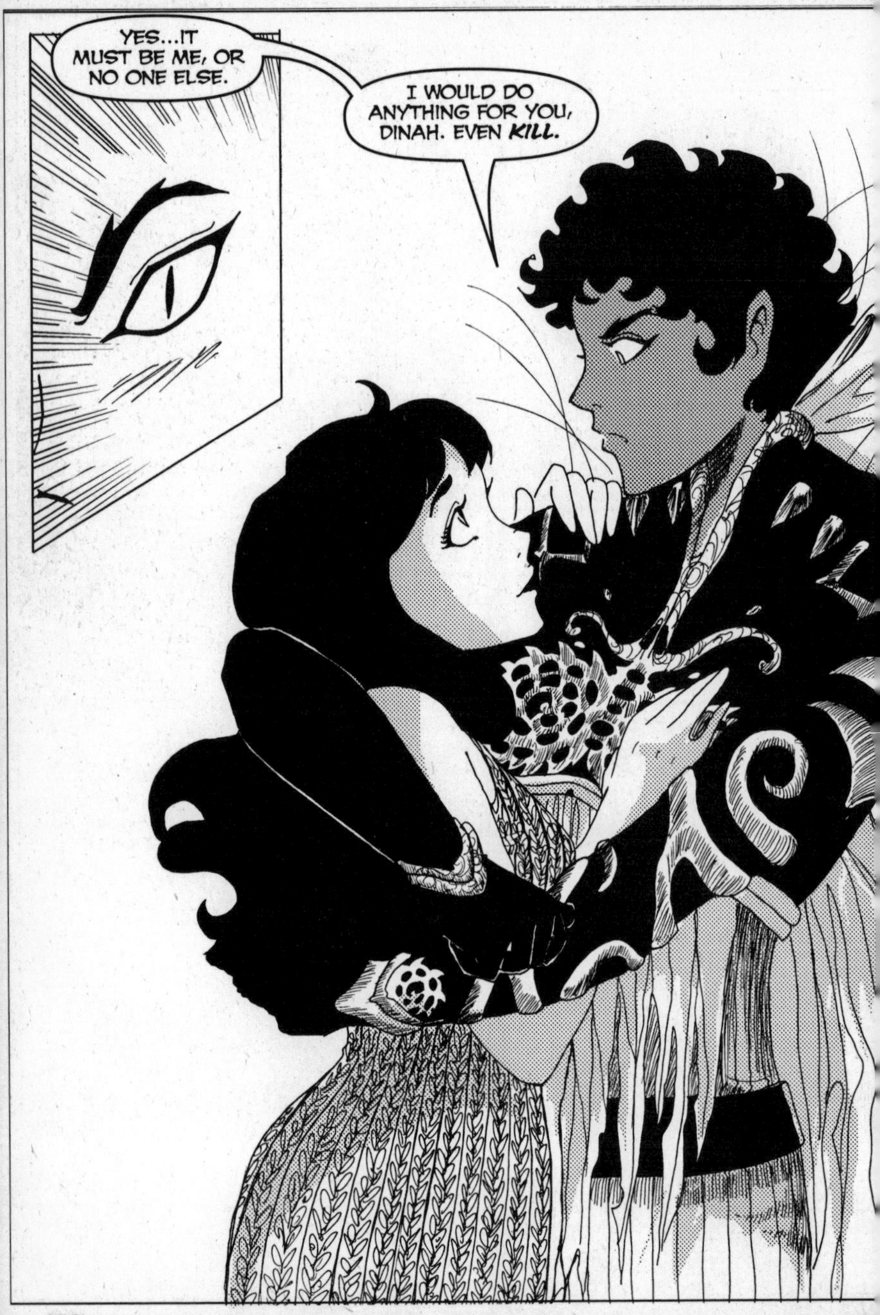
YES...IT MUST BE ME, OR NO ONE ELSE.
I WOULD DO ANYTHING FOR YOU, DINAH. EVEN KILL.

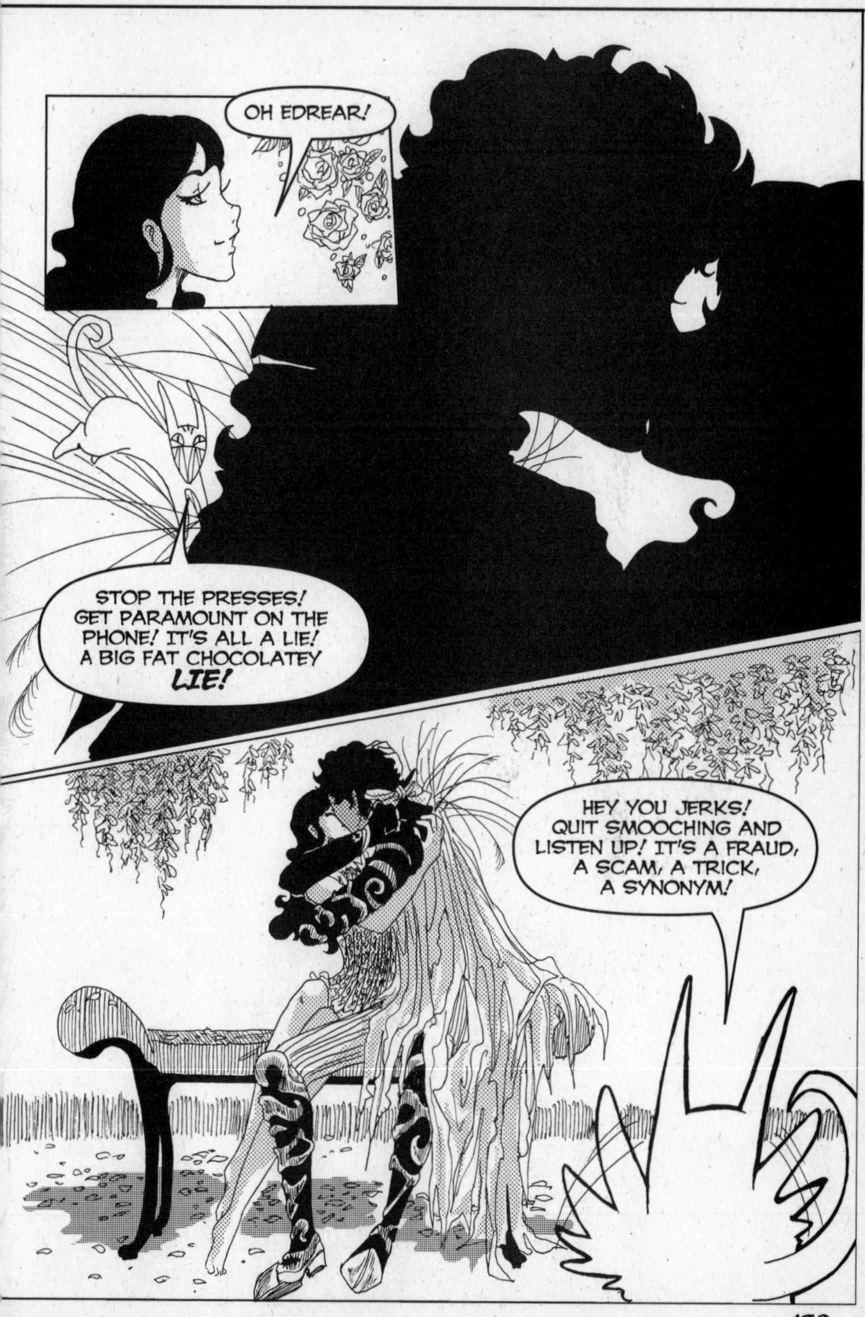
OH EDREAR!
STOP THE PRESSES! GET PARAMOUNT ON THE PHONE! IT'S ALL A LIE! A BIG FAT CHOCOLATEY LIE!
HEY YOU JERKS! QUIT SMOOCHING AND LISTEN UP! IT'S A FRAUD, A SCAM, A TRICK, A SYNONYM!

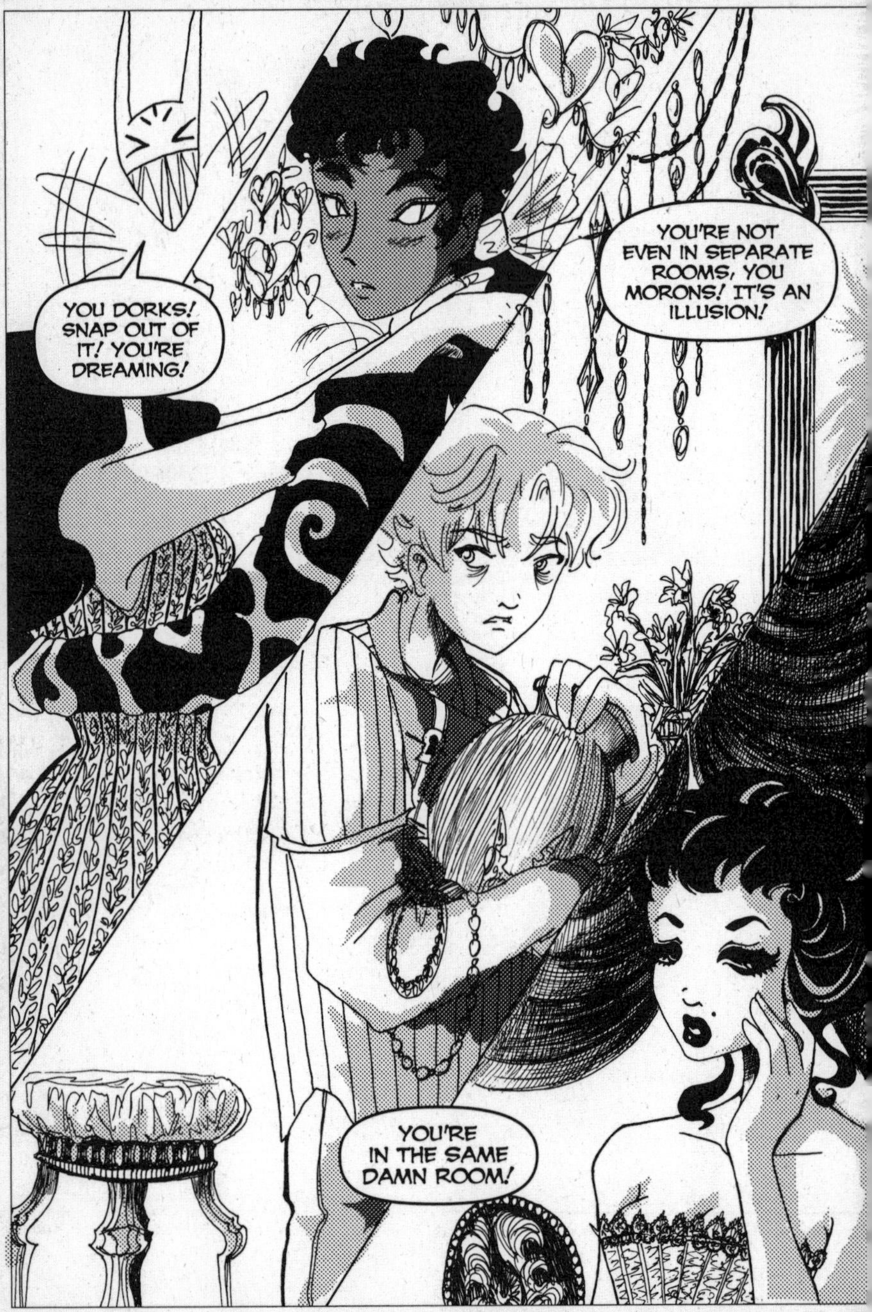
YOU DORKS! SNAP OUT OF IT! YOU'RE DREAMING!
YOU'RE NOT EVEN IN SEPARATE ROOMS, YOU MORONS! IT'S AN ILLUSION!
YOU'RE IN THE SAME DAMN ROOM!

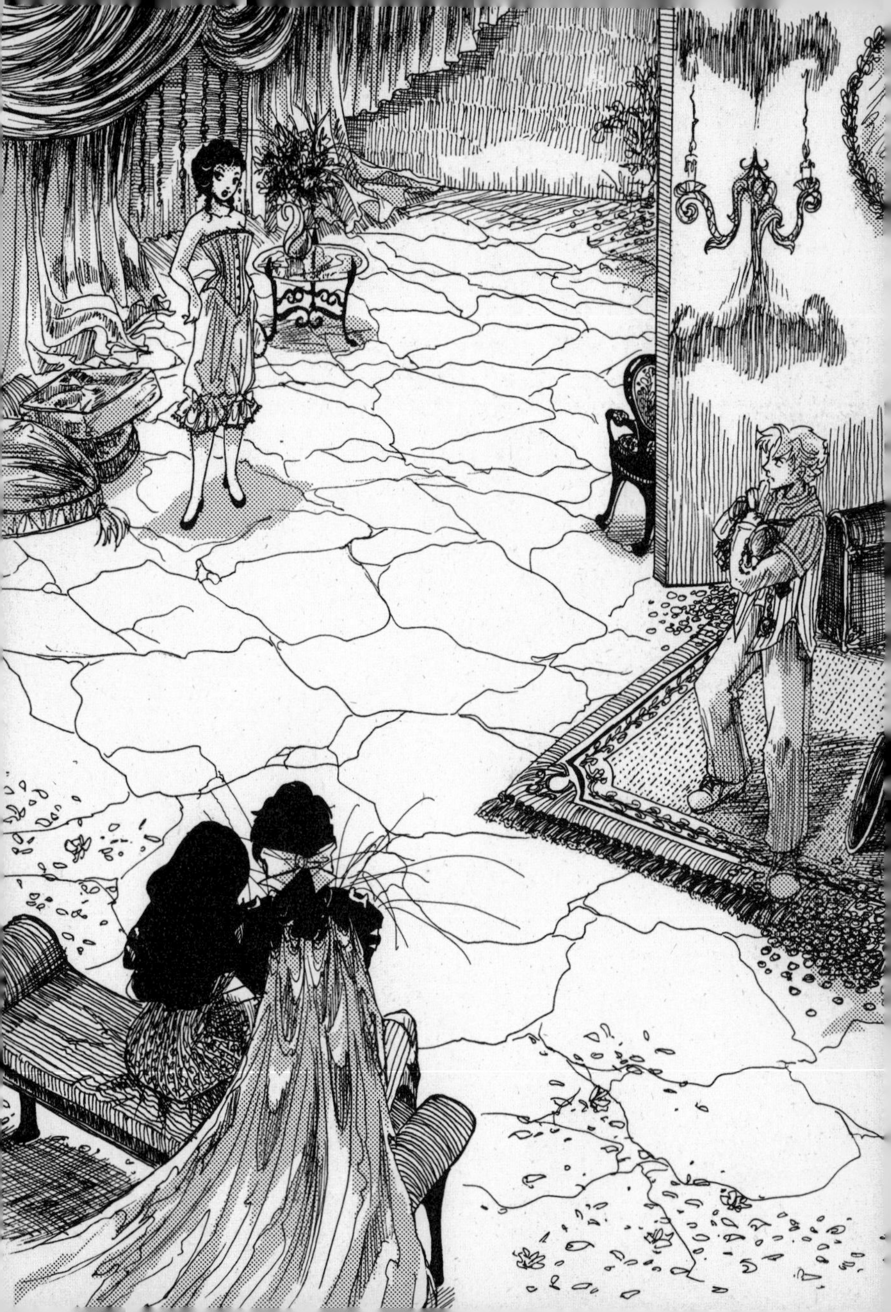

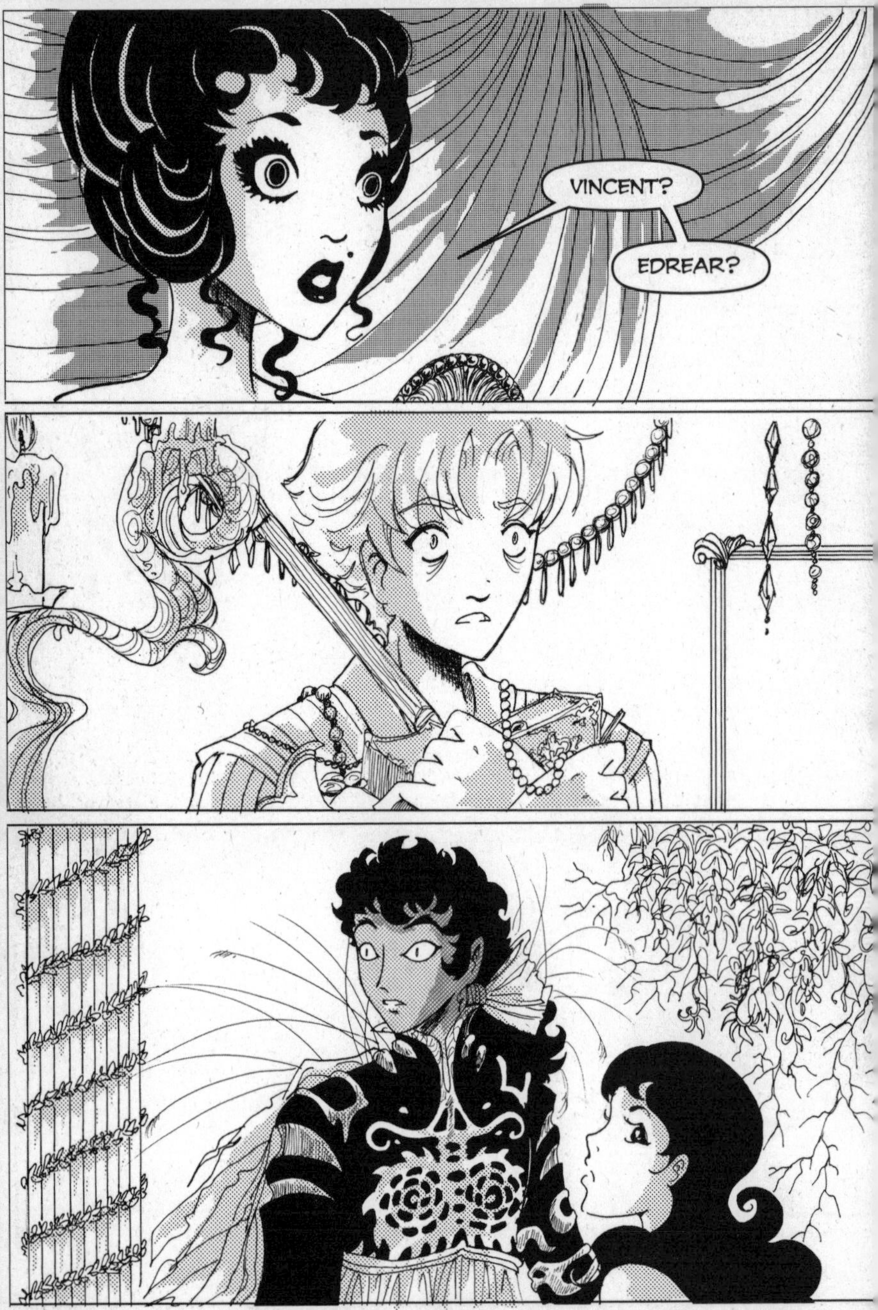
VINCENT?
EDREAR?

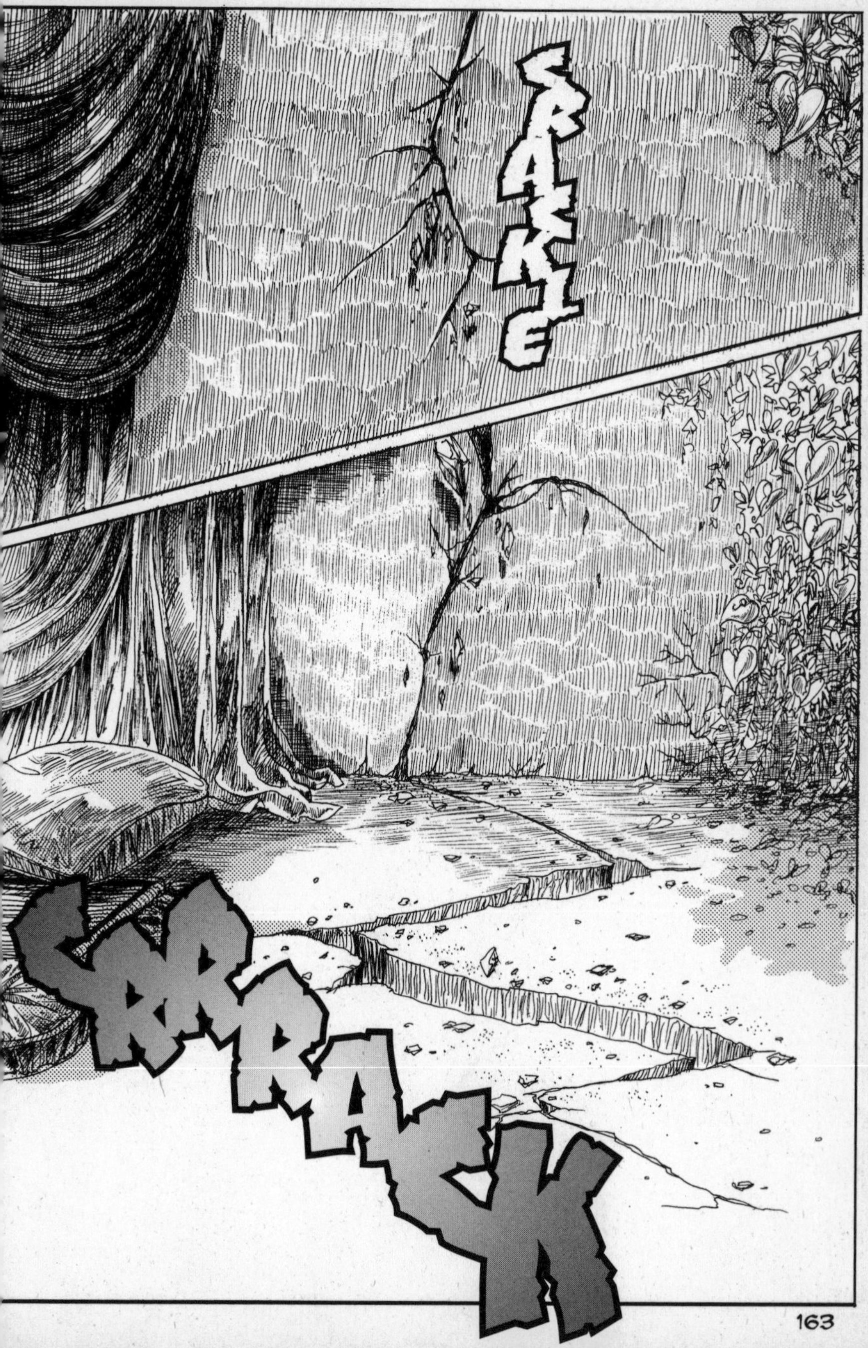
CRACKLE
KRRACK

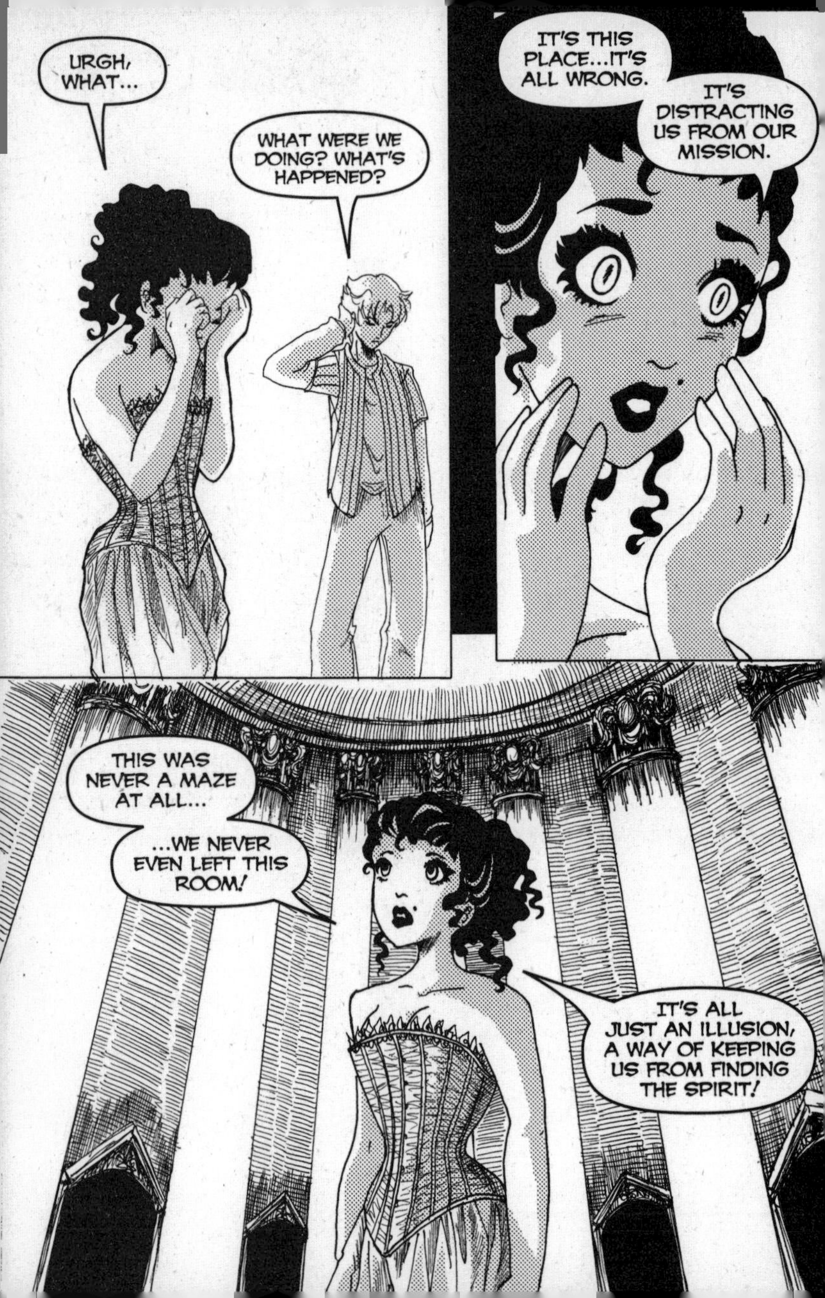
URGH, WHAT...
WHAT WERE WE DOING? WHAT'S HAPPENED?
IT'S THIS PLACE...IT'S ALL WRONG.
IT'S DISTRACTING US FROM OUR MISSION.
THIS WAS NEVER A MAZE AT ALL...
...WE NEVER EVEN LEFT THIS ROOM!
IT'S ALL JUST AN ILLUSION, A WAY OF KEEPING US FROM FINDING THE SPIRIT!

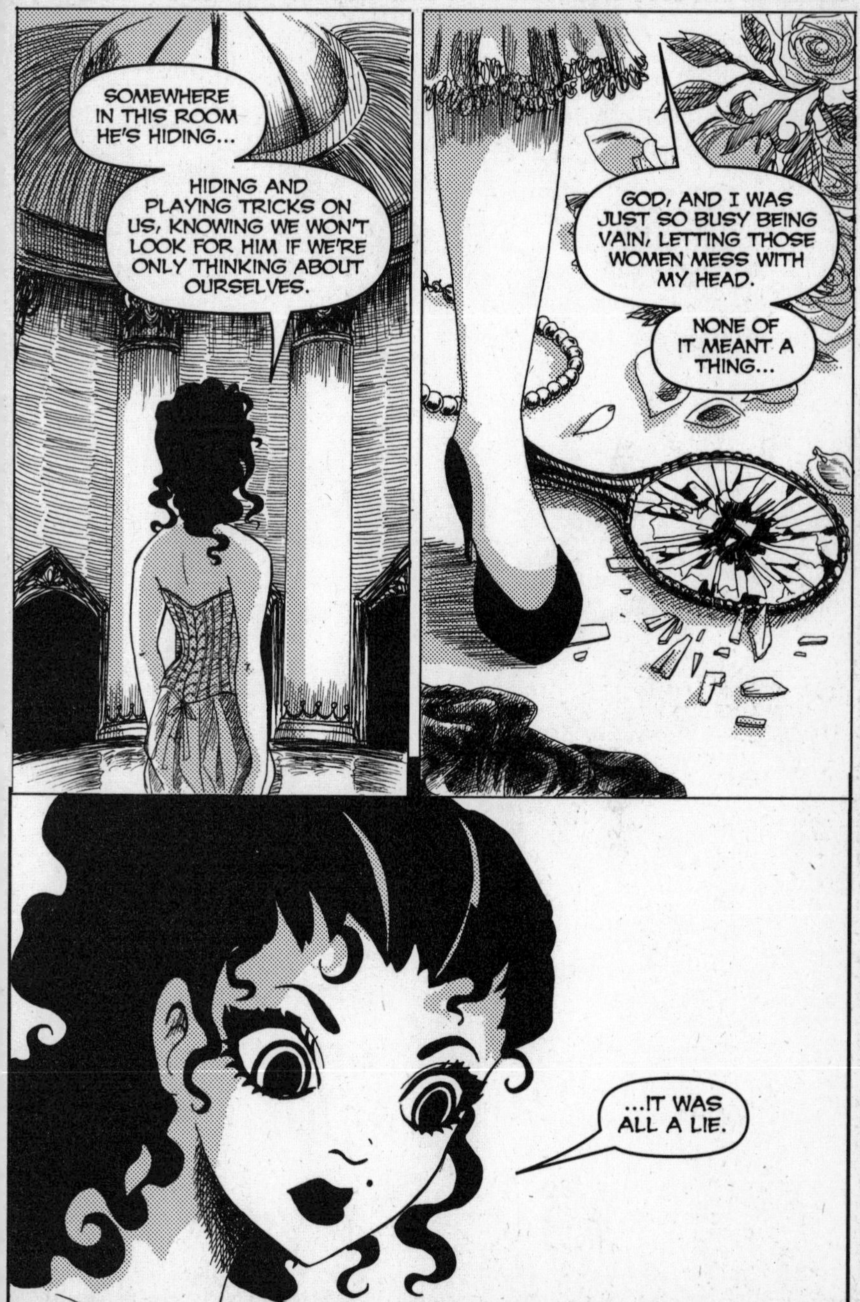
SOMEWHERE IN THIS ROOM HE'S HIDING...
HIDING AND PLAYING TRICKS ON US, KNOWING WE WON'T LOOK FOR HIM IF WE'RE ONLY THINKING ABOUT OURSELVES.
GOD, AND I WAS JUST SO BUSY BEING VAIN, LETTING THOSE WOMEN MESS WITH MY HEAD.
NONE OF IT MEANT A THING...
...IT WAS ALL A LIE.

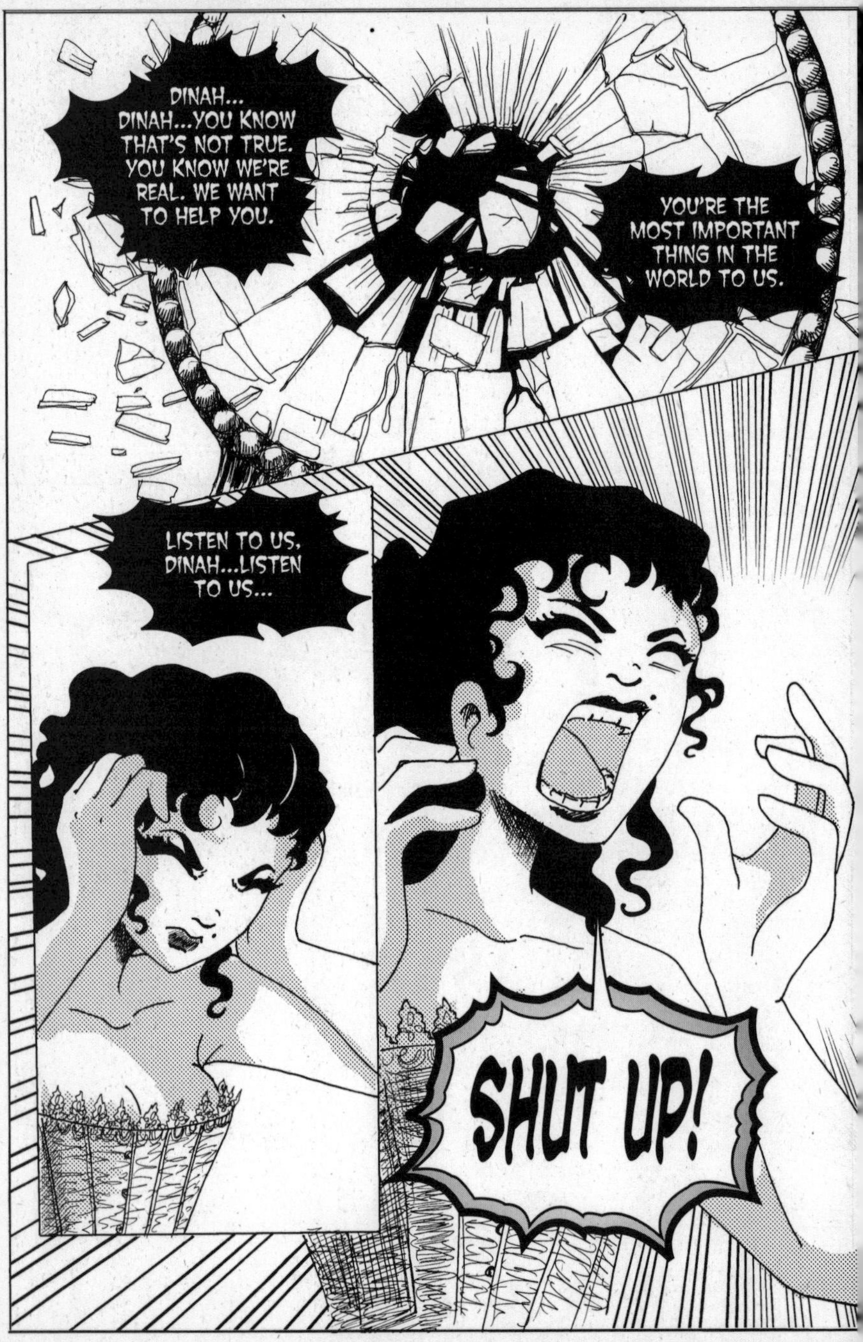
DINAH... DINAH...YOU KNOW THAT'S NOT TRUE. YOU KNOW WE'RE REAL. WE WANT TO HELP YOU.
YOU'RE THE MOST IMPORTANT THING IN THE WORLD TO US.
LISTEN TO US, DINAH...LISTEN TO US...
SHUT UP!

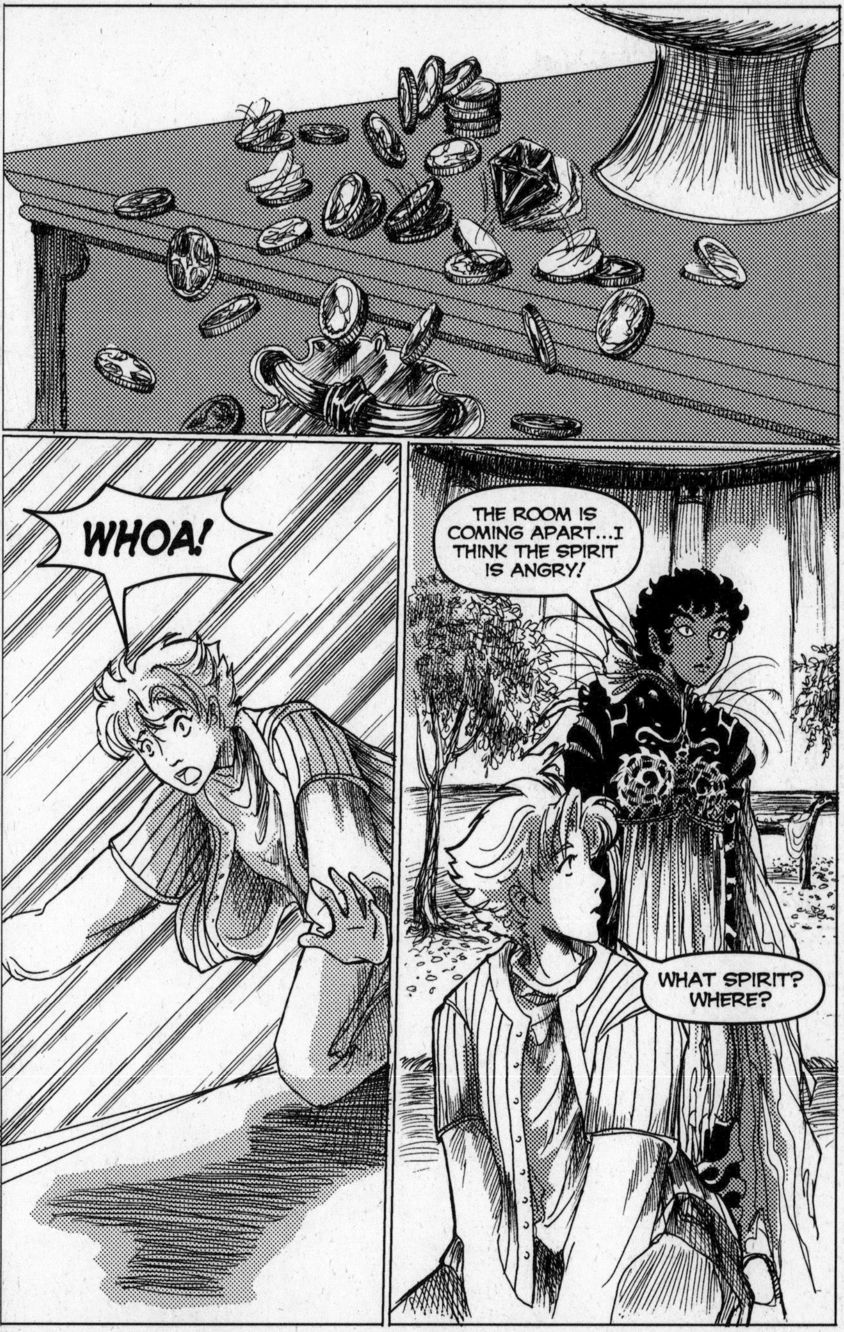
WHOA!
THE ROOM IS COMING APART...I THINK THE SPIRIT IS ANGRY!
WHAT SPIRIT? WHERE?

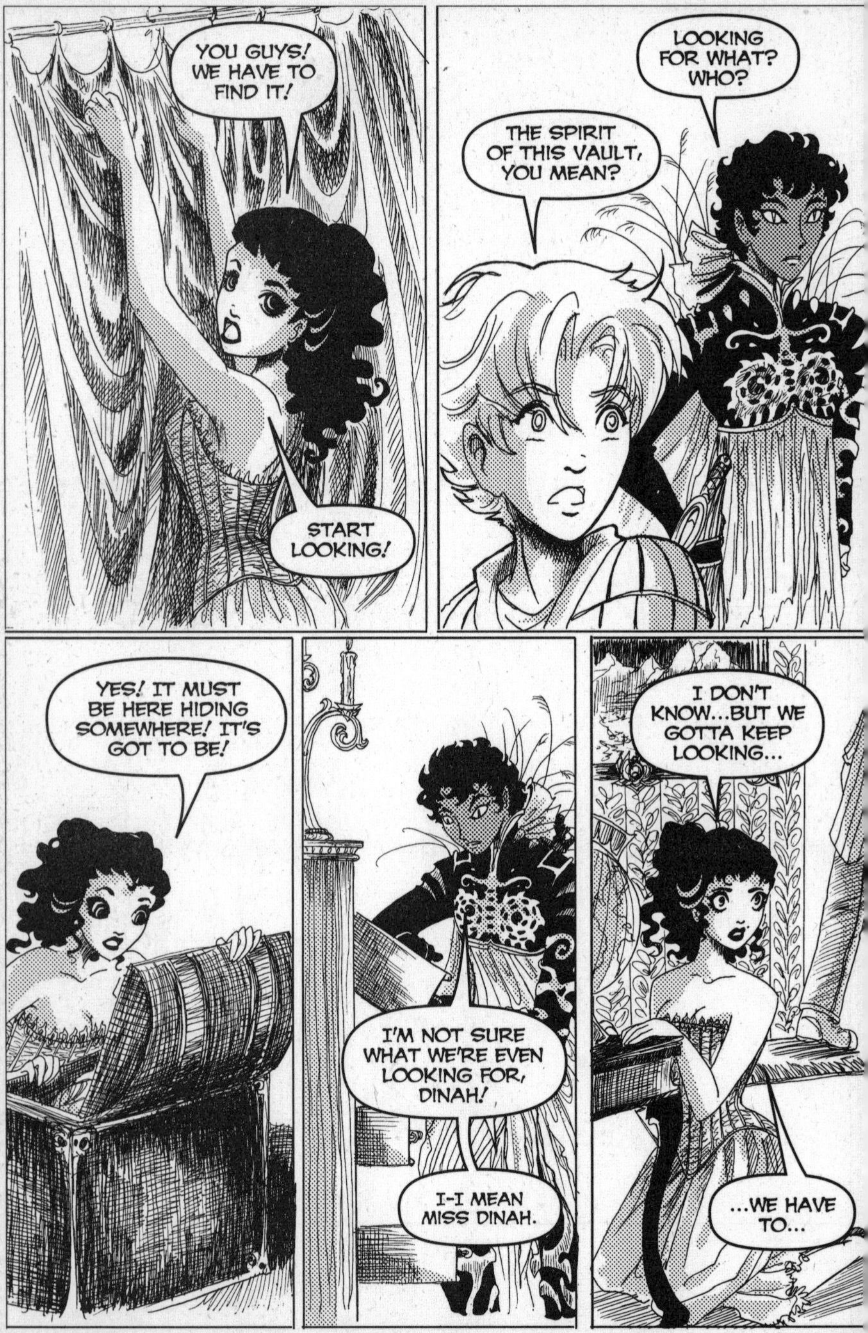
YOU GUYS! WE HAVE TO FIND IT!
START LOOKING!
LOOKING FOR WHAT? WHO?
THE SPIRIT OF THIS VAULT, YOU MEAN?
YES! IT MUST BE HERE HIDING SOMEWHERE! IT'S GOT TO BE!
I'M NOT SURE WHAT WE'RE EVEN LOOKING FOR, DINAH!
I-I MEAN MISS DINAH.
I DON'T KNOW...BUT WE GOTTA KEEP LOOKING...
...WE HAVE TO...

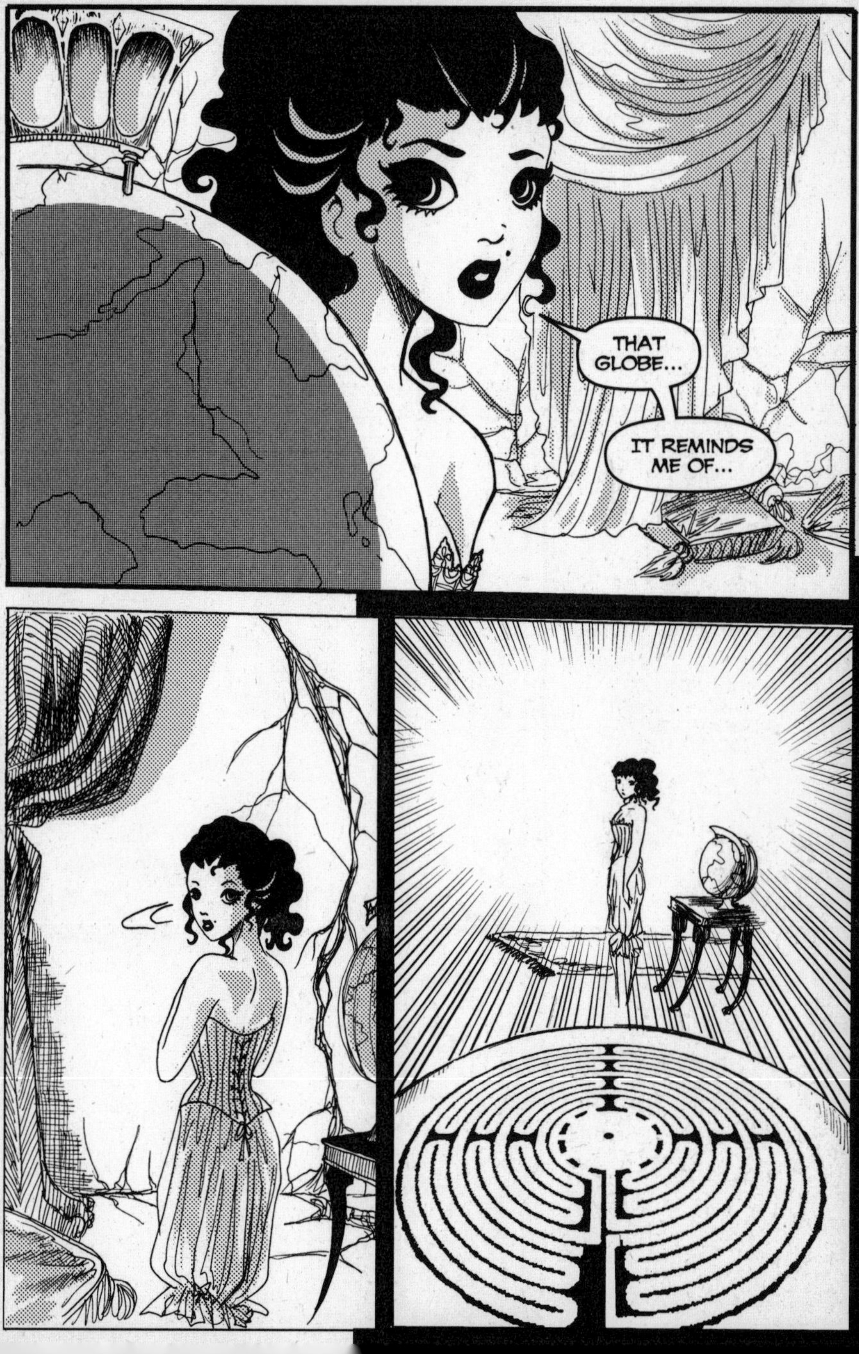
THAT GLOBE...
IT REMINDS ME OF...

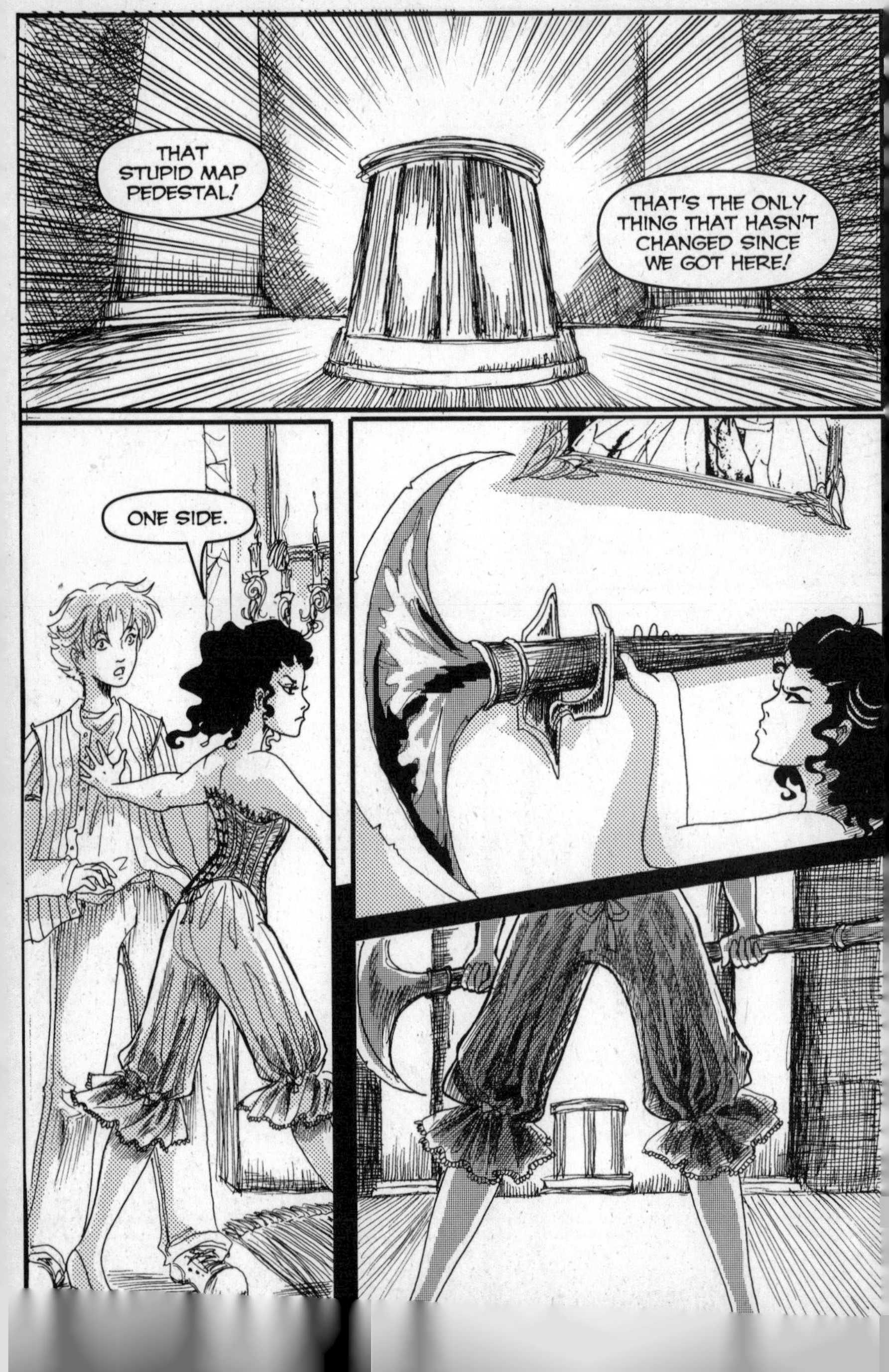
THAT STUPID MAP PEDESTAL!
THAT'S THE ONLY THING THAT HASN'T CHANGED SINCE WE GOT HERE!
ONE SIDE.

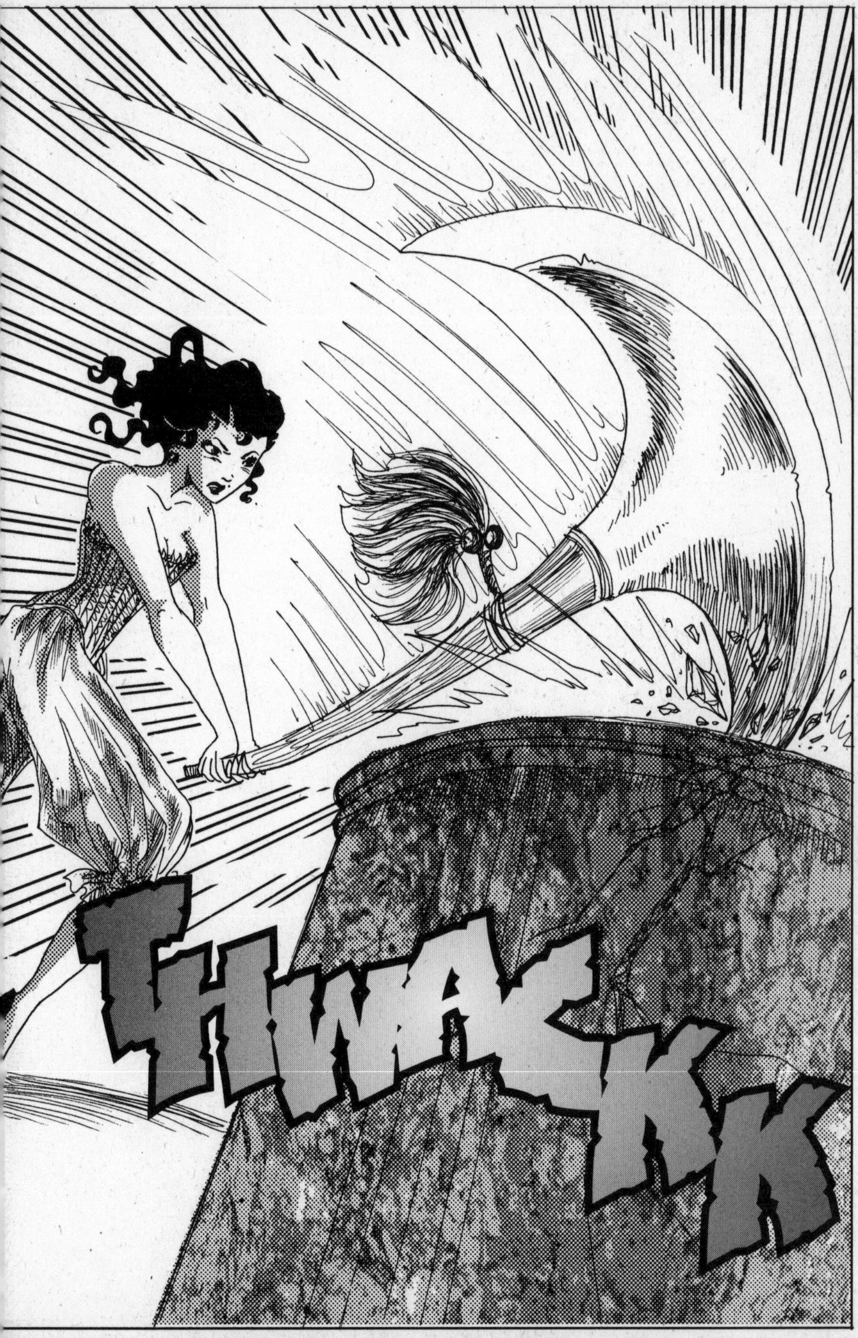
THWACKK

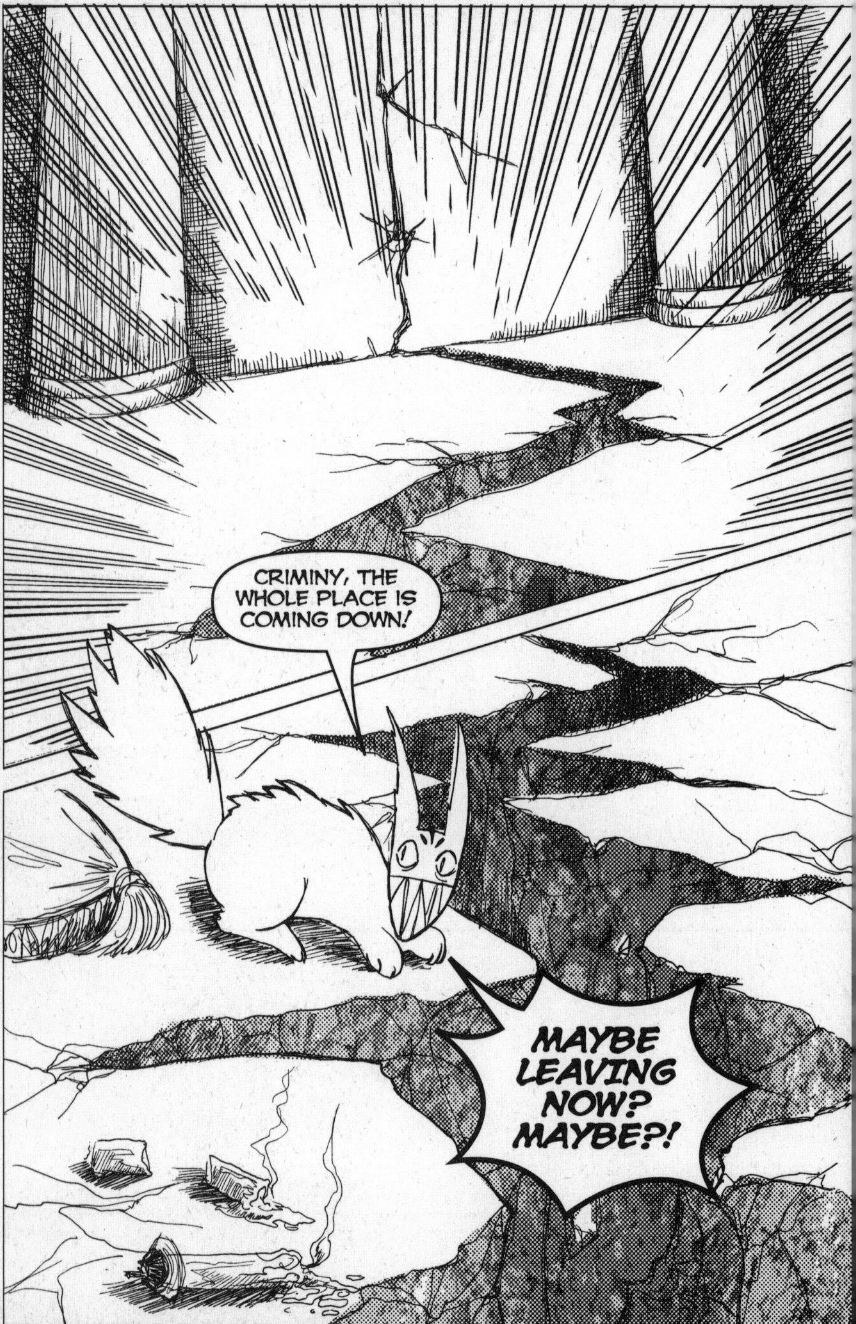
CRIMINY, THE WHOLE PLACE IS COMING DOWN!
MAYBE LEAVING NOW? MAYBE?!

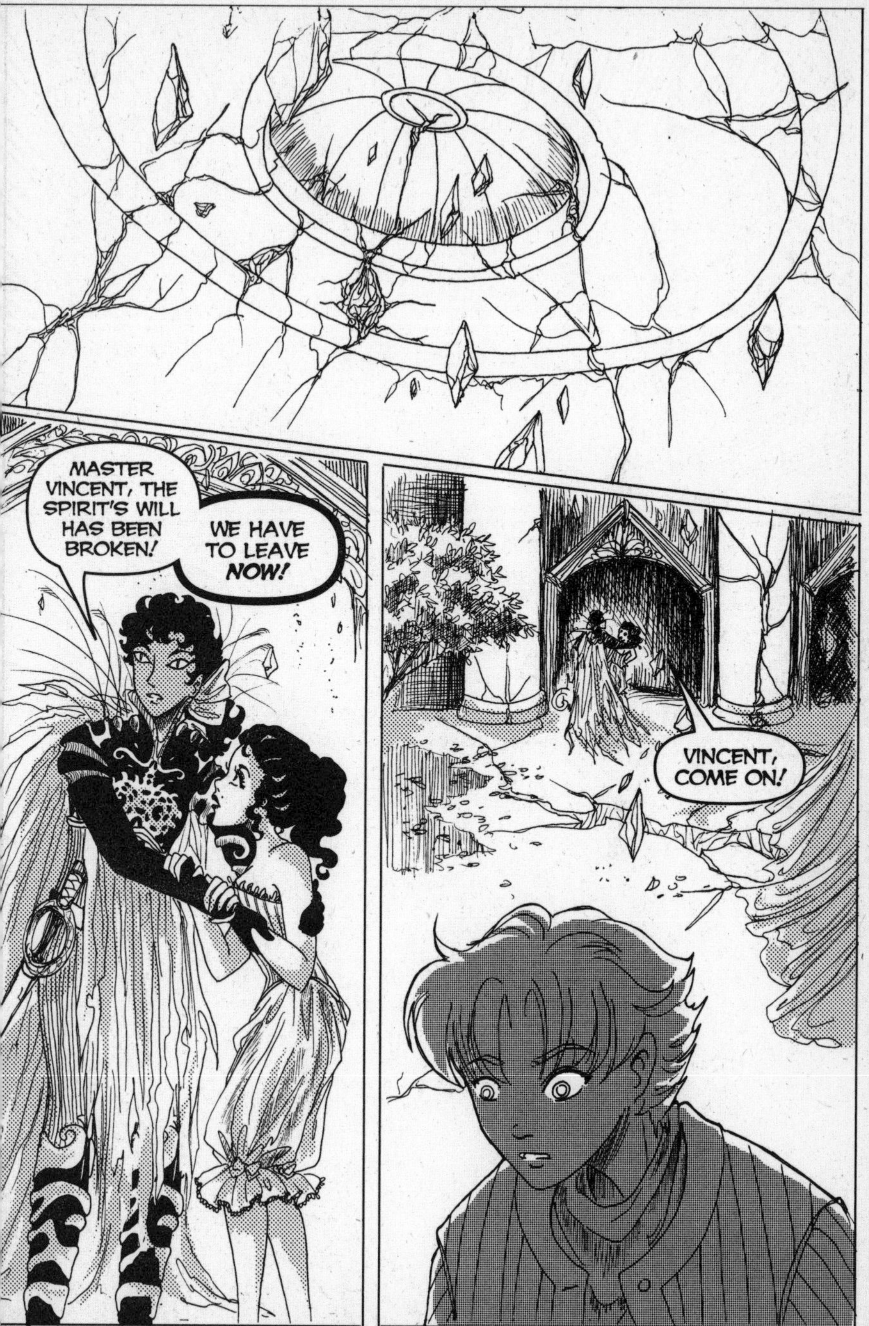
MASTER VINCENT, THE SPIRIT'S WILL HAS BEEN BROKEN!
WE HAVE TO LEAVE *NOW!*
VINCENT, COME ON!

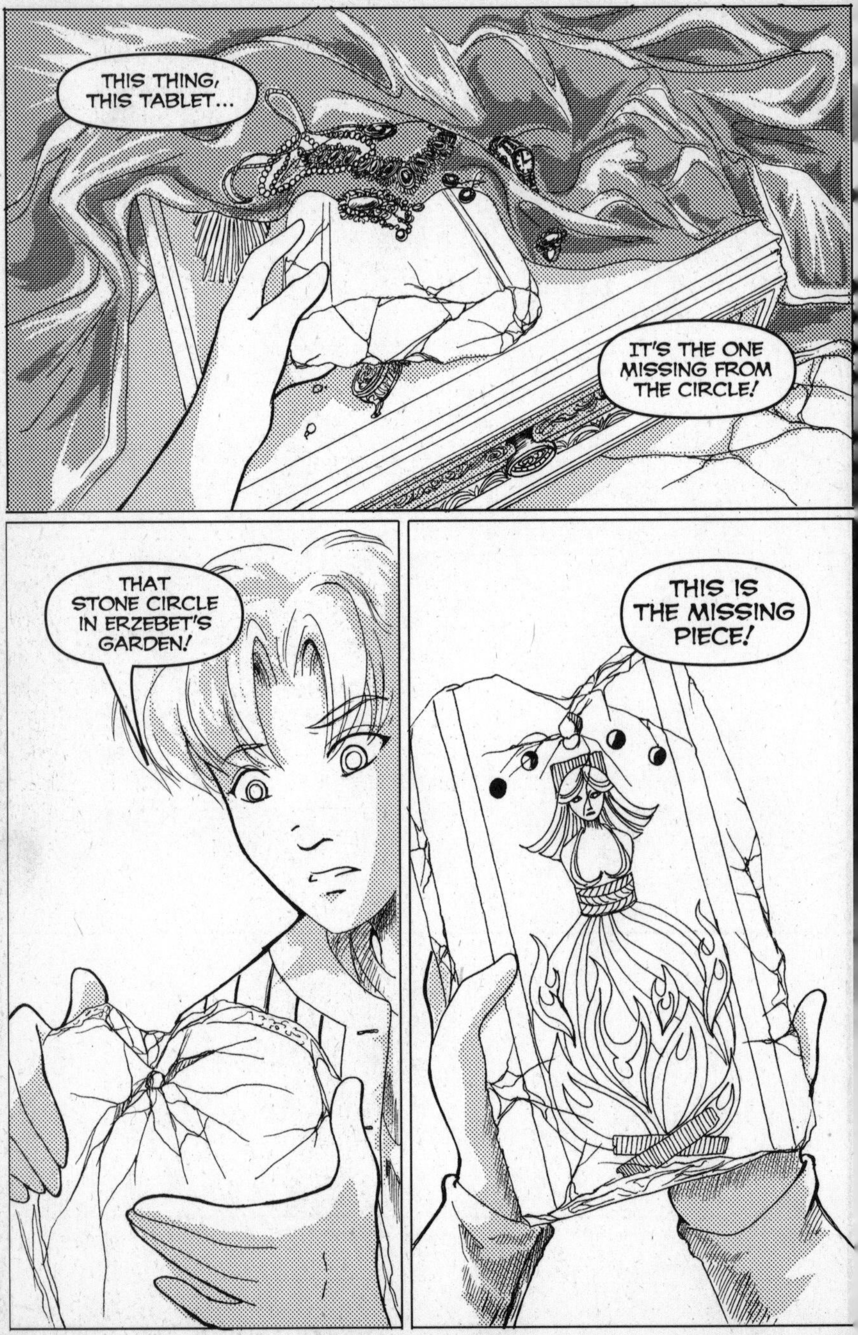
THIS THING, THIS TABLET...
IT'S THE ONE MISSING FROM THE CIRCLE!
THAT STONE CIRCLE IN ERZEBET'S GARDEN!
THIS IS THE MISSING PIECE!

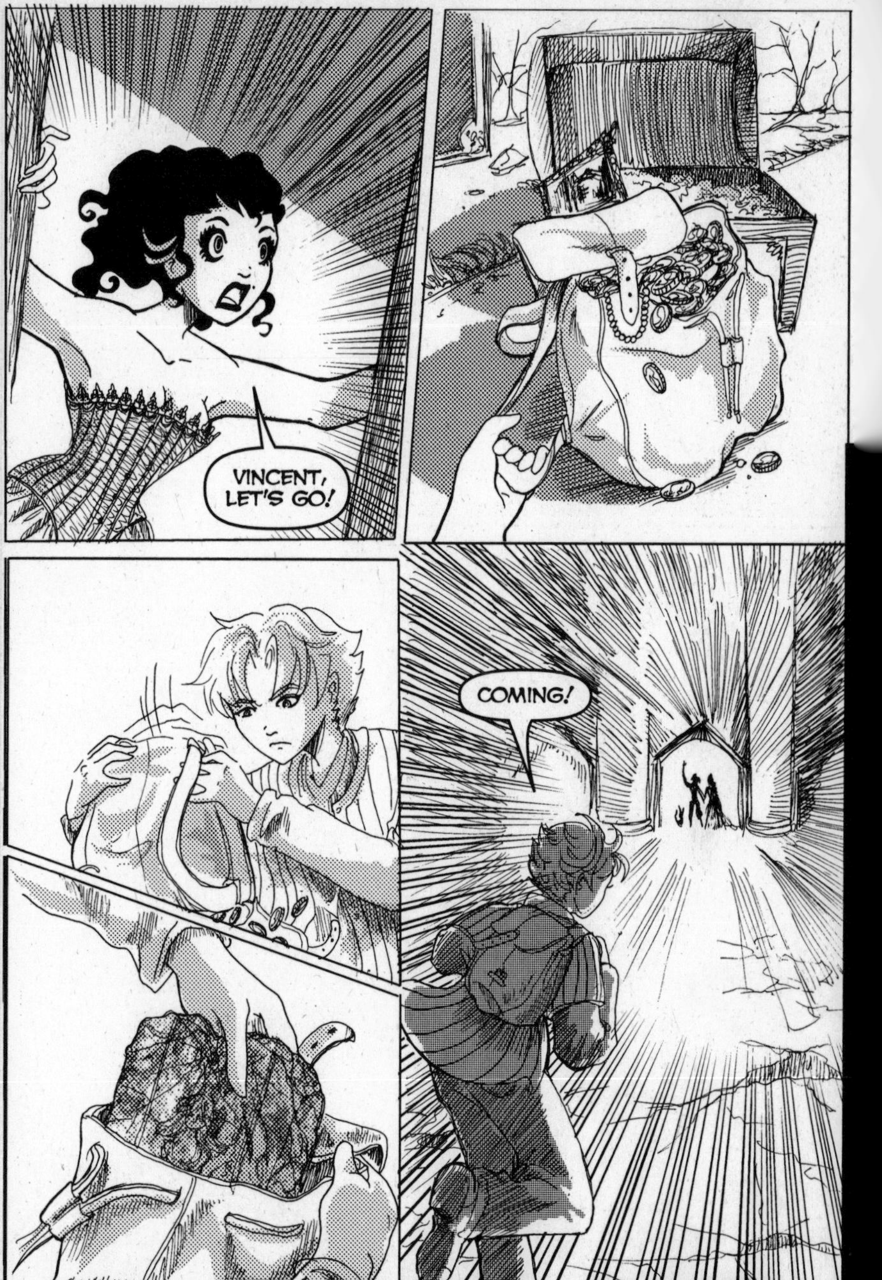
VINCENT, LET'S GO!
COMING!

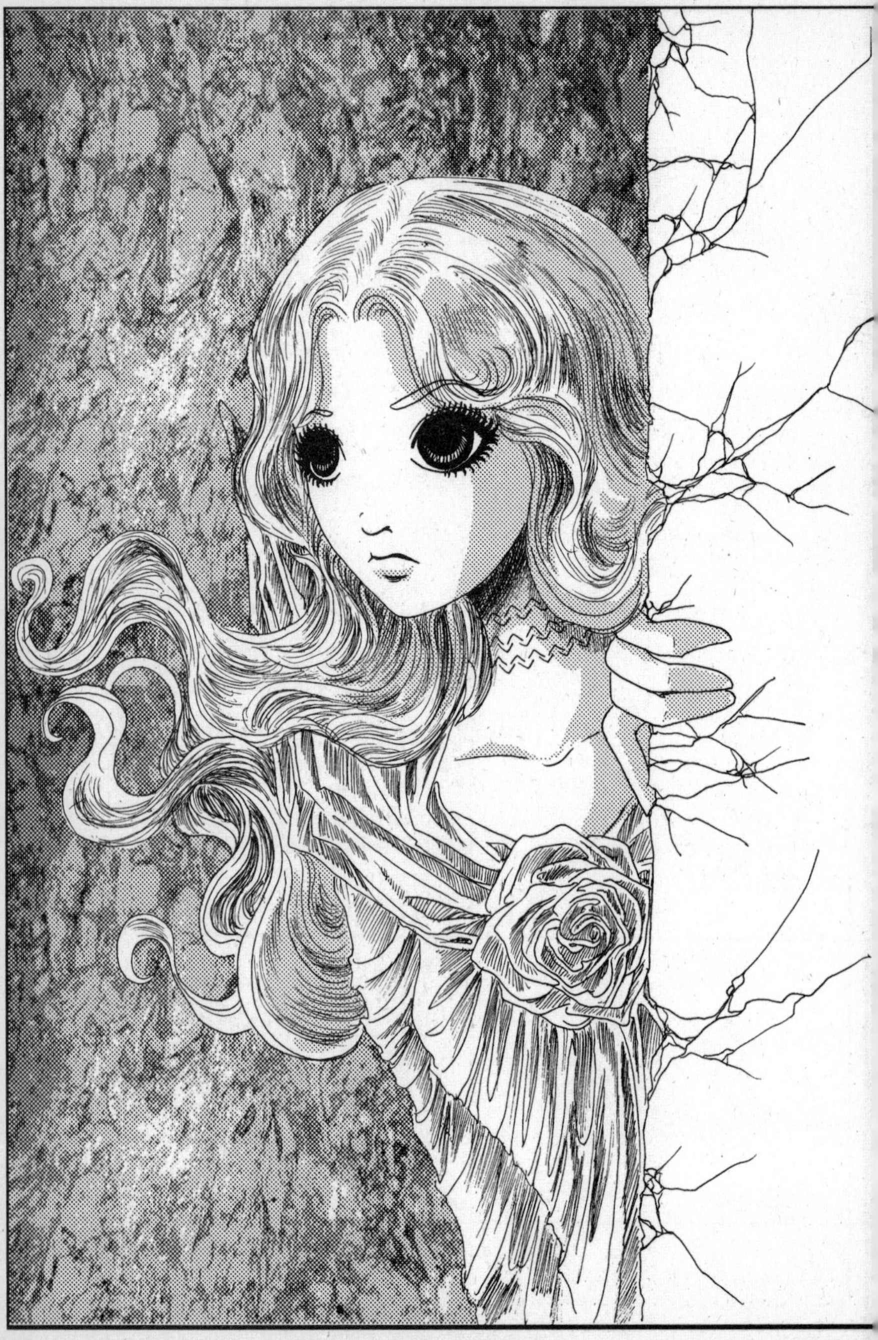

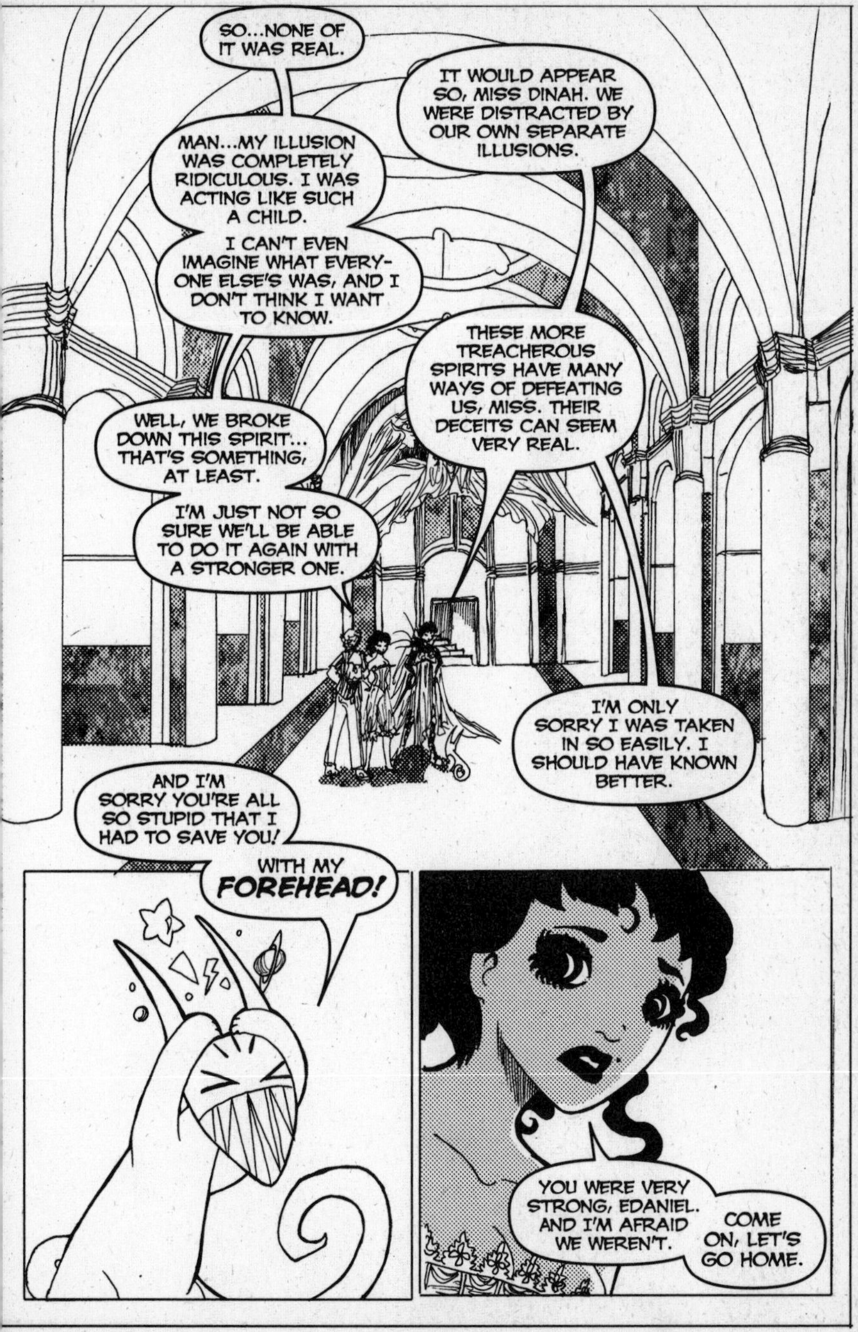
SO...NONE OF IT WAS REAL.
MAN...MY ILLUSION WAS COMPLETELY RIDICULOUS. I WAS ACTING LIKE SUCH A CHILD.
I CAN'T EVEN IMAGINE WHAT EVERY-ONE ELSE'S WAS, AND I DON'T THINK I WANT TO KNOW.
IT WOULD APPEAR SO, MISS DINAH. WE WERE DISTRACTED BY OUR OWN SEPARATE ILLUSIONS.
WELL, WE BROKE DOWN THIS SPIRIT... THAT'S SOMETHING, AT LEAST.
I'M JUST NOT SO SURE WE'LL BE ABLE TO DO IT AGAIN WITH A STRONGER ONE.
THESE MORE TREACHEROUS SPIRITS HAVE MANY WAYS OF DEFEATING US, MISS. THEIR DECEITS CAN SEEM VERY REAL.
I'M ONLY SORRY I WAS TAKEN IN SO EASILY. I SHOULD HAVE KNOWN BETTER.
AND I'M SORRY YOU'RE ALL SO STUPID THAT I HAD TO SAVE YOU!
WITH MY **FOREHEAD!**
YOU WERE VERY STRONG, EDANIEL. AND I'M AFRAID WE WEREN'T.
COME ON, LET'S GO HOME.

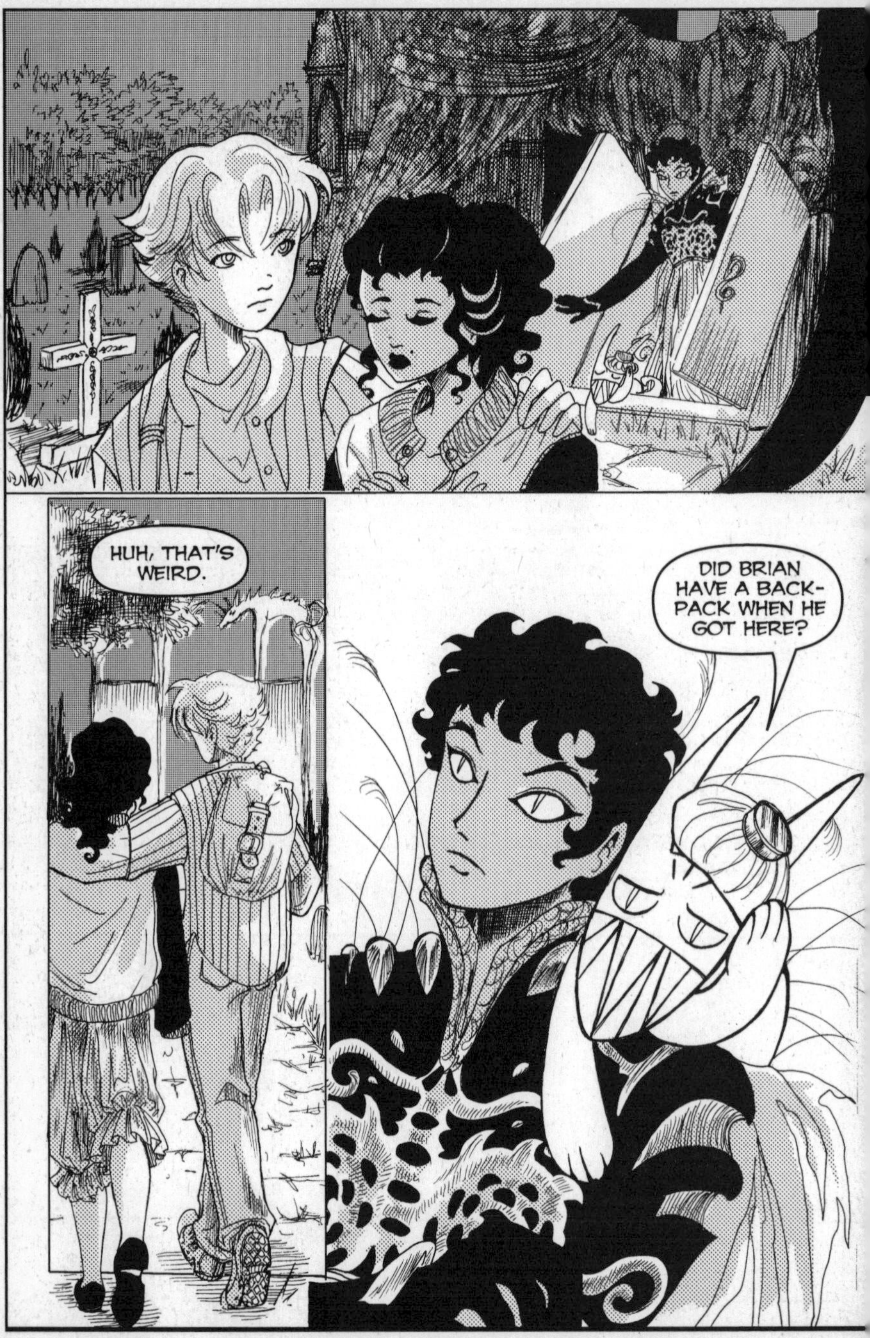
HUH, THAT'S WEIRD.
DID BRIAN HAVE A BACK-PACK WHEN HE GOT HERE?

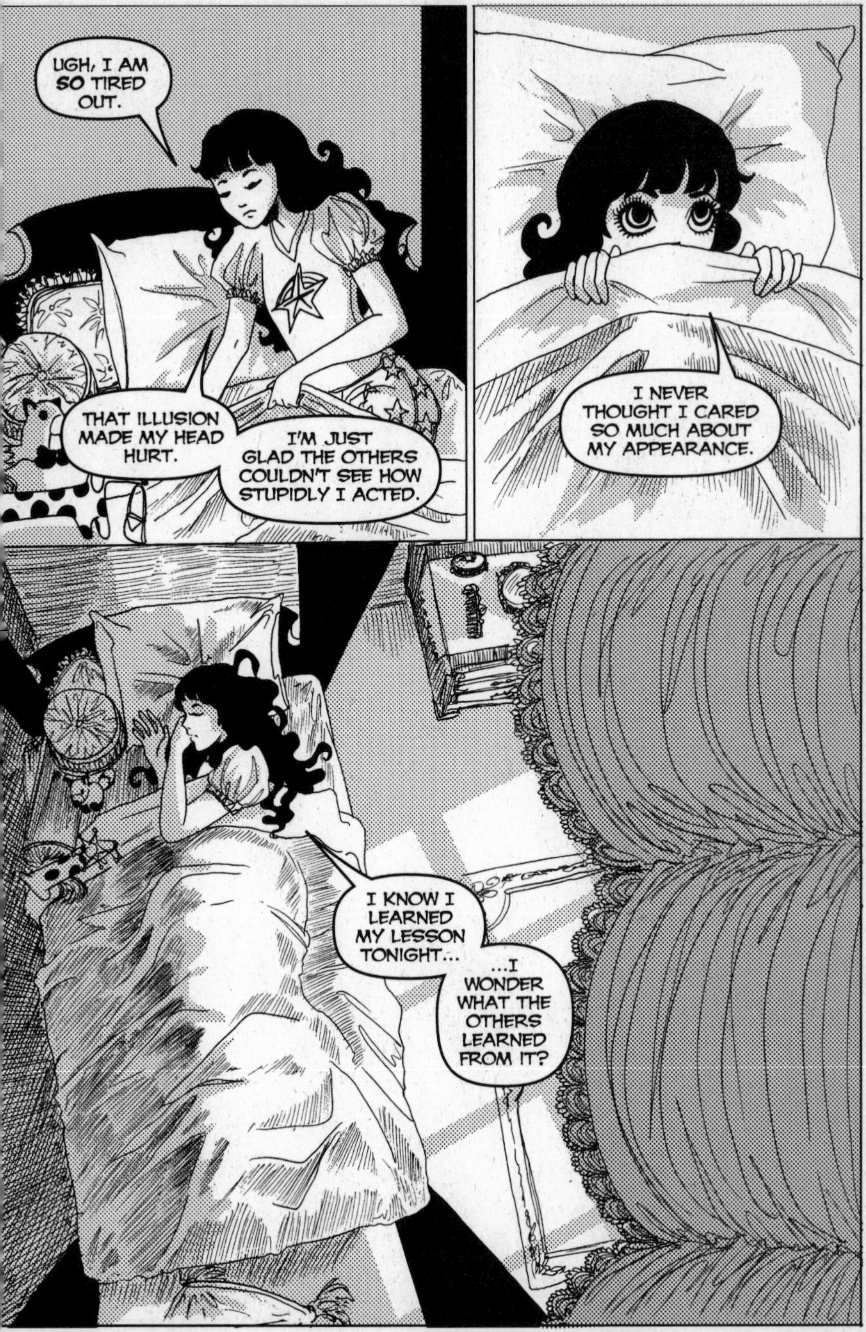

UGH, I AM SO TIRED OUT.
THAT ILLUSION MADE MY HEAD HURT.
I'M JUST GLAD THE OTHERS COULDN'T SEE HOW STUPIDLY I ACTED.
I NEVER THOUGHT I CARED SO MUCH ABOUT MY APPEARANCE.
I KNOW I LEARNED MY LESSON TONIGHT...
...I WONDER WHAT THE OTHERS LEARNED FROM IT?

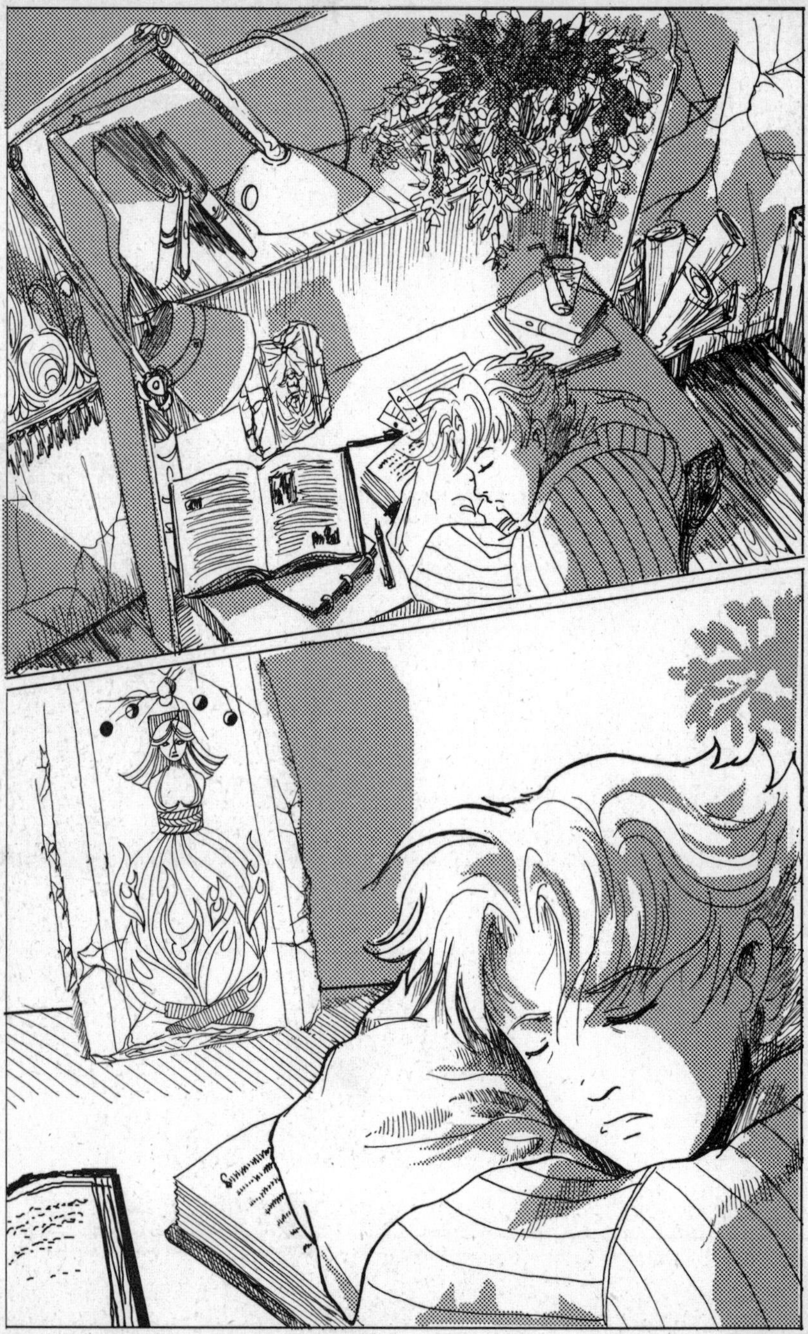

To Be Continued

In Volume Four of Bizenghast:

In the dark, hidden corners of the Mausoleum, Dinah begins to understand the true nature of the sacrifice Vincent has made to be with her. But mysteries from beyond the grave, both in the crypts and in Dinah's own home, prove to be distracting. As the riddles become more complex and intricate, their answers may be in the choice Dinah is forced to make between the lost souls and her closest friend...

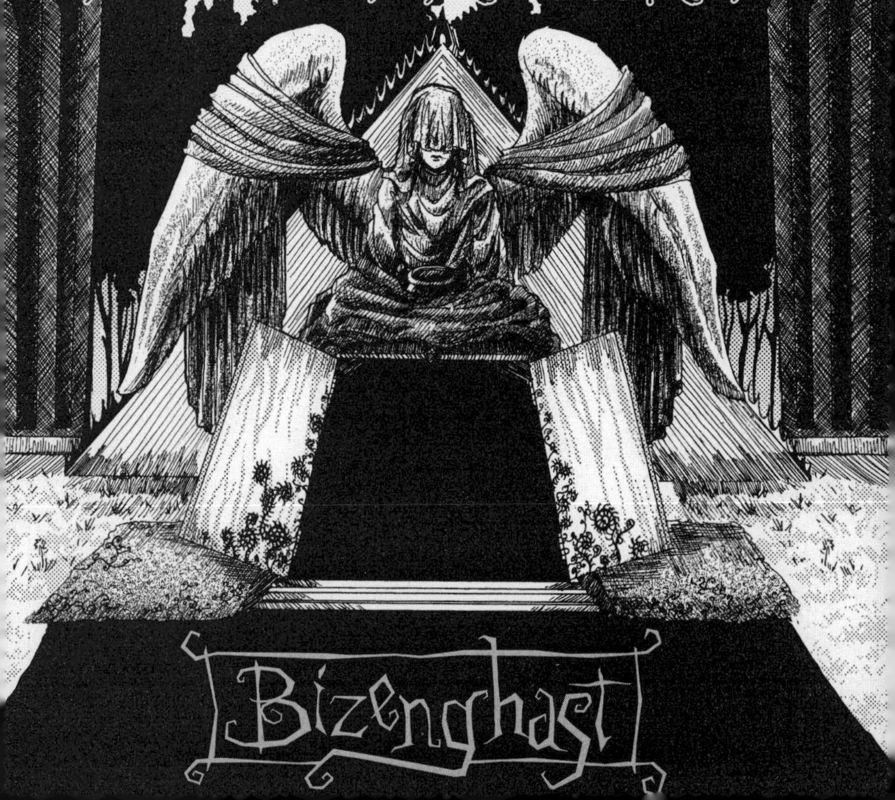
Bizenghast

Special Bonus Section-
M. Alice LeGrow & Cosplay

The only thing I love more than drawing is sewing, and I'm an avid cosplayer. Cosplay is the hobby of making reproductions of outfits seen in anime, manga, Japanese musicals, and even non-Asian sources. Cosplayers convene all over the world at conventions year-round. We do photo shoots, trade costuming ideas, and host very tough competitions! Sometimes I compete and sometimes I'm a judge at these cons. I've even cosplayed in Japan! But for me, the best part about cosplay is being with my friends and making group costumes together. Cosplay lets me meet new people and stay in touch with my friends who live far away. If it wasn't for my friends, I never would have started cosplaying in the first place!

I've made a lot of cosplay outfits over the last six years, but more recently I've started to cosplay from my own art. The following are four of my favorite Bizenghast-related costumes. I hope you like them!

-M. Alice

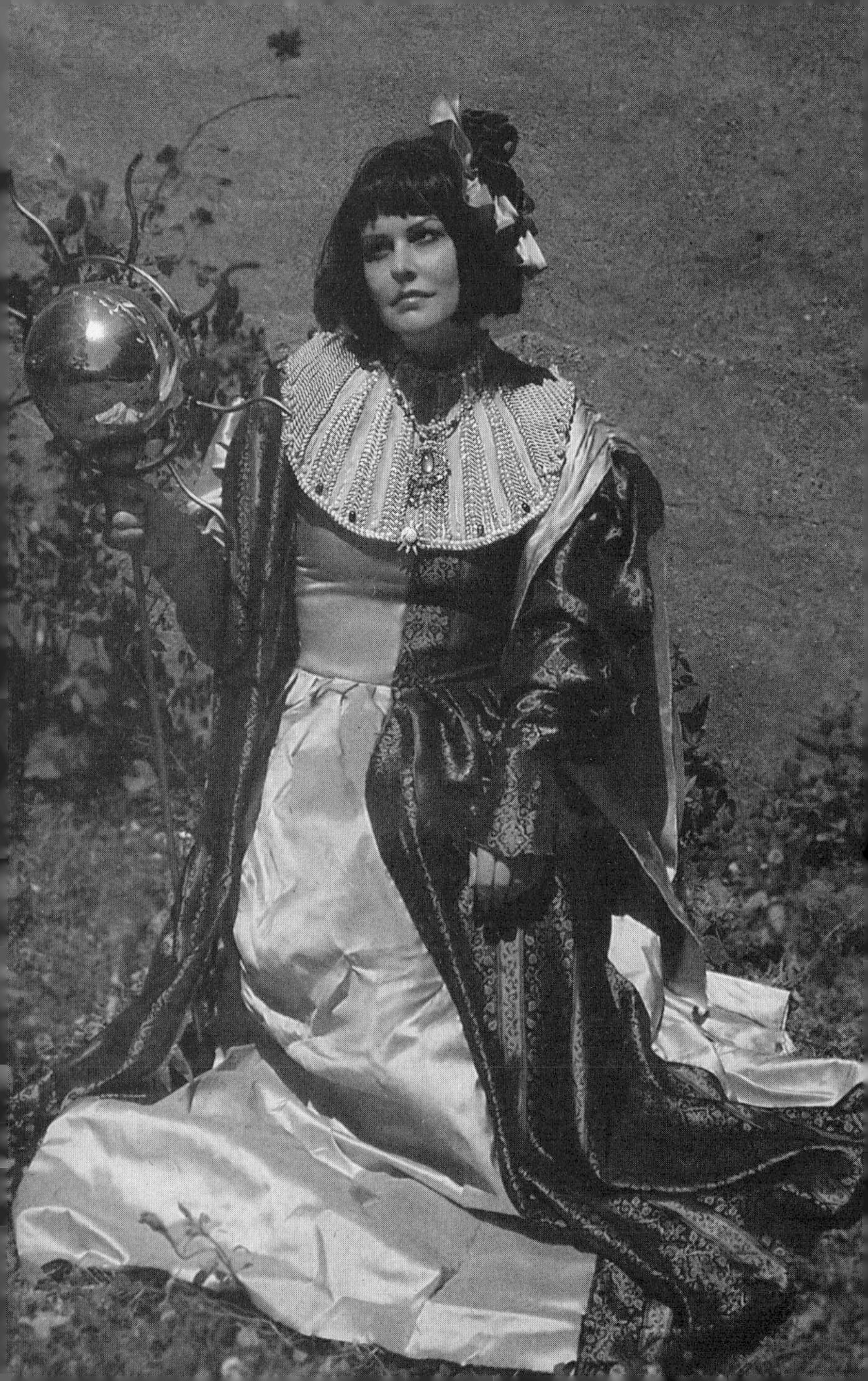

Name: IXI Dress

IXI is a very 'superficially complex' character...she presents a multi-layered and multi-patterned facade to the world. So I wanted to choose fabrics that would have patterns and stripes for her outfit. I also wanted the sun and moon to be her symbols and gave her a large sun staff.

My costume is actually based on earlier sketches of IXI before she was drawn into the comic, so it's a bit different, but overall reflects IXI's character, I think. Unfortunately I forgot to wear my little belt with sun medallions for the shoot, but I do have them!

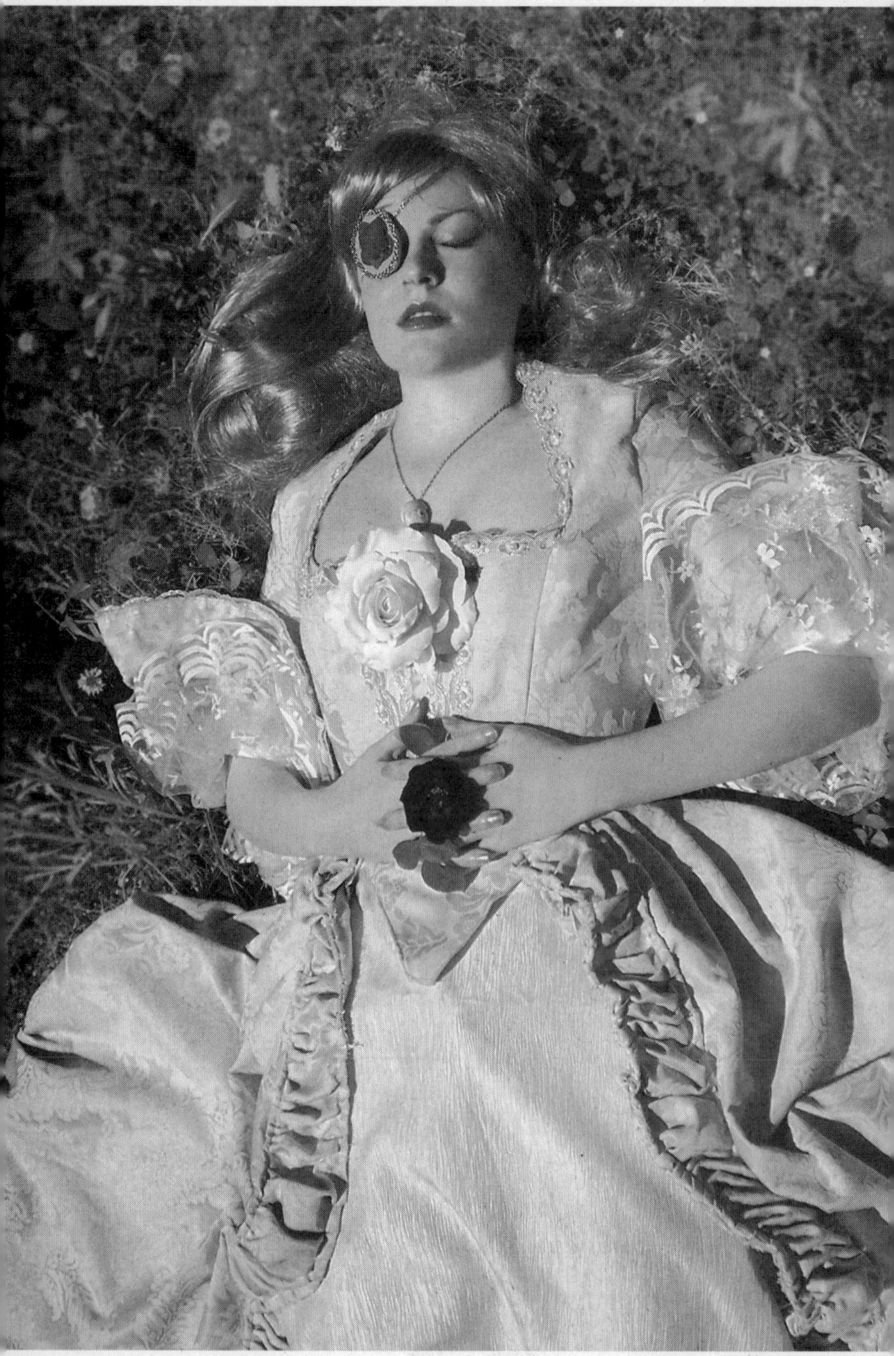

Name: Her Little Ladyship

The funny thing about this character is that she never had a name originally...
she was listed on the script simply as "ghost." Then fans began calling her "Her
Little Ladyship" and it just stuck with me, and that became her official name.

I like this dress very much, but I have to wear a corset every time I put it on,
and it's laced so tight I can hardly breathe! We were going to do a more
elaborate photo setup for this dress, but I was so out of breath from the corset
that I just laid down on the grass and we took the pictures that way.
The rose in my hand is from my own garden. I love my roses!

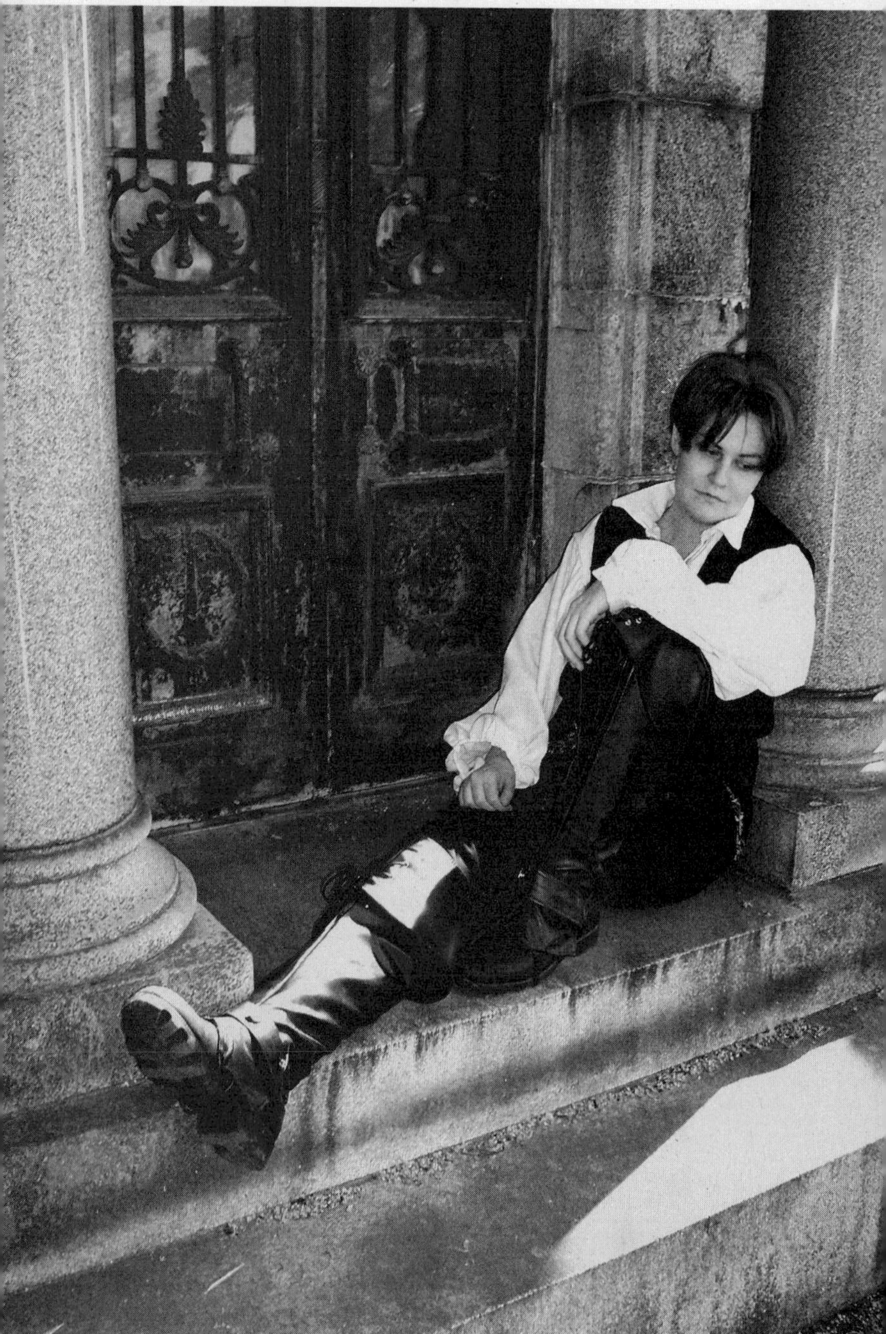

Name: Vincent

I always wanted to dress as Vincent just once! So when I designed his black embroidered vest for book 3, I decided that was the costume I wanted to make. I've only worn one other boy costume before (as Harry Potter) but it was pretty successful, so I didn't have much of a problem with this one. I felt like a pirate guy in this outfit. Boy costumes are SO much more comfortable to wear than heavy ballgowns!

DARK MOON DIARY

™

After losing her parents in a tragic accident, Priscilla goes to live in a new town with her aunt's family. As if adjusting to a new family wouldn't be tough enough, her relatives turn out to be vampires who live in the ghoul-filled town of Nachtwald! Priscilla tries hard to assimilate, but with a ghost for a teacher, a witch as a friend, and food that winks at you, can she ever adapt to life in her new town? Or will she pack her garlic and head back to normal-ville?

© Che Gilson and TOKYOPOP Inc